Wisdom Nuggets

Devotional

Hansen Mettle

MAPLE
PUBLISHERS

Wisdom Nuggets: Devotional

Author: Rev. Hansen Mettle

Copyright © Rev. Hansen Mettle (2023)

The right of Rev. Hansen Mettle to be identified as author of this work has been asserted by the author in accordance with section 77 and 78 of the Copyright, Designs and Patents Act 1988.

First Published in 2023

ISBN 978-1-83538-015-4 (Paperback)
        978-1-83538-016-1 (E-Book)

Book cover design and Book layout by:
    White Magic Studios
    www.whitemagicstudios.co.uk

Published by:
    Maple Publishers
    Fairbourne Drive, Atterbury,
    Milton Keynes,
    MK10 9RG, UK
    www.maplepublishers.com

Acknowledgements

This book is a reality because of the encouragement and contribution of many people. First, I acknowledge the support of my wife, Julie, who consistently pushed the idea to collate and publish these devotionals. I also thank Dr. Ralph Armah (University of Ghana) and his wife Barbara Armah who edited the scripts and packaged the devotionals into the book in your hands. My final acknowledgment goes to Mr. Aaron Parry (U.K) for his role in getting publishers for this book. I am grateful to you all and others who helped in diverse ways to make this book a reality.

God richly bless you always in all ways.

Rev Hansen Mettle

Contents

Gift of Life 16

Be Diligent 17

Request for a King 18

Do your seeds fall on unproductive soil? 19

Title Holder, Power Broker or Vessel? 20

Remember the Good Deeds of the Lord 21

She Came from Behind 22

Perfect Love 23

A True Friend 24

Forgive 26

God is Faithful 27

I will Make you the Head 28

In Pursuit of Knowledge 30

Be Faithful 31

Weak Indeed 32

Whole Armor 33

Turn from Your Evil Ways and Live 34

Choose God's Peace 35

Walk the Talk of Love 36

Break Fallow Ground 37

Temporary Applause or Eternal Relationship? ... 38

Called to Love, Not Condemn 39

Seek Godly Counsel 40

Character Versus Charisma 41

Take Good Care of Yourself 43

Temporary Trouble, Eternal Glory 45

Saved by Grace 46

Clean on the Inside 47

Passionate Correction 48

Spiritual Vigilance 50

Obeying God's Will 51

Student or Stooge? 52

Pay the Price for the Prize 54

True Joy is in Obedience.. 55

Ask God for Confirmation 56

The Undefiled Garment 57

Obedience over Service 58

Know God's Voice... 60

No One can Lose with God... 61

God's Instruction 62

Very Much Land... 63

Willing Hearts; Not Idle Hands 64

Stay in Contentment Lane... 66

God's Will... 67

The One in You is Greater.. 69

A Father Disciplines.. 70

God's Presence... 71

Endure for Christ 72

Those Who are for You... 73

Who Do You Imitate? 75

Praise God for the Foundation 76

Seek Knowledge 77

Don't Throw Away your Confidence... 79

Faith through Actions... 80

Faith Demands Work 81

Be Eager to Help 82

Let the World See Your Light 83

Look to Serve, not to be Served 84

Faithfulness to God 85

Little by Little... 86

God works in partnership with us 87

Forget Not 88

God our Protector 89

Build Your altar 90

His Rod or Your Spear? 91

The Potter and The Clay 92

Your Worth is in Christ... 93

The Yoke is Broken 94

His Goodness and Mercies 95

Be Vigilant.. 96

Dead to legalities; Alive to Pleasing God.................................... 98

The World's fact and God's Truth... 99

Be Truthful.. 100

God's Calendar... 102

Goodbye Fear, Welcome Faith.. 103

The example of John the Baptist... 104

The Unchanging One and His Promises 105

At thy Word.. 106

He Will See You Through.. 107

Serving in Love 109

Those who are For You... 110

United We Stand... 111

Do it Wholeheartedly 112

Stay with Him... 113

You've Been Chosen & Anointed... 114

Speak the Word 115

Rely on God.. 116

God's direction.. 117

It's Time: "Arise and Go"... 118

The Sweet and the Bitter 119

Love above Law 120

Are you A Partner or Parasite?...121

Just a Touch..122

Sin cannot offer security 123

Give No room to Laziness..124

Seek his counsel and secure your future 125

Realities of life 126

Call God 127

Thus says the Lord 128

Faith and Works *129*

Purpose and Pursuit...130

A New Dawn 131

A broken and a contrite heart 132

Godly living...133

God's Promise 134

Victorious Shout...136

Souls Over Pigs 137

Hall of Prayer 138

Embrace God's Purpose for your Life 140

Take His Yoke and Learn of Him 141

Enjoy Life...142

God Can Do Anything Through Anybody 144

Do Right, Pursue Truth 145

Define Your Moral Borders..146

Stay in Your Track...148

Jesus Christ has no Equal 149

Don't Flirt with Sin 150

Operate within your area of calling....................................151

Be patient with God 153

Recover it All 154

Eternally minded, yet not earthly-dormant....................155

Appreciate Your Pastor 156

Get Up and Go Out 158

God Will Come 159

Retreat and Rest.. 160

Be Content 161

Refuse to be Distracted 162

Be Faithful 163

Shun the wrong, Stand for the right.................................. 164

Choose Your Friends Carefully 165

Safety in the Word 167

Hidden Treasures 168

Praise God in All Things 169

Accept Your Strengths... 170

God's Work Over Factionalism 172

Healing for Broken Relationships 174

A Solid Foundation.. 175

Don't Lose Your Flavour 176

Honour Your God 177

Atmosphere for the Presence 178

Be Discerning.. 179

Don't Worry 180

Your Plans, God's Direction 181

Take Back Your Joy 182

You will Rise Again.. 183

Confront the Darkness.. 184

Take a Stand.. 185

Wise as Serpents, Harmless as Doves............................... 186

Pray or Become Prey 187

Praise God in Trials 188

The Right Time 189

God Decides 190

Eagle's Nest... 191

Thank God for His Work 192

Praise the Lord in All Things 193

Strengthen Your Brothers 194

Shake Off Gloom 196

Value in Service 197

Accept God's Rest 199

More Than Conquerors 200

Pursue Knowledge of God 201

The Light of His Face 202

Strength to Deliver 203

God's Provision 204

Be Rich Towards God 205

Wait on the Lord 206

God's Grace 207

God's Comforting Arm 208

Seek God's Will 209

Prepared Receptacles 210

Draw Your Satisfaction from God 211

Live for Christ 212

Live within Your Means 213

Set God at Your Right Hand 214

Your Light Will Shine Again 215

Cherish God's Presence 216

Be A Chanel of Liberation 218

Sow in Tears, Reap in Joy 219

Wait for Your Elevation 220

Safety in Authority 221

Loyalty 223

Let Your Yes be Yes 224

Stay Away 225

Run in His Strength 226

Walk Circumspectly 227

He Hears.. 228

Have Faith in God... 229

Don't Live in Fear 230

Gratitude... 231

Move on to Where You are Accepted................................ 232

Commit to being Faithful... 233

Your life is in the hands of God 234

Preparation Precedes Manifestation................................ 236

God's Ministry is About Service 237

Jesus' Love Never Fails... 238

Have Realistic Expectations of Your Relationships 239

Thank God for Each Day 240

The Spirit is Poured out on You 241

Live Like You're Saved 242

Contend for the Truth 243

Jesus Christ, the Only Way 244

Honest Fathers... 245

Our Glory is in our Unity 246

Do What God Says... 247

Hold Your Peace 248

Praise God amidst Challenges 249

Be Slow to Judge... 250

Apply the Word to Your Life.. 251

Your Armor-Bearers 252

Godly Leadership involves Giving 254

Embrace Your Calling 256

From Rejected to Cornerstone 257

God will Reward... 258

All Power Belongs to God.. 259

God will Restore Your Praise 260

A life of Balance 261

Die to Sin..262

Intercede for One Another..263

God Will not Abandon You...264

Stay in Your Lane 265

Dirt and Death 266

Answer Herod with Silence 267

Do Right, Give Justice, Be Honest 268

Love Your Enemies..269

Give Your All 271

Be Your Brother's Keeper...273

Foundations are Important 274

Give God some Praise 275

Dealing with Rejection 276

Sin Must Not Rule 277

Live Each Moment Like It's Your Last...............................278

God wants a Shobi 279

Time will Tell 280

Productivity is Key to Prosperity 281

Embrace Change...282

Let the Children Come to Jesus Now 283

Stay Humble...284

You will Overcome..285

Sharing is Caring..286

Lamp of the Lord 287

God Will not Let you Down 288

Miracles are only Signposts..289

God Accepts You...290

Don't Show Partiality 291

No Longer Afraid of Death...292

God will Speak for You and through You 293

Preservation in God 294

Go, Preach, Teach 295

God will Prove Himself...296

Do it Now 297

A "Little" Disobedience...298

You are God's Property 299

You are Who God says You are...300

Home in God...301

The Stones will Cry Out...302

Enslaved by Blessings? 303

Outshine the Darkness...304

Do Justly, Love Mercy, Walk Humbly 305

Continue to Trust God in the Darkness 306

When Jesus Owns You 307

Love the Lord's Presence 308

Choose to Serve 309

Love, Forgiveness and Restoration 311

Recount the Goodness of God...312

He Will Surely Help You...313

Put on the Armor of Light 314

Your Reward in Due Season 315

Numbers Do Not Guarantee Success...316

All Power Belongs to God...317

Jesus Is the Answer...318

Rejoice in The Holy One...320

Finish the Race 321

Preparation Before Possession 322

God Has Your Back...323

Celebrate Life 324

Acknowledge Your Helpers 325

Maintain the Momentum...327

Remove the Grave Clothes 329

Your Defined Audience Will Accept You...................................331

Beyond the Pain...332

Covet God's Presence..334

Discipline...336

Endure the Waiting 338

Turn the Wanderer..339

Lessons from the Transfiguration..340

Don't be Like a Horse 342

Focus on Jesus..344

Thank God for Your Foundations 345

Be a Blessing to the Burdened...346

You Can be Free 347

Divine Determinations..348

Forgive and Let Go...350

Fulfill your Ministry..351

Faithfulness 352

Plan with God..353

Appreciate the People in Your Life 354

Things that Accompany Salvation 355

Service will Elevate You...357

Draw the Line..359

God Will Reward You..360

Contend for The Faith 361

Clothed in Divine Glory...363

Ride the Storm..364

Closer Than You Can Imagine..365

Let God Make You 366

Pursue Knowledge of God...367

Everybody Needs Somebody...368

The Presence of The Holy Spirit..370

No Condition is Permanent 371

Let God Lead 372

Desperate Times Demand Focused Prayers 373

Hosanna to The King of Kings 374

Follow Where He Leads 375

Battles You Fight Alone 376

Chosen for A Purpose 377

Look Beyond the Pharisees 378

Jesus Christ Paid It All 379

Opposition Can Be the Ladder to Your Position 380

Close That Door 381

Peace to You 382

Your Healing has Come 383

Maintain the Momentum 384

Fleeting Glory 385

Open Your Mouth 386

You Are Your Brother's Keeper 388

Deliverance is Assured 389

Love Your Enemies 390

Be Grateful 392

Dare to Be Different 393

Love is a Liberating Force 395

Passion for Praising 397

Let's Pray For Each Other 399

Spread the Word to the World 400

Fall in Love with Jesus 402

Pray for Long Life 403

Delivered from The Grave 405

It Shall Not Stand 406

Sing Through the Storm 407

Power Belongs to God 409

Wisdom Is of God 411

The Light Will Prevail 412

Time to Sing Not to Sink 413

Stand in Your Place 414

Praise is a Game Changer 415

Morning Praise 416

Jesus Christ Reigns Supreme 417

Rise to The Occasion 418

Move When You Have to 419

The Voice of the Lord 421

Think Beyond Today 422

Rejoicing in Suffering 424

Adapt Quickly 425

His Faithfulness Is Forevermore 427

A heart of gratitude 428

Allow yourself to be mentored 429

Rise up and Work! 431

Wait, Your Herod isn't Dead Yet 432

But you have come to Mt. Zion 433

Greatness in You 434

Serve As you wait 436

Yea in Christ 437

You are God's Star 438

His Ways are not Our Ways 439

Your future is Hidden in Him 440

New Possibilities 441

Gift of Life

Matt. 13:16-17, NKJV

But blessed are your eyes for they see, and your ears for they hear; for assuredly, I say to you that many prophets and righteous men desired to see what you see, and did not see it, and to hear what you hear, and did not hear it.

The opportunity to live to see the advent of a new year is not a right, but a privilege. It is not by our goodness, but by his grace. If you are still stuck with some of the negative thoughts of the past year, it will help to reflect on what Jesus told his "congregation" in this passage of scripture and apply it to yourself: "...many righteous men desired to see what you see, and did not see it, and to hear what you hear what you hear, and did not hear it."

Indeed, there were many who passed away last year who are more "righteous" than you and I put together, in terms of good human behavior and character; and yet they died while God chose to keep us here. There were others who did not survive less serious health challenges than what you had to contend with. Yes, it was tough! Yes, it was rough; but the good news is that YOU ARE STILL HERE!! Today, if some thoughts should occupy your mind, let them be thoughts of God's mercies, and praise him for all it's worth.

You are highly favored to be counted among the living, and the space you occupy among the living is a precious gift from God himself. Truth is, you could have been dead. You don't necessarily have to be to be sick to die. In the quietness of your sleep, God could have closed the page on your unfolding story, and delegated you to the archives of history, but he chose to make you a part of the present.

God by that choice is saying, "you are still relevant to me. I haven't finished with you yet." Thank God for letting you hear and see the dawning of a new season of life. Hope for nothing, but the best. Wishing this year will be the most fulfilling year of your life yet.

Happy new year! God bless you

Be Diligent

Prov. 27:23-24, NKJV

Be diligent to know the state of your flocks, and attend to your herds; for riches are not forever, nor does a crown endure to all generations

In the first verse (23) of our scripture for today, there are three words I want us to consider; they are the words, "diligent," "know," and "attend." The word "diligent" means giving serious attention to something. One who is diligent is very conscientious and orderly. He is not careless but takes good care of whatever little he has.

The Word of God is saying that it takes diligence to know "the state of your flock." Every one of us has been given "flocks" and "herds" by God; these are in the form of gifts, talents, and resources. A man's true riches are reflected in his awareness of God, and the diligent use of all the resources the Lord has placed at his disposal.

We are not going to be here forever, and so are the "riches" (gifts, talents, and resources) God has given us. We are stewards, and not storehouses. We can only be fruitful through diligence, knowledge, and careful attendance to our "flocks" (gifts) and "herds" (talents). You can't afford to wait for gold before you go for God. You don't lean on what you don't have; that amounts to wishful thinking. Pay attention to what you have and make the best use of it.

It is not enough to "know" what you have. Diligently "attend" to it. Make quality time for God, and the people and things that matter to you most. It is a necessary investment that will produce growth and prosperity. Your focus on your "flocks" and "herds" is key to having fulfillment. Lack of diligence is an enemy to progress. If you desire success, commitment to diligence, knowledge, and work are not negotiable.

The wise have said that "no condition is permanent," so make hay while the sun shines. Good management and contentment always win for those who trust and depend on the Lord for a life of fulfillment. Living out your destiny is in your hands; you either make or mar it. The choice is yours. Be diligent, acquire knowledge, and do your best in whatever you do.

God bless you.

Request for a King

1 Sam.8:4-7, GNB

Then all the elders of Israel met together, went to Samuel in Ramah, and said to him, "Look, you are getting old and your sons don't follow your example. So then, appoint a king to rule over us, so that we will have a king, as other countries have." Samuel was displeased with their request for a king; so he prayed to the LORD, and the LORD said, "Listen to everything the people say to you. You are not the one they have rejected; I am the one they have rejected as their king."

The elders of Israel displayed gross insensitivity when they came to Samuel with a request for a king. They hid their real motive for asking for a king and pointed to the attitude of Samuel's sons as the reason. If they loved and cared about Samuel as much as he loved and served them, the elders of Israel would have refrained from pointing at a painful spot in his life as reason for demanding a king.

It is clear from God's response that the elders had been influenced by the style of government of the nations around them, and no longer wanted theocracy. The only way to get their desires fulfilled, was to exploit the crisis in the prophet's family. Instead of sharing Samuel's burden, and using their influence as elders to mobilize for prayer and intercession for him, they 'shot' him down; subtly accusing him of bad parenting.

Perhaps they were expecting Samuel to publicly denounce his children so they could have the opportunity to establish their own order of government. This posture did not please the LORD, and he who knows the secret of every heart declared to Samuel, "You are not the one they have rejected; I am the one they have rejected as their king."

Indeed, the elders needed some lesson from the father of the Prodigal Son, who despite the rebellion of his son, had a place of hope and forgiveness in his heart for him. It is unacceptable to use the unfortunate circumstances of anyone's family life to judge, denounce, or reject his integrity. Our selfish ambitions should not make us so callous, careless, and insensitive to the extent that we don't feel the pain and frustration of parents who are struggling with dysfunctional kids.

Let our young people also note that your acts of omission and commission, impact on how people see and behave towards your parents and family. Live in a way that will spare them heartache and embarrassment. It is obvious Samuel did not have a very happy ending; essentially because the elders exploited the problems in his family to reject his children as leaders in his stead, and by so doing rejected God.

We have a responsibility to help each other. The burden we bear becomes lighter, when we know there are friends and loved ones out there who care and are standing with us in prayer. No responsible parent needs to be reminded how bad his child or children are. What he/she needs is spiritual and emotional support and encouragement. Never ask him to give you a "king" because his kids are bad; find a better reason for your request, in order to spare him additional pain. If you cannot help him, don't hurt him.

God bless you

Do your seeds fall on unproductive soil?

Eze. 33:31-32

So, they come to you as people do, they sit before you as My people, and they hear your words, but they do not do them; for with their mouth, they show much love, but their hearts pursue their own gain. Indeed, you are to them as a very lovely song of one who has a pleasant voice and can play well on an instrument; for they hear your words, but they do not do them

---

When you expect too much from people you sacrifice your life for, you can become vulnerable to undue pressure and disillusionment.

A doctor friend sent me a news item about a pastor who committed suicide because he was frustrated with the lack of appreciation and love from his congregation. They pestered, pressured, and persecuted him until he could take it no more. Instead of pouring out his frustration, he bottled it up until it exploded in his face. We have no right judging him, but we can learn to avoid being pushed into taking that route.

Every parent, pastor, coach, counselor, and all other persons in leadership ought to know for a fact that we cannot always get people to respond the way we desire, relative to what we teach them. You can put in the best of efforts and resources to raise a child, and he may grow up to live a life contrary to all the values you taught him. That is never a parent's wish or dream, but it can happen, and indeed does happen.

As a shepherd of God's flock, it is dangerous to be overly concerned with the attitudes they show towards you. It is not your responsibility to change anybody. You don't make decisions for your children when they are grown enough to rationalize. God told Ezekiel that the people who came to sit before him were only pretending to be interested in his counseling, but each of them was going to walk away and do whatever they deemed fit.

As a parent, pastor, or counselor, you have to learn to leave your children, members of your congregation etc., in the hands of God. Do your best for them, but be careful not to raise the bar of your expectation so high that when they don't respond appropriately your entire world crumbles. When you have done your best for those you mentor, you know it, and so should not take the negative response too personal.

You have a life to live, and those you mentor are only a part of it, not all of it. If you are hurting, make no pretense about it. Talk about it with those who identify with your pain and despair. It is better to seek help than pretend you can handle it alone. God's Word provides you a wonderful resource base. Encourage yourself in this one thing; that you did your best, and cannot be held responsible for the rest. Let God be judge and interpreter of your actions and inactions.

You are not, and will not be the first or last to sow seeds that fall on unproductive soil. Your reward is in the hands of God, and it will surely come to you in due season. I pray for every hurting pastor and parent for God's grace and presence to keep and protect you always in all ways. May the good Lord give you His peace and joy in Jesus Name.

God bless you

Title Holder, Power Broker or Vessel?

Ezra 5:2, NKJV

So Zerubbabel the son of Shealtiel and Jeshua the son of Jozadak rose up and began to build the house of God which is in Jerusalem; and the prophets of God were with them, helping them.

When you have a family, church, or any organization for that matter, where everyone wants to be in leadership, no progress can be achieved. It is important to understand that even though one may have the gift of a leader, sometimes the best role to play is that of helps.

Speaking at a church leaders' conference a few days ago, I made a point that obviously did not go down well with my audience, but which I rigidly insist is the gospel truth; we are all called to lead souls to Christ, but not everyone of us is called to head a church. Our denial of this basic Biblical truth is one of the reasons for the Church becoming breeding ground for charlatans and false prophets etc.

If you are a sincere seeker of truth, please be well informed that there is more to leadership than being seen at the frontline. You may have the ability to give birth, but that does not necessarily translate into being a good parent. When you are in group, your greatest goal and ambition should be for the overall good of the group, not your personal parochial interest.

The achievement of the goals of your family, church, or organization should be strong motivation that overrides any selfish ambition. When the exiles returned to build the Jerusalem temple, Zerubbabel and Jozadak stepped up to begin the work without requesting help from the prophets, but the scripture records that "the prophets of God were with them, helping them." This gives us an example of how we can effectively commit to be a blessing anywhere we can offer help, without trying to show of our medals and certificates.

God does not need title holders, and power brokers; he needs vessels that he can use to achieve goals that will benefit more than one person. If you want to do it God's way, then take your eyes off yourself, and rise up and help.

God bless you

Remember the Good Deeds of the Lord

Ps.77:10-12, NKJV

And I said, "This is my anguish; But I will remember the years of the right hand of the Most High." I will remember the works of the LORD; surely, I will remember your wonders of old. I will also meditate on all your work, and talk of your deeds

---

We have had very difficult experiences with our orphanage work, and one such instance was when thieves raided the Children's home and took away a flatscreen television set for the nursery, office equipment, bags and dresses for the kids, and a good amount of cash.

When news reached us that Saturday morning about the robbery, we gathered to access the extent of damage and loss. After I was briefed on how much we had lost, my emotions began to tear my spirit apart...but God! His Spirit took my mind to the kids; none of them was hurt or killed. Indeed, they did not even hear any sound until daybreak when they saw the damage to the office door and tampering with the security camera at the gate.

God brought me from negative reaction to the things lost, to a positive remembrance of the lives protected. It was as if the Holy Spirit was asking me to sing, "Count your blessings, name them one by one." A new picture emerged in my mind. The Lord showed me that everyone's present circumstances hold two indelible pictures of the past; one of the good works of God, and two, of unpleasant painful experiences orchestrated by Satan.

What will give us peace and keep us strong in faith and joyful in life, is remembrance of "the years of the right hand of the LORD." My message to you is to keep trusting the Lord by thinking about his goodness that has brought you this far. The future is still an unpredictable and unexplored territory, but the God who kept you through yesterday's storm, will keep you through today's flood.

Cheer up, and don't crawl back. You may feel the pain, but don't let it drown your praise. Remember the track-record of your God. He is still the same; ever faithful, ever sure. Like the Good Book says, "the Lord who began this good work in you, shall also bring it to a perfect end."

God bless you.

She Came from Behind

Matt.9:20-22, NIV

And suddenly, a woman who had a flow of blood for twelve years came from behind and touched the hem of his garment. For she said to herself, "If only I may touch His garment, I shall be well." ...And the woman was made well from that hour

---

The protocols of the kingdom of God revolve around faith and obedience. From a cultural point of view, the woman with the issue of blood had no business touching Jesus.

The law clearly says in the book of Leviticus that "if a woman has a discharge of blood for many days, other than at the time of her customary impurity, all the days of her unclean discharge shall be as the days of her customary impurity. She shall be unclean," and anyone or anything she came into contact with, was equally unclean (Lev.15:25-27).

This woman did not only touch Jesus, but touched the HEM of his garment, which was laced with a material to remind the Jewish people of the law (Num.15:38). She was conscious of the law, but circumvented LEGALISM, and reached out to the LOVE of Christ. She applied the principle, that "man was not made for the Sabbath (the law), but the Sabbath for man." And what I find most interesting about her story was that SHE CAME FROM BEHIND.

The lesson here is, it doesn't matter how long you have been in Christ, if you don't develop an intimate relationship with the Lord, you may never receive any impartation from his Spirit. If you get stuck with legalism, it will hinder you from experiencing the love of God. Jesus had no problem with the woman's "violation" of the law, he was appreciative for her faith and understanding of God's heart of love.

Today, Jesus is asking you to keep your eyes on him. No matter how profuse your "issue of blood" may be, his grace overrides every judgment the enemy has placed on you. You may be physically sick, but you are not spiritually lost. You are not out because you are behind. Reach out and touch him. His mercy cancels every mess.

God bless you

Perfect Love

1Jn. 4:18,20, NIV

There is no fear in love; but perfect love casts out fear, because fear involves torment. But he who fears has not been made perfect in love...If someone says, "I love God," and hates his brother, he is a liar; for he who does not love his brother whom he has seen, how can he love God whom he has not seen?"

Whoever claims to love you, and at the same time fears you, has not yet come to a full understanding of what it means to love.

You cannot love someone and when you see him or get into his company begin to entertain fear; panic, feel unsure, and unsafe. In any healthy relationship, you feel safe in the company of the beloved than anywhere else. If a child feels unsafe, and uncomfortable in the presence of his parent, then something is not right; it might possibly be that the parent is abusive.

On the flip side, there is a positive aspect of "fear". We love God and fear Him; meaning we respect and honor him. This positive "fear" of the Lord works in tangent with love. Love demands from us respect for those we love. If you don't respect your child, brother, sister, parent, or spouse, there is a break in your love-circuit, and you need to fix it.

If you don't feel comfortable to let your spouse know what you earn by way of salary, there is a deficiency in your "love" for him or her, because God's Word says you have become ONE flesh. What belongs to you, belongs to your spouse; it may not be what you are experiencing right now in your relationship, but that is God's ideal. Otherwise, you simply are not walking in perfect love. Why? "Perfect love casts out fear." It has zero tolerance for fear.

The premise then is that since you cannot love the one you fear (the one who scares you), the only obvious choice is that you will either withdraw from him or hate him. There is no middle ground, and there is no neutral gear. A challenge comes with Apostle John's question to all of us, "If you cannot love your brother who you see, how can you love God whom you have not seen?"

The apostle says that position makes us liars. Therein lies the problem; if I am a liar, then how do I claim my place as a child of God? This is because Jesus made clear in Jn.8:44 that every liar is a child of the devil. Indeed, hatred has its source in the devil.

The pieces are beginning to come together now, and all of us have to do some reality check on our "love" claims. God is doing some serious repair work in my thoughts and attitudes through His Word and Spirit. It started 37 years ago when I gave my life to Jesus. It is an unfinished business, but I am enjoying the journey. At least I am not who I used to be. I am loving more, and getting blessed on a daily basis.

I welcome you to this spiritual walk with Jesus. Your love will be perfected, because your fears will be taken care of. The process can be long and painful, but the rewards are too good to ignore. It lasts from here (earth) to there (heaven). Welcome to the Jesus-love-club.

God bless you.

A True Friend

Eccl.4:9-10, NKJV

Two are better than one, because they have a good reward for their labor. For if they fall, one will lift up his companion. But woe to him who is alone when he falls, for he has no one to help him up.

One day in the month of April 1989, I fell on a street outside the Paris airport while trying to board a bus to the hotel where I was lodging. It was Springtime, and the ice had made the ground very slippery. Within a split second of that fall, I began to feel the cold bite into my bones.

Thankfully, I was with a beloved friend, Rev. Samuel Otu Pimpong, Senior Pastor of the University of Ghana Baptist Church. He graciously extended a hand to help me get up on my feet; that was one of the many times I have experienced the value of having true and caring friends in my life. Indeed, "two are BETTER than one".

We are created for relationship, not just any kind of relationship, but meaningful, healthy, and mutually beneficial relationship. Genesis 2:18 records, "And the Lord said, 'It is not good that man should be alone; I will make him a helper comparable to him.'" This clearly points to the fact that relationship is God's idea; and like everything else God loves and cherishes, Satan and his demons hate it with unrelenting aggression.

The devil attacked the first human relationship in the garden of Eden, and introduced fear, mistrust, and murder (Gen.4:1-20) and has since maintained notoriety for creating confusion among families and friends. Some of you have been wounded and "damaged" too often and so badly, you prefer to keep to yourselves. Too many people have taken advantage of you, and you no longer know who to trust. You cannot trust your pastor, your friends, and even your own parents. You have been hurt too much, too often, and for far too long, that you've locked yourself up in a world of isolation.

That may work for a time, but there is a BETTER way to live; it is the way God planned it to be from the beginning, and that is for you to build and MAINTAIN healthy relationships. Despite the past disappointments and hurt feelings, there are people God wants to bring into your life to give you that fresh spiritual, emotional, and physical back-up you need. God will need your 'permission' to do that.

If you maintain an entrenched position that everybody is bad because all the people you related to in the past ended up taking advantage of you, and left you wounded and bleeding, you may never see the right folks God wants to introduce into your life. You need someone to talk to. You need someone to be your "dung gate" - someone who is willing be at the receiving end of all your stress and distress garbage. I call such true friends, "emotional detoxification agents." You need such to survive.

By virtue of the work I do in the Lord's vineyard, I am almost always a victim of ministry "toxic wastes" of varying types, shapes, and degrees. I sincerely don't think I could have come this far without the extraordinary strength and support of my wife. She shares the pain and lightens the burden.

Your lifeline may not be your spouse (if he/she is abusive, and I hope not) but God has someone you can trust. Ask the Holy Spirit to open your eyes so you can see those assigned for your company. And while you wait, deepen your relationship with the One True Friend (Jesus) who can never stop loving you. May His Spirit lead you into relationships that build you up, and not tear you down.

God bless you.

Forgive

Mk.11:25-26, NKJV

And whenever you stand praying, if you have anything against anyone, forgive him, that your Father in heaven may also forgive you your trespasses. But if you do not forgive, neither will your Father in heaven forgive your trespasses.

God has clearly defined the perimeters for hearing our prayers. Jesus said if our prayers will be accepted, it will have to flow from hearts full of forgiveness. We can all assume God has accepted our prayers without reference to the conditions of our hearts.

Oftentimes when I asked the Holy Spirit to show me who I needed to forgive, I have been surprised at the list of people he would throw up at me; some of them not in any real relationship with me. I have learnt through those spiritual encounters, that we sometimes CHOOSE to be offended, and end up holding grudges that block our prayers.

In 1st Pet.3:7, the scripture says when a husband is not in right relationship with his wife, his prayers do not register with God. All of these put together shows that it is not enough to just get up and pray. It also indicates that much of what we call "prayer" is spiritual semantics, and sheer waste of time. When we don't meet the conditions set by God, we cannot obtain the answers promised by God.

As long as you harbor unforgiveness against a brother or a sister (no matter what they did to you), you tie God's hands and make it impossible for Him to forgive you (ref. v.26). Indeed, anyone you refuse to forgive, controls you. When you see that person, hear anything concerning him, or even think of him, you begin to experience diverse negative thoughts and emotions.

These negative thoughts and emotions trigger a chain reaction that can affect your health. God is saying you can't stand before Him with all that garbage and claim to be communicating with Him. He has too many things about you He can point to, and kick you out of His sight, but no! He CHOOSES to forgive you ALL, and He is saying if you want Him to listen to you, and release His blessings on your life, then treat others the way He treats you.

Forgiving someone doesn't necessarily mean you have to maintain intimate relationship with him. What it does mean is to settle it in your heart that whatever be the reason for whatever you hold against that person, you are releasing it and not allowing it to influence what you think, do, or say to him and about him.

You refuse to hold grudges against anyone, so you can have free access to the Presence of God and be heard when you pray. Forgiveness is sometimes a difficult choice, but always a healthy goal. It breaks down the barriers that hinders our prayers. If for no other reason at all, forgive so that God can forgive you, and your prayers will not be hindered.

God bless you

God is Faithful

Josh.21-43-45, NIV

So the LORD gave Israel all the land he had sworn to give their forefathers, and they took possession of it and settled there. The LORD gave them rest on every side, just as he had sworn to their forefathers. Not one of their enemies withstood them; the LORD handed all their enemies over to them. Not one of all the LORD's good promises to the house of Israel failed; everyone was fulfilled

---

The fathers who received the promise to possess the land, did not keep faith with God, so they did not live to see its fulfillment. Only Joshua and Caleb, out of the entire generation of Hebrews who left Egypt, partook of the blessing.

God is faithful to all his promises to us, even when we are unfaithful to him. If we are not ready to walk in his will, he is patient enough to wait for those who will be willing to run with the vision and fulfill the mission. Sometimes our attitude towards our Heavenly Father and his work, tends to give the impression that we are indispensable.

Beloved, I have lived long enough, and learned enough from God's dealings with his servants to conclude that if I choose to disobey God in what he has called me to do, it will not have any lasting effect on his eternal plan or purpose; he will always have someone to do what I refuse to do. The worst impact my disobedience can have on God's plan is to delay it, but I can NEVER dismantle, disorganize, or destroy it.

God will do what he says he will do, irrespective of whether we co-operate with him or not. It is in our own best interest, and indeed an honor, to be used of God. The generation that crossed the Jordan river under the leadership of Joshua, had a radically different attitude towards their leader, as compared to those who crossed the Red Sea under Moses's leadership.

The "Red Sea saints" frustrated their leader (Moses) to the extent he struck a rock out of anger, instead of speaking to it as commanded by God (Num.20:7-11). As a result of their intransigence, they received a promise they never enjoyed. Their children, the "Jordan river saints," inherited the promise and enjoyed its benefits. God gave them "all the land he had promised to their forefathers, and they took possession of it and settled there."

When God blesses, the book of Proverbs says he adds no trouble to it; so we see the children of Israel, not only possessing the land and settling in it, but also defeating their enemies and enjoying peace. Can I suggest to you, that it is out of place to claim the promises of God as if God owes you a debt that he has defaulted in paying; no, he doesn't. Get this understanding - whether we live or die, we live or die for Jesus.

We have been bought, and the buyer (Christ) OWNS us. We are his bonafide property. When you follow his leading, like the Jordan-river saints, you will possess the promise land. God will give you His peace, and he will subdue every enemy that rises against you. When God stands with you, and for you, no enemy can fight you and win. Hear me out; the bigger they come, the harder they will fall, and their curses will become cushions of blessing.

God bless you

I will Make you the Head

Deut.28:13a, KNKV

And the Lord will make you the head and not the tail

The first twelve years of my childhood life was spent in a community full of poverty, deprivation, and illiteracy. The things I saw and heard, left an indelible mark on my mind. When we relocated to what was considered a middle-income class environment, memories of the wonderful, but less privileged men, women, and children I had left behind stayed with me.

These memories served as motivation to do something with my life so I could contribute to help lift ALL of them to a level where they could experience more decent lives. There was one thing missing I failed to realize; I did not factor God in my plans. Fact is, I was not a born-again Christian. I dreamt of studying hard, making it to the top as a world-class professional, so I could reach down and lift those I had left behind up the social ladder. Everything within me rejected the illiteracy, deprivation, and abject poverty I experienced around me.

Sooner than later, I came to realize that without Christ, my best intentions were not going to be good enough. I was trying to MAKE MYSELF THE HEAD, which was clearly against God's divine order. I was behaving like Moses jumping to the defense of his fellow Hebrew, and later being questioned by the same people he was trying to defend, "who made you a king and a ruler over us?"

In saying all this, I want to encourage you to allow God to MAKE YOU! It is good to put your best foot forward in whatever your dreams are; but your best option is to do so with the leading of God. As a child of God, it is God who holds the key to who, and what you become. When He speaks of making you the head; it doesn't necessarily mean you are going to become the head of your company or president of your country today or tomorrow. That is possible, but it goes further and deeper than that; it means he is going to make you RELEVANT.

God is saying to you that he has the power to make something out of your nothingness. It doesn't matter whether you serve in a restaurant, are sick in bed, or an average student struggling to make good grades in school, God is well able to "make you the head, and not the tail." People will want to ask your advice before taking weighty decisions, while others will see in your company, a blessing you might not see yourself.

When God makes a man, that man doesn't push for recognition. Indeed, he restrains himself from being "crowned king" by the crowd. He becomes like Joseph, whose light shone from prison to palace. He becomes like Daniel, whose gifts could not be overshadowed by Babylonian captivity; and he becomes like Ruth, whose position as the last and the least known among the reapers in the field, could not stop her becoming part of the ancestry of David and Jesus.

Beloved, seeking to make yourself what God has not made you, is a dangerous adventure. One of the ways you can discern your drift towards that direction, is when you begin to desire to be somebody else other than yourself. Remember all "heads" are not of the same size, shape, or color. God made them without asking our input or opinions. If you don't accept yourself, nobody will accept or respect you. Untie the hands of God and let him MAKE YOU the head he wants you to be, and not the tail you are likely to become if you resist him.

God bless you and make you relevant in Jesus' name!

In Pursuit of Knowledge

Hos.6:3, NKJV

Let us know, let us pursue the knowledge of the Lord. His going forth is established as the morning; He will come to us like the rain, like the latter and former rain to the earth

---

Ignorance is very costly. You cannot own what you don't know, and you cannot know until you commit to learning. God wants to have a relationship with us based on love and knowledge. This knowledge is not acquired through "distance learning". It is knowledge gained through daily, progressive, intimate relationship with Jesus, as we spend time meditating on His Word, following His Ways, and fulfilling His Will.

It is knowledge gained in the prayer-closet, fueled by praise and worship, a life of love, discipline, sacrifice, integrity, and compassion. Despite the rare miracles worked through him by the Lord, the apostle Paul still expressed the desire " to KNOW Him (Jesus) and the power of His resurrection" (Phil.3:10a). This is not academic or head-knowledge. Paul is talking about "heart" or "full knowledge" (Greek word is "epignosis") - academics inclusive, not exclusive.

We are challenged to "press on" in pursuit of this knowledge, which suggests that there might be hindrances to that effort. When we don't feel like praying, that is when we must pray. When we don't feel like praising, that is when we must praise. When we don't feel like witnessing for Christ, that is the time to witness. The LEARNING process should begin with a LEANING posture. You cannot learn anything from God, if you are leaning on your own understanding. Lean on the Holy Spirit. He is our real Teacher in the School of God.

Sometimes I find myself hard pressed not to love some folks because they treated me really bad. The only way I come clean is to ask the Holy Spirit to love them through me, and He always does. He is so faithful, gracious, powerful, and consistent.

Beloved, Jesus Christ (our Bridegroom) is coming again. I don't have His flight schedule or arrival date, but I see the signs of His coming. The way He said it would be before His arrival, is what I am using to draw my conclusions. Everything is just fulfilling His Word. We (His Bride) must get ourselves ready for the wedding. Ideally, you cannot marry someone you don't know, and the more you know your future spouse, the better. You can look into his or her eyes on the wedding day with a heart bubbling with joy and love, because you know your beloved in a way that makes you feel safe and secure in his or her presence.

The King is coming. Let us "press on" to KNOW Him in a very personal and intimate way. Depending on the preacher to know God, is "long distance education". It is not recommended for kingdom elevation. Wean yourself from spiritual baby-milk. Learn to pray for yourself. Talk to God as a child talking to his or her father, and He will reveal Himself to you. He will come to you "like the rain...that waters the earth." God bless you and yours in Jesus' Name

Be Faithful

Prov.19:20, NKJV

A faithful man will abound with blessings, but he who hastens to be rich will not go unpunished

When people want to get what they want to get without any regard to integrity, truth, and moral values, they are unable to hold faithfulness as a principle of life. An unfaithful person is a liability in any community and relationship.

In this passage of scripture, we see that one of the things that breed unfaithfulness is greed, and an insatiable desire to get rich quick. This is a generation of speed and fastness. There's nothing basically wrong with that. The problem is when it makes corruption an acceptable way of life and equates vice with virtue.

As children of light, we must pay enough attention to Jesus' words that "man shall not live by bread alone..." and that there are consequences for unfaithfulness. Once it becomes evident that you have been unfaithful, you lose the trust people used to have in you and that means whatever blessing these people can be to you is truncated.

The Lord has a great incentive for you to be faithful. His Word says, "a faithful man will abound with blessings." Your faithfulness will position you for the blessings of God. Nobody can ignore you if you are faithful, so be faithful. They may not like you but will respect you for it. Be faithful to God, to yourself, and to all others.

God bless you

Weak Indeed

Prov.24:10, GNB

If you are weak in a crisis, you are weak indeed.

The depth of our faith, and the strength of our character and commitment, is hardly seen when things are going well with us. Anybody can claim to have faith in God when things are going well with him.

People can easily identify with you when they consider you as a "safe haven"; someone whose company benefits them. Once you give them a treat, and do not pose a threat, you are forever their hero. Your true lovers are those who stick with you when the heat is on, and you don't have anything to benefit them.

In the same vein, you are your own worst enemy, if you cannot stand up to crisis, because many of the crisis you will have to deal with, are people related. Whether you are a parent or a child, employer or employee, teacher or student, pastor or lay person, married or single, young or old, does not exonerate you from one form of crisis or the other.

The interesting thing about crisis is that it may come without warning; and even if you see it coming, you may not be able to stop or dodge it. The best you can do is to endure it, and that is where the grace factor comes into play, and prayer becomes crucial. Jesus had many shades of crisis in his days on earth. Gethsemane was the doorway to what amounted to the mother of all his earthly crisis. The path he pursued and survived, is the way to our victory; he prayed until sweat coming from his body looked like blood.

You cannot love life and wish away crisis. You can hope for it not to come but be prepared to stand and not sink if and when it comes. The writer of this proverb says clearly that one who is weak in crisis is weak indeed. When you are tempted to do what you know you shouldn't do, it is crisis time for you, and you must win over it. There is no formula to escape crisis, whether in the home, church, workplace, or anywhere else; we all face diverse kinds of crisis. You have to learn to live with and overcome it.

Jesus taught us to pray not to be led into temptation. It is key to winning over the crisis even before it strikes. You don't wait for the crisis to come before asking God for help; you make it a subject of daily prayer, asking God to give you strength to stand and overcome any crisis that might come your way. It is my prayer that if you are contending with any crisis today, the good Lord will give you strength and tenacity to be able to stand and conquer.

God bless you.

Whole Armor

Eph.6:11, NKJV

Put on the whole armor of God, that you may be able to stand against the wiles of the devil

Satan and his demons are not the figment of any human imagination; they are real, active, alive, and patently evil. You ignore them at your own peril. We must however be careful not to attribute every negative occurrence to Satan and his demons. That is another extreme likely to lead us into being obsessed with demonism.

But the truth as revealed in this portion of scripture is that; 1. We are involved in a spiritual fight against Satan. And when we talk about Satan, we are not referring to someone who is dumb, a nonentity, or a push-over. We are referring to a spirit-being who attempted a palace-coup in heaven and was able to get a third of the heavenly hosts on his side (Rev.12:7-9); someone who used deception to knock out our first parents in the garden of Eden, dared to tempt Jesus Christ our Lord (Lu.4:1-4), and possessed Judas Iscariot right in the presence of Jesus at the Communion Table (Jn.13:27).

2. Our second lesson from today's passage is to make sure to put on the spiritual defensive armor God has provided for us. It is clear that there are things God will never do for us. The command is for us to PUT ON the WHOLE armor of God. This must be done with diligence, if we are to survive against our number one arch enemy, Satan and his demons.

3. The devil has "wiles" or well-thought-out plans against us. He was here before we landed here. He knows what attracts our attention and distracts us from God. When one trick to trap us to sin against God fails, he doesn't go to sleep. He goes back to the drawing board and tries another strategy, so never lose your guard.

4. Satan has a very well-structured military hierarchy. When Daniel prayed, God answered immediately, but Bible says the "prince of Persia" (the territorial evil spirit of Persia) blocked the angel of God for 21 days. It took perseverance on Daniel's part to overcome the "prince of Persia." Indeed, God had to send the archangel Michael to deal with that high-ranking demon. Glory be God for the blood of the Lamb, we are no longer victims of the devil and his demons. Once we obey what the Word commands, we are safe from the treachery of the devil and his demons.

Put on the whole armor of God, and no weapon fashioned against you, your family, or church will prosper.

God bless you!

Turn from Your Evil Ways and Live

Eze.18:23, NKJV

Say to them: 'As I live,' says the LORD GOD, I have no pleasure in the death of the wicked, but that the wicked turn from his way and live. Turn, turn from your evil ways! For why should you die, O house of Israel?'

We are witnessing an interesting phenomenon on the spiritual landscape of our country, with an increasing number of "prophets," whose specialty is to curse the "wicked" and predict the death of prominent people in society.

The scripture does not endorse wishing evil or putting a seal of condemnation on sinners. It states clearly that God is not happy with the death of a sinner. He hates sin, but not the sinner. The sinner is God's lost treasure; a precious soul created in the image of God, and God is searching for him with relentless passion and aggression to restore him.

Everything about the life and mission of Christ is centered on this one thing: salvation of the wicked/sinner, not his death and destruction. The Word of God says, "there will be more joy in heaven over one sinner who repents than over ninety-nine just persons who need no repentance" (Lu.15:7). My understanding of what Jesus is saying here is that all the good guys in church put together, do not bring as much joy to heaven, as one "wicked" person who turns his back on sin and accepts him as Lord and personal Savior. You may have a problem with that, but you cannot change the rules of the game; God loves the sinner.

If wickedness will decrease, the gospel must be preached in its unadulterated form by all who have seen the light and been saved by His grace. There is no scriptural basis for cursing sinners, no matter what sin they have committed. There is no category of sinners who are disqualified from accessing the grace of God.

Let the Spirit of God plant seeds of compassion in your heart, so you can shepherd souls to heaven, not sentence them to hell. Remember this; for every "wicked" person or sinner who dies in his sin, God loses and Satan wins. It means when you rejoice over the death of a sinner, you are actually celebrating the "victory" of Satan.

Wake up to God's call to save the lost. Tell the world that hell is real, but God has prepared a better alternative for all who are willing to accept Jesus Christ as Lord and personal Savior. Let's get the job done. We are saved to serve, not to curse and condemn.

God bless you!

Choose God's Peace

Is.48:22, NKJV

"There is no peace," says the LORD, "for the wicked."

The word "wicked" used in this context, refers to one who has hardened his heart against the Word and Will of God. It is referring to one who lives in sin; one who enjoys and indulges the desires of the fleshly nature, and as a result is unable to access the peace of Christ. It is more of rejection than denial. It is not God deciding to deny the "wicked" person His peace; it is the "wicked" who chooses to reject God's peace, which is the fruit of God's Spirit.

A life yielded to the Holy Spirit cannot be controlled by the sinful nature. The writer of the book of Romans puts it this way: "Do you not know that to whom YOU PRESENT YOURSELVES SLAVES TO OBEY, you are that one's slaves whom you obey, whether of sin leading to death, or of obedience leading to righteousness?" (Rom.6:16).

For instance, you cannot insist on seeking revenge, and dream of having peace. That feeling of vengeance will place a yoke of unhappiness around your soul, and you cannot know the peace of God till you submit to the Word of God and forgive.

There is nothing as precious as the peace we have in Christ. It impacts every area of our lives. Our joy depends on it, our health depends on it, and our productivity is determined by it. If there is anything that can stand between you and God's peace, it is nothing but sin. It is not necessarily some gargantuan wicked activity like murder, or idolatry. When you worry, it is sin. Why? Jesus said we should not worry; so, when we worry, it is disobedience.

Anytime you choose to disobey the Word of God, you have made a decision to reject His peace and presence in your life. In very simple matters of life, you may fall prey to losing your peace. The scripture is serving you notice that whenever you lose your peace, you have lost touch with the Holy Spirit. Something is happening around you, or inside of your mind, that is stifling the free flow of God's peace, and must be dealt with immediately.

Remember the words of the prophet Isaiah (Is.26:3), "You will keep him in perfect peace, whose MIND is stayed on you..." Sometimes it takes conscious determination to win this battle of the mind, especially when the facts on the ground points to nothing but stress, pain, confusion and crisis.

But thanks be to God, who in all our struggles offers help if we turn to him in prayer. May you never deny yourself so great a blessing and privilege; to enjoy the peace of God always in all ways. God bless you and yours, with the peace that surpasses all human understanding in Jesus Christ's wonderful Name! Amen!

Walk the Talk of Love

1 Jn. 3:18, NKJV

My little children, let us not love in word or in tongue, but in deed and in truth

---

Talk is cheap, so anyone can say "I love you," without putting much thought to it. By the way, I learnt recently that the correct English word for describing one who talks much is "talker," not "talkative"; so, it is the norm for a talker, or talkative person to say things he really does not mean.

Indeed, the world interprets love to mean something different from what the Bible defines it to be. The world confesses love to you if it doesn't involve any personal loss or sacrifices. In many of my counseling sessions with young people preparing for marriage, their perception of life after marriage has almost always been one of romance, and happiness thereafter.

They come to the table with what I sometimes see as unrealistic expectations of getting, benefiting, and holding; little or no thought of giving, learning, and releasing. Such misconceptions clearly do not help in building strong foundations for successful marriage lives, and so I have found it forever important to call attention to the cost aspect of the marriage union during counseling sessions.

In his letter to the saints, Apostle John explained how important it was, and still is, for believers to go beyond confessing love, to actually manifesting it in deeds and in truth. He said you cannot ignore a brother in need when it is in your power to help him, and then turn round and say, 'I love you.' No, you don't! You must put substance to the 'sound of love.'

In Jn.3:16, God showed his love for us by giving us tangible evidence in his Son, Jesus Christ. Love that does not give, is a lie; and love that gives everything minus self, still falls short of God's expectations. If you love your wife, you don't deny her your physical presence and insist she should be happy because you provide everything she needs. Don't let the devil seduce you into believing your children are okay with just buying them goodies, and not being in their lives.

Put life into your love-life, and never miss an opportunity to let someone know and experience the love of God in you, both by the giving of your PRESENTS and your PRESENCE. Our world is suffering from acute love-deficiency, and many are those who are struggling with rejection. A little time you invest in showing them you care is all the spark they need to lighten their lives.

Walk the talk. Let your love find expression in good deeds. God bless you and make you a channel of divine love in Jesus Name! Amen!

Break Fallow Ground

Hos10:12, NKJV

Sow for yourselves righteousness; reap in mercy; break up your fallow ground, for it is time to seek the LORD, till He comes and rains righteousness on us.

The ministry of the prophet Hosea was an extremely difficult one. God asked him to marry an unfaithful woman; a woman he was to love, but who would consistently prove unfaithful by running after other men.

In that chaotic and murky marriage relationship, God painted a picture of how Israel was being unfaithful to him; while he loved them and stayed committed to his covenant with them, they betrayed and hurt him by going after other gods. Then the time came when Hosea raised the red flag and warned of severe consequences if the people would not repent and commit to serving the one true God only.

That call is relevant in our time too; a time when the Church has defiled itself so much that the dividing line between Christians and unbelievers in terms of attitudes and behavioral patterns, is almost non-existent.

Here is Hosea's Living message to Israel and the Church. First, the prophet declares, "sow for yourselves righteousness; reap mercy." The principle of Sowing and Reaping is clearly played out here; what you sow is what you reap. Nobody does the sowing for you. If you desire to access the mercy of God, then it is your responsibility to sow for yourself righteousness; that is, pursuing truth, shunning the wrong, and doing the right. The sun may shine for both the sinner and the saint, but the Spirit of God doesn't minister to both at the same level.

The second call is to "break up your fallow ground." Once again, we see here that the responsibility lies on us to break the "ground"; to prepare our hearts for God to do in us what we are not able to do for ourselves. You cannot do any serious and successful sowing on a "fallow ground". It has to be prepared through breaking, and that is akin to a hardened heart being softened through repentance and obedience; God's Spirit is not able to do any effective work in an unrepentant heart. It is not of weakness on the part of the Spirit, but of denial by the person involved.

Seeking God will only produce good dividends if it is done in a spirit of repentance. You must get rid of everything that defiles body, soul, and spirit, in order to enjoy the freshness of the rain of righteousness. When the ground is not prepared, weeds will choke out whatever is planted, and your effort will be wasted. God, like Hosea, is forever committed to his covenant of love for you, but you have a part to play in order to enjoy the full benefits of the covenant.

Sow for yourself righteousness and break your fallow ground. God will not do that for you. If there is an area in your life where you know "the ground is hard" through sin, take action today! Repent, and prepare your heart for "it is time seek the LORD, till He comes and rains righteousness on you!

Temporary Applause or Eternal Relationship?

Jer.32:17-18, NKJV

They sacrificed to demons, not to God, to gods they did not know, to new gods, new arrivals that your fathers did not fear. Of the Rock who begot you, you are unmindful, and have forgotten the God who fathered you.

These are words of a song composed and sang by Moses to the children of Israel in the wilderness. The words recounted the faithfulness of God to his people, and their response of ingratitude and rebellion. Before we pass judgement on them, we must first reflect on our own individual and collective attitudes towards God's grace and mercy towards us.

If Israel sacrificed to idols, it means they took the blessings they received from the Lord and used it to honor other gods. What it is saying to us is that our stewardship of whatever blessings the Lord gives us is important to him. You cannot use the money God gives you the strength to make, to promote ungodliness. All that God gives you must be used to promote people and programs that stand the test of righteousness. Where you spend your time, and how you use your resources should show your commitment to honoring the grace of God on your life.

The world is aggressively pushing idols of sex, money, power, and fame down our throats; and if we are not careful, we may tacitly endorse practices and lifestyles that are contrary to the Word of God. Satan has a way of drawing us away from God and making us worship the creation instead of the creator. When the world threatens you with sanctions and insist you bow to its filth, or face its wrath, you have to take a stand for Christ and truth. I know it is neither popular nor politically correct, but if you are given the choice between pleasing the Lord, and becoming popular with the world, where would you cast your vote?

Remember, the applause of the world is only temporary; your relationship with God is eternal. The "new" is always attractive and promises what it cannot deliver. Do not trade anything for your relationship with God. Keep your eyes on Jesus Christ, the author and finisher of our faith. Anything and anyone that exalts itself to the status of deity and demands your worship must go down the drain of rejection and contempt.

When they package evil and present it to you in the form of entertainment and modernity, refuse to yield to the deception. Jesus told Satan, "It is written; you shall worship the Lord thy God and serve him only." This is the most appropriate response for the "new gods" today's corrupt socio-political systems are churning out. Let your convictions be clear and above board. As much as the world is free to believe and worship its own gods, it should not impose its standards on you. Their freedom ends where yours begin.

God bless you!

Called to Love, Not Condemn

1 Sam.1:17-18, NKJV

Then Eli answered and said, "Go in peace, and the God of Israel grant your petition which you have asked of Him." And she said, "Let your maid-servant find favor in your sight." So the woman went her way and ate, and her face was no longer sad.

Lady Hannah had no child, and so went into the tabernacle to petition God for a child. She chose to pray quietly without making any show of her burden. Bible records that "she was in bitterness of soul and prayed to the LORD in anguish" (v.10).

It takes someone who has been through a situation similar to what Hannah went through to understand her frustration. In the comfort of his armchair at the door-post of the tabernacle, Eli the priest, looked at Hannah praying on her knees, and weeping; her lips moving without her words being heard, and he concluded that she was drunk. Here is the danger; judging people we don't understand on the basis of our limited knowledge of the circumstances of their lives.

Hannah respectfully protested against the priest's prejudiced position and said, "I am a woman of sorrowful spirit. I have drunk neither wine nor intoxicating drink but have poured out my soul before the Lord." How about that? How often do we not add to the burden others carry by making very insensitive, careless, and judgmental comments?

The priest Eli's response is worthy of our emulation and showed tremendous spiritual sensitivity and maturity on his part. When he realized he was wrong, he immediately spoke a word of compassion, blessing, and comfort into Hannah's life. The man of God was neither intransigent, nor defensive; he readily accepted his mistake, and spoke words that were proper and appropriate. The spirit of depression was lifted off the shoulders of Hannah, and she walked away happier and very much comforted. Indeed, she took no offense at the priest's unjustified rebuke. She received the blessing in faith, and God honored both her prayer, and the blessings Eli pronounced on her.

Let us be slow in coming to quick conclusions about the struggles and challenges others may be going through. We may not know as much as we think we know. Eli's formula for prayer, did not match Hannah's depth of frustration. The fact that someone stands to pray while you kneel down, doesn't make you more spiritual than him. The connecting point to God is the HEART, not the ACT. Let each exercise our freedom in Christ without being overly critical of others. We are called to love, not to condemn.

God bless you.

Seek Godly Counsel

1 Chron.13:1-2, NKJV

Then David consulted with the captains of thousands and hundreds, and with every leader. And David said to all the assembly of Israel, "If it seems good to you, and if it is of the LORD our God, let us send out to our brethren everywhere who are left in all the land of Israel...and let us bring the ark of our God back to us

---

There are many channels we can explore before taking major decisions; especially when those decisions do not affect us alone. One such channel is consultation with trusted "captains". Careful consultations bring constructive results.

When King David decided to change the location of the Ark of God, he took into consideration the reverence the generality of Israel had for the Ark, and so went into consultation with them. He refrained from taking a unilateral decision on an issue that demanded a united front and general consensus. As long as the people were one with him in spirit, David felt safe and comfortable in making them part of his decision-making process.

Indeed, it is unwise to take counsel with your opponents and detractors; it will be like putting a gun to your head and pulling the trigger. You need to consult but be careful who you consult. The next important step David took was to begin with the leadership; "the captains of thousands and hundreds, and with every leader." We all need "captains of thousands and hundreds" in our lives, no matter our level of knowledge and expertise. No one can claim absolute wisdom and knowledge apart from God.

Fortunately, he has given each of us a measure of his wisdom and knowledge that we can put together to achieve great goals. The way forward is to share your thoughts and burdens with those you can trust to help you sort them out. Discuss your fears and doubts with the "captains" in your life. They are part of the gifts and blessings the Lord has given you. There is nothing shameful about seeking help when you need it.

Indeed, if you are so self-sufficient that you never needed to consult anyone for advice - not your parents, not your spouse, not your pastors, not your seniors and elders, then you are like Moses sitting in judgment over Israel from morning till nighttime. You are not doing right; you are abusing your brain and body and inviting depression and frustration. Get people who sincerely care about the things you care about involved in decisions that are weighty and have far-reaching consequences.

It will be naive to suggest that you can tell everyone about everything. You cannot do that; but what you can, and must do, is to prayerfully identify the category of relationships you can confidently consult whenever the need arises. It will free you from stress and avoidable mistakes. It will wean you off pettiness and make you joyful in your daily pursuits.

God bless you

Character Versus Charisma

2 Sam.14:25, NKJV

Now in all Israel there was no one who was so praised as much as Absalom for his good looks. From the sole of his foot to the crown of his head there was no blemish in him

---

The great English writer, William Shakespeare, wrote in his classic play titled Macbeth, that "there is no act to find the mind's construction in the face." In other words, you cannot tell what a person is thinking, just by looking at his or her face.

Appearance can be extremely deceptive. King David's favorite son appeared to be Absalom. He indulged Absalom and showed a soft spot for his disobedience all through the young man's turbulent life. According to the scriptures, Absalom's physical appearance was that of a perfect gentleman, but the same could not be said of his character. The most handsome child of the king became the most disloyal and rebellious citizen of his kingdom. He used his beauty and charm to win the hearts and minds of even close associates and officials of his father. Absalom was handsome, but not honest. He was good-looking, but not trustworthy.

Listening to a news item yesterday on a Christian radio station, I was shocked at the statistics of Christian marriages ending in divorce over the past decade. Part of the problem can be attributed to entering into relationships with people who appear to be something they are not; a perfect Absalom-cut, and an excellent Judas Iscariot spirit. We are all vulnerable to such characters because it is impossible to discern the motive of everyone who comes into relationship with us. Perhaps our greatest weakness is the tendency to concentrate so much on the outward appearance that we become less sensitive to the promptings of the Holy Spirit, relative to the face behind the mask of the person we are dealing with.

A cousin of mine has always maintained that "a man in love is a mad man." If that is true (which I guess it is to some extent), then we need to do some spiritual realignment. The emotional pain we go through, as we come face to face with the Absaloms' in our lives can be minimized, if we take a little more time to ask the Holy Spirit to show us "the man/woman behind the mask"; because CHARACTER and CHARISMA are not the same. Jesus spent a lot of time with his disciples before calling them his friends (Jn.15:15). As a servant of the Lord Jesus Christ, I see too many saints wounded and bleeding emotionally because they fell into the trap of a "handsome Absalom."

I have been a constant victim myself, and sometimes tempted to think that "he who loves much, suffers much." If you are contemplating marriage or committing to any kind of relationship with a business partner, a leadership team in the church etc., please depend on the Holy Spirit to give you discernment so you can make an informed decision. Outward beauty and impressive human achievement are like the body of a car; it has absolutely nothing to do with the condition of its engine (the heart).

Look before you leap, because all that glitters is not gold. I pray that the Lord will minister grace to you in any area of your life where an Absalom has brought you pain and caused you grief. Your future is more important than your past, so free yourself from what happened that you cannot change and position yourself for greater possibilities and better relationships. May God guide and bless you in all your future relationships.

God bless you

Take Good Care of Yourself

Mk.3:9-10, NKJV

So He told His disciples that a small boat should be kept ready for Him because of the multitude, lest they crush Him. For He healed many, so that as many as had afflictions pressed about Him to touch Him

---

A common feature of the ministry of our Lord was the large number of people who always followed him. This account of Mark shows the pressure that was on Jesus, because "as many as had afflictions pressed about Him to touch Him." Faced with the possibility of the crowd crushing him to death, Jesus did the smart thing; he asked the disciples to keep a small boat ready for him. His reason for requesting the small boat was "because of the multitude, lest they CRUSH him."

The lesson for us is to be very objective and apply commonsense, even when we are doing something for God. We don't only have to work; we also have to work SMART. Jesus could have chosen to pray during this particular crisis, but that would not have solved the problem. The crisis he was facing, demanded a practical, commonsense approach, and immediate response, not a long-term spiritual solution. He was dealing with people who were desperate for healing. They had no patience to wait in a queue; and in such a frenzy and chaotic crowd, the safety of the Lord could not be guaranteed. Jesus did what was necessary to position and protect himself in a way that would be of benefit to everyone involved.

As a minister of the gospel, and one used to the push-and-pull of the people we are called to serve, I know of times when tiredness sets in, and yet the "multitude" clamor for your attention. Sometimes you tend to think if you don't keep going, despite the depleted energy, God's work will not get done. That is far from the truth. If it didn't stop after Peter, James, John, Paul, and all the apostles left the scene, why would it stop because you took a break? I have learnt how to stop when the energy level for ministry drops; to sleep and trust God to take care of his people until I am revived enough to run the next race. I have learnt that if you push yourself beyond what your physical body can endure, you might not live long enough to benefit as many as God plans for you to bless.

Beloved, Jesus Christ the Lord of life, was strategic in ministry. He did not make spiritual capital out of physical realities. He made provision for his protection; he asked for a "standby ambulance" in the form of a small boat. The Lord was willing to bless the multitude, but not prepared to be buried under their frustrations. Let me say to somebody out there working without taking time off to rest, "you are not doing right." Whatever work you are engaged in, follow the Master's example by providing a protective cover for yourself.

If you are in ministry, let me offer a word of caution; never sacrifice your family for the "crowd." Remember Paul's advice to Timothy, that if a man cannot take good care of his own family, he is not qualified to serve in leadership position in Christ's Church. Don't abuse your body, your relationships, your resources, your time, and opportunities, in the name of faith. Get a "small boat" standing by in case of an emergency. Don't replace PLANNING with PRAYER; identify the difference and give each its own place of priority. Take good care of yourself and your family first, and then you will have the peace and energy to serve others better and longer.

God bless you

Temporary Trouble, Eternal Glory

2 Cor. 4:16-17, GNB

For this reason, we never become discouraged. Even though our physical being is gradually decaying, yet our spiritual being is renewed day after day. And this small and temporary trouble we suffer will bring us a tremendous and eternal glory, much greater than the trouble

---

My head used to be covered with a mass of hair; there was no indication that I was going to experience baldness. Coming into the ranks of senior citizens, time began to reshape my hair, and baldness set in; the message was loud and clear that the "physical man is gradually decaying."

I appreciate the many efforts at developing age-defying chemicals and medicines to stop the process of physical decay; but the truth is that our best efforts can only delay the process of decay, but never stop it. We are better off coming to terms with what we cannot change than trying to fight it. Apostle Paul had to admit that he was suffering. His comfort was not in a present he could not control or change, but in a future that promises relief.

Following Jesus does not guarantee a life of daily ease and laughter. Sometimes we have to face pain and decay. This is because the principle at work in the universe today is still subject to the consequences of Adam's sin, and until Jesus Christ comes to restore creation back to divine order, everything in creation will continue to groan. Too many believers are in denial of this basic truth and are living in self-delusion; thinking that Christianity is a tea party. Please, it is not! We are in a chaotic spiritual environment, where Satan and his demons are still free to operate against us. We must face the fact and stand up to the fight.

There is climate change, and much pollution of air and water bodies, and the effort we need to put in to stay alive and healthy is more than little. Our joy and comfort therefore do not rest on the temporary struggles and challenges of this life, but on what lies beyond here. Encouragement comes with the remembrance that while our physical being is gradually decaying, the inner man of the spirit is gaining strength. What you are losing physically, is necessary for gaining what God has prepared for you spiritually.

Paul says, "this small and temporary trouble we suffer, will bring us a tremendous and eternal glory much greater than the trouble." Whether you consider the "trouble" you are going through to be small or big, take consolation in the fact that it is temporary. It cannot hold you forever, and the end result will be glorious. I encourage you once again to keep the faith and kick the fear. There are no hopeless situations with our God; every pain you endure will be adequately rewarded in greater measure with his glory.

God bless you

Saved by Grace

Gal. 6:14, GNB

As for me, however, I will boast only about the cross of our Lord Jesus Christ; for by means of his cross the world is dead to me, and I am dead to the world

---

The early church faced a crisis which is reflected in our devotional scripture for today (Gal.6:14). The Jewish Christians wanted to marry the "dos" and "don'ts" of the Mosaic law to their newfound faith in Christ. They found it hard worshipping God without external rituals that gave them grounds to boast about their self-righteousness. They ignored the power of the cross; the source of their salvation, and highlighted their physical circumcision, the symbol of works of the flesh.

Apostle Paul had to remind them that our restored relationship with Father-God, and subsequent access to heaven has nothing to do with anything we have done or can ever do. Salvation begins and ends at the cross.

The number of souls you lead to Christ, and the amount of money you give to your church are not the reason God calls you his child. You are a child of God by virtue of the sacrificial death of the Lamb of God. It is the price Jesus Christ paid by shedding his blood on Calvary that makes all the difference.

Good works are not good enough to meet God's righteous demand for salvation, so if we should boast, let us boast in the fact that the BLOOD of Jesus has set us free from the bondage and consequences of sin.

God bless you

Clean on the Inside

Matt 23:27-28, NKJV

Woe to you, scribes and Pharisees, hypocrites! For you cleanse the outside of the cup and dish, but inside they are full of dead men's bones and all uncleanness. Even so you also outwardly appear righteous to men, but inside you are full of hypocrisy and lawlessness

This is hard stuff but guess who was preaching; it was "gentle Jesus, meek and mild." He did not sound like a motivational speaker, or a pastor who aims at keeping the people in church at all cost. Jesus loved his audience too much to allow them to continue living a lie.

The Scribes and the Pharisees were completely out of tune with the Spirit of the Law. Their worship was a display of self-righteousness; effectively replacing doctrine with dogma. They loved to put on a show to impress, while in their hearts (where it matters most with God), they were starved of truth and integrity. Jesus insisted on walking the talk. The Master's position is that those who confess God should have a heart-attitude that reflects in their actions. It is better to say you don't believe in Jesus, than to confess him and betray him; that is the bottom line.

It is not difficult to go through the motions of worship without any heart-commitment to God. Indeed, this danger of backsliding in heart is more a threat to those of us who have served the Lord for years, than it is to newly born-again believers. We can get so familiar with the move of God, that we stop moving along with him. The word "hypocrisy" Jesus used here, reflects a condition of pride; presenting a false image of who we really are. It is an unnecessary position to take, because even though we can deceive our fellow human beings with falsehood, our deepest thoughts and motives are constantly laid bare before the Lord.

What we reflect on the outside in terms of behavior, must correspond with what is on the inside in relation to belief. If you don't believe in something, don't endorse it. Let your works be a manifestation of your convictions. What you are before men, should be same as who you are before God.

The Lord is not enthused with the praise that only comes with the supply of bread. Faith in Christ is not merely about accumulating Bible quotations in your head, but the inner convictions of your heart, which translates to a life of humility, honesty, love, and integrity. Get your act together, and shine as a child of the light, if you really love my Jesus.

God bless you

Passionate Correction

Amos 5:10, NKJV

They hate the one who rebukes in the gate, and they abhor the one who speaks uprightly

---

Almost everyone knows our society is literally walking with its head on the ground, and legs in the air. You may not admit it, but you know it. Most of the things that are celebrated today, are mostly things we should be sad about. Some of the people we hail as legends and celebrities, turn out to be huge embarrassments, and an apology to everything decent and moral.

A random survey of some of the films shown on prime-time television, and the lyrics of most of the music being churned out today, points to one thing; our world is sinking in a quagmire of immorality. When we talk only about prosecuting sexual offenders, I know we are dealing with the symptoms and not the causes of the disease. We can do better by discouraging the creation of an environment and culture that promotes sexual promiscuity. As the old saying goes, "prevention is better than cure."

What we should be doing, if we want decency in our private and public lives, is to uphold the Biblical standards of morality. We must reinvent the wheel of correction and rebuke, encouraging Godliness and integrity. If a brother or sister is hooked on pornographic stuff and you know it, God expects you to help him/her out by being bold enough to speak up against it. As long as you live in an environment that takes away the sanctity of sex and makes it an "over the counter" commodity, and you condone it, many souls are bound to fall victim to its devastating effect.

This generation hates the Bible because it doesn't speak its politically correct language of compromise, when it comes to issues of sin. They tell you it is not right to speak against evil because no one is perfect. Somebody please give this boy a break. God's Word says the opposite; it says as "iron sharpens iron," so are we to look out for each other's interest. One important way to "sharpen" me, is to rebuke me if you have to. You don't rebuke me of sin because you are perfect, but because we are collectively in pursuit of righteousness.

You don't protect me by watching me live in sin and keeping quiet about it. If you want to avoid the "hate" of the world, you can never walk in obedience to the Word. Jesus did not only comfort, encourage, inspire, and save people, he also rebuked sin when necessary. Look at the scripture for our devotion again. It says, "they hate the one who rebukes in the gate." What is the purpose of a gate? It gives access when opened and prevents entrance when closed. That is what "rebuke" does in our lives.

When applied according to scripture, it opens the door to righteous living, which ultimately brings rich rewards. When it is compromised, it closes the door to repentance and subsequent restoration, and the end result is judgment. Nobody who keeps quiet and withholds rebuke, when you are pursuing a path that can destroy you, can claim to love you.

Rebuke is neither rejection nor condemnation. Rebuke is another word for correction. I choose to call it "passionate correction," because I believe it takes passion to see a loved one redeemed from self-destruction; to be able to rebuke him. Pay more attention to the people who correct you, than those who compromise with you. One who loves you, will not keep quiet over what can destroy you.

God bless you

Spiritual Vigilance

Lu.9:30-32, NKJV

And behold, two men talked with Him, who were Moses and Elijah, who appeared in glory and spoke of His decease which He was to accomplish at Jerusalem. But Peter and those with him were heavy with sleep; and when they were fully awake, they saw His glory and the two men who stood with Him.

Jesus took three of His disciples up a mountain. You can imagine what effort they might have put in to get up the mountain. I had a mountain-climbing experience only once in my life in 1979 at Abeokuta, Nigeria. I must confess I never liked it, so anytime I read about people going up mountains, I applaud them. I see them as 'strong' people.

The three disciples who went up the mountain with Jesus obviously fall within that category and will forever have my appreciation. However, these mountain-climbing companions of Jesus, nearly missed the wonderful experience and encounter God had purposed for them on the mountain. They were meant to SEE the glory of Jesus, not to SLEEP on the mountain. It appears they were not anticipating anything unusual.

Being with Jesus had become a daily routine for them. They had witnessed Him heal the sick, feed thousands, and raise the dead. What more could happen with Him that they had not seen? Familiarity was breeding contempt - unconsciously. They were tired and ready to give in to sleep; but suddenly they saw a unique phenomenon. Moses and Elijah appeared, and with them came the glory of God. Bible says, "and when THEY WERE FULLY AWAKE, they saw His glory." What is God saying to us? You cannot SLEEP and SEE the glory.

Spiritual vigilance is required of all who desire to SEE His glory. You may have been a believer and in expectancy for something you may consider to be taking too long a time to manifest. The delay is taking its toll on your faith and commitment to the Lord. You have slackened in your spiritual life - no more reading of the Bible, no private prayer time with the Lord, and not much committed to fellowshipping with the saints.

You still believe in Jesus. You have not completely renounced your faith in Him. You just feel tired, discouraged, uninterested in the things of God, and are just about to sleep on the mountain - in His Presence!! Don't sleep yet. God is saying to you, the time to SEE His glory is closer than you can ever think or imagine. You cannot come this far with Jesus and miss your miracle on the mountain!!

Stay expectant and be open to the Holy Spirit. He can and will surprise you on the 'barren mountains' of your life.

God show you His glory now and always in Jesus' Name!

God bless you!

Obeying God's Will

Jn. 4:34, GNB

My food," Jesus said to them, "is to obey the will of the one who sent me and to finish the work he gave me to do."

When we talk about food, we are referring to a key sustainer of our human bodies. In this scripture, Jesus tells us what his priorities in life are. First, he talks about obeying "the will of the one who sent" him. He recognizes that he was not to live to please himself.

Jesus acknowledged that he was subject to the will of the one who sent him; any deviation means disobedience. He was sold out on his assignment; focused, determined, unwavering, and resolute.

Our difficulty in the Church today is that we are so much in love with our RIGHTS, we have lost track of our RESPONSIBILITIES. The word "obedience" scares us and tends to imply limitation to our liberties. The truth, however, is that unless we submit to God, we have no real freedom. I see two different dimensions of "freedom" in the Holy Bible. it is either FREEDOM FROM SIN, which is borne out of a sense of obedience to God's will, or FREEDOM TO SIN, which is a by-product of living to please self and the worldly system.

Jesus makes it clear that there is no middle ground between obedience and disobedience, as far as the will of God for our lives is concerned. You choose to obey or not to obey. There is no room to pick and choose. For you as a blood-bought child of God, your only choice is to take on a posture that your very survival depends on obeying God's will for your life, as revealed in his Word. The second revelation Jesus gives us here, is his determination to "finish the work he (God) gave me to do." It is good to encourage ourselves and rejoice in how far God has brought us, but that should not make us complacent and lose sight of the finish-line.

Finishing "the work he gave" us to do, is more important than how far we have come, and how much we have achieved. History is full of great men of God who at the apex of their ministries went down in shame and disgrace, because they lost focus and became complacent. When men congratulate you on what you might have done for the Lord, be careful it doesn't get you intoxicated to the point you take your eyes off the ultimate goal.

Unless you finish the assignment, you have failed your God. Place more emphasis on obeying God's will than following man's way. The two are not the same, and do not produce the same results. Stay focused on the things that are important to God; your role in impacting souls for the Kingdom of God, beginning from your home to the wider world. God bless and strengthen you with grace enough to obey him and finish your life's assignment on a glorious note.

God bless you.

Student or Stooge?

Jer.5:30-31, ESV

An appalling and horrible thing has happened: the prophets prophesy lies, and the priests' rule at their direction; my people love to have it so, but what will you do when the end comes?

Has anything much changed since Jeremiah spoke those words? Have prophets stopped peddling falsehood and lies; "directing" God's people to the world, instead of drawing them to the Word?

The present economic difficulties and challenges (especially in our part of the world) has created a market for abusing the prophetic ministry. The number of people falling victim to the antics of false prophets is quite alarming; going by what we hear and see on a daily basis, the worse is yet to come. What makes the situation even worse is the fact that God's "people love to have it so."

When you have a situation where people are not willing to read and study the scriptures for themselves, their "lack of knowledge" becomes the very tool for their exploitation. In the final analysis, we see that the false prophets thrive on our unwillingness to obey the admonition to "study to show yourself approved unto God." We need a paradigm shift that will make us students of the Word, instead of being stooges of prophets; many of whom only trade in the gospel and take advantage of our desire to have our ears tickled with half-baked truths. They tell us what we want to hear, because they know what we want to hear.

Let me take some liberty here; isn't it funny that some of us believe that by typing "amen" to a so-called prophetic declaration, we are going to be instant millionaires and billionaires? Come off it my dear, there is a world of difference between MAGIC and MIRACLE. God gives manna when you are in the wilderness and can't help yourself. Once you are in an environment where you can work and improve your lot, the dynamics change. God then gives you "power to create wealth." You can never associate laziness with the God of the Bible.

If you don't want to be a victim of prophetic manipulation, here are four tips for your consideration - (1) Be a student of the Word of God. (2) Use the Word as litmus test for every prophecy that you receive, no matter who is prophesying. It is about your eternal destiny, and you ought not treat it lightly. (3) Guard against pre-determining what God must say to you. Keep an open mind when it comes to what God is saying to you. (4) Live your life with the end in mind. Jeremiah poses a very important question, "but what will you do when the end comes?" When the chips are down, your life is about you. It has nothing to do with the prophet, or Facebook declarations, no matter how nice they sound.

If you walk in faith and obedience, you are covered. Prophecy is important because it is one of God's ways of giving direction to his children. But the truth of the matter is that you don't need prophecy to live a productive life. Put your faith into action instead of waiting on a prophet to tell you who is your enemy, when to work, and where to go. If you do that, you will be opening yourself up for deception. Think on these things, and the good Lord help you to live by faith, and not by running after prophets.

God bless you.

Pay the Price for the Prize

Judges 5:7, NKJV

Village life ceased, it ceased in Israel, until I Deborah, arose, arose a mother in Israel.

One of the major deficiencies facing the world today, is the lack of Godly, bold, faithful, and selfless leadership. From the home to the church, and from the political ruling class to business executives, decisions are generally made on the basis of personal convenience, and not to sacrifice for the good of others.

When the prophetess Deborah told Barack that it was God's will for him to go and deliver Israel, the gentleman was excited about the prospect of fame and popularity that was to come from that pursuit, but at the same time, he shied away from what it would cost him to be named in the people's Hall of fame. Barack wanted someone to face the bullet whilst he stayed at a safe distance so he could avoid the prospect of being killed; at the same time, he was keen on being part of beneficiaries of any possible booty, if the battle favored them. He insisted on Deborah going with him, and the prophetess obliged on condition that she was going to claim the victory at the end of the battle.

When the mission was accomplished, Deborah celebrated the victory in song, describing how hopeless the situation was in Israel before she stepped in and fought for the salvation of her people. Herein lies another lesson for us; those who stand up to the fight, have a legitimate right to celebrate their victories. Every parent knows what it takes to raise a child in today's environment; an environment that is hostile and alien to morality and commonsense. If, by the grace of God, you are able to raise a child who is walking with the Lord, and pursuing worthy goals, you have cause to be thankful and happy. Meanwhile, there is something you can do if "village life" has ceased in your family, church, or business.

If the peace, calmness, and love you use to know is now history, rise up to the challenge to pray for restoration. If the "city life" of blurring car horns, traffic jams, and unending human activity is taking a toll on you, rise up like Deborah and do something about it. There will be no change in your situation until you change your position. Deborah inspired faith in others when they saw her not only expressing faith in God but acting it out in battle. She had to step out of her primary calling of prophetess, to lead the battle against Israel's enemies. She teaches us that God is able to use us anywhere we are willing to serve, if our motives are right.

When we desire to do what will benefit others, God will give us the grace to succeed. It doesn't matter how difficult the circumstances may seem to be, if you will take the initiative, God will make a way for you. Until Deborah arose, nothing happened; the bondage continued. God was still for them, but that did not change the status quo. Leaders take initiative, and that is what you've got to do, if you want things to change in your family, church, business, or community. If you allow others to fight your battles, then be prepared to be denied of the joy of victory. This is the time to arise and do what must be done. Get up and take that first step. Keep moving, until you establish your presence and be the one who brings joy, peace, and prosperity to your family, church, and community.

God bless you.

True Joy is in Obedience

Ps.119:56, GNB

I find my happiness in obeying God's commands

Many years ago, when I did not know the Lord, I aggressively pursued things and people I believed could make me happy. It was a wild goose chase. Nothing, and nobody satisfies like Jesus. Different things and people brought some measure of happiness into my life, but only for limited periods of time. The times and moods of happiness never lasted for long and did not show consistency on my life's graph sheet. Some of the people and things I looked up to, for my happiness, later became burdens and painful memories.

When I gave my life to Jesus Christ, my old ways of seeking happiness continued with me for some time. It is however too clear to me now than ever, that the only way to live a consistently joyful life, is to commit to obeying God's Word. We are wired by God in ways we cannot fully understand. It takes the "manufacturer" to explain how the product works, and only God can give us instructions that will enable us to function properly. When God "commands," he does not intend to turn our lives into a military boot camp. When God says "don't touch that fruit," it is because he knows the consequences will not be good for me; so, the fact that he "commands" it, gives me joy in obeying him.

The commands of God, rightly interpreted, are instructions that give direction. When you understand it this way, it puts no pressure on you. Rather, it gives you pleasure. When I look back at my journey with Jesus, my greatest joy is that obedience to his Word has brought me great rewards of peace, joy, and contentment. I testify to this, so that you can test God in that area of your life. I would rather pray for grace to obey Christ, than live in sin and make excuses. If there is something in your life that needs to be dealt with, do your part by confessing and confronting it. Are you ready to receive the joy of the Lord? Then obey his word, and it will transform your world.

God bless you.

Ask God for Confirmation

Jos.9:22, NKJV

Then Joshua called for them, and he spoke to them, saying, "Why have you deceived us, saying, "We are very far from you," when you dwell near us?

In the journey to the promised land, Israel under Joshua, created fear and panic as they advanced from place to place, overrunning every enemy that rose against them. When the Gibeonites heard that the people of Israel were within 'firing range,' they adopted a strategy to pre-empt any attack from Joshua's army.

The Gibeonites went and presented themselves as coming from a very far country with gifts; seeking for a covenant under oath that Israel would not attack them. Fortunately for the Gibeonites, Joshua and his entire leadership team fell for the deception. Despite Joshua's commitment and consistency, he became a victim of complacency, and failed to cross-check the information he had received from the Gibeonites.

Scripture records in Joshua 9:14, "Then the men of Israel took some of their provisions; but they did not ask the Lord." Later on, when it became clear to Joshua that the Gibeonites were close neighbors, and had deceived them, he did what I believe every believer should do (especially those in leadership position as parents, pastors, group leaders etc.) The verse 22 reads, "Then Joshua called for them, and he spoke to them, saying, 'Why have you deceived us?' This obviously firm, but gentle confrontation is very necessary, if we are to eliminate the canker of deception in the home, the church, and everywhere it rears its ugly head.

You see, beloved, a deceptive person is a very dangerous person. The only way to help him out is to take him on. There is nothing spiritual about seeing someone deceiving people and keeping quiet about it. What you should not do is smile with him as if nothing has happened and talk about it behind his back. It will not help him, but rather harden him. The exposure may hurt, but when he heals, you would have helped a brother. Silence is not always golden, so as "iron sharpens iron," let us not shy away from helping each other out of unhealthy habits like deception.

If the people you are relating to in the home, school or workplace are not being truthful to you, don't brush it under the carpet; bring it out in the open and deal with it. No relationship can thrive in an atmosphere of lies and deception. Thank you for choosing the Joshua path in dealing with issues of deception, and always remember to ask God for confirmation of the information you receive from "strangers". Don't just dance because you hear the sound of good music.

God bless you.

The Undefiled Garment

Rev.3:4, NKJV

You have a few names even in Sardis who have not defiled their garments; and they shall walk with Me in white, for they are worthy.

Like attracts like; if you identify with Jesus, you will be with Jesus. As the good Lord rejoices over us, we have to respond appropriately FOR him, and rejoice IN him. Our reason for rejoicing should be with the deepest understanding of our privileged position in Christ Jesus. God has clothed us with a very extraordinary spiritual garment, which is in the form of a robe.

Adam's sin de-robed us of our spiritual covering. Before the fall, man had no need of clothes. There was no nakedness to be covered, because Adam and Eve wore robes of purity, righteousness, and absolute innocence. The glory of God enveloped them. When sin entered, everything changed. They were stripped naked and exposed to shame and embarrassment.

If you are like me, you will understand the time and effort that goes into "covering our nakedness" (naturally speaking). I like to dress simple, smart, and sharp - not enthused at all about gay and loud colours. My confidence level is good when I dress to my taste and satisfaction. The truth however is that since the day of my birth, I have worn all kinds of clothes, and none of them ever seem to last for long. Here comes Jesus, when I was BORN AGAIN, and He clothes me with just ONE spiritual garment in the form of a robe, and presto, the lost covering and glory is restored.

The Father offered Adam and Eve animal skin to cover their nakedness, but gave us His Son, Jesus Christ, to cloth us in His own garment of righteousness. How blessed we are, to be wearing the best spiritual-designer clothes made by God Himself. This is the basis for my joy. It's not about money, people, popularity, possessions or position. All of that may have their place in life, but none of them is a lasting "garment".

We can and will lose all of those one day. When you stand before God, you either stand naked like Adam and Eve (as an unrepentant sinner) or clothed in the righteousness of Christ (as a saint redeemed by the blood of Jesus). No other dress to choose from. Friend let us rejoice, for the Lord has done us good. He has clothed us with garments not made with human hands but woven out of His saving grace and mercy. Let's put it on anytime and every time. It is the difference between us and the world; that difference is clear, and it must show.

God bless you.

Obedience over Service

1Kings 6:11-12, ESV

Now the word of the LORD came to Solomon, "Concerning this house that you are building, if you will walk in my statutes and obey my rules and keep all my commandments and walk in them, then I will establish my word with you, which I spoke to David your father."

During King David's lifetime, he wanted to build a temple to honor the Lord for his grace and mercies towards him. After consulting with the prophet Nathan, David was given the thumbs up to go ahead and build the temple. The prophet never felt the need to pray about David's proposed temple-building project. Nathan assumed that anything that is done by anyone which appears to benefit the kingdom of God, should be acceptable to God. However, in the wee hours of the night, the Lord told Nathan that he would rather have David's son, Solomon, build the temple.

God's purpose for David, did not include the building of a temple; he was anointed to build a united kingdom of God's chosen people, and that was how far his assignment was supposed to go. The lesson here is that no matter how lofty our plans and ideas may be, if it is not part God's will for our lives, it will not stand the test of time. It is important therefore, to take our plans to God in prayer, before we take a step towards its accomplishment. The fact that it sounds good doesn't mean pleases God. It may not necessarily be a bad idea but could be a misplaced goal.

When Solomon ascended the throne, he made the temple project a top priority, and that was a delight to the Lord; but beyond what Solomon was doing, God highlighted something that was more important to him than activity. God's heart desire was that Solomon would walk in obedience to his laws and statutes. The temple minus obedience was a non-starter.

Today, grace has located us, and we are free from the clutches of the Mosaic Law as a condition for pleasing God. Christ has fulfilled the demands the Law makes on us. It is however important for us to always remember that we are operating under a new law, which is THE LAW OF THE SPIRIT (Rom.8:2). This law is not written on stones, but on the tablets of our hearts. This law has moral principles that have no expiry date. This Law of the Spirit doesn't claim perfection from us but challenges us to pursue righteousness. It doesn't excuse sin, but embraces repentance and rights the wrong, where and when possible.

God is saying to us that we should not limit our relationship with him to service without submission to his Word and Will. He rewards obedience, and that is something we should always keep in mind. He uses the conditional clause ("if") to let Solomon know that his service was accepted, but his continued obedience was necessary, if he was going to experience a complete fulfillment of the promises God had made to David concerning his inheritance.

We have to keep obeying God's Word. Living a life that does not glorify God is taking a path that can hinder you from experiencing all that God has planned for you. Samuel's advice to King Saul is relevant to this and every generation of believers: "to obey is better than to sacrifice" (1Sam.15:22, NIV). God loves your service but puts priority on your obedience. Obey the Word of God. It will make you glow and glitter with His glory. Building a temple while living in sin, is a sheer waste of time and effort. The blessing will come, if you commit to obeying the Word.

God bless you

Know God's Voice

Jn.10:14,27, NKJV

I am the good shepherd; I know My sheep, and am known by My own... My sheep hear My voice, and I know them, and they follow Me

---

We used to have a very friendly dog my wife named, "landlord." He did stuff that surprised us, because he was not formally trained to do them. Personally, what excited me about "landlord", was his quick response to my voice. When I was not in the mood to play, and I communicated that to him, he would oblige and lie down quietly beside me. That was my dog; he knew my voice and could interpret my mood.

The understanding I get in reading the New Testament is that God became like us, so that he can relate to us at a personal level. Under the Old Testament dispensation, people could only hear from God by consulting a prophet, or seer. That was the norm. That was so because the "curtain" of sin, was intact, separating us from God. When Jesus died on the cross, that curtain was split into two, giving everyone who believes in his redemptive work direct access to God.

In that context, therefore, our otherwise dead spirits that could not hear the voice of God, was made alive to hear him. The sheep now has the capacity to hear the voice of his shepherd. That ability to "hear" is directly linked to the willingness to obey what he has already said in his Word, the Holy Bible. The ability to hear comes from your level of sensitivity to the Holy Spirit, which is an offshoot of the amount of time you invest in prayer, and other spiritual commitments.

If you keep a newborn child away from any human contact, by the time he gets to the age of six, you will clearly see that he will not be able to communicate as he should. It is the intimate relationship between the good shepherd and his sheep that makes it possible for the animal to "understand" the language of the human. It is okay to ask others we consider as being more spiritually matured than us, like our pastors for instance, to support us in prayer, and help clarify what God might be saying to us.

Indeed, it is very good and necessary to SEEK counsel from them. The problem arises when we let them stand between us and our Father; when everything we hear from God has to come from them. Can you imagine always having to go through a third party to talk to your own father, or to know what he has to tell you? You can never reach the point of knowing your father's voice. Learn to hear from God for yourself; and to do that, it is extremely important for to commit to studying the scriptures.

The Bible is the important communication tool God uses to talk to us. Once you receive Christ, and the Holy Spirit takes residence in you, trust God to speak to you and direct you. You may not get it right all the time, but you grow in it the same way a child learns to understand a parent's language, one day at a time.

God bless you

No One can Lose with God

Lu.24:5, NKJV

Then they went in and did not find the body of the Lord Jesus.

My wife left home at dawn after her morning devotion to buy food items for the children in the orphanage. She came home tired, but fairly excited all went well, only to find out later that her money purse was not in her bag. The confusion was huge, because her bank card and a good amount of cash was inside the missing purse. It was late night when she made the discovery so we had to wait till the following day for her to go back and see if she could locate it. We prayed about it, and the Lord did us good by letting her find it.

Reading this scripture literally brought me back to how we both reacted when my wife reached her hand into her bag looking for her purse and realized it was not there. These loyal women had gone to Jesus' tomb to embalm his body. When they got there, they found the tomb empty; the body, like my wife's purse, which held all that they cared about, was gone! It was disappointment beyond imagination, but again like my wife's purse, the body they were looking for, was not lost forever.

The disconnection was just a temporary separation. The missing body was the resurrection blessing. No one can lose with God. You may never get back something you lost, but you will have the Lord's Presence with you. Your empty tomb: that feeling of God not hearing your prayer, and not loving you enough, does not reflect the reality on the ground. God loves you and will show up again when it matters most. The empty tomb is your entry point into new territories and deeper experiences.

Your present disappointment is for a season, an open door to a pleasant destination. You don't keep looking for the things and people you cherish in a tomb. The tomb is a place for the dead, and God is saying to you today that he is emptying your tomb so he can restore your joy and give you fulfillment. The reason you cherish what you kept in the tomb is because you have no expectations for change. All you know to do after evidence of burial, is to embalm and "honor" your dead buddy. God says, "hold it there; I am an expert in reversing the irreversible. Your dead shall rise again." If you can believe this, you can receive grace for a new beginning at the place and point you think you are finished. It is well. God bless and restore hope to you in Jesus Name.

God's Instruction

Ps.32:8-9, GNB

The LORD says, "I will teach you the way you should go; I will instruct you and advice you. Don't be stupid like a horse or a mule which must be controlled with a bit and bridle to make it submit."

The language of communication with a horse is radically different from that of a dog. Horses on their own do not follow instructions like dogs generally do; horses have to be controlled and manipulated. They would rather follow their natural instincts than their master's instruction. Lack of trust in the leading of God can push you into that corner, where you are likely to depend more on your understanding, than divine direction as revealed in God's Word.

The Bible calls such an attitude, "stupid." Yes, it is stupid for us to ignore the direction of the one who created the world and all that is in it and assume control of our own lives when we don't even know how we arrived here in the first place. My heart bled last week when I read about a law being passed in New York, USA, to allow babies who have reached the full nine months term to be aborted. This is where human knowledge and wisdom is leading us, on a path of self-destruction and obvious stupidity.

I watched the National Geographic documentaries on television and see animals protecting their babies, only to turn to the news the next moment to hear educated human beings, in an advanced country like America, sign a paper to approve the murder of innocent babies in cold blood. No matter how hard we try to justify this evil practice, it still comes down to the fact that we are disconnected from our creator. We have rejected his Word and embraced the world. The consequences of our actions stare us in the face; the greater our exploits in technological advancement, the weaker we become in terms of the true essence morality and values of life.

Beloved, God has a better option for you and me. He says, "I want to teach you the way you should go." He is not forcing, he is not pushing, and he is not imposing; he is deliberately appealing to our conscience. God wants our hearts before he acts. It is possible that the confusion you are going through right now is because you are not considering the God-factor in the way you are living your life. This is not about praying, reading the Bible or going to church. All that is good and proper, and an essential part of receiving teaching from the Lord; but you can do all that, and still do what you want to do without reference to what God is asking you to do.

In that circumstance, the only choice left for the Lord to bring you to order to prevent you from destroying yourself, is to apply "bit and bridle" to make you submit. That in itself is not how God wants to relate to his children and is a far cry from the choice he might make. When we reject his direction and refuse his correction, he respects our freedom of choice, and in the end, we harvest unpleasant consequences. May we become students of God's Word who read the scriptures to receive teaching and instruction, and not as a religious obligation to numb our conscience against guilt.

God bless you.

Very Much Land

Jos.13:1, NKJV

Now Joshua was old, advanced in years. And the LORD said to him: "You are old, advanced in years, and there remains very much land yet to be possessed

---

I am barely months away from my seventieth birthday, and sometimes I wonder how I got here so fast. I still remember my early years in school and can't believe I've been around here for almost seven decades. In retrospect, I thank God that at least I've done something with the life he gave me, just because his grace has been sufficient for me. However, a little reality check shows me how much work still remains to be done in the kingdom of God, and how limited we are in terms of what we can do for God.

As in the case of Joshua, we shall all one day wake up to the realization (if we have not done so already), that we can only do as much as grace will help us to accomplish. Every one of us has a role to play in shaping lives and bringing God's kingdom into manifestation on earth. We are living lights that must shine and brighten every corner we are located. What we cannot do, is to work as if we have the capacity to do anything and everything. You can do a lot, but you cannot do more than grace, time, resource, space and energy will allow you.

Looking at the extent of work that remains to be done, can drive you nuts and make you feel like a failure. Don't go to an early grave trying to do everything, being everywhere, and undertaking every task for everybody. Do your best and let God be the judge. Do your best, but don't kill yourself. You are better off taking good care of yourself and living to be of value than stretching yourself thin and breaking down beyond recovery. The best of sports men have their "expiry date." Usain Bolt is a legend, but he has called it quits, because his strength has waned. You may be only 16 today, but that is only for today. Sooner than you think, you will be where I am today; the position of the numbers will turn. Yes, from one-six (16) to six -one (61). And when you arrive here, and you look ahead, you may see that there is still "much land to be possessed."

You need not be disappointed with the results. Thank God for whatever little land you were able to possess and be an inspiration to the next generation of battle-ready young men and women, whose time and turn has come to fight for the remaining land. Thank God for being part of his eternal plan and take a good rest. Go on a vacation, if necessary. If you don't have the stamina to run, please walk. Remember you can only do your part. When your role is acted out, your best bet is to slow down, or to opt out.

God bless you.

Willing Hearts; Not Idle Hands

Mk. 6:36-37a, NKJV

When the day was now far spent, His disciples came to Him and said, 'This is a desert place, and already the hour is late. Send them away, that they may go into the surrounding country and villages and buy themselves bread; for they have nothing to eat. But He answered and said to them, "You give them something to eat."

When you have a mind to help people, God gives the means to meet their need. We started our work with destitute and orphaned children at a time when we were at "ground zero" financially. The opposition, persecution, and frustration were ruthless and fierce; it was literally speaking, our daily bread.

I remember a pastor "friend" scheduling a meeting with me and claiming the Lord is saying my decision to quit my job and build a home for orphaned children was not part of God's purpose for my life. His analysis of our circumstances was clearly discouraging. It was heartbreaking. This was someone I considered a true man of God, and someone I trusted and confided in (I no longer do, for obvious reasons). Through much prayer, coupled with God's grace and mercy, we stayed the course.

Today, we are counting the number of children we have been able to lead to Christ and help through school. Some have come out of tertiary institutions and are either working or doing their national service. We answered to Jesus' command, "YOU give them something to eat," and are so fulfilled, content, blessed, and at peace with God. Beloved, when God takes you to the wilderness, He will supply the bread you need to feed the multitude. What He needs from you is to give what you have; your little mustard-seed faith, resource, time etc.

The problem with many who fail in their calling is fear of losing out, and unwillingness to sacrifice. Someone gave out his few loaves of bread and fish before the miracle was effected. Jesus knew the disciples had nothing, and yet he commanded them to feed the hungry multitudes. He did that for two reasons. First, to make them aware that without Him they have nothing to offer. Secondly, that when God commands them to do something, He has already made provision before making the call. There is no basis for doubts and fears. All they needed to do was to wait for direction.

The same God who took Moses to the wilderness and fed a whole nation with manna for forty years, was the same God who fed the multitudes with bread in the wilderness through the hands of the apostles. He is looking for human channels who will not choke the supply by thinking only about themselves, but are willing to obey the Master's call to "give them to EAT." God is looking for willing hearts, not idle hands. If you are willing to share God's "bread and fish" to the hungry, get ready for a journey to the "desert side" where the needs are. He will show you where the needs are, and what to do about it.

Your "little" is somebody's "much". Spiritually, physically, emotionally, and financially, there are people God wants you to help. Don't look at what you don't have. God is your source of supply. Stretch out your hand in faith. Take the piece of bread and fish he puts in your hands. Don't hide it. Turn round and begin to share, and you will be amazed the extent it will go, and the impact you will make. You can turn someone's pity-party into a joyful celebration, so go ahead and obey the Master's command to "give them something to eat."

God bless you.

Stay in Contentment Lane

Ps.131:1-2, GNB

Lord, I have given up my pride and turned away from my arrogance. I am not concerned with great matters or with subjects too difficult for me. Instead, I am content and at peace. As a child lies quietly in its mother's arms, so my heart is quiet within me

You can't eat your cake and have it; or if you like a reverse order, you cannot have your cake and eat it. You always have to give up something, if you want to go up somewhere. You have to give out, in order to get back. The psalmist's confession reveals to us a man who used to be (1) proud in a very negative way (2) arrogant (3) meddled in matters "too difficult" for him; probably issues that should be left to God to sort out.

We learn from what he is telling us that his attitude robbed him of peace and contentment, which by all intents and purposes, are the real riches of life. I don't know about you, but I'd rather have peace and contentment than all the treasures of this world. The drive and desire to be something God never meant you to be, is only an indication of unbridled pride and arrogance. Let's face it, because it is easy to cover up such dysfunctional attitudes; you can pretend to be operating at a higher level of faith, when in actual fact, pride and arrogance is the name of the game you are playing.

Believing that you can afford to live at the same financial level as your CEO, is not faith; it is a moral failure. Indeed, it is a character flaw called "pride". It is not wise to put yourself under undue pressure because you want to create an impression. If God wants you to do something for him, he will give you the capacity to do it. He does not pressure you to do what he has not prepared you to handle.

If you are a bishop, and God gives you a congregation of fifty, preach the same way you will preach if he gives you a congregation of 5,000. Don't metamorphose into a prophet and begin to say what God has not said, all in a prideful adventure to gain popularity. Stop engaging yourself in "matters too difficult" for you. If the shoe is not your size, please don't wear it. It will hurt your feet. Save yourself the pain and the problem.

Take a look at a baby sleeping in the arms of his mum; no fears, no fretting, no hustle, nothing to worry or be anxious about. He is at peace, because he is in mummy's arms. What a beautiful picture of the kind of peace and contentment you can experience when you put away pride, arrogance, and matters too difficult for you. Life is much easier to handle when you accept yourself; when you make the best of what you have, instead of coveting what others have.

May the good Lord help us all to take the step to stay in contentment-lane, so that we can daily enjoy the peace of God that passes all human understanding.

God bless you.

God's Will

Matt. 26:42, NKJV

Again, a second time, He went away and prayed, saying, "O My Father, if this cup cannot pass away from Me unless I drink it, Your will be done."

Jesus was faced with a peculiar challenge at this time in his life. The "honeymoon" was over, and he was torn between saving his skin, and surrendering to the will of God. That "will" made it mandatory for him to suffer extreme shame, embarrassment, torture, and death. Wait a minute! Is the Bible saying my suffering can sometimes be "a cup" that "cannot pass away from me unless I drink it?" Exactly so.

That is why you don't have to allow anyone to subject you to feeling guilty about the challenges you face. There are a lot of believers out there, who have no peace because they have been deceived into thinking they are not doing enough, and that is what accounts for their challenges and suffering. Jesus' response to what was obviously an unanswered prayer was to submit to the will of God.

Be very circumspect about what you say when you see a brother or sister going through challenging circumstances. You may not know God's perfect will in that particular person's situation. I have heard some preachers talk about how they never got sick since accepting Christ, and I praise God for their lives; but to suggest that any believer who gets sick lacks faith, is unscriptural. Indeed, it is an obvious untruth. Elisha died a sick man (2Ki.13:14), and Apostle Paul spoke of leaving Trophimus sick in Miletus (2Tim.4:20).

I strongly believe Paul might have prayed fervently for Trophimus' healing, but his own testimony was that at the time he left the young man, he was still sick. It may be that sometimes God allows these things to happen to remind us that he is the ultimate healer, and deliverer, not us. Somebody's SUBJECTIVE EXPERIENCE should not be used to define God's OBJECTIVE TRUTH. The sovereignty of God is the overriding factor in all His dealings with us. No one can undo what God plans to do in his or her life, and sometimes what God allows may be contrary to our expectation.

His appointments may involve some disappointments. In the garden of Gethsemane, Jesus show-cased his humanity, as the Father took him through that route. Though he never tried to fight the will of his Father, he did attempt on two occasions to negotiate his way out of that part of the deal that involved pain and suffering. When he realized how unproductive his position was, he asked for God's will to be done; not because the process was comfortable for him, but because it was necessary for our salvation.

None of us would like to go through pain and suffering, and God knows that more than we do. He has promised healing, deliverance, et al; and he is indeed faithful to his promises. Yet he is Sovereign, and can allow, do, and undo, as he pleases. Ours is to keep trusting, stay faithful, obedient, and submissive, and allow God's will for our lives to be established.

Scripture says Christ was exalted above all, because he suffered above all. As long as the challenges persist, keep asking God to intervene, but never let anyone put a guilty verdict on you because of your peculiar circumstances. If it happened to Jesus, it can happen to you; and thank God that in Christ, he who endures to the end, enjoys through eternity. May that be your story in Jesus' Name.

God bless you.

The One in You is Greater

1 Jn.4:4-5, NIV

You, dear children, are from God and have overcome them, because the one who is in you is greater than the one who is in the world. They are from the world, and therefore speak from the viewpoint of the world, and the world listens to them.

Everyone is entitled to his or her opinion on any subject under the sun. Indeed, there are basically two opposing viewpoints when it comes to issues of morality and spirituality. There is the viewpoint of the world, and the firm declaration of the Word of God. The world takes its position on issues based on what is "politically correct," whilst the Bible aligns itself with what is morally right, and spiritually healthy.

Apostle John wrote to the saints, describing them as overcomers, because of WHO was in them. Referring to the unbelievers, John states, "they are from the world, and therefore speak from the viewpoint of the world, and the world listens to them." There are three key truths revealed that we need to take note of, in order to be able to hold onto our integrity when dealing with unbelievers.

First, we must understand where they are coming from; that they are products of the worldly system, and therefore cannot accept our concept of life. Mango trees do not produce blue berries, neither can you pick pawpaw from orange trees. The fruit is always determined by the seed, and not vice-versa. Secondly, once we understand where they are coming from, we can begin to understand why they believe and behave the way they do. Being products of the world, the unbeliever can only think the way the world thinks, and of course talk the way the world talks, without reference to God's Word or Will.

Thirdly, "the world listens to them." The world listens to them even when what they say is morally corrupt, intellectually bankrupt, and spiritually barren. The reason is simply because they are of the same breed. Like attracts like, so do not be surprised or offended, when you face challenges from people who don't subscribe to the faith you confess, use language that seek to hurt your sensibilities, or project a viewpoint that can best be described as stupid. Now you understand why their viewpoint does not tally with yours, and why their behavior towards you should not bother you.

You know your source, that "you are from God." You know your position, that you "have overcome them." You have not overcome them in a physical fight, or verbal combat, but you have prevailed over them because of what God through His Word has deposited in you. They may have something you don't have, but you have SOMEONE greater than anything they can ever have, no matter how poor your physical condition may be.

If you want to win with God, then you must be prepared to swim against the tide of what is popular with men and walk in the path of what is acceptable to God. Sometimes, that choice can cost you relationships and other material advantages, but that is the price you pay, for the privilege you have as a child of the living God. Hold on to your integrity and let the Word of God be your point of reference every day, in every way.

God bless you.

A Father Disciplines

Deut.8:5-7,9-GNB

Remember that the LORD your God corrects and punishes you just as a father disciplines his children. So then, do as the LORD has commanded you: live according to his laws and have reverence for him. The LORD your God is bringing you into a fertile land - a land that has rivers and springs, and underground streams gushing out into the valleys and hills...There you will never go hungry or ever be in need.

This was a generational promise to Israel in the wilderness, which has relevant lessons on discipline to all who desire a deeper walk with the Lord. Moses told Israel that disciplined and ordered life was necessary for the preservation of inheritance. He said there is a reason for maintaining discipline through correction and punishment. God does not correct us to embarrass us. When he allows us to go through the fires of affliction without immediate intervention, he has the end-result in mind, not the immediate relief.

Every wilderness experience we go through is not to break us, but to build us up. The Lord corrects us when he sees us take a route that would lead to our ultimate destruction. The discipline of God is neither bullish, nor selfish. It is targeted to build in us the CHARACTER we need to make a difference wherever he positions us. King David did well (with the help of God) to subdue all the nations around him, and left for Solomon an inheritance of national cohesion, peace, and prosperity.

Unfortunately, David's legacy did not survive the test of time. This was because the moral laxity in his own life, regarding women, disoriented the family structure. The domino effect was disappointing. His sons manifested the same traits of personal indiscipline. Amnon raped his half-sister, Tamar; Absalom staged a palace coup, while Solomon had 300 wives and 700 concubines, many of them from nations God had warned Israel not to marry from(1Ki.11:1f). Solomon's foreign wives eventually led him into idol worship, which laid the foundation for the destruction of David's legacy of a United Kingdom of Israel. The issue with David's sons was lack of self-discipline.

The best form of discipline is self-discipline, and if we don't adhere to it, then God, as a loving and responsible Father, reserves the right to discipline us in areas we may need to be disciplined. When we are disciplined by God, it is part of the process to bring us to "an expected end". Sometimes the discipline will confine us to the "wilderness." The "wilderness" is only a period of transition, and our submission to God's dealings will determine how long or short the journey is going to take.

You are on your way into "a good land" (a good place, both here and in the life hereafter). A place of water and fountains - speaking to us of abundant life. Be of good cheer. You are in safe hands. Even in times of God's discipline, and seeming chastisement, God is focused on your ultimate good. Nobody loves and cares for you like Jesus does. Submit to his leading and accept his rebuke and correction. God wants you to enjoy his abundance without abusing it. May his peace be with you and yours today and always in Jesus' Name.

God bless you.

God's Presence

Ps.51:11, NKJV

Do not cast me away from Your presence. And do not take your Holy Spirit from me.

A child of God who lacks the Presence of the Spirit in his life, can be likened to fish out of water. When Adam sinned, he lost the Presence. He began to run and hide from his creator. God did not walk away from Adam, and indeed does not remove himself from anyone who sins against him; it is sin itself that creates the barrier between us and Father-God. Sin comes with consequences, and the first and most devastating is separation from God, which is another description of death.

David knew the negative effect of living "outside" the Presence of God. He saw King Saul struggle with mental derangement anytime the Lord's Presence left him. Saul would go into a frenzy and would need the anointed music of David to gain calmness. Nothing in life holds together in perfect harmony without the Presence of God. Wherever God shows up becomes heaven, and wherever he walks out of, becomes hell. You cannot exchange anything with the awesome Presence of the Lord. Many of us crave for power, peace, and prosperity, without realizing that all of these are in the PRESENCE of the Lord. You cannot have God's peace, power, and prosperity without his Presence.

Our greatest joy should not rest in what God does for us, but in who he is to us; he is our "Immanuel" (God WITH us). The reason Jesus died on the cross is to redeem us from sin, and the reason he sent the Holy Spirit is to ensure his permanent presence in our lives. It's all a work of grace, but it is not a license to continue living in sin. Light and darkness cannot dwell together. To enjoy the continuous Presence of the Lord, you must honor him by living in Christ's holiness.

Let your life without, reflect the light within. When the Spirit convicts you of any wrongdoing, restrain yourself from justifying it; go to God in repentance. It is our loving Father's joy to be a part of our lives. He grieves when we erect barriers between us and him by indulging in sinful living. Let us humbly come to a place of repentance anytime we sin against him; and like David, may we be consistent in praying, "Do not cast me away from your presence. And do not take your Holy Spirit from me." Amen, and glory be to the Lamb of God, who lives and reign forever and ever.

God bless you.

Endure for Christ

Jn.16:21-22, GNB

When a woman is about to give birth, she is sad because her hour of suffering has come; but when the baby is born, she forgets her suffering, because she is happy that a baby has been born into the world. That is how it is with you: now you are sad, but I will see you again, and your hearts will be filled with gladness that no one can take away from you.

The normal term a woman carries pregnancy, is nine months; but sometimes children are born pre-maturely before the full nine-month term is due. However, the climax of the whole process is not so much the time, as the actual delivery of the baby. The woman goes through pain to introduce a new life into the world.

Jesus, speaking about what the disciples were going to experience when he leaves them, explained that it was going to be rough, tough, and painful. To give a graphic view of what they were going to go through, he used the analogy of a woman in labor; what she goes through during the process of giving birth, and her reaction after the child is born. It begins with crying and ends with laughter.

The pregnancy period is long and dreary, and such is our time here on earth. As a pregnant woman looks forward to the birth of her baby, even so should we as believers anticipate the joy of our reunion with Christ when he comes again in his glory. Meanwhile there are birth pangs to endure before we enjoy the fruit of our labor on earth. With some of the apostles and disciples of old, it was persecutions that ended in executions.

What is the lesson for us? Following Jesus comes with a cost for those who would wear the crown of victory. To narrow our worship of God to the temporary joys of this life, is to miss the point for our salvation, which is to bring us into everlasting glory with Christ in His kingdom. Our hope does not lie in what we get or hope to get here, and now; it hinges on something greater, bigger, better, and larger than this life. It is possible to suffer loses, pain, and setbacks in many ways in this life. They are the birth pangs preceding our entrance into God's eternal rest in Christ. When that day comes, what joy we shall have. The process will end, and we will see our "baby", the reward for our faithfulness and endurance.

Expand your horizon. Everything will not always go the way you planned, and some of the bad things that happen to you are not meant to be avoided; they are meant to be endured. If you refuse to endure for Christ, you are on the road to causing spiritual abortion. It means you go through the pain without producing the life you are meant to produce. Beloved, the Christian life involves a certain measure of pain, but always remember that there is joy beyond the birth pang.

Be strong. Keep the faith and kick the fear. "Soon and very soon, we are going to see the King." I ask the good Lord to give you all the grace you need to go through your full term of pregnancy, to endure the pain of delivery, and bring forth triumphantly as you enter God's promised rest in Christ when the roll is called in yonder.

God bless you.

Those Who are for You

1 Chron.12:1-2, NIV

These were the men who came to David at Ziklag, while he was banished from the presence of Saul, son of Kish (they were among the warriors who helped him in battle; they were armed with bows and were able to shoot arrows or to sling stones right-handed or left-handed; they were kinsmen of Saul from the tribe of Benjamin).

Rejection is a very damaging weapon of Satan. It has the capacity to make you feel inadequate, unwanted, and unloved. David was a man who suffered much rejection but stood his ground and prevailed to become all that God, through the prophet Samuel had said he was going to become. In this instance, young David was thrown out of the presence of King Saul because he was becoming too popular. Now, that was a heavy price to pay for a man whose only crime was that he was loyal to his king, devoted to his nation, and very committed to his job.

Being kicked out of the king's presence meant he lost his job, his "best" relationships, including his beloved friend (Jonathan). But in his time of rejection and isolation, God showed another side of life; that no matter what happens to a child of God, it is impossible to isolate him. Those divinely ordained to be a part of your life will be drawn to you, and they can never leave you. They may be physically far from you, but you will be eternally alive in their hearts.

The people who rallied around David were exactly the kind of people he needed for the fulfillment of God's purpose for his life; they were seasoned soldiers, who needed no training. Like David, they had fought and won battles and so they were ready to be used by God to establish the future kingdom of Israel. They were people who loved David from a distance; at a time when his privileged position in the king's palace wouldn't allow them to come near a man they respected, loved, and so much cherished. When the chips were down, and King Saul fired David, they stepped forward and stood out to be counted.

All of us are sometimes forced to swallow the bitter pill of rejection. We are shown the red card by friends and loved ones when we least expected. You wake up one day to hear your close pal, spouse, or other relevant relation say to you, "please count me out of your company. It's over and am checking out." If you've ever walked through it like I have, you know the pain that rejection brings. If you are just going through the experience now, you can testify that it is no fun. What is important, however, is to avoid trying to hold to what obviously is an irreversible situation. You have done your best, but it doesn't seem enough to salvage the broken relationship. There is every indication that you are no longer an attraction, but a distraction; it is time to move out of "King Saul's house."

Always remember that those ordained to align with you, will not come to you until you are willing to let go of those who do not want to associate with you. Everyone who joins himself to you with a view to getting something out of you without giving anything back to you is on a visit and will get off your bus sooner or later. It is not about you; it is about their motives and expectations. Let them go. Those who are appointed to be part of your life's journey will come to you prepared like David's men, ready to fill every gap and space that will benefit your course. They will love you for who you are, and not for what they can get out of you.

Your limitations, failures, weaknesses, and shortcomings will not be "breaking news" for them; it will serve as opportunity to show you how much they care. Rejection can actually be God's way of restructuring your life and bringing you into proper alignment with the people you should connect to, in order to find your rhythm towards success. Stop beating yourself up because someone walked away from you. If they must stay with you, they will not be amplifying what they consider to be your faults and mistakes.

Be generous enough to forgive them, but not careless enough to pursue them. You are better off being alone than relating to someone who simply doesn't want to have anything to do with you. There are times when the best medicine for a sick relationship is in the word "goodbye." When it is said to you, sail above it, don't sink under it in despair. Love yourself and live to the fullest.

God bless you.

Who Do You Imitate?

Phil. 3:17, GNB

Keep on imitating me, my brothers and sisters. Pay attention to those who follow the right example that we have set for you. I have told you this many times before, and now I repeat it with tears: there are many whose lives make them enemies of Christ's death on the cross.

Your greatest legacy is not the amount of money you leave behind when you die, or the extent of your popularity. Your greatest legacy is the influence and impact you make on others to make them better human beings, by bringing them to a saving knowledge of Christ, and helping them live God-honoring lives.

One time in his ministry, Jesus had to caution the people not to imitate the lifestyles of their spiritual leaders. He described the Pharisees and Sadducees especially, as hypocrites and liars. He insisted that even though they taught the right doctrines, they lived contrary to what they preached. Years after Jesus ascended to heaven, the Church faced a similar crisis, and apostle Paul had to address it upfront. These cracks are still appearing in our walls. Whether we like it or not, all of us are influence-peddlers; parents influence their children, teachers influence students, pastors influence congregants, politicians influence voters, friends influence each other, and the list can go on further.

The influence we exert, or that we accept, may either be negative or positive. Paul's position is that who, and what we imitate as Christians should be on the side of what is morally right and good. We cannot just follow anybody and everyone who shows up and claims to be for Christ; their fruit must inform our decision to go along with them or turn away from what they stand for. The scary part of this admonition is that Paul's complaint was about believers, and his conclusion was, "there are MANY whose lives makes them enemies of Christ's death on the cross." Imagine for a moment that God sees you as an ENEMY of Christ's death on the cross, while you consider yourself a Christian, maybe even a preacher!

That means you have identified with the camp of Satan. Bad example borne out of self-deception. Let's do a little introspection today and find out what kind of influence we are having on others. Can you say you are a good example for others in promoting peace and unity in the home, church, and larger community? Or are you a "mob-rouser", forever set on a path of destroying relationships, promoting sinful living, fighting everything that enhances faith in God and purity of life?

Your influence will live in the hearts and minds of your relationships long after you are dead and gone. Be careful how you live. If you claim Christ as Lord, live a life of love, which will drive you towards being an everlasting witness to the Light.

God bless you.

Praise God for the Foundation

Ezra 3:11, NIV

With praise and thanksgiving, they sang to the LORD: "He is good; his love to Israel endures forever." And all the people gave a great shout of praise to the LORD, because the foundation of the house of the LORD was laid.

Those of us addicted to building lives and structures, know how important foundations are; a foundation marks the beginning of what used to be a mental picture. It is the beginning of a journey that ignites hope and confidence in future possibilities. It is worth celebrating and thanking God for, but in many instances, we get excited and invite friends to celebrate with us, only when we have the house completed and ready to be occupied.

Friend, every foundation you have laid in your life is an achievement. If you look too far into the future, you may not see so clear what is near you now. Be careful you don't cross your bridges before you get to them; worrying about tomorrow when you should be thankful for today. The nature of foundations is that they are usually buried under the ground; not seen with the natural eye, and that is exactly how your efforts and sacrifices may appear to be right now.

You have fasted and prayed. You have trusted and waited and you're beginning to wonder if it was worth the while. The answer is a big, loud "yes!" There is absolutely nothing like wasted time and effort in the kingdom of God. You make a mistake ignoring your "foundations." If you do, the picture you get about yourself will always be one of failure. Everyone who started building with you may have completed their life's project, but that should be none of your business.

Remember that Noah was called to build an ark, Moses was assigned to build a tabernacle, while Solomon was mandated to build a temple. All of these structures had different time frames for completion. If Noah had tried to build a temple, he would have been a failure. You are not called to imitate someone else's life and assignment. Drive in your defined lane. Praise the Lord for grace to grow in your role. Your foundation is evidence of a glorious future, not only in this life, but in the hereafter.

You have a beginning; foundations of what you have deposited in time, space, and people. That is where the party should begin, and that should be your anthem of praise. Give God some high praise and get ready to raise the structure to the next level. Peace and prosperity to you.

God bless you.

Seek Knowledge

Lu.12:47-48, GNB

The servant who knows what to do, but does not get himself ready to do it, will be punished with a heavy whipping. But the servant who does not know what his master wants, and yet does something for which he deserves whipping, will be punished with light whipping. Much is required from the person whom much is given; much more is required from the person to whom much more is given.

Many years ago, as a student-journalist, part of our studies involved reporting court proceedings. The idea was to give us insight into how the law works, and how to undertake court reporting without being charged with contempt because you misrepresented proceedings in the court. It was during that period of schooling in the court that I learnt that "ignorance is no excuse in law"; the fact that you did not know it is wrong to do something, doesn't exonerate you from prosecution if you commit that offense.

In other words, it is your responsibility to know what can get you into trouble with the law and avoid it. The implication is, "you will be held accountable for every act of omission and commission, whether you did it out of ignorance or not." The only difference in the judgment pronounced may be its relative severity. If the court establishes that you know what you did was wrong, and yet you went ahead and did it, you are likely to be punished severely than the one who did same out of ignorance; even though he will also suffer a measure of punishment.

Jesus is speaking the same language here. First, the Master wants us to understand that we will be held responsible for whatever we do with the gifts, relationships, tasks, time, and opportunities God has given us here on earth. We cannot escape the scrutiny of divine accountability for what we have been assigned to do. Secondly, he makes clear that there are two categories of servants; those who know what to do, but do not get themselves ready to do it. Jesus said their punishment will be "heavy"; the reason being that they had KNOWLEDGE of what was expected of them but failed to PREPARE themselves for the assignment.

Do you know what God wants you to achieve by the end of this year? How much preparation are you putting into achieving that goal? Knowledge puts you a shade ahead of the ignorant person, so failure to apply the knowledge through preparation means you are not being responsible, and so your punishment will be "heavy." You've got to avoid it. Unfortunately for the one who would want to hide behind the curtain of ignorance, the Lord says your excuse of lack of knowledge will not give you total respite from punishment. It is your responsibility to SEEK KNOWLEDGE of what is required of you as a "servant." You have God's Word of assurance that if you seek, you will find; so, if you choose to sit and not seek, you have punishment (lack, need, poverty etc.) over the abundant life Christ promises to those who trust and obey.

If you know what to do to bring peace and prosperity to you and your family, do it. Knowledge that is not applied is worse than ignorance. And in case you don't know what you must do to fulfill God's purpose for your life this year or any day, engage the Holy Spirit's help, as you prayerfully search the scriptures for knowledge and wisdom. He is more than ready and willing to teach, lead, and anoint you towards fruitfulness.

God bless you.

Don't Throw Away your Confidence

Heb.11:35-36, NIV

So do not throw away your confidence; it will be richly rewarded. You need to persevere so that when you have done the will of God, you will receive what he has promised.

Your confidence is what you need when you are confronted with delays, setbacks, and opposition. Fortunately, you have started this year with some level of confidence in what you hope to achieve. This confidence is the stabilizing force of your goals and objectives. As long as you hold on to it, you are sure to navigate through the challenges that are bound to come your way, and that is why the writer of the book of Hebrews strongly suggests to God's people in very clear language: "...do not throw away your confidence."

This means every one of us can get to the point of feeling discouraged, disappointed and disoriented. When this happens, the tendency to give up on our dreams may be stronger than the desire to go on. If you read John's account of the reaction of Peter and his friends immediately after the death and resurrection of Jesus, you see a classic example of this (Jn.21:1-13). For three years, the disciples had Jesus with them every day. Life was interesting and exciting, and they looked forward to each day with eager anticipation of miracles, signs, and wonders. The job description was well cut-out, and there was some level of predictability and security.

Suddenly, the light went out; Jesus was absent much longer than they were used to, and they did not know exactly what to do next. They threw away their confidence; Peter gave the cue by saying, "I'm going out to fish," and the rest responded, "We'll go with you." He was their inspiration, so the moment he threw away his confidence, the rest could not hold on to theirs. As God's chosen people, no matter where we find ourselves, we have an innate leadership role because of the light of Christ within us. No matter how difficult your circumstances may be, there is one thing you don't have to do; throw away your confidence, because the Word of God says, "it will be richly rewarded."

If you are convinced that you are doing your best, and not consciously fighting God's will for your life, then keep on keeping on. The journey may be long, but the joy awaiting you at your destination will be worth the long wait. Hold on to your confidence. Keep praying. Continue praising. Your miracle is on the way. Men may write you off, but God has already counted you in. Persevere, and your day of laughter will come; "after you have done the will of God." I pray for you that the good Lord himself will strengthen and empower you to stand tall and strong through every storm and struggle; that in the end, you will come out like gold refined in fire.

God bless you.

Faith through Actions

Matt.9:1-2, NKJV

"So He got into a boat, crossed over, and came to His own city. Then behold, they brought to Him a paralytic lying on a bed. When Jesus saw their faith, He said to the paralytic, "Son, be of good cheer, your sins are forgiven you."

The focal point of our discussion on this scripture is the statement, "when Jesus SAW their faith." The immediate impression one gets here is that faith can be seen! If Jesus SAW their faith, then faith is tangible. Let us proceed from that premise and find out how Jesus SAW their faith. The conclusion is simple. Jesus saw their faith in what they did, in their actions.

You can go to church all your life, but if you do not develop a personal relationship with the Lord by reading the scriptures, praying, committing to acts that will help you grow in the faith, you will forever remain a spiritual minnow. The inspiration you get from the Word of God should be translated into action. Whatever you want to achieve in life, believing for it is only the starting point. Stepping out and confronting the challenges is the real deal.

It is not enough to walk with God; you must WORK with God. That is what bring positive results. God will take you up where you show up. Let me remind you that you don't get what someone has worked for, through "faith" that never wants to pay any price. That kind of wishful thinking is called "covetousness." It is unhealthy. It is evil. What you believe, can be SEEN in what you do; so, put your hands to the plough and act out your faith. God is ready to take you to the next level when He sees your faith expressed in your actions.

God bless you

Faith Demands Work

James 2:26, NIV

As the body without the spirit is dead, so faith without deeds is dead

When God called us into full-time ministry, we believed His promise to lead, guide, protect, and provide. There was no question of anyone giving us financial or material support. We had to step out in faith and believe God for every meal and need. Indeed, the only choice we had, and still have, is to believe in every single promise in the Bible relative to God's faithfulness in providing for his children.

We embraced the eternal truth of God's Word, that he never puts his saints to shame. We had no illusions that accepting to throw away our personal and collective ambitions to pursue God's call on our lives was going to be easy. Little did we know that the challenges of full-time ministry, especially for fresh starters like us, was going to demand more than a part of us, but all we have to offer.

Today we understand fully what the Apostle James means by "faith without deeds is dead." We worked and toiled to come this far. God did not just show up and say, "hey guys, I am happy you have consented to do my work so take this check and go to the bank. I have instructed the manager to give you all the money you need to fulfill your ministry." We worked and wept for years before having anything you can describe as enough.

It is in what you do that your faith is manifested. True faith in God, will drive you to pursue goals that will be a blessing to you and others. It is impossible to have the "God-kind" of faith the scripture talks about and do nothing. The measure of your faith in God is revealed in how far you are prepared to go to serve the course of Christ and humanity. Sitting and doing nothing is evidence of lack of faith. Those who do nothing, get nothing done.

You can have the best of dreams, but if you don't commit yourself to having a plan of action, your dreams will forever remain an illusion. God never does for us that which we can do for ourselves. Faith is like a key that opens a door for you. Once the door is open, you are responsible for stepping inside and getting what you want; so, don't just believe, but act on your faith. If you want to win, then you must get to work.

God bless you

Be Eager to Help

Matt. 8:5-7, ESV

When he entered Capernaum, a centurion came forward to him, appealing to him, "Lord, my servant is lying paralyzed at home, suffering terribly" And he said to him, "I will come and heal him."

When it comes to responding to human need and suffering, no one among men comes close to Jesus, the Christ. Whenever and wherever Jesus saw a need, he offered his service. He was extremely liberal in giving to all people his time, his power to heal and his ability to deliver from Satan's stranglehold, regardless of race, social status, gender, or color.

Jesus never charged any consultation fees, nor demanded special treats before putting in an appearance to do the work of the Kingdom. The centurion who asked Jesus to heal his servant, knew his position had no influence on what Jesus was capable of doing. This was a man who obviously was not a push-over. He was a military commander (Matt.8:9). He probably had heard and seen enough about Jesus to conclude that he was dealing with someone who did not only have power to heal, but who does so with compassion and integrity. This was confirmed by Jesus' response to his request: "I will come and heal him."

Is there someone asking for your help that you are ignoring? What is your response to God nudging you to help a vulnerable child, a struggling single mum, a discouraged and dispirited teenager? Let your answer be like your Master; "I will come and heal him." The one who needs your help may not be a believer, or as spiritual as you are, but he is still a child of God, created in the image of God; the same God who created you and I. Yes, this world is sick and needs the Savior. Your willingness to be used by God to "heal," opens the door for your empowerment. You will not need to be physically present always to make the desired impact. Your prayers (words) need no visa to cross geographical boundaries.

Many of us wake up each morning feeling miserable, and end the day unfulfilled, because all we see, hear, think, and feel are matters that concern us alone. Your feeling of loneliness for example cannot survive your pre-occupation with helping others. Listen to the voices of frustrated 'centurions' in your family, church, school, and workplace who are calling for your spiritual, emotional, and physical help, and go and "heal" them. Where you cannot go physically, send your word or your "wealth." That is what you are worth; saved to serve. Go ahead and use every tool and talent God has given you to bless someone today. Send this word of comfort, "I will come and heal (help) you."

God bless you.

Let the World See Your Light

Esther 1:10-12, NIV

On the seventh day, when King Xerxes was in high spirits from wine, he commanded the seven eunuchs who served him - Mehuman, Biztha, Harbona, Bigtha, Abagtha, Zethar and Carcas - to bring before him Queen Vashti, wearing her royal crown, in order to display her beauty to the people and nobles, for she was lovely to look at. But when the attendants delivered the king's command, Queen Vashti refused to come. Then the king became furious and burned with anger.

This story of King Xerxes and his beautiful wife who refused the king's request to make a public show her of beauty and glamour, has some semblance to how we sometimes behave towards Christ our husband and King of kings. Like Queen Vashti, we often tend to forget that we owe our position in life to Jesus Christ our Savior and King. We forget too easily that we come to a place of glory, not based on our own wisdom and power, but only through the grace and mercy of Almighty God.

No matter how far our natural beauty and intellect plays a part in our elevation, we should never forget the King whose decision makes the difference in our promotion. One of the lessons one can learn from Queen Vashti's demotion, relative to our relationship with Christ, is that he has glorified us so we will glorify him. He has called us to stand before the unbelieving world as light. Christ has saved us, and made spiritual investment in our lives, so we would serve him by leading others in the same path of grace. We are in the palace by grace and can only maintain our position through obedience to God's will.

Sometimes the "command" may not be convenient, or even make sense to you. Permit me to suggest to you that if you want to walk with the King of glory, you will have to prepare yourself for lots of inconvenience and senseless stuff. It's not about how you feel, it's about what the King desires you to do. The beauty bestowed on you was not made possible by human intervention. God brought you out of a spiritual dung hill; washed you with his own precious blood. He put his name on you and enveloped you in his glory. He did not do all that, so you go into hiding.

The King is proud of his bride and wants to put you on display to the world. Step out from behind the curtain, and let the world see the light that you have become, because of the extraordinary love of the King of kings. By all, and every means, the light within you must shine to brighten the path of those in the darkness. Turn it on, and the Holy Spirit will empower you to do what you need to do.

God bless you

Look to Serve, not to be Served

Mk.10:42-45, NIV

Jesus called them together and said, "You know that those who are regarded as rulers of the Gentiles lord it over them, and their high officials exercise authority over them. Not so with you. Instead, whoever wants to become great among you must be your servant, and whoever wants to be first must be slave of all. For even the Son of Man did not come to be served, but to serve, and give his life as a ransom for many."

In the secular world, people are generally defined by their titles and positions. In my beloved continent of Africa in particular, people who have titles like presidents, chiefs, ministers/secretaries of state, pastors/prophets etc. expect, and sometimes demand special treatment, attention, and advantages. Society is structured in such a way that the higher you go on the social ladder, the greater your access to attention, authority, power, and service. Your position demands that you be regarded as lord of all you survey and be served.

Jesus posited a radically different view of leadership in his kingdom. His kingdom demands SERVANT-LEADERS and has no place for those who are looking for greatness for themselves. Jesus made clear that the disciples should not expect to be anything than SERVANTS. Unfortunately, the Church today is not walking in the Master's path. Leadership is about power, and we end up with hero-worship in the very courts of God. Our impact is waning, because the world is infiltrating our ranks with its brand of leadership ideas, which is based on master-servant relationship; the bishop is in a different class than the congregation, and so instead of serving the people, the order is reversed, and the flock end up serving him.

There must be a restoration of kingdom principles of leadership among God's people. Your commitment to service, determines your level of productivity. Beginning from the home, we must drop the craze for titles and the desire to be served. When everyone decides to give our lives to others, our burdens become a blessing. There is so much joy and peace that we'll all experience. Jesus made clear that there is a huge difference between the leadership style of the secular world, and that of the people of God. He put himself forward as a perfect example, stressing that he did not come to be served, but to serve and "give his life as a ransom for many."

If there is anything we can do to make the lives of others better, let us do it without counting the cost. You don't need to be called an evangelist to lead a soul to Christ. You don't need to be called a bishop to minister prayer and counseling to one overtaken by discouragement and frustration. There is a difference between what people call you, and how God our Father sees you. Ministry is not about titles, authority, and a flamboyant lifestyle. It is about sharing your life "as a ransom for many." Look for opportunities to serve, not for a position to be served. That is the heartbeat of Jesus.

God bless you

Faithfulness to God

2 Chron.31:20-21, NIV

This is what Hezekiah did throughout Judah, doing what was good and right and faithful before the LORD his God. In everything that he undertook in the service of God's temple and in obedience to the law and commands, he sought his God and worked wholeheartedly. And so he prospered.

When we confess prosperity, we must look at what made people like Hezekiah prosper, and follow their example. There are five things associated with Hezekiah's prosperity. First, we are told he did what was good. You cannot do wrong and get the right results. Jesus Christ was identified with doing good. Bible says he was anointed by the Holy Spirit, and he went about doing good. The act of doing good, is more an act of love, than a demand of law. It attracts blessings and lessens burdens. It is impossible to do good and feel bad, so do good.

Secondly, Hezekiah did what was right. He went beyond doing good; he did right. When the motivation to do good has no linkages to ensuring you do the right thing, your goodness is not good enough. Thirdly, Hezekiah prospered because he was faithful. Being good and doing right, does not make a person faithful. Indeed, a faithful person will always pursue what is good and right. It is however possible to have someone doing good and being right, without being faithful.

Judas did all that was good and some right things for Jesus, but he was unfaithful. His covetousness weighed heavier than his desire to be faithful to the Lord. Faithfulness is a fruit of good and right, and not vice versa. There are spouses who do what is good and right in the home but are not faithful outside the home. King Hezekiah got it all properly figured out, and so he prospered. The fourth thing he did that unlocked the doors of prosperity in his life, was seeking God. He was not complacent. He depended on God totally, because he knew human wisdom and effort alone was not enough to bring him prosperity.

He was so prayerful that he was able to reverse Isaiah's prophecy that he was going to die. God added fifteen years to his life, because he had faith enough to pray and ask God for life-extension. If you want to prosper as a child of God, you must seek God daily. And finally, "he worked wholeheartedly." The king did not name and claim things. He worked with passion, and God blessed his efforts. The path to prosperity has been laid bare to us by King Hezekiah. Let us begin to walk the talk and God willing, we shall thrive and prosper in accordance with the plans and purposes of God for our lives.

God bless you.

Little by Little

Ex.24:28-30, NIV

I will send the hornet ahead of you to drive the Hivites, Canaanites and Hittites out of your way. But I will not drive them out in a single year, because the land will become desolate and the wild animals too numerous for you. Little by little I will drive them out before you, until you have increased enough to take possession of the land.

God does his work in our lives with our best interest at heart. Every blessing we seek from the Lord Jesus Christ is already in store, and ready to be delivered. What he is not prepared to do, is to give us something we are not adequately prepared for. Evidence abounds of people who displayed such humility in their time of need to the point one would think it was part of their nature. When their needs were met, and their status changed, they became the very epitome of pride and arrogance.

Most people can easily connect to situations like the one cited here, and that is why God told Israel that he was going to drive out their enemies alright, but he was not going to do in a single year. "Little by little," he said, "I will drive them out before you, until you have increased enough to take possession of the land." If you agree that our God does not change, then you should admit that his principles do not change. There are some things God will give to you immediately you ask for it, but there are others that may delay. This may not sound good, but it is true; the period of your preparation for certain things may go beyond this year, so brace yourself for any eventuality.

There are so many factors that come into play in determining what we get or do not get in answer to our prayers, but God is saying to us that "prepared blessings are for a prepared people." Apostle Paul prayed fervently for healing, but God's answer to him was, "My grace is sufficient for you." If you are going to be a strong believer in Christ, you will need to understand that answers to your prayers will not always come at the snap of a finger; and the fact that the answer to a particular prayer seems to be dragging is not a sign of God's denial.

There may be enemies lurking around you, posing as friends, who may attack you because of the blessing. You may have some innate weaknesses that may surface and destroy you if the Holy Spirit does not root them out. It is very important to God that he deals with these, and other potential threats, before he brings you to the place prepared for you. It is not wise to start a car in fifth gear, and so the Lord is taking you through a process to ensure the end will be glorious and peaceful.

If you are like me, you may often think that what you are asking the Lord to do, is not something that requires any further delay, so he has to do it here and now! However, we must take comfort in the fact that God knows what we do not know, and sees what we do not see, so it is in our best interest to allow the process of preparation to continue as long as God our Father desires. Keep praising and praying. You are on God's mind, and He is preparing the way for your glorification. Rise up and live! All things are working together for your ultimate good.

God bless you.

God works in partnership with us

Jn.11:44, NIV

The dead man came out, his hands and feet wrapped with strips of linen, and a cloth around his face. Jesus said to them, "Take off the grave clothes and let him go."

God will never do for you that which you can do for yourself. When Jesus' friend was sick, the sisters sent to call him. Jesus did not come as quickly as they had expected, and that resulted in Lazarus death. Four days later, Jesus showed up and after some words of encouragement to the deceased's family, he went to the tomb, and raised the dead man to life. But the Lord's instructions before and after this episode have a few lessons for us; key among them is that God will never do for us that which we can do for ourselves.

The first thing the Lord did when he got to the tomb was to ask them to roll away the stone that sealed the tomb. God wants to meet our needs, but he desires us to do first things first. You cannot build without a foundation. If you want God to bless your home with peace, it is your responsibility to remove attitudes and tendencies that hinder peace. When Lazarus rose from the dead, his hands and feet were still wrapped in funeral clothes. Jesus did not remove the clothes; he asked the family to play their part in the miracle journey.

God works in partnership with us to fulfill his purposes for our lives. When you pray for something, you must step out in faith and work towards achieving it. Waiting ON God, is quite different from waiting FOR God. In the first instance, you enter the sphere of prayer and seeking direction. Beyond that, you hit the road doing whatever you can, while waiting in expectation for God to give you what it takes to achieve your goal. If you are looking at your resurrected Lazarus and expecting God to remove the grave clothes for you, it's not going to happen.

If you are a student and want to improve your academic performance, you do well to pray; but after the prayer, you have to dedicate quality time to your books. If you are having marital problems, God is willing to help you sort them out, but recognize that someone in the equation has to do what God will not do for you; compromises must be made, to accommodate what cannot be changed; and changes made where possible. May grace abound to you to see all the grave clothes in your life and relationships and remove them, so that your lost peace, and joy will be restored.

God bless you

Forget Not

Jer.18:19-20, NIV

Listen to me, O LORD; hear what my accusers are saying! Should good be repaid for evil? Yet they have dug a pit for me. Remember that I stood before you and spoke in their behalf to turn your wrath away from them.

One of the most common features of life is the canker of ingratitude. Jeremiah was surprised that the very people he had been praying and asking God to forgive and bless, could turn on him so viciously. He asked a question that most of us have asked too many times: "Should good be repaid for evil?" The answer is "no", but the reality is "yes"; we can easily forget the good that friends and family have done for us and be ungrateful to them. Today if there is any lesson we must learn, it is to REMEMBER the good others have done to us in times past and refuse to dismember them in a Khashoggi-style heartless murder, even if they offend us one way or the other.

The preceding verses of our devotional scripture indicates how Jeremiah responded to the ingratitude of the people; he prayed judgment on them, and these are scriptures we often hear believers quote in justifying the curses they invoke on those who offend them. Fact is, Jeremiah is not our perfect example. Jesus Christ is the deal, so whenever we are confronted with issues like this, we should reflect on what Jesus did and said in similar circumstances. He blessed his enemies and asked us to do same.

Ingratitude can never be justified, but it is part of our human weakness, and we should be careful not to yield to it or respond in ways that do not conform to scripture. Every one of us should learn how to appreciate people for what they do for us. Even those who tend to irritate us, can be God's instruments to mature us. Pay special attention to your family and friends, because each of them is part of God's blessing package. Take time to tell those who help you in word and deed, how much you appreciate their love and friendship.

If you are a husband who never made any comment about the meal your wife puts on the table, except when it doesn't taste good, you have a problem. I hate to tell you this, but you are not being grateful and need to change. You see, a gentle holding of the hand and saying, "thank you for the wonderful meal", will not kill you, it will boost your relationship. If you are a student, you have something to thank your parents for; you can tell them how grateful you are to them for taking good care of you.

The price we pay for being ungrateful is as huge as the reward we get when we show gratitude to those who have been a blessing to us. The most excruciating part of ingratitude is when you go beyond not appreciating your benefactor to targeting him with false accusations et al. It is interesting the extent to which ingratitude can go. Listen to Jeremiah declaring, "they dug a pit for me." If you won't thank me, why would you thrash me? Let's be fair to each other and appreciate the blessing God meant us to be to each other. If we do, we shall be fulfilling God's divine law to be each other's keeper.

God bless you.

God our Protector

Is.30:2-3&5, CEV

You trust Egypt for protection. So, you refuse my advice and send messengers to Egypt to beg their king for help. You will be disappointed, completely disgraced for trusting Egypt...But Egypt can't protect you, and to trust that nation is useless and foolish.

A man called me on phone after my morning radio program and said he was in extreme difficulty and needed immediate relief from the challenges he was facing. I asked if he had given his life to Jesus, and whether he was a practicing Christian. He said no, so I tried to explain to him why he needed to accept Jesus Christ as his Lord and personal Savior, but he was not interested. All he wanted was someone to pray his problems away, and command miracles into his life.

I graciously explained to him that it does not lie in my power to solve people's problems. I guess that might be the job of occultists and magicians, and fortunately for me I am not one, and do not even have what it takes to be one. I am too intoxicated with love for Christ to be recruited by demons. The long and short of it was that he ended the conversation. He was obviously disappointed. He was angry. I called him back and appealed to him to calm down and listen to the gospel of salvation.

Beloved, if you think for once, that you can live without Christ and fulfill God's purpose for your life, it's like challenging God to a wrestling contest. You lose the fight before you enter the ring. It helps to seek counsel from people because one of the ways God speaks to us, is through people. The problem arises when we DEPEND on them to the extent that, we trust what they say than what God's Word admonishes. These people then become our "Egypt", and what the Lord is saying to us is, making a god of your own wisdom, of any person, thing, or place, and attributing to it or them, our source of blessing produces unpleasant consequences.

First, it brings disappointment. Nothing holds and gives constant satisfaction outside of Christ. Second, depending on "Egypt" brings disgrace. Wherever grace is missing, dis-grace is bound to manifest. Third, we lose divine protection when we remove ourselves from trusting the Lord and seeking His direction for our lives. There is no guaranteed protection outside the name and blood of Jesus. The fourth consequence is hopelessness born out of foolishness. Not my word; that's exactly how God's Holy Word puts in the Contemporary English Version of the Bible.

If there are issues you haven't committed to God in prayer, do so now. God is interested in every nitty gritty of our lives. He cares about all the details - both big and small. He is not enthused about us running on our own steam and tangent and turning to Him only when we mess up. Begin your day, week, month, and year with Jesus. You cannot do any better than that, because no one loves and cares for you more than Jesus Christ does. With Christ, you always win, no matter how long you must wait. Trust in the Lord, and he will do you good.

God bless you.

Build Your altar

1 Sam.7:15-17, GNB

Samuel ruled Israel as long as he lived. Every year he would go around to Bethel, Gilgal, and Mizpah, and in these places he would settle disputes. Then he would go back to his home in Ramah, where also he would serve as judge. In Ramah he built an altar to the LORD.

There are some things you may never have to stop doing. One of our mentors told my wife that one of the things she has learnt in family and ministry life is that you never cease to be a parent. Your age does not free you from getting involved with the lives of your children and grandchildren. No matter what they do, they always have a place in your heart and mind.

Somewhere, somehow, your retirement plan will always have to include a non-retirement package of timeless, unscheduled counseling, mentoring, hosting of both your spiritual and biological children and grandchildren. That was exactly what we see the prophet Samuel doing here. As prophet and judge of the nation of Israel, Samuel did a circuit EVERY year to settle disputes. Of course, he did not ignore his relationship with God; and to ensure that his family was not sacrificed for ministry, he built an altar to the Lord in Ramah, his hometown.

Some of the things we were doing in the past year calls for continuity. A new beginning doesn't mean everything we were doing in the past year is no longer relevant. Unless you've got a new job, you have to keep going to the job you were doing last year. If something has to change, maybe it is you; your attitude to work, compatriots etc. Some things need to go through a cycle of repetition. Sometimes the repetition is needed to get the job done. That kind of routine demands a good dose of self-discipline; indeed, if it is your calling, it will be as fulfilling as it may sometimes be boring.

What you should always keep in mind is the need to build "an altar" in your Ramah (home/family/business etc.) Give God's presence in your church, your home, and/or business top priority. Go wherever the Lord or your job assigns you to go, even if it has become a mundane routine. This one thing you must always remember; that no matter where you go, your family and friends must continually sense the presence of God. You must shine for Christ. The "altar" (presence of God) should not disappear until you appear. Make Jesus Christ an institution in your family; not by force, but by choice based on love.

Jesus Christ is our ALTAR, on which our sacrifice of praise and worship is offered to Father-God, through the Holy Spirit. Jesus is the Centre that holds everything together. Begin the year by ensuring this Altar is not altered in your home and other sphere of influence. Stay connected to him, as you walk daily towards greater possibilities.

God bless you.

His Rod or Your Spear?

Joshua.8:18, NKJV

Then the LORD said to Joshua, "Stretch out the spear that is in your hand toward Ai, for I will give it into your hand." And Joshua stretched out the spear that was in his hand towards the city."

Joshua learnt under the tutelage of Moses. He was very much used to the Lord telling Moses to stretch forth a rod, but when he took over the leadership, the same God instructed him to stretch out a spear.

The difference in their callings and ministry was as different and unique as the difference in their ages, and generations of people they led. Moses led a wandering people, who were like sheep, and needed a shepherd's rod of correction, direction, and comfort. Joshua's ministry was centered on fighting to occupy land and property, so he needed a spear not a rod.

You may be failing at something because you are bent on using somebody's else's "weapon." It is good to learn from people, but we should be careful not to try and be the people we admire. Their waistline may not be same as yours; and even if they are, you still have to wear what fits your taste and style. What works in the countryside may not work in the city. Learning from others is not same as copying them and trying to be who they are.

I remember how we used to write letters, affix stamps to envelopes, mail them and wait anxiously for days and weeks for replies from dear ones. Today, thanks to technology, we no longer take that route; communication is much faster, and easier. If you insist on using the old in the dispensation of the new, you will not achieve much. Find out what works for you best and use it. God has given you gifts and talents that befit what he has purposed for your life. Forget about "Moses' rod" and use your spear. That's where your victory is going to come from.

God bless you

The Potter and The Clay

Is.64:8a, NKJV

But now, O LORD, You are our Father; We are the clay, you are the potter; And we are all the work of your hands

---

For starters, a potter specializes in fashioning varieties of items out of clay. The clay is his primary raw material, while his hands serve as his major work tool. He is an artist with extraordinary flair in using a material that others may consider useless. The potter decides what he does with each piece of clay he scoops out of the mass. He does not consult with the clay, neither does he negotiate with it. He knows what he wants before he touches the clay.

The product is finished in his mind before he begins the process. The potter does the formation to bring about the transformation that will meet the purpose intended for each piece of clay. Everything begins and ends with him, and not the clay. Even so, are we in the hands of God (the Master Potter). We cannot be anything more or less than God has predestined us to be. There may be a lot of things you wish you had accomplished in the year which did not materialize. As long as you did the best that you know to do, there is no point in beating yourself and forever counting your losses. If there are lessons to be learnt in order to do better next time, learn them quickly and move on.

Anxiety can paralyze your ability. God may restore some of the loses. What does not need restoration, or is beyond restoration, he may replace, all with a view to making you who and what he created you to be. He is the One who calls the shots. You are safe in the Master Potter's hand. Even when he crushes you to the ground, he does it with a view to REMOLD you, not to REJECT you. Get ready for greater and better experiences with God. Let your desire be to be in his hands. Give him the liberty to break you, melt you, and mold you according to his divine purpose for your life. It keeps your eyes off the other pots (people).

The Master Potter's touch is all you need to survive the unpredictable challenges of life. The molding and remolding process can be painful, but the Master Potter's ultimate goal is to fashion you into his divine image, and give you peace, joy, and gladness. May God our Father touch you in a very special way, and prepare your body, soul, and spirit for triumphant living.

God bless you

Your Worth is in Christ

Lu.1:53, NKJV

He has filled the hungry with good things, and the rich he has sent away empty.

God does not subscribe to any ideology that embraces poverty, and/or insists on all men sharing everything in common irrespective of what they do. God is not against us being rich. We must place Luke 1:53 in its proper context. If you place a literal interpretation on it, you will lose the message it is conveying to us. The God who says in his Word that he gives us strength or ability to make wealth, cannot turn around and fight us for being rich.

The "rich" he is talking about here, are those who boast in their own abilities, strength, and achievements, without acknowledging that it is God's grace that makes them who they are. People who have that mindset have little or no respect for anyone who doesn't belong to their "class." Jesus told a parable about a man who boasted in his riches so much that he incurred the displeasure of God (Lu.12:16-21). As far as the Rich fool was concerned, his wealth had nothing to do with God. He worked for it therefore he congratulated himself for it. God had nothing to do with his wealth, so he went ahead to develop an "enjoyment and consumption plan" that centered on himself alone. Such attitude towards life breeds contempt for others less fortunate than the rich.

Unless you know who you are in Christ, being in the company of such people can be very intimidating. Mary knew her family was not among those the religious aristocracy considered as worthy of frontline attention; but then here she was, counted among the poor by men, yet numbered among the rich by God. Please, it is important for you to understand, know, and acknowledge, that your real value as a human being created in God's image, is not in your material treasures. It is in your spiritual connection with Christ.

Your worth should never be measured by your wealth. It should forever be interpreted from the perspective of your standing with Christ. You are as big and important as the God you worship, no matter your financial, social, health, or academic status. When nobody took notice of Mary, God paid attention to her, because she removed herself from competing with others. If you can read this message today, it's an indication of God's grace towards you.

Every breath you take is a gift from God. Every trial you face is a chance to grow, and an opportunity to glow. No condition is permanent, and your situation can change any second from now. Complaining isn't going to make things better for you. No one wins by whining. Continue trusting and relying on God, and he will fill you with good things. The God of Mary is the God of Miracles, and yours is on the way.

God bless you.

The Yoke is Broken

Jer. 28:2,4 NKJV

Thus speaks the LORD of hosts, the God of Israel, saying: "I have broken the yoke of the king of Babylon...And I will bring back to this place Jechonaiah the son of Jehoiakim, king of Judah who went to Babylon," says the LORD, "for I will break the yoke of the king of Babylon."

When Israel sinned against God, he sent the prophet Jeremiah to warn them to repent, or risk being taken into captivity by the Babylonians. Instead of following through with the call to repent, God's people decided that God's messenger was the problem. They subjected Jeremiah to ridicule, harassment, and persecution, until God's divine judgement fell, and they were taken into captivity. The Babylonians became a YOKE around their necks.

Their frustration was captured in a song (Ps.137), which speaks about sitting by the rivers of Babylon and weeping. They could no longer sing the songs of the Lord, because they were "in a strange land." It was in this condition that the Lord promised to deliver them; and indeed, in Ps.126 they testified of that deliverance: "When the LORD brought back the captivity of Zion, we were like those who dream. Then our mouth was filled with laughter, and our tongue with singing (v.2-3)."

Mercy triumphed over judgement. Peace replaced pressure because the Babylonian yoke was broken. He is the same God yesterday, today, and forever; full of grace and mercy, never happy to see his children messed up. The yoke in your life shall be broken. If there is any area in your life that needs to be yielded to God, don't hold back; surrender it to him. Making excuses for sin only increases the weight of the yoke in your life. It will be a disservice to yourself. Give God space to work out your release. The Master yoke-breaker is at your door. The yoke in your life shall be broken.

God bless you.

His Goodness and Mercies

Lu.1:46-48, NKJV

And Mary said: "My soul magnifies the Lord, and my spirit has rejoiced in God my Savior. For He has regarded the lowly state of His maidservant; for behold, henceforth all generations will call me blessed

---

God loves it when we appreciate his goodness and mercy towards us. He loves it when we express our appreciation in praise and worship to his Holy Name. Having been assigned to be the mother of the King of glory, Mary verbalized her joy and gratitude in praise to God. Her lips revealed the state of her soul and spirit. While her "soul magnified the Lord", her spirit "rejoiced in God."

The connection between body, soul, and spirit is very important in worship. Bible says those who worship with their lips minus their hearts, do "worship in vain." Give your entire being to the Lord as you thank him, not only for the things he has done for you in the course of the year, but for WHO he is. Mary first acknowledged what the Lord had done for her, and then proceeded to declare what she expected in the future. She said, "For He has regarded the lowly state of His maidservant; for behold HENCEFORTH ALL GENERATIONS SHALL CALL ME BLESSED" (Lu.1:48).

When you know what God has done, you can declare what he will do. You don't wait to see it before you say it. Check your spiritual clock; it is time to praise the Lord, worship him in the beauty of his holiness, and declare the great future awaiting you. Like Mary, let your body, soul, and spirit come before him in joyful adoration. Do it, even if you don't feel like it. The just shall live by faith; a higher level than feeling. God will honor your gratitude; what you declare into your future, and that of your family, career etc. will surely come to pass.

I declare to you in the name of Jesus Christ, the King of glory, that you are blessed and highly favored. Henceforth ALL generations shall call you blessed. Lift your voice and praise the Lord for his grace, glory, goodness, and greatness. Go beyond what he has done and announce greatness into your future. If you dare believe it, you will receive it. Praise the Lord, and the good Lord bless you forever!

Be Vigilant

Matt.2:7-8, NKJV

Then Herod, when he had secretly called the wise men, determined from them what time the star had appeared. And he sent them to Bethlehem and said, "Go and search carefully for the young Child, and when you have found Him, bring back word to me, that I may come and worship Him also

---

The motive of a worshipper is of paramount importance to the Lord. Herod, like many folks in church today, was worried that wisemen would make a trip to Jerusalem to pay homage to another king, while he was the recognized king of the land. He felt threatened by that development and settled on eliminating the newborn King. To carry out his diabolical plan, he had to apply the weapons of pretense and deceit. He told the wisemen to come back when they locate baby Jesus, so he would also go and worship him. His real motive was to kill the baby.

While filled with jealousy, hatred, and rage, Herod put on the mask of a believer. It took divine intervention to neutralize his evil plan. Let the redeemed of the Lord take warning; it is not everyone who sings with you, who sides with you. Not everyone who hears your vision and expresses interest, shares your values, and intends to contribute towards its realization. Being human, and being limited in knowledge, wisdom, understanding, and discernment, you should make it a habit to ask for God's continued guidance and direction in all your relationships; especially in relating to "strangers."

Paul told Timothy to "know them that labor among you." Sometimes we think we know people enough, just because we have been with them for long periods of time. If that were true, there would hardly be any divorce in marriages; but we see people who have been married for decades, suddenly turning their backs on their spouses, and treating them like dung. This happens even among Christians; indeed, we are becoming leading contenders for the crown of divorce. The statistics speak for itself. It is because we cannot know everything about everyone we relate to, that we are prone to be victims of those who relate to us for what they can get, not because they care.

Full knowledge is the preserve of God alone. Do not be too sure and over-confident when you have not taken quality time to discern the motive for a relationship. This is not to suggest that you live on the edge of fear and suspicion. It is a call to be totally dependent on God, instead of your human wisdom. Remember, the people Herod was dealing with, are described as wisemen; yet Herod was able to deceive them. Don't take anything you hear at face-value. People do not always believe in what you are doing, even though they may not say so. Take time to wait till you get God's leading (till you see the star).

If you fall in love with your eyes shut, you will wake up one day to find your deliberate blindness has produced a burden, instead of a blessing. Many great and lofty dreams have been killed because the "wisemen" behind those dreams fell victim to 'Herods' of mischief, betrayal, and blackmail. Love all men but protect your 'baby king' from Herod by being spiritually vigilant and seeking God's direction, not man's suggestions. You can never tell the real intentions of men, even when they profess to worship with you. Trust and depend on God always in all your ways.

God bless you.

Dead to legalities; Alive to Pleasing God

Mk.10:47-49, NKJV

And when he heard it was Jesus of Nazareth, he began to cry out and say, "Jesus, Son of David, have mercy on me!" Then they warned him to be quiet; but he cried out all the more, "Son of David, have mercy on me!" So Jesus stood still and commanded him to be called. They called the blind man, saying to him, "Be of good cheer. Rise, He is calling you."

Here was a man called Bartimaeus, blind and desperate for healing. When he heard that Jesus Christ was within his community, he knew it was a rare opportunity to receive his healing. Bartimaeus was well aware of his limitation. He could not see, so it was impossible to locate exactly where Jesus was in order to go to him. The blind man, however, reckoned that the lack of sight had nothing to do with the power of sound. He could make use of his voice to reach the goal of receiving his sight. (Take note; what you lack, should not stop you from using what you have.)

When Bartimaeus started crying out to Jesus, the people standing there (some of whom probably also needed Jesus' attention for their healing) told him to shut up. They said the blind man was breaking protocol. In a sense they were saying that it was not the right way to pray; too much shouting and crazy prayer and praise, distorts the status quo. That reminds one of Hannah praying in the temple and the High-priest, Eli, taking her for a drunk. The underlying truth revealed in this episode is that no prayer formula can match the cry of a desperate heart. What gets God's attention is not THE ORDER OF SERVICE, but THE HEART OF WORSHIP.

When blind Bartimaeus cried out to Jesus, his heart and soul was poured out to the Lord in absolute surrender. He was literally saying, "Jesus, you are the Only answer to my anguish. If you don't do it for me, it will never get done by anyone." Those who thrive on legalities and protocol, told him to follow the status quo, but he refused. His faith, determination, resilience, persistence, and perseverance paid off. If you have been talked into being "decent" with your prayer, praise, and worship, then that explains why your "blindness" persists. Isn't it interesting that when Jesus finally heard the shout and asked that the blind man be brought to him, the same self-acclaimed "prayer experts", were the same people who told blind Bartimaeus that Jesus was calling him?

Sometimes, in your moments of distress, the only person to listen to, is the voice of God's Spirit within your own spirit. If the world says "silence", and your spirit says, "shout", go ahead and shout. It is your spirit that bears witness with the Holy Spirit. Let your relationship with God be PERSONAL, not PROFESSIONAL. If blind Bartimaeus had played to the niceties of Church order and protocol, he might never have received his sight. Break free from any limitation in your prayer life. You don't need any "thee" and "thou" to talk to your Father in heaven. Speak the language of your soul; simple, straight, and sincere. Shout, when you feel like it. If nobody likes it, Jesus loves it, and you've got to live it. That's where your healing is.

God bless you.

The World's fact and God's Truth

2 Ki.6:17, NKJV

And Elisha prayed, and said, "LORD, I pray, open his eyes that he may see." Then the Lord opened the eyes of the young man, and he saw. And behold, the mountain was full of horses and chariots of Fire all around Elisha.

It can be very frustrating trying to explain your vision to a "doubting Thomas." Elisha found himself in a similar situation. The king of Syria had sent soldiers to arrest him for revealing his battle plans to the king of Israel. While the Syrian forces marched towards Elisha, he appeared to be unusually calm and unruffled. When his servant called his attention to the present danger, Elisha's response was, "Do not fear, for those who are with us are more than those who are with them" (2Ki.6:16).

However, it appeared the young man was not convinced. He would have preferred they make a quick dash for the door to save themselves from being slaughtered. He had a problem with his spiritual sight. He was spiritually short-sighted, so he stopped at what the natural eye could see. The young man had no idea that there is a world of difference between FACT and TRUTH. It was an established fact that they were surrounded by enemy forces, but the truth is that they were also PROTECTED by God's divine presence. The armies of God spiritually assigned to ensure their safety, far outnumbered the soldiers of Syria physically dispatched to effect their arrest.

Beloved, never make the mistake of underestimating the protection God gives you 24/7. Some of us indeed need the kind of prayer Elisha prayed, for God to open our spiritual eyes of faith to go beyond hearing the rich promises of God's Word (logos) and actually SEEING its reality (the rhema). What is against you today, tomorrow, and forever, is far outnumbered and outweighed by what is for you. Your Savior's ARM is more powerful than Satan's ARMY. Ask God to remove the scales of doubt from your eyes so you can see and soar above the storm.

Limiting yourself to the facts, will deny you knowledge of the truth. Jesus said, "you shall know the truth and the truth shall set you free." Accumulating present facts without reference to eternal truth as revealed in God's Holy Word, will enslave you. It takes KNOWLEDGE of the truth of God's Word to be set free from fear. I pray that your spiritual eyes be opened, so that your vision will always be on the overwhelming blessings God has FOR YOU, and not the insignificant bullets the enemy fires at you.

God bless you.

Be Truthful

Ps.101:6-7, NKJV

My eyes shall be on the faithful of the land, that they may dwell with me; He who walks in a perfect way, he shall serve me. He who works deceit shall not dwell within my house; He who tells lies shall not continue in my presence.

Because the company he keeps was bound to impact his conduct, the king was very selective and discriminatory in who served in his court. Indeed, it was important to him that those who served in his house be counted as faithful. There are two categories of people he refused to confide in; (1) "He who works deceit" and (2) "He who tells lies." The simple reason is that you cannot be safe with a deceiver and a liar. Anyone who has the tendency to tell lies and deceive, is a ready tool for Satan's use. He can destroy at random, and literally kill without a second thought.

Relationships are too important to be toyed with. You must have clearly defined lines regarding what you expect in a relationship, and you should be prepared to treat others the way you expect them to treat you. If you cannot be trusted, don't expect to be entrusted with valuable information. People may deny you what you may think is your due, simply because they cannot trust you. My late father would always insist that every liar and deceiver is a potential thief. As a child, it did not fail to make an impression on my mind; and now as an adult, I fully understand how important it is to be faithful and truthful.

The peace of friendship and family is dependent on how faithful we are to each other. If you are married, can I suggest to you that as long as you hide things from your spouse, you are living a lie? You may have been pushed into taking that route as a response to the way your spouse treats you, but that doesn't change the fact that both of you are caught in a quagmire of deception. You are completely outside the borders of Biblical love and need to do something about it. Jesus once asked the question, "Why call me 'Lord, Lord, and not do the things I say?" That's how deception works; it says one thing and does exactly the opposite. It promises a full cup of tea and delivers an empty cup instead.

If you have a reason not to do something, let whoever you are relating to, know your position. Don't keep your friends and family expecting you to deliver on something you know from day one that you aren't going to do. You are giving them the impression you are unfaithful and untrustworthy. Once you are classified as a liar and deceiver, you lose respect and whatever you say or do is subject to doubt and scrutiny. People are not going to trust you because you ask them to; no, they are going to define you by your commitment to truth and integrity. It is therefore in your best interest to be faithful.

Sometimes it will cost you. Those who thrive on deception and lies will attack your person and character, because the light you exude exposes their rot. Keep standing for truth. You should have no other choice. You will attract the best of people and things. Doors will open for you in ways you cannot imagine. The eyes of the Lord will be on you, and you will be counted on "to serve in the courts of kings." God will entrust you with treasures, and people will share their deepest secrets with you, because you will be seen as a safe port in their turbulent waters. Be faithful. It has great rewards.

God bless you.

God's Calendar

Lu.1:13-14, NKJV

But the angel said to him, 'Do not be afraid, Zacharias, for your prayer is heard; and your wife Elizabeth will bear you a son, and you shall call his name, John. And you will have joy and gladness, and many will rejoice at his birth.

No prayer of a child of God is ever wasted. What you are asking and believing God for, may be taking "too long", by your reckoning. You may even be wondering if God ever heard that prayer, because like Zacharias, you may be running against time, or time may be running against you. Your calculation is that if you don't get it now, you are not going to need it tomorrow. Your reason? Tomorrow may be too late. No. God's tomorrows are never too late. Your reason is not lining up to His season.

A careful look at God's answer to Zacharias' prayer reveals the following truths. First, God understands our fears. The angel began his discourse with the priest by allaying his fears. He said to him, "Do not be afraid, Zacharias..." That was a shot in the arm. A timely word for a tired soul. God is sending me to say same to you today. Do not be afraid. He is in charge and will discharge. Keep doing what you are called to do in His kingdom. The enemy will love to see you stop "burning the incense in the temple." Don't stop. God is about to send an angel to meet you there.

The second revelation is that God always hears our prayers. The angel's next statement was, "your prayer is heard." That seals the deal. Once we know God hears the prayer, we should trust Him to deal with the issues. No prayer is wasted. Keep praying and trusting. Third, God's answers to our prayers are not cut to fit our myopic ideas. They are tailored to fulfill His higher purposes. The child was not to be given to show that the priest too has a son, but to fulfill a divine assignment. He was not to be a private, exclusive "property" of Zacharias and Elizabeth, but a gift to the world. That is what the blessings God gives us are meant for - to bless the world.

When Hannah asked for a child (1Sam.1), she promised to make him available to God, and God used him to bless the world. God's answers to our prayers are meant to give joy to a wider audience. In the verse 14, we read, "And you will have joy and gladness, and MANY will rejoice at his birth." Not EVERYONE will rejoice at his birth. Some may be offended by your breakthrough, but MANY will rejoice "at his birth". The Lord will surely change your story. That which you are believing for, will come, and "you will have joy and gladness, and many will rejoice at his birth." If you learn this lesson of faith, you will experience God's season of joy and gladness; a season of answered prayers and angelic visitations in Jesus' Name.

God bless you.

Goodbye Fear, Welcome Faith

Lu.8:50, NKJV

Don't be afraid; just believe, and she will be healed.

Jesus was invited to heal a sick girl, but by the time he got there the girl had died (Lu.8:40-55). As far as the affected family and friends were concerned, it was a useless case; if God had something to do about it, it could not be AFTER the death of the girl. Jesus was to prove them wrong. While they saw the end, he contemplated a fresh beginning for the girl. Jesus diagnosed their problem as two-fold, fear, and lack of faith. He dealt with both negative tendencies directly with the admonition, "Don't be afraid; just believe, and she will be healed."

What is it that is causing fear and panic in your life? What is it that is making you doubt God? You are entitled to live a life of victory, but to be able to do that, there are some things you must learn to deal with in your own life. One of them is FEAR. When things don't seem to work out the way you want, some of the people around you can become part of the problem of the fear you have to contend with. They may mean well alright, but that does not take away the fact that their "mourning" can drive fear into you and create doubts about whether your dead situation can ever come back to life. You've got to do what Jesus Christ did; put the "mourners" outside and keep those who are trusting with you inside.

There are some areas of your life that is like your home. You are not supposed to allow just anyone to enter and do what he or she likes. If you think everybody can enter every area of your life with their doubts and fears, then you better get ready for defeat and unnecessary setbacks. It is okay to have people sympathize with you in your moment of grief, but none of them should arrogate to himself the right to decide what God can do or not do in your life. In the verse 52 of our devotional scripture, the people laughed at Jesus when he asked them to stop wailing with his explanation that the girl "is not dead but asleep." The following verse said, and I quote, "They laughed at him, KNOWING that she was dead."

This is the catch; sometimes our "knowledge" and experience can become a hindrance to our trust in God. Jesus ignored their fear, which was based on their knowledge of the fact of death. He went ahead to ACT on the basis of his faith, affirming that with God ALL things are possible. You will do yourself a lot of good if you shut out the voices of "mourners" who keep telling you that your situation can never get any better because of what they know. Beware who you allow into the inner chambers of your life. You are better off listening to genuine sympathizers who inspire hope than professional mourners who induce fear. There are no dead ends in Christ. Your light will shine again. Keep trusting.

God bless you.

The example of John the Baptist

Matt.3:4-6, NKJV

Now John himself was clothed in camel's hair, with a leather belt around his waist; and his food was locust and wild honey. Then Jerusalem, all Judea, and all the region around the Jordan went out to him in the Jordan, confessing their sins.

John the Baptist wore clothes that dated back to the days of Elijah; completely unfashionable. He ate food that would not attract enough patronage in a restaurant to keep it in profitable business, and yet he was an attraction. Why? His dress-code, and the anointing on his life spoke volumes of his intent, purpose, and calling. He did not make any attempt to attract people to himself. He concentrated on leading them to God.

The anointing was the attraction, not the dress or the food he ate. In his ministry, we see a careful balance between the physical and the spiritual, the natural and the supernatural. There is no overkill in either the way he dressed or the food he ate. Let God's people take note that our callings and blessings have nothing to do with what we eat or wear. You don't carry a special anointing because you wear the latest designer suit or eat at a five-star hotel. As you receive God's blessings, watch out against "eating and dressing" above your budget, with a view to show off.

God will not take responsibility for your frivolous spending. Manage the resources God places in your hands carefully. Faith is neither foolishness nor presumption. Always remember that no power can distract FROM you, what God attracts TO you. If you are a single lady who believes in Christ and believing him for a marriage partner, you don't need to dress half-naked "to strike gold." You need the glory of God to overshadow you, and it will attract the right person to you. Keep yourself well. Dress sharp, but with moderation.

Position yourself where God has made provision for your gift and ministry (John's place was the Jordan river), and all that should come to you will come to you. Anything short of that may frustrate you because you spend so much money and effort, and yet do not get the attention you think you should get. John the Baptist shows us what a combination of trusting God, self-acceptance, and contentment can do in the life of any believer; you become an attraction and inspiration to others.

Your dress may not be extraordinary, and your meal may not be the choicest, but you can still make an impact in your "desert". Take your eyes off what you lack, and let your heart be in what you have to offer the world. What must come to you will come to you, and that is prosperity in God's reckoning.

God bless you.

The Unchanging One and His Promises

Joel 2:26, NIV

You will have plenty to eat, until you are full, and you will praise the name of the LORD your God, who has worked wonders for you; never again will my people be ashamed.

God is speaking of the ultimate, your future, not the present. One of the things that the enemy uses to attack our faith and trust in God is time. God usually looks at the bigger picture when he communicates his will to us. He talks about the finished product, while we think about the present challenges and the raw materials available that don't seem to hold any prospects for the future. We tend to forget He is the God of the impossible, who calls the things that are not as if they are and causes them to come into being.

Your present situation may be pointing to a different direction than the Word of God is declaring right now but know this for a fact; life has not frozen below zero degrees yet. There is constant movement inside and outside of you. God is in constant motion, putting the pieces together for that manifestation of his promise of providing you food to "eat in plenty and be satisfied." He is not referring to mere physical food, but a decent life that projects his goodness, and provides you dignity; never placing you in a perpetual state of shame.

Someone has rightly said that "the music of God never stops. Only the dancers get tired." How I wish and pray that you keep dancing to the promises of God, and never get tired, even when your feet are hurting, and your faith is wavering. You should acknowledge that keeping you alive throughout the years, despite the challenges, gives occasion "to praise the name of the LORD your God, who has worked wonders for you." Beyond that, he is giving you a firm and solid assurance that "never again will my people (including you) be shamed."

Affirm and confirm with a big amen. Beloved, God is faithful to his promises, and once he says "never", it simply means never. Let all hell break loose, and Satan invent new weapons against you; Once God has spoken, Satan's scheme will not stand. Get up. See your redemption coming and sing praise to the King whose word concerning your life is irreversible.

God bless you.

At thy Word

2Chron.11:4, GNB

"Do not attack your fellow Israelites. Go home, all of you. What has happened is my will." They obeyed the LORD 's command and did not go to fight Jeroboam.

When our desires contradict the will of God, we have no option than to go along with what God wants. Rehoboam, the son of Solomon, who succeeded his father, was faced with rebellion soon after ascending the throne. Jeroboam led the rebellion which brought about the division of the kingdom of Israel. In response to the secession, Solomon's son (Rehoboam) mobilized troops to forcefully crush the opposition to his rule. Unfortunately for him, what appeared a rebellion to his rule, was in the perfect will of God.

His father's marriage to foreign women, and worship of idols in his old age, provoked God's anger, leading to a prophecy that his son and successor would bear the consequences of a divided kingdom. Rehoboam was humble enough to accept what obviously looked like an unfair response to his plan to go to war. This is the area in which we all can get "upset" with God; when we suffer for wrongs we have not done or are denied answers to our prayers. Sometimes we are convinced what we are asking for, is in the very center of God's will, and yet it is delayed and sometimes denied. Take for instance, an issue of praying for the recovery of a loved one who is sick. God's Word, which shows us God's will, says clearly that his will for us is to be healed of all our infirmities, and yet healing is denied.

Apostle Paul said, when he prayed three times about his infirmities, all he got from God was assurance: "My grace is sufficient for you." Keeping faith alive in Christ, also means giving room for his unexplained workings in your life. On this side of heaven, we simply won't get everything going the way we want, not even in our dealings with our Heavenly Father. There was no reason for Job to go through what he went through, except that God's will was at play. He did not even know that all that was happening around him was a result of God's confidence that he would never deny Him.

Can you imagine the time, money, and weaponry Rehoboam had used in preparing for the battle before God sent to stop him? It might have been a very embarrassing spectacle for the king, and the temptation to kick against God's will could have been strong, but King Rehoboam submitted to God's will. You may be struggling with something that you expect God to change and have trusted and prayed but God does not appear to be coming through for you. Let His will be done. Don't go to war. Keep trusting. His grace will always be sufficient for you in the good times, and in the bad times.

God bless you.

He Will See You Through

Jer.46:27, NIV

My people, do not be afraid, people of Israel, do not be terrified. I will rescue you from that faraway land, from the land where you are prisoners. You will come back home and live in peace; you will be secure, and no one will make you afraid

Living in a foreign country as a non-citizen is never the same as being within the borders of your own country. When you are visiting a country other than your own, you do not have the same rights as someone who is a citizen, or even one with a resident permit. So to think of being taken away as prisoner into a foreign land paints a very gloomy picture. In that condition, there is nothing like having a real dream or vision, because you are limited in what you can do. Your choices are skewed, and you live at the beck and call of another human being. Your status changes with the involuntary change of your geographical location. Israel found itself in this unacceptable situation.

Jeremiah warned them about an impending judgment that would make them slaves to the Babylonians, but they ignored the warnings. In fact, they assaulted and insulted the prophet of God for daring to speak to them about their sinful condition and the consequences it was bound to trigger. In the fullness of time, the prophecy came to pass, and God's chosen people found themselves slaves in a foreign land. The treatment they were subjected to, drained them of any self-confidence and self-esteem. They became fearful and faithless but thank God for his goodness and mercy. The same voice of Jeremiah that pronounced judgment was the same voice God used to inspire hope in his people.

God promised four blessings of restoration. First, he was going to bring them home. If you never travelled out of your home before, you never appreciate the adage, "home sweet home." You may not appreciate the freedom you have, only because it has never been taken away from you without your consent. Indeed, life outside of Christ is a spiritual prison, captivity, and slavery; and to that extent, all of us were slaves to Satan. Jesus brought us "home." This is the beauty of it, our release from slavery. The second restoration message God gave Israel was to bring them home to "live in peace." A home where there is no peace is merely a house, a dwelling place without God's divine presence. Jesus Christ is our Prince of Peace, our Melchizedek (King of Salem/Peace). May his peace be established in your home now and always.

My prayer for you is that no matter the amount of pain, disappointment, and suffering you have endured, or may still be going through, God's grace will locate and be with you. The third restoration promise was security. Whatever door of opportunity God opened for backslidden Israel to become victims of slavery was going to be closed. Mercy was going to once again triumph over judgment. God was going to protect them, and no one could harm them any longer.

I am trusting God to protect you from evil. Our security begins and ends with him. Finally, God says to Israel, and by extension is saying to us, "no one will make you afraid." If you can trust in God's promises to restore, keep, protect, and give you his peace, you should have no fear of the threats of men. Faithful is he who has promised, and he will also do it.

God bless you.

Serving in Love

Jn.13:5, NKJV

After that, He poured water into a basin and began to wash the disciples' feet, and to wipe them with the towel with which He was girded

---

This singular act of Jesus is one of the most extreme expressions of his love for all mankind. After having what was to be the last supper with his disciples and pronouncing the birth of the New Covenant with the breaking of bread and blessing of the cup of wine, the creator of all things took off his outer garment, poured water into a bowl, picked up a towel, and began washing the feet of his disciples. If you read this passage without deeply reflecting on it, you might miss very important lessons therein. Can you imagine any head of today's church, stooping to washing the feet of his members? We are not talking about neat feet pulled out of shoes. We are talking about feet that were dirty and filthy from trekking long distances through desert sand.

The role Jesus took upon himself was not fitting for his 'status;' but like everything he did while on earth, he set us an example of what it means to be a Godly leader; you serve, not seek to be served. Those who want to lead on the Jesus team, should be humble enough to do whatever needs to be done in the interest of God's kingdom and his people, without counting the cost to their interest, convenience, or reputation. Unless, like the divine Master, we are willing to make ourselves "of no reputation," we have a long way to go in attaining the fullness of his image and making the desired impact. And come to think of it, Jesus washed the feet of ALL His disciples, including Judas! That is the aspect that surprises me.

In all sincerity, without this extraordinary example, I would never agree to wash the feet of any "Judas" in my life. What would you have done, knowing that the dirty feet you are washing, will be running to invite your enemies to kill you soon after you've got it cleaned up? It takes the grace and Spirit of God to do what Jesus did, and fortunately you have that Spirit dwelling in you. God expects you not only to forgive those who have offended you one way or the other, but also to "wash their feet;" show them some love.

Walking this love-walk is what separates you from the unbeliever. This call to forgive and be gracious to those who may even be planning to hurt you while you are helping them is not negotiable. It's not easy if you narrow it down to doing it in your own strength. If you are willing to obey what the Lord commands, I bet God is ready to give you the power to do it. Show some love. The rewards are more than you can think or dream of.

God bless you.

Those who are For You

Lu.11:23, NIV

He who is not with Me is against Me, and he who does not gather with Me scatters

---

Jesus never kept quiet about his detractors' lies. Information brings clarity and neutralizes falsehood, so anytime he was falsely accused of casting out demons "by Beelzebub, the ruler of demons," he responds to it honestly without hostility. In this particular instance, the Lord was obviously not enthused by this lie by people who should have known better. If it were gentiles who were sabotaging His ministry, it would have been understandable. Indeed, it would have been narrowed down to their ignorance; but here are God's own people (church folk) going on the rampage to destroy the work of God out of spite and hatred for the Lord of life. Jesus immediately defined their fate; if you are not FOR him, then you are AGAINST him. If you don't gather WITH him, you scatter WITHOUT him. There is no middle ground between allied forces and enemy troops.

Whatever you undertake for God, family, and your good self, God will draw to you helpers, and the enemy will also throw in opposers. You must be spiritually vigilant to stay above Satan's gimmicks, and keep pursuing God's assignment for your life. Your opposers can be very ruthless with their tongue. Jesus said when they go on a mission to destroy his disciples, they may think God approves of it. You must protect your spirit from descending to their low level of thinking. Keep encouraging yourself with this reminder that if they did it to Jesus, they are bound to take you through the same route. The channels of attack may change, but the enemy remains constant and resolute.

Clearly identify those who are FOR you, not with a view to fighting your opposers (that is the Holy Spirit's job). Do this to avoid being distracted. This demands lots of prayer, patience, and discernment. You may have to contend with some "Judas Iscariots" along the way, but that should not discourage you from searching out those who are FOR you. One of the reasons the enemy will consistently push detractors your way, is to create mistrust and fear in you, and by so doing isolate you. Satan knows he cannot take your life, but he also knows he can stop you by isolating you. Loners don't achieve much. Don't succumb to the opposition. Confront it with fresh zeal and passion.

God already has people prepared FOR you at every stage of your journey in this life. There are no constants; people will come, and people will leave, but you are never without lovers. They may not be loud, but they are full of love for you, and believe in you. Be focused, and always remember you cannot get everyone appreciating what you do, but you will always have someone standing with you, by you, and for you. Dwell on the light, not the darkness, and may the good Lord protect you always...in all ways.

God bless you.

United We Stand

Lu.11:17, GNB

But Jesus knew what they were thinking, so he said to them, "Any country that divides itself into groups which fight each other will not last very long; a family divided against itself falls apart.

Jesus had been accused of using Satanic power to cast out demons and heal the sick. Responding to this attack on his integrity and ministry, he explained that it was impossible for him to fight against Satan if he was on the devil's side. He went on further to rationalize that division does not bring strength, but weakness. In this encounter with his detractors Jesus teaches us that it doesn't matter how populated, popular, powerful a country, family, team, or church might be, if it is not united, it's chance of survival is zero. A united family, church, or country is the team with the biggest chance of success. If you are trying to work with someone dragging the opposite end of the rope, you are in a very long-distance race you cannot win, because it is leading to nowhere.

You cannot force anyone to accept or love you, but what you can do is to insist on building your life with people who have faith in you, and who are prepared to stand by you even when they don't agree with you. If you are on a job, in a relationship, or any form of team whose vision you don't identify with, you will do yourself a world of good if you check out. Any time you spend trying to create something out of a determined divided front, is going to yield hollow results. Where the division is not MISUNDERSTANDING between you and the group, but OPPOSITION to its set objectives, you don't simply belong there. Please check out immediately.

My personal research has shown that one major reason for poverty in many countries is lack of unity fueled by greedy political juggernauts. The name of their game is, "divide and rule." Indeed, it has a historical precedent in the colonial era in Africa when the continent was divided into bits and pieces. The history of the Church is no different; we are still breaking away from each other and fighting each other, never realizing that our division and its attendant weaknesses are the reasons for the growth and spread of other religions.

The reason for dysfunctional family relationships is not money. It is lack of unity of purpose. Everyone wants to have his or her own way, so the captains are too many to do the ship any good. I wish I could say this is not the case in our churches, but no. Perhaps it will not be an understatement to say that it is worse in God's House. If it were not so, the number of pastors licking wounds, suffering burnout, and committing suicide would be less than we are witnessing today.

People live in houses they cannot call "home" because there is neither love nor life. At best, the unwritten law is, "each one for himself, and God for us all." Jesus' position is that it doesn't work that way; we either look out for each other's interest, or God looks out for nobody's wellbeing. A house divided against itself cannot stand. It will fall. It may take a long time to fall, but it will fall. Our strength is in being each other's keeper. Our very survival in all our relationships is in one word: unity. Remember, a house divided against itself cannot stand. Be a unifier, not a destroyer.

God bless you.

Do it Wholeheartedly

Col.3:23-24, NKJV

And whatever you do, do it heartily, as to the Lord and not to men, knowing that from the Lord you will receive the reward of the inheritance; for you serve the Lord Christ

---

How people act or/and react to your best efforts may sometimes be disappointing, discouraging, and disheartening. You may help people who may later turn their backs on you. Some may even malign you and speak evil of you to anyone who cares to listen to their 'crucifixion' story. You will be surprised to know who some of your long-standing haters have been; people who have said too many times that you are wonderful to the highest heavens. The wound they inflict on you can be very deep and long lasting. To mitigate the hurt feelings associated with such behavior, we are admonished to look at everything we do as service to the Lord.

When your actions are driven by the understanding that God is the ultimate benefactor, and any reward or appreciation will come from him, you are in a better position to accommodate ingratitude. The hurt is deep when our expectations are high. Lower your expectations of how people should respond to the good you do to them, and you will not have to struggle when they react in negative ways. Your entire life is meant to be lived serving the Lord, and that translates into serving human beings; many of whom do not have any value for showing gratitude. Servants are rewarded by their Masters, not their colleagues; even so, your reward as servant of the Lord is from the Lord, not the brothers and sisters you serve and bless. There will be those who will appreciate your efforts and thank you for it. Take such compliments as bonus, not as the blessing.

The "inheritance" which is God's promised blessing, comes from him alone. God rewards our services in ways we may not see or understand. His rewards are of greater value than what any man can give us. The devil is an expert in using things like ingratitude from those we have helped in the past to stifle our desire to continue doing good in the present. Yielding to that temptation, is like locking yourself up in jail. Free your mind and continue serving and doing good. That is God's will for you. Do it and experience the continued wave of God's blessings.

God bless you.

Stay with Him

2Pet.1:18, NKJV

And we heard this voice which came from heaven when we were with Him on the holy mountain.

Before his death in Rome, Apostle Peter wrote his last letter to the Church, and here in this verse, he refers to his experience with Jesus on the Mount of Transfiguration (Mk.9:1-8). He testified to the glorious affirmation of the deity of Christ by Father-God, and the voice from heaven that confirmed Jesus Christ as the beloved "Son" of God (1Pet.1:7). Our take this morning is on the phrase, "we heard this voice which came from heaven WHEN WE WERE WITH HIM."

Intimacy is key to knowing God, and hearing his voice is dependent on how close you are to him. The only disciples who heard this voice on the Mount were Peter, James, and John. They did not only hear the voice but knew exactly where it was coming from; that it was coming from heaven. These three had a higher and deeper relationship with Jesus than all the other apostles. They were the only ones chosen to go with Jesus on the mountain, and obviously there must have been a reason for that; you get what you want and reap what you sow. God is no respecter of persons. In his sovereignty, he may make choices that are not influenced by what we do or do not do, but we can at the same time get used by God according to our willingness and availability.

You have to get close enough to God to feel his heartbeat. The closer you get to God, the stronger the bond of friendship and intimacy becomes. If you are not hearing from God, it might be because you have forsaken your first love. Let's do some spiritual laboratory test: (1) Do you READ the Bible? (2) Do you MEDITATE/THINK on what it says? (3) Do you OBEY its instructions? (4) Do you PRAY for the Holy Spirit's help? (5) Do you PRAISE & WORSHIP God regardless of your circumstances? I can humbly suggest to you that doing these very basic spiritual exercises can radically transform your relationship with God. Forget about hearing some exoteric audible voice declaring, "I am the Lord..."

The Holy Spirit is within you to connect you to divinity. Talk to him and listen to what he says to you through the Word, your circumstances, Godly people, and you will not miss your way. You see, the three disciples who heard the voice were not with Jesus on comfortable ground like the rest of the disciples; they had to do the tough job of climbing the mountain with Jesus. That means sometimes there may be something you need to sacrifice to get that special intimacy with God. It may be spending less time on the internet, fasting for a few days, or it may be investing your money in Christian books, it may be forgiving a friend, spouse etc. The fact of the matter is that something must give way, for Jesus to come in. Come with me to the mountain. Let us meditate daily on God's Word; praying, praising, and worshipping until we hear him speak his peace into our hearts, healing into our bodies, and deliverance to our souls.

God bless you.

You've Been Chosen & Anointed

Ps.89:20-24, NKJV

I have chosen My servant David; with My holy oil I have anointed him, with whom my hand shall be established; also My arm shall strengthen him. The enemy shall not outwit him, nor the son of wickedness afflict him. I will beat down his foes before his face, and plague those who hate him. But My faithfulness and My mercy shall be with him, and in my Name his horn shall be exalted.

Instead of preoccupying yourself with thoughts of who is against you, spend time meditating on who is FOR you. Satan and his cohorts know too well that if they can get your attention on themselves instead of on the Lord, you will become mincemeat for them. Here are rich and exciting promises God wants you to claim for yourself. Settle it in your spirit today, that God has placed you in a very unique position as His child. The psalmist points to some of the extraordinary changes that happened since you gave your life to Jesus Christ. The best way to enjoy the blessing is to know and accept its dynamics.

First, you have to reckon that as a child of the Most High God, you are anointed with oil from above. This far supersedes any physical oil any man/woman of God can pour on your head. The power of the Holy Spirit dwells in you; making you more than a conqueror in Christ. You may experience some physical and emotional weaknesses, but your spiritual strength never fluctuates or changes. It is a constant factor, eternally sealed with the blood of Jesus.

Secondly, God's hand is on you to "establish" you. You may not be seeing it now, but it is there. You are in God's hands. Nothing that happens in your life surprises or confuses him. Whether it is good or bad, Jesus is working it out for your good. Thirdly, there is assurance that "the enemy shall not outwit you." When you depend on the wisdom of God, every trick the enemy plays on you to weaken your faith and expose you to harm will be exposed and neutralized. Satan is not smarter than God, so don't make him bigger and heavier than his actual size and weight. You have the mind of Christ if you meditate on the Word of God, and with that level of Godly wisdom, Satan and all the armies of hell cannot outwit you. They can disturb you, but they cannot dethrone you. You are seated with Christ "in heavenly places," whether rich or poor, sick or in good health.

Fourthly, you have the Lord himself taking up the fight and beating down your "foes before his (your) face, and plague those who hate him (you)." If you try to take on battles meant for God, you will wear yourself out before the whistle is blown for the fight to begin. Trust him to take care of the opposition. And finally, you have his promise to remain faithful to you, and be merciful to you. Stop stressing yourself about who is doing what against you. God has your back covered, and that's all you need. He will lift your "horn" (strength) IN HIS NAME. You are blessed and your enemy knows it. Live like you know and believe it.

God bless you.

Speak the Word

Eze.2:4-7, NKJV

The people to whom I am sending you are obstinate and stubborn. Say to them, 'This is what the Sovereign LORD says.' And whether they listen or fail to listen-for they are a rebellious house-they will know that a prophet has been among them. And you, son of man, do not be afraid of them or their words. Do not be afraid, though briers and thorns are all around you and you live among scorpions. Do not be afraid of what they say or terrified by them, though they are a rebellious house. You must speak my words to them, whether they listen or fail to listen, for they are a rebellious house

---

Fear of society's reaction towards the truth we stand for, is making some of us tow the line of compromise. When you listen to the news and hear the shame and disgrace individuals and families have to endure because of one person's moral indiscretion, nobody will tell you that this generation needs a true prophetic voice; "a voice of one crying in the wilderness, prepare ye the way of the Lord." (Matt.3:3). God has called us to speak life into dead situations. A critical study of lives and ministry of the apostles and early Christians testifies to one fact; this call is neither a romantic adventure, nor is it for the faint-hearted. There is no grey area between light and darkness.

What we are called to address is not trivial; it is a stronghold that enslaves the souls of men. To break its hold, we must hear what God is saying in His Holy Word and tell the world exactly that. God does not speak a diplomatic language. He expresses love without embracing lies. The God of the Bible says what he means and means what he says. If God is sending you to speak to issues relating to sin, go ahead and say it like it is - in love. It is strange that we only hear today's 'prophets' pronouncing blessing even in situations where there is obvious evidence of people living in sin, and badly being in need of repentance. Messages on righteous living are scarce commodities because they do not attract the crowd.

If you want to serve God's purpose in saving the lost, your only option is to say what God is saying, not what society is suggesting. You don't have to be bothered by the tag they put on you. God says, "you must speak my words to them; whether they listen or fail to listen." That means people will respond differently to the truth of His Word. Your assignment is to declare God's truth, and not to demand its acceptance. Go ahead therefore and speak and uphold the truth of God's Word. It is the only hope for a hopeless world, and the most urgent business God's Spirit desires your participation and input.

God bless you

Rely on God

Lu.22:35-36, NKJV

And He said to them, "When I sent you without money bag, knapsack, and sandals, did you lack anything?" So they said, "Nothing". Then He said to them, "But now, he who has a money bag, let him take it, and likewise a knapsack; and he who has no sword, let him sell his garment and buy one."

A self-styled revolutionary statesman of Latin America once said, "When circumstances change within 24 hours, tactics must be changed". This is more a Christian principle than a revolutionary rhetoric. At one time in His interaction with His disciples, Jesus sent them into the mission field with instructions not to carry along any provisions. The people they were going to minister to, would take care of their needs. It was a short-term assignment and would not burden their hosts. But when Jesus was about to exit and the disciples were "NOW" going to go on long-term, life-time missions, He changed the rules.

The first arrangement no longer applied. This time around, the disciples were told they had to plan and make provision for what they would need on the mission field. They were no longer going to live at random and at the expense of others. God was going to provide alright, but they needed to strategize on managing what God provides judiciously. The import of Jesus' advice is that we cannot live off the generosity of friends and relatives for the rest of our lives. We must live in such a way that "when circumstances change within 24 hours, tactics must be changed". This is not about being inconsistent, it is about being responsible.

God does not want us putting our faith in what others can do for us all our lives. The fact that God used me to meet a need in your life, doesn't mean you wake up every morning expecting that it's going to be the norm. Miracles are exceptions, not the rule. You must plan for your future based on your income, not on my salary. Jesus said, "But NOW, he who has a money bag, let him take it..." And I beg your indulgence to add, "let him who has no money bag (bank account) buy/get one."

Time changes without prior notice. A child of God should not take delight in parasitic living - always expecting others to help. The battles of life are not fought at the same levels with the same strategies. God may cause you to receive some blessings without you working for it, but that is not an endorsement to always expect handouts. Wean yourself from being a perpetual receiver. Time to believe and work towards being self-sufficient.

God bless you.

God's direction

Ps.32:8-9, NKJV

I will instruct you and teach you in the way you should go; I will guide you with my eye. Do not be like the horse or like the mule, which have no understanding, which must be harnessed with bit and bridle, else they will not come near you.

When you are making a journey and not sure of the route to your destination, the obvious thing to do is to depend on someone who knows the way. In today's world of technological advancement, most people depend on GPS to navigate their way to wherever they want to go. But whether it is a human guide or technology, they both have limitations. How many times have we not heard about a car or plane crashing because of equipment failure? In some of our trips abroad, we have asked for directions from people who we thought should be able to help us find our way around, only to realize later they had misdirected and misled us.

God offers us guidance that is consistent, reliable, dependable, unfaltering, and solid. He makes it clear to us that his offer to guide is for free, and not by force. He created us in His image; meaning we can choose either to obey his instructions or not to follow his leading and direction. Whatever choices we make, comes with consequences. God has opted to be a part of our lives because of our vulnerability to sin, failure, and defeat. He loves you too much to allow you to go through life without availing himself to you as teacher, guide, and counselor. He loves you so much that even though you are the ultimate beneficiary of his grace, he refuses to treat you "like the horse or like the mule, which have no understanding, which must be harnessed with bit and bridle, else they will not come near you."

As much as the LORD desires for you to come and access his guidance, he is saying, 'I am not going to force you as if you don't have any brains in your head. You are not an animal. You were created in my own image. Exercise your will and come, and I will help you.' This is the power of his love, no threats, no rejection, and no condemnation. You can answer this invitation today. You can access God's direction right now. All it takes is to ask for it. Instead of depending solely on your political leaders, pastor, doctor, driver, pilot etc. to sort you out, make a call to heaven first. Let God be the One using the people, things, and circumstances to shape your destiny. Pray and commit it all into his hands. Listen to what he says and follow where he leads. You can never go wrong with Jesus. He is waiting. Take that first step and don't ever plan without him.

God bless you.

It's Time: "Arise and Go"

Lu.15:17-20a, NKJV

But when he came to himself, he said, "How many of my father's hired servants have bread enough and to spare, and I perish with hunger! I will arise and go to my father, and I will say to him, "Father, I have sinned against heaven and before you, and I am no longer worthy to be called your son. Make me like one of your hired servants. And he arose and came to his father...

For some of us, all we need to do to see a change in our miserable, stagnant, and unproductive lives, is to tread the path of a "prodigal son." We have either wasted, missed, or messed up opportunities, and now find ourselves locked up in a situation that is making life difficult and distressing. The chances we miss because of wrong choices we make, can put us where we ought not to be. The good news, however, is that there is nothing impossible with my God and your God, and so whatever changes we determine to make, we can do it.

The parable of the Prodigal Son gives some positive steps towards reversing the consequences of bad choices. The first is to come to the awareness of your sorrow state. The scripture says, "but when he (the Prodigal son) came to himself..." You need that awareness of not living up to your full potential, because as long as you are complacent, apathy will set in and you will be rejoicing over something you should be rejecting. If you are not doing enough to better your lot, you should know it more than the prophet Isaiah. The young man had to admit that he had blown his best chance.

Once the awareness came, he began to count his losses. This is key: If you don't know what you lost, there will be little or no motivation to initiate any movement towards change or recovery. Having clearly satisfied himself that indeed he should be living better than what he was doing, the Prodigal son took the most important decision that was to lift him from the status of an ordinary servant, to that of a dignified son. He said, "I will arise and go..."

Maybe as you read this today, you are missing out on some blessing because you made a wrong decision or choice regarding something, someone, or some place. I dare suggest to you that if awareness has come to you, and that opportunity is still there, you have to bury your pride and "arise and go." You may not get exactly what you lost, but it is better to gain back your status as a son, than live in your complacency, pride, and rebellion and continue eating with pigs! Some of us have believed, fasted, and prayed over somethings long enough, and all we need to do now is to "arise and go."

The only missing link is our commitment to do what needs to be done. This narrative clearly shows that no matter how much faith we confess, we cannot achieve certain goals until and unless we are prepared to work towards same. Prosperity is a prize and reward for hard work, not laziness and excuses. God will never help you beyond what you can do for yourself; so if you have "come to yourself" about something that needs to change in your life, then "arise and go." Take action; change your attitude, humble yourself, and the result will be different from what you see right now.

God bless you.

The Sweet and the Bitter

Eccl.10:9, ESV

He who quarries stones is hurt by them, and he who splits logs is endangered by them.

God has a sense of humor. It was in a time of personal stress from ministry burdens and frustrations that the Lord gave me this scripture; saying to me that you cannot work with sheep and avoid the smell of sheep. This should be a great word of encouragement to you too, if for one reason or the other, you are at a point of giving up. Whatever you choose as a goal or career path, comes with its own challenges. The one who "quarries stones is hurt by them".

If you don't want anyone getting too involved with you, then marriage is not for you. Marriage has bumpy roads and unpredictable hiccups. It is impossible to predict the long-term commitment and faithfulness of a partner; not even if the person is a tongue-blasting, Bible-rattling preacher of the gospel. This, however, should not be a reason not to marry. It will be like saying you won't ride a car or fly in an airplane because of the possibility of an accident occurring. You don't run from life's challenges, you confront them.

Every activity that has a blessing, also has burdens. Whatever choices you make, you should brace yourself to be "hurt" to get to your ultimate destination or goal. If you choose to marry, you must understand that you are not only going to enjoy assets, but liabilities too. The life partner you choose, is not cut in a perfect mold; that person is coming into your life with years of accumulated assets and liabilities. Stop dreaming of a life without hurts because it is a fantasy and an illusion. It simply doesn't exist anywhere in this world of sin.

The further people are from you, the less likely they are to hurt you. Those who don't break stones, are least likely to be hurt by stones. Continue your good work with the consciousness that you have a God who heals. When it hurts, you don't quit; you report at His "clinic" and you shall surely receive healing through grace. Friend, if you dare "split logs," they will be a danger to you, but protection and wisdom from above will bring you to a glorious ending. Don't be disheartened. God is working with you in the log-splitting business of your life. Rise up and ride on. You will succeed.

God bless you.

Love above Law

2 Ki.4:27, GNB

But when she came to Elisha, she bowed down before him and took hold of his feet. Gehazi was about to push her away, but Elisha said, "Leave her alone. Can't you see she's deeply distressed? And the LORD has not told me a thing about it."

The woman referenced here, was in deep distress. She had just lost her only child who was born through a prophetic declaration by prophet Elisha. In her frustration, she ran to the man of God for help. When she got to Elisha, the first thing she did was to bow down and hold the prophet's feet. This was no act of worship; it was a show of humility on her part, and sign of respect for her spiritual father.

It is good and important to honor the men and women who sacrifice their lives, time, resources, and life's ambition to mentor, lead, intercede, and equip us in the things of God. While this act of the grieving woman touched Elisha's heart, it offended Gehazi's protocol. The prophet's assistant was so concerned with law and order, that he had become insensitive to suffering and sorrow. Elisha had to point him to what matters most when confronted with human suffering and anguish; everything else must be put on the back burner, and the negative circumstances given priority attention.

You cannot continue to preach while someone is dying right at your feet. Religion that takes human life for granted, has nothing to do with the Christ of Calvary. Elisha said, "Leave her alone. Can't you see she is deeply distressed?" Think about that for a moment. You may be so busy with 'holy projects,' you hardly "see" the hurting people God want you to help. Elisha showed us that God does not have to tell us everything before we show sympathy and concern; and to the modern-day prophets who claim to know everything about everyone, here is a classic lesson in prophetic ministry: A prophet cannot know anything, or indeed everything about everyone, anytime he chooses. Absolutely unscriptural and impossible!! Prophecy does not come by a man's will or decision.

You don't decide to prophesy or see a vision. If God doesn't reveal it to you, you cannot see or know anything about anyone or circumstance. Any other way, the source of your prophecy cannot be God, but Satan, the deceiver. That is the position of God's Holy Book, the Bible. Meanwhile, let each of us ask the Lord to sensitize us to the needs of those who are hurting. A word of hope and comfort, a gentle hug, and a listening hear, can be the lifeline to someone's deadline. The Gehazi spirit is a spirit of discouragement, division, and destruction. God's holy people do not need that. Be an Elisha to some disadvantaged child, confused man, or distressed woman. Let him/her take hold of your 'feet.' Don't push him/her away. Your 'feet' is the only source of solace, hope, and comfort they can relate to. If you must break the Sabbath to save a soul, go ahead and do it. Put Love above Law.

God bless you

Are you A Partner or Parasite?

Ruth 1:16-17, GNB

But Ruth answered, "Don't ask me to leave you! Let me go with you. Wherever you go, I will go; wherever you live, I will live. Your people will be my people, and your God will be my God...May the LORD's worst punishment come upon me if I let anything but death separate me and you.

It is very easy to align ourselves with people we can benefit from. Many relationships have weak foundations because the motive for the connection is not what one gives away, but rather what one stands to gain from it. This is the chore of many marital crisis, and the reason for many other unhealthy relationships. If Ruth had analyzed Naomi's financial and material worth, and used that as a yardstick to follow Naomi, she would never have taken the decision she took. Indeed, when Naomi painted a gloomy picture of her past and present, and then spoke of a future without prospects, Orpah who had earlier showed the same affection towards Naomi, opted out.

Herein lies the difference between selfish Orpah, and selfless Ruth: (1) Ruth saw something in Naomi that Orpah did not see. Ruth saw beyond Naomi's present material impoverishment and physical limitations. She discerned the spiritual glory of God that could not be quantified in terms of money. Orpah's self-centeredness and focus on material gain, blinded her from seeing the great privilege of associating with a woman of God, and being counted among the people of God. (2) Orpah gave Naomi her HEAD, while Ruth gave Naomi her HEART. Naomi did not only LIVED with Naomi; she LOVED the Godly old lady without reservation. (3) Orpah was unwilling to associate with Naomi if she was not going to get anything out of the relationship, but Ruth chose to sacrifice herself for the comfort of the helpless senior citizen.

In the end, Orpah's story ended with her decision to walk away from Naomi. That is what happens when we enter into relationships with our selfish interests being the motivating factor. Those who marry with their minds set on what they can get out of the union, rather than how they can be partners in building healthy homes and families, are more likely to live in disappointment and unhappiness. Ruth was blessed beyond her wildest imagination because she triggered the divine principle of "sowing and reaping."

If you are always intent on serving where you are likely to be seen, applauded, and rewarded, you will never realize the blessing of Ruth. If your idea of choosing a marriage partner, friends etc. is to look for those who are rich and affluent in material wealth, you cannot be a trusted friend or partner. The truth is, when the money dries up, your love will die out; and that is a very serious moral weakness. Ruth got more than she could ever ask for and became grandma of King David. You cannot go any further than what you are willing to sacrifice for a healthy relationship. Love people for who they are, not for what you can get from them. Be a PARTNER, and not a PARASITE.

God bless you.

Just a Touch

Matt.8:14-15, NIV

Now when Jesus had come into Peter's house, He saw his wife's mother lying sick with a fever. So he touched her hand, and the fever left her. And she arose and served them

Those who serve the Lord faithfully, always gain his attention in times of crisis. Peter had come home with Jesus, after what possibly could have been a long time away from home on a mission's trip. At least the context does not indicate any of them had previous knowledge of Peter's mother-in-law being sick. The important thing, however, is that Jesus gave her his immediate attention.

There are three lessons here for us: the first being Peter's mother-in-law staying in Peter's home as a result of poor health. Even though the scripture admonishes married couples to be separated from their parents, it never said to forsake, neglect, or deny them. The fact that we are to "leave and cleave" to each other, should not be reason to be disconnected from our parents. Peter sets us an example of how to relate to our parents after marriage. We may not necessarily have to bring them into our homes, but we still can "touch" them by calling to find out how they are doing and show them we care.

The second lesson comes from Jesus. He walked into a crisis; he was confronted with a suffering woman. That was not the time to quote scriptures and pontificate on whether Peter was right or wrong in allowing his wife's mother to move in with them. The law must wait, because there was a life to be saved. Remember the letter kills. It is the Spirit that gives life. The principle of loving your neighbor as yourself, effectively puts to rest all legalistic arguments against Peter's act of kindness. And finally, when the mother-in-law received her touch of healing, the scripture said, "she arose and served them."

She did not take Peter's act of kindness for granted. She did not try to impose herself. She humbled herself by SERVING. Pay attention to your family. Share in their struggles. Fight for their salvation. Demand deliverance for those Satan has taken captive. No condemnation. No judgment. No cursing. Touch them with your prayers, if you cannot reach them with your hands. Bless them, and the Lord will bless you.

God bless you.

Sin cannot offer security

Prov.12:3, CEV

Sin cannot offer security! But if you live right, you will be as secure as a tree with deep roots.

The stability of a tree depends on the depth of its roots. When a storm hits, it takes firm roots for a tree to survive. This is the picture the scripture is painting, relative to how we live our lives. Making wrong and ungodly choices weakens the moral fiber of the believer. Adam and Eve were fully covered with divine protection until they sinned. The security they used to enjoy eluded them. They began to live in fear and panic. God's presence was no longer something they cherished. Once the covering is removed, a crisis is introduced.

This cycle of sin and its consequences continues. Wherever sin is accepted as the norm, the presence of God is rejected, and divine security is lost. Apostle Paul cautions is in these words: "Quench not the Spirit." Living right is right. You may not make Godly choices all the time, but even when you make the wrong choices, it shouldn't be deliberate. Don't decide to do what you know does not conform to the Word and Will of God; that amounts to rebellion, and the prophet Samuel told King Saul that rebellion is another name for witchcraft(1Sam.15:23).

In other words, to rebel against the Word of God, is the same as practicing witchcraft. If for whatever reason you are caught in living a sinful life, you can break out of it right now. You are where you are because you decided to be there. Nobody can stop you from living for Christ, but yourself. Align your thoughts and actions with the Word of God. When you do that, your "roots" gain depth that brings security. There is no better way to live. You may not be perfect, but you can live a Godly life; a life of honesty, integrity, love, caring and sharing. You are just a decision away from it; go for it, and you will have God's guaranteed protection.

God bless you

Give No room to Laziness

Neh.4:6, KJV

So, we built the wall; and all the wall was joined together, unto half the height thereof: for the people had a mind to work.

If you are engaged in a project that demands working with others, and you desire to see positive results, then your best bet is to ask God to draw to you the kind of people with "a mind to work." That was the secret Of Nehemiah's success, and that has always been the case with individuals and corporate bodies who make impact; whether religious or secular. In the sporting world, you find that great teams are always a result of individual commitment towards a common goal. Laziness doesn't win laurels. What we need to understand is that there are people out there, who just love to be part of a winning team.

They have no desire to work, and it is not advisable to accept such folks on your team. They don't want to dirty their hands, but want to feed their stomach. Their eyes are on the booty, never on the battle. When you have such people on your team, you have nobody, and you are simply going nowhere. Your vision will suffer; not because God is not on your side, but because your team is tearing it apart. If you want to BUILD something that will last, look for a 'Nehemiah team'; men and women who have "a mind to work." This is especially important for all in leadership.

Winning begins in the MIND. As long as you lead a team that does not have 'a mind to work', you are at a big disadvantage in getting the job done. This is one of the major issues with our society today; we want everything fast, without making the necessary sacrifices. The truth of the matter, however, is that once your team's mental attitude is right, adrenaline levels rise to conquer and overcome every obstacle. A winning team becomes a matter of course.

Build the walls of your life with people who have "a mind to work" for success, not those who wait for manna from heaven. Such waiting has neither life or logic; it's a sheer waste of time. The brand name for such behavior is "laziness." Don't fall for it. Look out for builders, not 'babies' who consume without producing.

God bless you.

Seek his counsel and secure your future

Ps.33:11, NKJV

The counsel of the Lord stands forever, the plans of his heart to all generations.

Planning is a very important part of life. It is aptly said that one who does not plan, actually plans to fail. A plan helps you to map out the direction you want to go, otherwise you will go everywhere and get nowhere. As a child of God, you don't do solo planning. You plan with God; and the reasons you must do so are two-fold. The primary reason is because God already has a plan for your life, and secondly because it is God's plan for your life that will ultimately prevail. Moving in opposite direction to God's plan for your life will only create delays, dead ends, and frustrations.

So, what is the solution? Seek counsel from God. Ask God to show you His unique plan and agenda for you. The wise have said that "all that glitters is not gold." All your peers may be moving in a certain direction and succeeding in their pursuits, but that may not be the place of your calling. Don't be a carbon copy of someone else's script. Be original. A good manager may not necessarily be a good teacher, so always do some serious introspection before launching out "into the deep."

Mere qualification is not enough to make you successful. Peter was a competent and qualified fisherman but caught no fish until Jesus intervened. Spend quality time with God in prayer everyday. Read and meditate on his Word. It will throw light on your ideas, and give you wisdom and direction. You may not always get it right, but you can trust God to work it out for your good because you ask for his counsel. Remember that after all is said and done, it is the will of God and the plans of his heart that will prevail. Seek his counsel and secure your future.

God bless you.

Realities of life

Ex.18:12, NIV

Then Jethro, Moses' father-in-law, brought a burnt offering and other sacrifices to God, and Aaron came with all the elders of Israel to eat bread with Moses' father-in-law in the presence of God

---

Accepting certain realities of life, will make it easier for you to survive betrayals, blackmail, and ingratitude. You must understand and accept that there are people who attend your "party", sit at your table, and eat your bread, who can never like or appreciate you. Before Judas Iscariot did it to Jesus, Aaron did it to Jethro; and someone, somewhere, somehow, may do it to you. Our devotional passage today is a narrative of Moses' father-in-law hosting a feast or party during a visit to Moses and her daughter, who happened to be the wife of Moses.

Aaron was at the party alright, but he was later to sit with Miriam and backbite Moses for marrying a foreigner. One would have expected that since Aaron disapproved of Moses' marriage to a foreigner, he would graciously have excused himself from a celebration organized by the woman's father; but no, here is what the Bible records: "Aaron came with all the elders of Israel to eat bread with Moses' father-in-law IN THE PRESENCE OF GOD." Aaron ate bread provided by the father of the woman he did not like. Probably he even joked and danced with her "IN THE PRESENCE OF GOD." Wao! Get the drift?

It is always important to remember that not everyone who benefits from your time, resource, counsel etc. is likely to appreciate the sacrifice you make in their lives. If you convince yourself that none of the people God has used you to bless can ever turn their backs on you, attack your person, or betray your trust, you may not find it easy overcoming the shock and pain that comes with it. Mark my words! When it comes to issues of who loves or likes you, they are purely matters of the heart, and you cannot do anything about it.

Take consolation in the fact that God will always put people in your life who will love you for you. They may never have the opportunity to sit at your dining table, but from the distance where they sit or stand, they appreciate you so much and love you so deeply. Keep an open mind when God use you to bless people. If you don't expect too much, when the "party" is over and you hear those who dine with you "IN THE PRESENCE OF GOD" (fellow believers) dent your image and betray your trust, it won't hurt that much.

God bless you.

Call God

Jer.33:3, NKJV

Call to Me, and I will answer you, and show you great and mighty things, which you do not know.

Ignorance is the reason for much of the suffering and underdevelopment we see all around us. You cannot break the cycle of poverty in a society where the majority of the people are uneducated and live in ignorance. Indeed, one of the most effective ways of enslavement is lack of knowledge. When you don't know your worth and value as a human being created in the express image of God, you allow just anyone to define you and ultimately devalue you. God, speaking through the prophet Jeremiah, is asking you to call to him. He says he will not only answer your call, but more importantly, "show you great and mighty things, which you do not know."

Beloved, it is impossible to know more than what we know, and absolute folly to pretend to know everything we need to know, that we don't already know. In dealing with God, we first have to accept that we are limited in what we know and cannot be empowered to be fruitful unless we are willing to be taught; and that if God would teach us, then we have to take the initiative and humbly ask him to do so. Prayer is not punishment. Prayer is a way of showing how dependent we are on God. It is a sign of trust, and God promises answers to our prayers. He knows what we don't know and doesn't need an interpreter to understand whatever language format we use to communicate with him.

God wants to give you a revelation that will introduce you to your elevation. He is talking about showing you "great and mighty things." That is a bold challenge to your blind life. It takes only God to bring things that are beyond our thoughts and imagination to manifestation. So, where do we go from here? Place that "call" and see God at work in your life. Don't just believe for anything; trust for the "great and mighty things," because that is what he has promised. This is not being presumptuous; it is about praying according to the perfect will of God. He is saying he will show you great and mighty things, and so praying for anything less is praying against the will of God.

I sincerely believe that there are "great and mighty things" regarding your life and circumstances that you are completely ignorant of, and God want to bring you revelation to help you out. What he doesn't want to do is to impose anything on you, and that is why he is asking you to invite him to come in with what he has to offer. Call him today. Call him every day. You cannot prevail, until you learn to travail.

God bless you.

Thus says the Lord

Eze.36:33-36, NKJV

Thus says the Lord GOD: "On the day that I cleanse you from all your iniquities, I will also enable you to dwell in the cities, and the ruins shall be rebuilt. The desolate land shall be tilled instead of lying desolate in the sight of all who pass by. So, they shall say, 'This land that was desolate has become like the garden of Eden; and the wasted, desolate, and ruined cities are now fortified and inhabited.' Then the nations which are left all around you shall know that I, the LORD, have rebuilt the ruined places and planted what was desolate. I, the LORD, have spoken, and I will do it.

Our salvation is a well-planned and properly executed divine agenda. Our God is not a "politician" and does not operate a propaganda outfit. He doesn't need to lie to get our votes. What God promises He is always sure to deliver. The salvation package of the cross of Calvary goes far beyond washing with the blood of Christ. God does not save us from sin and leave us to struggle all our lives. The word of God says God "will ENABLE you to dwell in the cities, and the RUINS shall be rebuilt"v.33).

Quite often we get emotionally disoriented due to the perception that nothing can change in our lives because we are too limited in resources and opportunities. Expectations are not being met and we are even losing the little that keeps us hoping and believing for a better tomorrow. God has your situation under control and promises to "enable you" to live in a much more conducive environment. You will dwell in "cities" - beautiful places full of unusual challenges - and succeed because God will give you enablement.

Your life is not over yet. God want to use you as advertising signpost to attract others to His saving grace. He wants to turn on the light in the dark areas of your life "so they will say, 'This land that was desolate has become like the garden of Eden; and the WASTED, DESOLATE, and RUINED cities are now FORTIFIED and INHABITED.'" Just check the words highlighted in capitals. It's about you and the restoration God is determined to bring into your life. Claim the fullness of the blessing of Calvary. Don't wait till you get to heaven before enjoying your new life in Christ. There are issues you don't have to worry about because only God can work them out.

I woke up this morning with a heavy load of challenges waiting to bury me alive, but I just beat the heat by casting "all my cares on the Lord" because He cares for me. Fact is, if you and I hadn't gotten up from bed today, life would still be going on as usual. Take God at His Word, and free yourself from stress. Jesus has vested interest in your success and that is why your breakthrough is guaranteed. God is saying to you, "I, the LORD, have spoken it, and I will do it"(v.36b)." Pray, rejecting life's worst, and Live expecting God's best. God is making your life like the garden of Eden. Embrace the glory and rejoice in His goodness. Thank God for what you have now and trust Him for what He has promised.

God bless you.

Faith and Works

Jn.10:25, NKJV

Jesus answered them, "I told you, and you do not believe. The works that I do in My Father's name, they bear witness of Me.

The messenger's lifestyle should reflect the message he or she preaches. The two are inseparable. Jesus said, "The WORKS THAT I DO in My Father's name, THEY (the works) BEAR WITNESS OF ME." In context, he was making reference to the signs and miracles that formed part of his ministration, but by application we are looking at its totality in terms of what we DO as believers. Charisma without character is dangerous. When the service is over, the benediction is shared, and the "amen" is said, what we do outside of the confines of the chapel walls speak volumes of who our God is.

That is why we should move away from anything that dents our witness for Christ. Jesus walked the talk, and we must do same. Even the secular world maintains that "Actions speak louder than words." Let your tolerance level for anything that does not glorify God drop to zero. When we live what we preach, we reach the hearts of those who do not know the Lord as their personal Savior. The impressions we make on the lives of others are largely due to what they see us DO. Never ask people not to look at what you do, and just go along with your message. They have no choice. They will expect you to authenticate your message by the way you live your life.

So, go ahead and show up. One act of love, mercy, and compassion is more powerful than ten thousand promises that never got fulfilled. As a child of God, your whole life should be a testimony of who your God and Father is, so that even if you don't say it, people will see Him in you. Your "works" (not only your words) should bear witness to your faith in Christ. This was what Jesus was driving at when he said, "by their fruit (works) you shall know them." You cannot know people well enough by just listening to what they say about themselves. You can be deceived. Your best bet is to look at what they do and tie it in to who they claim they are, and that way you have a better picture of your "clients".

This same standard should be the measure by which you live your life. Your faith cannot be seen on your face. Your faith will be seen in your fruit - how you behave, relate, and conduct yourself in private and in public. People may not be interested in your looks if you don't act right towards them. The apostle James wrote: "But someone will say, I have faith, and you have works. Show me your faith without your works, and I will show my faith by my works"(Jam.2:18). We may not get it right all the time, but it should still be our goal to get it right as much as we can, God being our helper. And now may the works that we do in our Father's name bear witness to our confession of His Son's grace in our lives.

God bless you.

Purpose and Pursuit

Ex. 35:25, 30-35(MSG)

"All the women who were skilled at weaving brought their weaving of blue and purple and scarlet fabrics and their fine linens. And all the women who were gifted in spinning, spun the goats' hair...Moses told the Israelites, "See, God has selected Bezalel son of Uri, son of Hur, of the tribe of Judah. He's filled him with the Spirit of God, with skill, ability, and know-how for making all sorts of things, to design and work in gold, silver, and bronze; to carve stones and set them; to carve wood, working in every kind of skilled craft. And he's also made him a teacher, he and Oholiab son of Ahisamach, of the tribe of Dan. He has filled them with skill to do all manner of work of the engraver and the designer and the tapestry maker, in blue, purple, and scarlet thread, and fine linen, and of the weaver-those who do every work and those who design artistic works."

When a child of God says he doesn't know God's purpose for his life, the real problem has to do with his inability to locate, or perhaps even accept God's calling on his life. The real issue is not lack of gifts or talents. No one is born into this world by accident. No human being is a mistake. Solomon was born out of a murky marriage relationship between David and Bathsheba, and yet look what God did with him. Without apology, I am pro-life. I believe in the sanctity of human life. I believe God created you a man or woman for a specific purpose.

In order to fulfill His purpose for your life, God has gifted and wired you in a way that guarantees your success. Moses could never have been able to do the job of the craftsmen and women. He simply was not gifted and trained in that line of duty, and recognizing that, he looked for those gifted by God to play that role. He was smart enough to know that the gifting of God is not limited to gender. God can use anybody irrespective of your age, education, location, or gender. Accept yourself for what and who God has called you to be.

The kingdom of God is made poorer when everyone gravitates towards doing the same thing. Everyone want to be a prophet. Everyone want to be the bishop. In the end, there is so much duplication with little or no impact. Confusion and strife become the norm where people operate outside their area of calling. You cannot be happy doing a job you are not conditioned spiritually, emotionally, physically, and technically to undertake. Otherwise, there will be no need for teaching and training. That was why God did not only fill Bezalel with "wisdom, and understanding, in knowledge and all manner of workmanship" (v.31-NKJV) but also gave him ability to TEACH others.

Here is the catch! If you don't know or accept your God-given gifts and abilities, how do you impart it to others? Finding your purpose in life begins with exploring what God has placed INSIDE you, not your outside environment. Prison gates could not stop Joseph from interpreting dreams, and becoming what God purposed him to become. Exploring what God has put in you gives you power to exploit what is around you. There are some things and needs that can only be met with your input. If you insist on being something God has not made you to be, you may lose the job satisfaction that goes with it. Don't let that happen to you. Let the pursuit and use of your gifts and talents be the focus of your life.

God bless you.

A New Dawn

Mic.4:7, AMP

And I will make the lame a remnant, and those who were cut off a strong nation; and the Lord shall reign over them in Mount Zion from this time forth and forever.

The goodness of God is very much revealed by the grace he bestows when all we deserve is judgment. The prophet Micah came onto the scene at a time when both Israel and Judah had turned their backs on the living God. The divided kingdoms had become so corrupted, it was not possible to differentiate between them and the pagan nations around them. The entire society from prophets, priests, kings, and ordinary citizenry, was caught up in sinful living. While prophesying about God's impending judgement, the prophet pronounced a word of hope for those who kept faith with God. He said the Lord was going to restore them. God was going to restore "the lame."

Take note that those who are lame have no power in their legs. Their movement is limited and they need help to be able to move about. They become perpetually dependent on someone or something, to go where they needed to go. God's word of assurance is that if you continue to keep trusting him, and refrain from compromising with the world, he will restore you. He will turn your life in the direction of victory. The Almighty God will empower you to be able to move on your "paralyzed feet." Nothing is impossible with God. Sometimes his timing is irritating to our human spirit.

We feel no justification for the Lord keeping us in suspense, when everything is pointing to the fact that there is no better time for us to have what we want to have than NOW! However, we have hope that cannot be cut off, if we hold to his promise of restoration. No matter how dark your world becomes, and deserving of divine judgement, grace will always speak on your behalf. The finished work of the cross of Christ will turn your lameness into laughter.

Don't allow the present darkness to drain you. Whatever you have lost; from job to joy, will be restored. God is in the process of making you "a strong nation". The pain in your lame feet (challenges you face), are birth pangs of a new day in your life; it's going to be your day of resurrection, restoration, and rejoicing. May you receive it in Jesus Name.

God bless you.

A broken and a contrite heart

Ps.51:17, NKJV

The sacrifices of God are a broken spirit, a broken and a contrite heart - these, O God, you will not despise.

Religion teaches and endorses 'doing' without 'being'. Religion makes demands that exclude relationship. It says that God is beyond your reach and so all you need to do to be acceptable to him is to perform rituals like washing of the body, bringing offerings, giving to the poor etc. The difference between Christianity and every other religious belief is in this; our God requires RELATIONSHIP with us.

He offers a love-relationship that can only be satisfied by our connecting through repentance from sin, and submission to His will. A "broken and contrite heart" is fertile soil for Holy Spirit investment. It marginalizes pride, and accepts that without God, nothing is worth living for.

It comes so low, making God the highest reference point. It 'sees' the holiness of God, and admits its wretched state of sin. From that platform of humility, it appreciates and embraces the love of Calvary and is ready to offer true, unadulterated worship. Come into that place of peace and power, with a "broken and contrite heart", and you will leave His Presence a blessed and joyful spirit. God be with you and yours. Loving you always in all ways. Shalom.

God bless you.

Godly living

Mic.6:8, NKJV

He has shown you, O man, what is good; And what does the Lord require of you, but to do justly, to love mercy, and to walk humbly with your God?

It is unwise to live as if we are not accountable to anyone. It is even more unfortunate to pretend we don't know what the Lord requires of us. Conscience alone speaks to our hearts concerning good and evil, and right from birth to death, one of the ways God speaks to us is through our conscience. In the center of our conscience there are three things the scripture endorses as necessary for Godly living. They are (1) to DO justly. This implies a determination to DO what is right in all things to all men.

It means you don't treat me well because you know me or can gain something from me and treat the other person like dung because he doesn't look like he has anything to offer you. (2) We are entreated "to LOVE mercy." I guess if you don't love it, you can't have it, and if you don't have it, you can't show or manifest it. We are in a world where there is so much suffering and pain. Our faith demands of us mercy towards those in this bracket of darkness. People don't have to "deserve" to be shown mercy. Mercy is an overflow of divine grace. Love it and God will manifest it through you.

The third demand God's Word and conscience are making of us is to "walk humbly with your God". Nothing brings us closer to God (aside of the blood of Jesus) than humility. Indeed, if there is one thing God repeatedly denounces and "hates" in scripture, it is pride. God honors humility. It is not a weakness, as some wrongly assume. It is a very simple but essential need in every believer's life. It is a door to elevation. Nobody walks humbly with God and stays under.

Failure cannot contain the humble, because God goes where they go and lifts them from nothing to something - always. May God grant us the grace to do justly, love mercy, and walk humbly with Him in Jesus' Name.

God bless you.

God's Promise

Is.46:3-4, MSG

Listen to me, family of Jacob, everyone that's left of the family of Israel. I've been carrying you on my back from the day you were born, And I'll keep on carrying you when you're old. I'll be there, bearing you when you're old and gray, I've done it and will keep on doing it, carrying you on my back, saving you.

Growing old is an uncomfortable thought to many. It is interesting how we wanted to be regarded as being of age during our teenage and youthful years, and then as we progressed into the middle years of our lives, we suddenly do everything in our power to stay young. We literally fight the idea of being considered as senior citizens until the evidence becomes so strong in our looks and movements that we hung up our gloves. I remember when I hit age 16 and suddenly, I had this wonderful ego I can do "all things" all MEN do.

At almost 70 I longer have the passion to be seen as matured and of age. It's gone. I can't stop time from moving and change from coming. The good news is that without even knowing it or seeing with the natural eye, my Bible says God has carried me on his "back" all these years and has promised to keep carrying me right there to the end of my life. What a privilege?! Let someone show me one (just one) of the so-called gods of this world who gives such extravagant love and particular attention to his worshippers. The gods of this world drive their worshippers under a yoke of fear.

It's a zombie-kind of relationship. They give the command, and the followers must obey. Period. No questions asked, no personal communication, nothing but dry and empty rituals that produces a people of anger, hatred, bitterness, vicious, ruthless and violent to the chore. Not so with this Jesus we worship. Just imagine for a moment, God's promise of "carrying you on my back from the day you were born, and I will keep on carrying you on my back..." Here is a God who is a mother extraordinaire. Put your fears to rest. You are in safe hands, riding on the back of God. What an imagery!

You need not be bogged down with fears of what the future holds. God holds your future, and what He holds no one can take from His hands. The lines on your face may change. You may wobble on your feet and be weak in your hands. If you are a lady, you may battle a good portion of the wrinkles on your face with make-over to shape up. You may try and succeed in looking young and beautiful as long as you wish, but sad to say, no make-over treatment can bring you to the exact place of youthful exuberance you so much desire as the years roll by. Change can be delayed but cannot be stopped. It's like running water. It will always find its own course.

God is offering us a free ride on His "back" into the future. On his "back", your feet are off the ground and can only go where He takes you. Your future becomes His concern. Your trust is in Him alone. He becomes your unfailing spiritual GPS - personally navigating your entire life from beginning to the end. Take hold of God's promise. It never fails. Be at peace with yourself. It shall be well with you. To all the young people out there who love my Jesus, trust His leading and do not be led astray by the attractions of this evil age. It's all subject to change and decay. Enjoy God's love and stay hooked on His back. There is no better, safer place.

God bless you.

Victorious Shout

Ps.66:1, NKJV

Make a joyful shout to God, all the earth! Sing out the honor of His name; Make His praise glorious."

A shout is no mere noise. A shout is a heavy sound that carries a specific message. When you hear spectators shout at a sporting event, it probably could mean their team won a game, tournament, or their idol won a race etc. It could mean somebody on the team they support missed a goal, touch down, or wasted an opportunity. The point is people don't shout for nothing. There is a shout of joy and shout of defeat. God is inviting us to join His winning team with shouts of joy. For us, every game of our lives is over before it begins, and the victory is always ours.

Christ has done for us what we could not and cannot do for ourselves. He did it while we were still sinners. He died to set us free from the penalty of sin. Don't begin another day with a defeatist attitude. If you yield to thoughts of frustration and failure, you will be frustrated and have a greater chance of failing. Praise God all day long. You may not get space where you are at the moment to verbalize your praise. Your present location may not be ideal for a shout, so you may be wondering what to do. I am sitting in my car writing this devotion this morning. In my spirit I am already in joyful mood and "shouting" in the deep recesses of my soul.

I am celebrating the goodness of God, and thanking him for what I have not seen, touched, known, or experienced. I am dictating the way my day goes. I am not "feeling" like it, but I am committed to praising anyway - even in my car!! The Jericho walls of life have no chance against your shout of joy. Every limitation before you will turn to liberation as you praise the Lord today. Making your praise glorious means letting it be born out of extravagant love.

Your praise should not be a ritual. Let it come out of a heart full of gratitude. Indeed, you must be grateful to live to see another day. Your bitter experiences are doors to better days. Praise the Lord with a shout, and His glory shall go before you. Stay blessed in Jesus' awesome Name, as you keep praising always in all ways.

God bless you.

Souls Over Pigs

Matt.8:33-34, NKJV

Then those who kept them fled; and they went away into the city and told everything, including what had happened to the demon-possessed men. And behold, the whole city came out to meet Jesus. And WHEN THEY SAW HIM, THEY BEGGED HIM TO DEPART FROM THEIR REGION."

Why should a whole city BEG Jesus to go away? This is the dilemma of human addiction to sin and evil. The city had been tormented by two demon-possessed men for years. According to the scriptures, these men lived in a cemetery and were "exceedingly fierce, so that no one could pass that way"(v.28). Jesus had an encounter with this fierce duo, cast out the demons into some pigs which run into the river and got drowned (meaning there are no demon-possessed pigs around anymore so you can continue enjoying your pig meat if you wish).

One would have thought the city folks who have lived in fear and harassment from these demonized men for so long would embrace and celebrate Jesus - maybe even honor him with a "key to the city". Surprisingly enough, they kicked him out. Their reason was because they lost a few pigs. They preferred the continued torment and suffering of their fellow human beings to losing a few pigs. The bondage and loss of human souls was no business of theirs, as long as their personal business interests were served and secured.

Beloved we have not moved away from this 'leave my pigs and let a soul die mentality' in the Body of Christ. Many of us have areas in our lives that Jesus is not welcome. As long as we can eat and dress well, our hallelujah is loudest. We give tithes and offerings in beautiful chapels with the best of music and after the benediction we say to Jesus, "leave my city until we meet again in church." There is no human touch to our spirituality and so the "demon-possessed" are coming out of the "cemetery" every day to torment us.

When all our time, money, and totality of our work and efforts are daily geared towards making our lives comfortable without any attempt to reach the lost, support the weak and vulnerable, feed the hungry, and clothe the naked, it is a tacit admission that we don't want Jesus in our "city". Self-centeredness never appreciates the need for the other person to have a little bite of what we have enjoyed for so long. God has given us cake, but we are offended and upset because He just gave somebody bread.

You can either keep or kick Jesus out of your life by how you respond, first to the needs in the lives of other people; and secondly, by your response to what God does in the lives of other people. Look carefully into the "closets" of your mind - into its different compartments and find out for yourself people whose lives you are not reaching, touching and/or affecting because helping them will make you lose some of your "pigs". Put people over and above pigs, and Jesus will never leave your city.

God bless you.

Hall of Prayer

Is.38:2-3, MSG

Hezekiah turned away from Isaiah and facing the wall, prayed to God: God, please I beg you: Remember how I've lived my life. I've lived faithfully in your presence, lived out of a heart that was totally yours. You have seen how I've lived, the good that I have done. And Hezekiah wept as he prayed - painful tears."

God's messenger should not be the object of your attention or worship, and the fact that someone prophesied to you doesn't make the prophecy a done deal. You see, my friend, Isaiah was a very unique prophet and Hezekiah knew that. Today's theologians call him "the Messianic prophet" because he prophesied concerning Christ more than any other prophet in Holy Book. God at this point sent him to go prophesy to King Hezekiah that his time on earth was over and that he was going to die. The essence of the prophecy was for the king to set his house in order (maybe write a Will) so that there would be no confusion after his death.

The king accepted the prophecy as a word from God because he knew the caliber and integrity of the prophet Isaiah. But beyond acknowledging the prophet's credibility, King Hezekiah knew his (the king's) personal faithfulness and acts of goodness. He knew these were not enough basis to demand salvation, but enough reason to expect audience and reward from God. I love his next move; he turned his back to Isaiah, "faced the wall" and began to pray and negotiate the extension of his lifespan with God. If today's believers will take a cue from Hezekiah, many false prophets will be jobless by the close of day today. If we will focus on pleasing God with acts of goodness, mercy, faithfulness, love and integrity, we shall be in a position to move the unmovable.

Instead of panicking and bowing before the prophet and asking him to "bath" him with oil and pray for him (like today's average Christian will do), the king literally said by his action, "thank you prophet for the prophecy, but you are only a messenger and not the owner of the message. You are only a man like me, not God. I have some reasons to tell God why I shouldn't die now. You have no idea about my relationship with God. Watch my back, I am not going to discuss the prophecy with you. Thank you." The next thing you know Hezekiah was praying for God to spare his life, and God agreed and added fifteen more years to his age. He would have died asking the prophet to pray for him.

So, what is God's word saying to us today? It is saying our personal relationship with God is more important than the prophecy of any man or woman of God. We are not saved by our good works, but our good works win us favor and they are rewarded by God. God is looking for a people who will come into intimate relationship with Him and refuse to live at the beck and call of "prophets". God is looking for a generation of "King Hezekiah's" who know what to do when things are not going right in their lives - a people of faith, and a people of prayer.

A people who can tell the "prophet", "I appreciate the message, but that is where it ends; I am not going to waste time discussing it with you. I am going to talk to the CEO myself." My goodness!! If you and I will take that stand, nothing shall be impossible with us. Welcome to the "King Hezekiah Hall of prayer". You are not a stranger to the court of heaven. You are a child of God, with equal rights as any apostle, archbishop, pastor, or prophet. If you can believe and petition heaven on your issues, God will answer. Ask, and you will receive.

God bless you

Embrace God's Purpose for your Life

Lu.4:42-43, NKJV

Now when it was day, He departed and went into a deserted place. And the crowd sought Him and came to Him, and tried to keep Him from leaving them; but he said to them, "I must preach the kingdom of God to the other cities also, because for this purpose I have been sent."

This passage of scripture is an eye-opener to how important it is to stay focused on God's purpose for your life, and not be swayed by people's opinion about your call. Jesus Christ came for the entire world, but after a successful preaching tour of the synagogues of Galilee, the 'congregation' wanted to turn the Savior of the world, into a local hero. Bible says, "And the crowd sought Him and came to Him and TRIED TO KEEP HIM FROM LEAVING THEM" (note my emphasis). It was a CROWD (a mega church) that tried to KEEP Jesus. The applause was loudest, and the feeling obviously might have been great.

Can you imagine how many men of God in our world today would trade such a big congregation for "a deserted place?" That is where the scripture says Jesus went after leaving the crowd; and when he had to respond to the pressure they were exerting on him, Jesus said "for this purpose I have been sent." His focus was on his purpose, not the people or his popularity. The crowd was only a PART of the purpose, but not the TOTALITY his purpose. To stay with the crowd, was to stifle his purpose. Friend, you may be hurting because you are not getting enough "crowd" attention and may have been convincing yourself that you are not fulfilling God's purpose because you don't have a huge crowd cheering in the stands.

Indeed, there are ministers of the gospel who are frustrated because they are doing everything right, and yet missing out on the crowd. They have fallen victims to the false indoctrination that if they don't have the crowd, they are not serving the Christ. If you are in that category, I encourage you to wake up. Numbers will not cure your numbness; it takes knowledge of God's purpose for your life, to love and enjoy God's call on your life. If you make the crowd your priority, and allow the crowd to "keep" you, that same crowd will kill your purpose. You may look flamboyant and successful in the eyes of men, but the dearth and scope of your spiritual impact may be very shallow.

Everything God has for you; from present to future is packaged in his purpose for your life. Don't let the crowd make you a local hero when God's purpose for you is to impact the world. Stop mourning about the lost crowd and keep moving towards the call of Christ. If you don't embrace God's purpose for your life, you will never enjoy the blessings that comes with it. God's power and prosperity for you, are in his purpose for you. Walk away from the "crowd" illusion to the Christ solution; it's all about PURPOSE! And your purpose is as unique as your fingerprint.

God bless you.

Take His Yoke and Learn of Him

Matt.11:29-30, NIV

Take my yoke upon you and learn from me, for I am gentle and humble in heart, and you will find rest for your souls. For my yoke is easy and my burden is light

---

Life in Christ comes with responsibility. It is a responsibility that is shared between us and the Lord, and key to a restful life in the Spirit. There are two things we are asked to do to come to God's promised rest. First is to TAKE His yoke (not our yoke) upon us. This suggests to me God doesn't force us to do anything we don't want to do. He loves to work with people who are willing and hearts that are open. If you don't believe in a course, it is better not to associate with it than pretend to share in the vision. It puts unnecessary stress on everyone involved and slows down progress.

The call of God is not an imposition. It is a proposition. "Whosoever will come", says the ancient hymnal. The onus is on you and I to be willing to "take" the yoke of the Lord and partner with Him in building His Kingdom, if we desire to have the rest He promises. The second important step to accessing the "rest" of Christ is to LEARN of Him. We are to relate to Jesus as apprentices learning a trade. We come to the spiritual "job site" with a humble heart to LEARN from the Master.

The learning process demands paying close attention to the Master, staying close enough to hear His instructions, and see His performance. I said it before and I want to repeat that when it comes to Jesus and things of the Spirit, "distance learning" doesn't apply. We've got to stay close enough to hear, see, and serve. In the "taking" of the yoke, and "learning" of the Master, we enter His rest. I ask the Lord to let us all abound in a daily dose of grace that will help us TAKE His yoke and LEARN of Him so we can enter His rest.

God bless you

Enjoy Life

Eccl. 5:18, NIV

Then I realized that it is good and proper for a man to eat and drink, and to find satisfaction in his toilsome labor under the sun during the few days of his life God has given him - for this is his lot."

God did not create us to endure life. God created us to enjoy life. That was why He set everything in place and pronounced all "good" before creating Adam. And of course, He did not leave Adam and Eve to roam in a forest but put them in a "garden". The scripture testifies that "the joy of the Lord is our strength". A joyless life is a miserable life. Any form of worship devoid of music, and expression of joy, is mundane, and hardens the hearts of men, making them ruthless and vicious. There are enough examples around us not too difficult to find. Any home where there is no fun, is no different from a prison. Check it out and prove me wrong.

Every blessing of God comes to enhance His desire for our joy. Don't get yourself so worked up you have no time for fun with family and friends. Jesus told the disciples to ask so they could receive. Why? So, they could have complete joy. In Jn.15:11(NKJV) Jesus said, "These things I have spoken to you, that my joy may remain in you, and that your joy may be full." This joy Christ offers is not dependent on what we have, where we are, what is happening to us, who loves or hates us, or how we feel. It includes being happy, but it is far more than that. It is like a river that flows from the Holy Spirit to water our emotional dryness and set us free to have the audacity to love ourselves, laugh at ourselves, and go about our daily chores as if we are the latest billionaires on the block.

This is something no amount of money can give you. You can have all the money in the world, and still be the most miserable person that ever walked this earth. Otherwise, why should some millionaires commit suicide? History holds record of many millionaires whose lives ended on a sad note. God want you to have what He has to offer and be joyful. And after you work so hard and earn money for your hard work, spend some of the money on yourself. Don't keep working till you drop dead without enjoying the fruit of your labor. You are blessed to be a child of God. If for nothing at all, as part of your salvation package, Jesus Christ through the Holy Spirit, has deposited His joy in you. It is part of the fruit of the Spirit. Eat it. Decide that you are going to flow in the joy of the Lord. Truth is, if you are in a sad mood right now, it is because you have decided to be sad.

Yes. Your mood is largely determined by you. Things will definitely happen that threaten your joy, but you can always bounce back and tell the devil you aren't accepting being miserable as a lifestyle. When sad moments come into your life, treat them as guests not permanent residents. Don't give your negative moods any bed of roses. Get them out with the song of the Lord. The will of God is for you to be joyful. Anything short of that is semantics. It is unacceptable noise and disturbance. Turn it off.

After working so hard, you are entitled to "eat and drink" (not alcohol please, it is toxic and a polluting agent). The devil should not tie your joy to any sinful activity. The source of the believer's joy is INSIDE of himself - He is called the Holy Spirit. Recognize His presence as you meditate on who God says you are. Step into this and every morning with confidence in what God can do, not what you can't do. Guard your heart against anything that tries to steal your joy. Enjoy every moment of everyday, including today. This is God's will for you.

God bless you.

God Can Do Anything Through Anybody

Mk. 6:2-3, CEV

The next Sabbath he taught in the Jewish meeting place. Many of the people who heard him were amazed and asked, 'How can he do all this? Where did he get such wisdom and the power to work these miracles? Isn't he the carpenter, the son of Mary? Aren't James, Joseph, Judas, and Simon his brothers? Don't his sisters still live here in our town?' The people were very unhappy because of what he was doing."

Being in the will of God can attract hatred, jealousy, and outright condemnation. Many of the issues you will have to deal with are not going to come from some weird monster with horns and hoofs. People who know you are people who will nail you. We all have to take warning and be careful how we interpret God's dealings in the lives of people we know. Sometimes the limited "knowledge" we have about others can make us draw conclusions that contradict the truth of who they really are in God's divine plan and purpose.

The people from Jesus' community could not accept His ministry for the simple reason that they knew who His parents and siblings were. As far as they were concerned, the I.Q of a carpenter should not, and could not, be equated to that of a professor. They did not benefit from the miracle-working power of Christ because of their "knowledge!" In the end, the good He was doing became a problem and an offense to them. This is a trap we can so easily fall into in our dealings with people we are too familiar with.

God can choose, change, and use even a murderer without our permission. The first apostles had to query the genuineness of Paul's conversion until Barnabas stepped in to assure them it was no fluke. Don't let your limited knowledge of anyone in your family or church destroy your confidence in what God can do through them. When it's about God, anything is possible - a David can kill a Goliath, dry bones can come back to life, and a virgin can conceive without having any intimate relationship with a man. If you doubt anyone God want to use to bless you, it will cost you big time, because God never gives us the option to choose who He uses to bless us.

Don't let what you "know" bring you that low. Fact is not always truth. It may be a fact that you know your child, brother, sister, friend etc., as a non-performing person, but the TRUTH is that God is able to turn him or her around to become the most powerful asset in your life. Be careful what you call impossible. The carpenter of Galilee is the Savior of the world. You may know him alright. That's a fact, but that fact doesn't affect the truth. In your own personal life, don't be discouraged by opinions of people who claim to know you more than you know yourself, and therefore cannot believe you have what it takes to do what God assigns you to do.

Jesus left his hometown and he flourished. Do same if you must. Knowledge that questions your credibility and ability has no heart in it. Put it behind you and move on with God. Do what God says to do. Certified or uncertified by those who claim to know all the reasons you cannot do any good. Stay blessed and keep flowing for Jesus.

God bless you.

Do Right, Pursue Truth

Prov. 21:3, NKJV

To do what is right and true is more pleasing to the Lord than an offering.

Religion zeroes in on the ACT minus the HEART. We satisfy our conscience by relegating our moral responsibility to the background, while we major in 'bribing' God. What we tend to ignore, or probably misconstrue, is the fact that what we do to men, is as important as what we give to God. Apostle Paul wrote a whole chapter (1Cor.13) on this eternal truth, stressing that anything we do outside the perimeters of love, doesn't register with God. If it's just a matter of giving to God and pleasing him, then it may be okay to steal money and give to the church. But no, God want us to live by principles of truth and goodness; to be guided by his Word and a good conscience.

David said God desires "truth in the inward part" (Ps.51). How sad for a child of God to think his obligation towards God begins and ends with an "offering". Let the saints take note that God doesn't run his kingdom on money earned out of wrong doing. He is not in a financial crisis, has never and can never be in one. The creator of the universe has no pleasure in money illegally earned; so, if you are engaged in drugs, prostitution, or fraud of any shape, kind, or color, God's demand of you is to repent, and do right and pursue truth; not to give an offering.

Don't be deceived by the applause of men. It does not define the approval of God. When you do what is right, and pursue the truth, you attract divine elevation. Yes, God loves a cheerful giver; but not giving gained from deception, fraud, stealing, or any form of wickedness. Whenever you give an offering to the Lord, be reminded that his greatest desire is for you to live right and pursue truth. Anything short of that, makes mockery of the faith we profess in Christ. Give your heart before you give the offering. The offering is most acceptable when the heart is readily accessible to the Lord. Put your heart before the act.

God bless you.

Define Your Moral Borders

Matt.14:6-10, NKJV

But when Herod's birthday party was celebrated, the daughter of Herodias danced before them and pleased Herod. Therefore, he promised with an oath to give her whatever he might ask. So, she, having been prompted by her mother, said, "Give me John the Baptist's head on a platter." And the king was sorry; nevertheless, because of the oaths, and because of those who sat with him, he commanded it to be given to her. So he sent and had John beheaded in prison."

The seductive dance of Herodias' daughter, her mother's evil advice, coupled with Herod's own moral weakness as a national leader and head of his family, created a perfect platform for the murder of John the Baptist. Every one of us is "dancing" before the world. Our lives are dance-forms that are advising and influencing those within our "catchment area", consciously or unconsciously. What began in Herod's house as a very harmless birthday party, ended with the murder of a prophet of God - a man who was born out of many years of waiting by his aged parents.

A man who was chosen by God before his birth to herald and announce the coming of the Savior of the world. A man Jesus Christ himself declared as being greater than any man born of a woman, except those born of the kingdom. This outstanding prophet had his head cut off to satisfy the whims and caprices of an adulterous woman, whose daughter broke the weak moral fiber of an immoral king with one seductive dance. One demonically inspired dance was all it took to confuse a king and had him kill a prophet of God. Can I suggest to you that you and I can easily become tools of "murder" in the hands of Satan through our dance-forms (lifestyle) - the things we say, and the decisions we make, based on the advice of our own company of "moral rascals"?

You see, if Herod had played it fair and right, and had not married his brother Philip's wife, Herodias, then her rogue daughter would have been nowhere near his party table to initiate that gruesome murder, which obviously invoked God's curse on the entire family. The secular world says, "prevention is better than cure", and I do concur to it. Don't get intimately involved with people, places, and things that obviously do not conform to God's moral standards. It can be the beginning of your "Herod birthday party". If you commit yourself to watching pornographic films or keeping company with guys or gals whose language and vocabulary is simply on the wrong side of decency and morality, you are planting seeds of evil and creating an appetite for sexual perversion that would lead you astray.

Those who don't defend themselves defeat themselves. Samson was a prophetic child - born to bring deliverance to God's people, but who ended his life in shame and disgrace. The deliverer of God's people at the end of his life, needed deliverance from God's enemies. He chose his bad ending by sleeping on Delilah's thigh. That was not a bed God approves of, and so Samson woke up to realize too late that the anointing was gone. I don't know about you, but I for one wouldn't want a "Samson-ending" to my life and ministry. I wouldn't want to be caught in a spiritual cobweb of moral depravity - a "king" (pastor and father) stripped of his spiritual and moral authority by the seductive dance of a demonized teenage girl and her adulterous mother. God have mercy. No!!

And so, the way forward? I try as much as possible to keep a safe distance from "Herod birthday parties". I am not called to evangelize in brothels, so I don't go there. Wisdom defines my borders of ministry. Don't play with fire if you don't want to get burnt. The Apostle Paul advised Timothy to "flee youthful lust". He didn't say he should "pray" about it. He said, "get out of there!" Period!! Make a decision today not to be a victim of any Herod birthday jam. Anything that has the tendency to draw you away from God is a seductive dance from Herodias' daughter. Avoid it like a plague before you sleep on Delilah's thigh and lose your light and life. Sincerely loving you always in all ways.

God bless you.

Stay in Your Track

Jn.12:49-50, NKJV

For I have not spoken on My own authority; but the Father who sent me gave Me a command, what I should say and what I should speak. And I know that His command is everlasting life. Therefore, whatever I speak, just as the Father has told Me, so I speak

---

God loves variety; and this shows even in the way he assigns, prepares, and delegates each of us to our life's assignment. There is a marked difference between the ministry of Isaiah, and that of Jeremiah, even though both of them were prophets. All the apostles of Christ were called into the same gospel ministry, but each had a different style of approach, audience, and reception. Peter never tried to be like John, nor did Paul waste time imitating Matthew. They complimented each other; never competed with anyone. This was because they clearly understood the dynamics of God's call on each person's life.

Jesus said he only spoke what the Father gave him to speak. He had his eyes on the ball. He did not have to be concerned with pleasing the crowd. He carried one message, and that was all he was prepared to present to the world. Nothing else mattered. What a great lesson for all of us; to do that which God has called and equipped us for, instead of pushing for what is not within our area of calling. God will only give you authority in the area of your calling, so that you can withstand the challenges that come with it. You can be frustrated in life and ministry if you choose to operate outside the perimeters of your calling.

You may very much desire the prophetic ministry for instance, but if God has not called you to be a prophet, you better keep your mouth shut. If you take a different route, you may end up embarrassing yourself, because God is under no obligation to honor something you say that he didn't ask you to say. His authority will not back your ill-advised utterance. God want to use you more than you can wish or hope for, but he wants to be the one who call the shots, not you.

He created you and knows you more than you can ever know yourself. God knows your exact role in his team; he 'cut' you to fit a specific role. If you move out of that 'space', you become a square peg in a round hole. Resist the temptation to talk, walk, run, or dance like the stars. You may be God's moon; meant to show up only once in a month. Stay in your track. That is what will please your Father in heaven, and give you ultimate joy, peace, and satisfaction.

God bless you

Jesus Christ has no Equal

2 Cor.1:19-20, NIV

For the Son of God, Jesus Christ, who was preached among you by me and Silas and Timothy, was not "Yes" and "No," but in him it has always been "Yes." For no matter how many promises God has made, they are "Yes" in Christ. And so through him the "Amen" is spoken by us to the glory of God.

Commitment to truth, unwavering faithfulness, and absolute trustworthiness; these are distinct attitudinal traits and attributes of our God. If you name the name of Christ and still live with the deceptive spiritual propaganda peddled around by some religious faiths that we all worship the same God, I am sorry to announce to you that you haven't connected to Jesus yet. Get this straight, Jesus Christ has no equal. He is "the WAY, the TRUTH, and the LIFE" and NO ONE (absolutely NO ONE!!) comes to Father-God except through Him. You choose another door; you end up in hell.

If my Bible or my faith offends you, too bad. I am not going to throw away my Bible and faith in exchange for your acceptance. It's NEVER going to happen even after "death do us part". This may sound politically incorrect, and I know it, but thank God I am not a politician. It may even sound "intolerant" or "rude" to those who have arrogated to themselves power to define and decide what we preach and how we preach. If you love my Jesus, don't allow the world to define and interfere with the Word. The world is on an obvious "war path" to deface and destroy the impact and influence of the Word of God, and it is high time the people of God stand up for the Truth and let the chips fall where they may.

God does not offer us a message that means one thing in California and another thing in Casablanca. God says what He means and means what He says. Of course, Jesus would never have been crucified if He lived all His life preaching the kind of "liberal gospel of convenience" many of us are preaching today. The so-called "motivational messages" that avoid the call to Godliness and conviction of sin, does not have what it takes to prepare the "Bride" (the Church) for the "Bridegroom" (Jesus Christ). When you and I call sin a "mistake," we ourselves are making and living a mistake. Sin is more than a mistake. It is falling short of God's standard.

You cannot sort yourself out of the consequences of sin without reference to God. That is why we are called to REPENT when we sin. We are children of God and we must be known as people of truth. Our "yes" must be "yes", and our "no" must be "no". There is no middle course between heaven and hell, so please tell it like it is and get some souls saved. Beyond that, in your relationship with others, please don't pretend to love someone you don't love. When you shake my hands and smile and say "praise the Lord" when in the depths of your heart you wish me dead, you are living a lie.

You may deceive me, but not the God I worship. I read your lips, but He reads your heart. Every day that passes by, we are losing our grip on this life here on earth and moving closer towards the exit door. Let us continually pray for grace to be like Jesus - being truthful and faithful to God, to ourselves, and to all others.

God bless you

Don't Flirt with Sin

Matt.18:9, GNB

If your hand or your foot makes you lose your faith, cut it off and throw it away! It is better for you to enter life without a hand or a foot than to keep both hands and both feet and be thrown into the eternal fire.

There is nothing more important than your salvation. Jesus made what we might consider to be a very radical statement here; the import being that no price should be too high to pay if you want to gain entrance into the kingdom of God. Considering how important our hands and feet are to us, it will be a suicide-mission to try to cut them off. However, if literally speaking, they pose threat to our walk with God, Jesus' unambiguous position is that they must go.

In real terms, Jesus is telling us what our priorities should be; faith in God and obedience to his Word should forever precede the quest for fame, fortune, comfort, or convenience. We are being admonished not to allow ANYONE or ANYTHING come between us and God. Whatever pulls you away from God, must be dealt with decisively. You must cut it off. If your best friend makes you worse off by enticing you to sin, he or she should lose the status of "best friend."

You are not to hate that person, but you cannot maintain the relationship at a level of intimacy because it weakens your commitment to God. TO FLIRT WITH SIN IS TO PLAY WITH FIRE. Take stock of your life and find out areas that appear not to help your spiritual growth. It may be people, places, things, or attitude. If you cannot reform, refine, or re-tune them, go ahead and remove them. Your obedience has everything to do with your eternal destiny. Don't trade it for temporary pleasure. The consequences are not pleasant. Wake up!!

God bless you.

Operate within your area of calling

2 Chron.26:16-18, MSG

"But then the strength and success went to his head. Arrogant and proud, he fell. One day, contemptuous of God, he walked into the Temple of GOD, like he owned it and took over, burning incense on the Incense Altar. The priest Azariah, backed up by eighty brave priests of God, tried to prevent him. They confronted Uzziah: 'You must not, you cannot do this, Uzziah - only the Aaronite priests, especially consecrated for the work, are permitted to burn incense. Get out of God's Temple; you are unfaithful and a disgrace."

The Call of God is not a license to misbehave and overstep the boundaries of our specific ministries. It is worth noting how humble Uzziah was, until God gave him so much success and fame. Success, fame, and prosperity are areas in our lives we all have to watch carefully. Our attitude towards God and others when God elevate us will either make or mar our history. Our end should be more important to us than where we are today. It doesn't help to be God's darling boy or girl today (when you have nothing) only to fall from grace to grass (after God has prospered you) as a result of pride and indiscipline.

The only way we avoid becoming victims of this kind of pride is to be mindful of the fact that we cannot make ourselves what God has not made us. Not everyone has the call of a pastor, and even among pastors, not everyone has the apostolic call to establish a church. If you drive and don't stay in your lane but veer off into the lane of vehicles coming from the opposite direction, you are bound to cause an accident that could easily be avoided. The problem is neither the condition of the car, nor the state of the road. It is all about you, the driver. The Church in these last days is experiencing a similar situation. Everyone is arrogating to himself or herself the right to lead.

Fewer and fewer people are willing to submit to God and His delegated leadership. There are people with the title of "Reverend" and who claim to be pastors but have no congregation at all. You cannot call yourself a leader if you have nobody following you; and if you are serving in God's House, be careful you don't assume a role God or His delegated authority (the Lead Pastor/ Bishop) has not assigned to you. "Burning incense" may seem to be no big deal, but if God has not given you that responsibility, please stay off the "altar". Whether in the home, school, church, or in public life, knowing and keeping to our defined roles, without recourse to doing what is not our area of calling, brings peace, growth, and prosperity to all.

Don't be jealous of another person's call. Use what God has given you, to do what He has assigned you to do. You are not a Billy Graham and you can never be one. God created you for who you are and what He wants to use you for. Accept your assignment with joy, and when promotion and elevation come, embrace it with humility, always being mindful of the fact that you can only operate within the limits set for you by God. Prosperity and success can threaten your walk with God if not carefully handled. Stay vigilant. Stay humble. Operate within your area of calling, and the end of your story will be something to celebrate. God bless you more than you can ever think of or imagine. Stay blessed in Him.

God bless you.

Be patient with God

Ps.40:1-3, ESV

I waited patiently for the LORD; he inclined to me and heard my cry. He drew me up from the pit of destruction, out of the miry bog, and set my feet upon a rock, making my steps secure. He put a new song in my mouth, a song of praise to our God. Many will see and fear and put their trust in the LORD.

Walking in the will of God demands a lot of patience. If you can't wait for God's timing, you can't win in life's battles. The temptation to run at our own speed is quite high because this is the age of "fast" everything. We have fast forwarded everything from food to marriage, so waiting for God's timing has become a huge task for all of us. The major technological advances we have witnessed over the last few decades has worsened the situation. Everything is done at the push of a button and there is little or no time to wait for divine input.

Our brains and fingers are too busy to compromise with waiting. Despite the "rush hour" lifestyle we are all engaged in, exercising patience with God is much more rewarding. First because God is the only one who knows every detail of what our future holds and has our best interest at heart than anyone else. Secondly, He has invested too much in our salvation to allow us to mess up. Last, but not the least, God want us to become a testimony of His goodness to the world.

The scripture says, "Many shall see it, and fear. And put their trust in the Lord." What are the "many" going to see? They are going to see the Lord hear your cry, bring you out of the miry clay, plant your feet on a rock, and put a song of praise in your mouth. Come on!! Give the Lord a shout of praise!!! Hallelujah to the Lamb of God. Keep waiting, praying, trusting, and praising. The God who has promised is faithful and He will do it. I see your feet coming out of that miry clay of sickness, loneliness, fear, rejection, disappointment, and frustration.

The process of your deliverance has begun, and it won't stop till you are out of the "pit". Be patient with God and He will give you power to overpower and glow in glory. You are marked for a miracle and chosen for a testimony to "many". God minister grace to you in your season of waiting.

God bless you.

Recover it All

I Sam. 30:18-18, NIV

David recovered everything the Amalekites had taken, including his two wives. Nothing was missing young or old, boy or girl, plunder or anything else they had taken. David brought everything back

---

If you are prepared to fight for what God has ordained for you, the odds are that you will recover every lost ground and glory the enemy has stolen. There came a time in David's life when he had to run away from King Saul's aggressive agenda to eliminate him. David became a fugitive with no fixed home address, because the king had unleashed a whole national military force to search him out and destroy him. While managing his own strategies to outwit Saul, there was unexpected invasion of David's camp while he was away on a mission. The invaders took away his family, properties, and those of his associates.

After a brief moment of shock and frustration, during which time his own colleagues threatened to stone him, David "strengthened himself in the Lord," and took a step of faith to recover all he had lost. The first thing he did was to pray about the problem. David could have just pursued the invaders, being an astute warlord with a gang of seasoned fighters on his side, but no, his initial reaction was to pray and seek God's direction and help. Many times, we fail, not because we don't know what to do during crisis, or not equal to the task confronting us, but because we count ourselves too sufficient to need help from God. As a child of God, it is good to be confident, but dangerous to be over-confident.

When David had God's approval and assurance of help, he knew the mission was accomplished before it began. He mustered courage and went after the enemy. He put in his best shot and got back everything he had lost. What have you lost in your life that you desire to take back? You have to be realistic and prayerful about it, because it is not everything that you lose that you can recover; the dead cannot be brought back to life, and spilt milk doesn't deserve one tear drop. However, there are things you may have lost that you don't have to give up on. It may be a failed project, a dysfunctional family, spiritual dryness, or an emotional disturbance. Beloved, if you pray and pursue, you can "recover all" or at least some.

You cannot spend all your life weeping over a "looted camp." Sitting in one place and complaining about the loss is a fruitless adventure. It is counter-productive, and absolute waste of time and energy. If you want a change, you must take the initiative to effect that change. Whatever you have lost remains a loss until you begin to pray and take steps to recover. God wants you to be happy, so identify what is yours by divine right and go for it. May the good Lord help you to recover everything you have lost in health, family, career, spirit, soul, and body before this year runs out, in Jesus Name!!

God bless you.

Eternally minded, yet not earthly-dormant

Lu.21:5-6, NIV

Some of his disciples were remarking about how the temple was adorned with beautiful stones and with gifts dedicated to God. But Jesus said, "As for what you see here, the time will come when not one stone will be left on another; every one of them will be thrown down."

Some of Jesus' disciples were captivated by the sheer beauty of the Jerusalem temple, and thought it was something worth celebrating. Jesus, responding to their remarks, however indicated that the temple had no lasting value; it was going to be destroyed in due course. Indeed, history records that it was destroyed by invading forces some years later. Today, in that very place, stands the Mosque of Omar. The beautiful temple is gone, in fulfillment of the prophecy of Christ.

Beloved, signs and symbols should not blind us to the Unseen realities of life. It is good to pay attention to the world around us. Indeed, it is a must. We cannot be so spiritually minded; we are no earthly good. There should be balance. The other side of the coin is God's desire for us to live with the understanding that everything we acquire and admire here today, has an expiry date. Have you ever tried to figure out how much it cost in monetary terms to keep your body functional in a year?

All the money you spend on education, the sacrifices you make getting up early to go work, the financial investments etc., are geared towards creating a world of comfort for your body and everybody else who by virtue of relationship, you are bound to care for. The truth, however, is that your beautiful body (which is the temple of the Holy Spirit) is not going to last forever. Time and age will take its toll on it, and "no stone will be left on another."

While you have it, enjoy it. Use it the best you can. Be eternally minded, without being earthly-dormant. Every day you live is an opportunity to be a blessing. God did not give you your body just to admire and adorn with clothes, shoes, and jewelry. It is meant to be used for his glory before it becomes useless. Even if your body is weak from sickness and pain, don't miss the opportunity to sing and praise the Lord. Time is not on our side; let us continually watch, work, and worship before the "temple" goes down.

God bless you.

Appreciate Your Pastor

Heb.13:17-19, MSG

Be responsive to your pastoral leaders. Listen to their counsel. They are alert to the condition of your lives and work under the strict supervision of God. Contribute to the joy of their leadership, not its drudgery. Why would you want to make things harder for them? Pray for us. We have no doubts about what we are doing, but it's hard going and we need your prayers. All we care about is living well before God. Pray that we may be together soon

Despite its paraphrasing of the scriptures, the Message Bible many times give more clarity to the meanings intended. The month of October is supposed to be Pastors' Appreciation Month, and we shall be better off paying tribute and giving honor to the men and women who have sincerely and genuinely sacrificed their lives to be under-shepherds of our souls. Many pastors have not survived the ministry, not because they are not committed or lack faith in the God who called them, but because of persecution and ingratitude from the very people they sacrificed their lives to serve.

When a pastor spends precious time praying, studying, preaching, teaching, and counseling for days, weeks, months and years to ensure the spiritual, physical, and material well-being of his flock, only for them to turn around to viciously attack his person, family, and ministry, he will need special grace to stand on his feet. What we tend to forget is that God doesn't call people into leadership because they are perfect, so if you want to find fault with your pastor, you may find more than you intended. If you are looking for a thousand, you may end up locating a million.

Except in a situation where a pastor is LIVING in sin and is unrepentant, it is absolutely unwise, unfair, and unacceptable for anyone to sit in a church and assign himself the role of a Pontius Pilate; consistently judging and criticizing the man or woman he calls his pastor. It gets interesting sometimes, when one considers the kind of people who attack the pastor without any justification; more often than not, they are people he had fasted and prayed for. They are people he had shared their pain and struggles in a very personal way; visited them on their sick beds at odd hours, depriving himself of quality time with his own family.

When they begin to enjoy the fruit of the pastor's labor, they take the freedom to frustrate him. As a pastor, I have been there too many times too often, not to know. I have friends who love the Lord, the flock, and the call, but who have had to quit the ministry because of emotional stress from the very people they set out to serve. They suffer burn-out and respond to it by walking out. Sometimes the attacks from the congregation is extended to the pastor's wife and children. The pastor's child is regarded as a special species and is not supposed to make the common mistakes that other kids make.

The dress and looks of the pastor's wife become an issue; big enough to be gossip for the week. Such unkind and blatant disrespect towards your pastor does more damage to his ministry than all the fiery darts Satan throws at him. You can do yourself, your pastor, and the kingdom of God a world of good by praying for your pastor and his family. Lighten his burden by praying for him, instead of preying on and pulling him down. Where there is a need to advise him, do so graciously without insisting he plays by your rules. If you are not comfortable with his or her style of leadership, find yourself another church. It is your right to make that choice.

What you don't have the right to do, is sitting in judgment over him, peddling falsehood, and saying mean things to undermine his person, family, and ministry. Only Satan can give you such an assignment. God NEVER destroys his chosen ones. He loves them for who they are, and for what they do. When they fall, he rebukes and disciplines them. If they repent, he restores them. He never rejects them. Appreciate your pastor. He is a gift from God to you. Pray for your pastor; and pray for me too. I need it every day more than yesterday. Thanks for praying and God bless you for appreciating your pastor. He deserves it.

God bless you

Get Up and Go Out

Ruth 2:2, KJV

And Ruth the Moabitess said unto Naomi, let me now go to the field, and glean ears of corn after him in whose sight I shall find grace. And she said unto her, Go, my daughter."

When we move, God moves. Ruth wanted a change in her circumstances. She had made a commitment to spend the rest of her life with Naomi. That commitment required sacrifice. Naomi was an old lady who had lost everything that could make life meaningful for Ruth.

The young lady made a careful study of her new environment, accepted the challenges that confronted her and decided to take action. She knew exactly what she wanted to achieve and how to arrive at her set goal. Her next step was to seek the permission, wisdom, and blessing of a mature person. When she had walked through this process, she stepped out and miracles began to unfold. What are we grasping here?

A combination of careful planning, seeking Godly counsel, and stepping out in faith can change anyone's destiny. Ruth would have forever lived in obscurity without these positive traits. Don't sit in one place and complain for the rest of your life. No politician can make your life better. They will forever be the way we have known them to be - making promises they don't intend to keep, for the sake of gaining fame, power, and its attendant goodies.

Forgive my drift, but truth of the matter is, if you don't like where you are right now or what you are doing presently by way of your job, initiate a process of change. Don't make any presumptions. Assume responsibility, pray, plan, and seek Godly matured counsel. When the lines are clear, get ready to work. The beginning may be small, but with tenacity, hard work, sacrifice, and faith in God, you will reach your goal.

Ruth did not go to the field to take a leadership role. She did not go looking for a husband. She just needed a job to put food on the table for herself and her old lady, Naomi. She ended up first being promoted, then getting married to the C.E.O of the farm, and finally being grafted into the family-line of Jesus Christ.

Careful planning, Godly counsel, the will to sacrifice for someone else (Naomi), faith in God, and initiative shot her to the top. You can also get there by getting up and going out. Go, and may the good Lord open doors of glory for you in Jesus' Name.

God bless you.

God Will Come

Is.35:4, NIV

Strengthen the feeble hands, steady the knees that give way; say to those with fearful hearts, "Be strong, do not fear; your God will come, he will come with vengeance; with retribution he will come to save you."

Emergency situations call for radical solutions. God understands this more than any of his creation. After negotiating with Pharaoh for Israel's release from Egyptian captivity and not getting the desired result, God decreed death; a radical persuasive tool that forced Pharaoh to yield to his demands.

When his chosen people came to the Red Sea and could not cross over, the Lord once again had to do the extraordinary; parting the Red Sea to make a way of escape for them. This same God, working in accordance with the same divine order, principle, and power, is asking for your cooperation so he can lift your oppression. Your hands represent your works, and once you become disinterested in your work because you are not seeing the results you expect, you begin to lose out.

The motivation to continue will begin to run dry. The dryness introduces weakness, and sooner than later, frustration sets in, and your world begins to crumble. Don't let that happen to you. If you have suffered, this is your time to thank God you survived, and move up to the surface. Encourage yourself in the Lord and trust him to come through for you. Your God will come.

He may come in the form of an idea, a word of inspiration from the Bible, counsel from the Holy Spirit or a spiritual leader, or friend. He may most likely come through an unusual source. If the situation seems impossible, then you need a miracle; and those who need miracles in their lives, are in good company when they put their trust in God.

The God who opened the Red Sea, will give you a Red-Carpet treatment. Take him at his Word, and he will lead you all the way to victory. May the good Lord re-enforce His grace in your life.

God bless you.

Retreat and Rest

Is.26:20, NKJV

Come, my people, enter into your rooms, and shut your doors behind you. Hide yourselves for a little while, until the indignation is past

In military warfare, there is something called "tactical withdrawal". When the battle is fierce and the enemy is gaining more grounds than you, you beat a retreat so you can re-strategize and launch fresh attack. The wisdom in "tactical withdrawal" is that it saves you from fighting a battle you clearly cannot win and gives you enough room to maneuver.

As believers, we are in a battle against three very powerful forces - Satan and his demons, the worldly system, and our own carnal nature or flesh. We need times of retreat to be refreshed. God is our Commander-in-chief. He knows the spiritual terrain better than we do, and so it is to our good and advantage to pay attention to His Word. The daily hustle and bustle we go through saps our strength. Sorting out challenges at home, school, church, and at the workplace can wear us down spiritually, emotionally, and physically, and if we keep going without retreating for renewal of strength, we are going to lose out.

Many pastors have suffered and are suffering from what we call "burn out" because there is nothing like "tactical withdrawal" in their battle plan. Please, if you are a leader of God's people, don't ever deceive yourself into thinking that taking a two-week vacation will collapse the church. If it does, then that's a personal weakness in delegating responsibility to others. If you are a parent, worker, student, or someone engaged in a scheduled activity, this comes to you too. Do your work with the consciousness that if you die today the world is not going to come to a stop.

The sun will still rise from the east and set in the west. People will mourn you, if they have to, but they will all go back to their daily routine as if nothing happened. That's the way life has been before we came around here, and that's the way it's going to continue to be till Jesus Christ comes. When you feel spiritually and emotionally weary, tired, overstretched, and dry, there is a place of rest you can always retreat to.

It is in Jesus Christ, the Son of the Living God. When you feel physically upbeat and worn-out, take a vacation. Don't work till you drop dead. That is not the life God planned for you. There are better days and things ahead. Relax. God will take care of the unfinished business.

God bless you.

Be Content

Prov.16:8-9, NIV

Better a little with righteousness than much gain with injustice. In his heart a man plans his course, but the Lord determines his steps

Greed, covetousness, and a desire to live above our means, are driving some of us to plan and pursue goals that do not take into consideration the 'God-factor.' We want to have what we want to have, regardless of how we get them. Pleasure and power, minus honesty, and purity, is what dazzles our world, but distorts God's Word, and confuses our walk.

There is no conviction against taking what doesn't belong to us. If nobody sees us take what does not belong to us, then we are not stealing. This behavior is another way of saying we are not accountable to anyone for our actions and inactions, not even to God, which actually amounts to self-delusion. Every one of us will give account to God for every act of omission and commission. Our salvation is secured in Christ, but our rewards will be determined by our obedience. It is better to live within your means, than live a lie.

Truth is, you are who you are, and not what you pretend to be. Cheating, stealing, manipulating and exploiting people and situations to service your appetite for inordinate wealth is a mark of dishonesty. Prov.16:8-9 is a good reminder that even though we have the right to make our plans, the ultimate outcome is in the hands of God.

Sometimes you work harder than your peers, but they get more results than you do. Instead of being jealous about what they have, celebrate your little harvest, while trusting God for more. It is self-imposed punishment to be pushing for what obviously isn't meant for you. Acknowledge God's desire to bless your efforts and bring your plans in line with his will.

Pursue justice and truth. Be wary of trying to impress the crowd; it might push you into the arena of compromising your faith. The lying, cheating etc., might bring you a lot, but the bigness of your wealth is not the same as the beauty of your worth. Be content with your lot.

God bless you.

Refuse to be Distracted

Neh. 6:2-3, NIV

Sanballat and Geshem sent me this message: Come, let us meet together in one of the villages on the plain of Ono. But they were scheming to harm me; so I sent messengers to them with this reply: "I am carrying on a great project and cannot go down. Why should the work stop while I leave it and go down to you?"

When Nehemiah heard about the broken-down walls of Jerusalem, he decided to do something about it, but in the course of pursuing his vision of rebuilding the wall, the enemy struck. The strategy was to stop the wall from being built by distracting him. Here is the catch: Distraction causes delays, and detractors undermine success. You will not be able to meet deadlines and get anything tangible done until you learn how to refuse meeting detractors.

It may sound a bit harsh, but there is a Biblical principle of not paying attention to people who try to stop or slow you down in what you seek to achieve. Scripture records Jesus' mother and brothers seeking audience with Him while he was busy preaching in public. Jesus' response was that his mother and brothers and sisters were those who listen to the Word of God and do it. He loved his family, but that love could not be reason for not doing what he was supposed to do for God.

This was same position taken by Nehemiah when he led the project to rebuild the walls of Jerusalem; and this should be the position of anyone who has a goal and want to achieve it. You've got to get your priorities right. Time to work should not be used trying to pacify detractors. Time to work should not be spent on people who have an agenda to reverse the gains you have made or are making. Enemies of your efforts do not deserve your attention. If you give it to them, you will be committing a very serious mistake that can jeopardize your very life's vision and mission.

This becomes especially important when what you are doing has to do with God. Get ready for the Sanballats and Tobiases. They will come against you with the venom of vipers, but like Nehemiah, you just have to stay focused. Keep two things in mind - (1) you are never going to stop what God has called you to do, and (2) you are never going to give audience to your avowed detractors and pretentious sympathizers. Identify those who believe in you and your cause. Work with them and confide in them.

Those who are with you, are those who are for you. Don't waste any more time arguing or explaining issues to those who are determined to frustrate you, who before they ask to meet you, have already determined the outcome of the meeting - to destroy your vision, and undermine your mission. Stay vigilant. Be resolute. No coming down to their level. Keep moving in response to your divine calling. God grant you tenacity in Jesus' name.

God bless you.

Be Faithful

Matt. 25:21, GNB

"Well done, you good and faithful servant!" said his master. "You have been faithful in managing small amounts, so I will put you in charge of large amounts. Come on and share in my happiness!"

Nothing matters to God more than faithfulness. When you are faithful, you meet all the requirements of effective ministry. Your ministry doesn't have to be "mega" to gain God's appreciation and approval. When the roll is called, and we stand before the throne of God, He is not only going to ask how much we did. He will question how FAITHFUL we were in what we did. What God gave you, in terms of talent, resources, time, relationships, opportunities etc., is what you will be asked to account for.

This should be encouragement for you to focus on doing the best with what God has given you, instead of trying to be something God has not made you. Beloved, earthly titles are not the same as heavenly trophies. You can put on yourself all the accolades and titles under the sun, but if you are unfaithful you are on the wrong side of God. Many of the things that impress the world today will have no value in God's presence tomorrow.

The scripture says it is not the quantum of the work you did, but the quality of the life you lived. For instance, if you cannot tithe on a hundred, you cannot tithe on a 1,000. If you are adept in deceiving your immediate relationships, you will soon major in deceiving the wider community, as and when the opportunity presents itself.

Your best bet is to remember God's measuring rod for success - i.e., faithfulness. Egocentrism and the desire to show off are subtle threats to remaining faithful. You have nothing to prove to anyone. Stay faithful to whatever you have to do for God, family, and community. Let God be the judge. Go your way rejoicing with whatever little He has given you. Only one thing is required of you: to be faithful.

God bless you.

Shun the wrong, Stand for the right

Lu.17:1-2, AMP

Jesus said to His disciples, "Stumbling blocks [temptations and traps set to lure you to sin] are sure to come, but woe (judgment is coming) to him through whom they come! It would be better for him if a millstone [as large as one turned by a donkey] were hung around his neck and he were hurled into the sea, than for him to cause one of these little ones to stumble [in sin and lose faith]."

If we examine these words of Jesus critically, we are bound to concede that the responsibility for sin, or doing something wrong, does not only lie with the sinner, but also with the one who is the immediate cause of the sin. Indeed, the one who lures into sin, bears the greater judgment. This calls for a lot of vigilance and caution. Your influence on anything anyone says or does, commits you to the consequences.

In the light of this eternal truth, you must be careful how you live your life. Whether in dealing with children or adults, you must be mindful of how your words and actions will impact their lives. You are not an island, and even islands have influence on the ecosystem. You cannot immunize yourself from impacting some lives.

What you can do is to ensure that your life and counsel do not encourage wrongdoing. Jesus says if you cause someone to sin, you will bear the greater judgement. That should not be your portion, so point people to the right path, and refrain from provoking anyone to sin.

Of course, taking that stand will not make you a favorite of those who want your endorsement to do wrong; but what does it matter, if that will spare you God's judgment, and mark you out as one who obeys and honors your Father in heaven? Shun the wrong and stand for the right.

God bless you.

Choose Your Friends Carefully

Prov.12:26, NKJV

"The righteous should choose his friends carefully, for the way of the wicked lead them astray."

I have lived long enough to endorse the fact that not everyone can or should be your friend. Anytime you enter into a relationship as deep and intimate as friendship without paying attention to this wise Biblical counsel, you set yourself up to hurt yourself. The command to love is not a license to be stupid or careless in matters of relationship. The NIV version of the Bible renders Prov.12:26 in a much clearer light: "the righteous is CAUTIOUS in friendship."

The question you may be asking is, "why should I be cautious in friendship?" The answer is because your friends influence your present and impact your future. There are levels of relationships and you must draw the line between who is an acquaintance and who is a friend. There is a "transference of spirit" with those we relate to as friends. You don't meet somebody today or relate to him for a week and go about touting him as a friend.

A young man was in my ministry, pretending to be everything you want him to be, and all that time he was pushing for a position in the pastorate. When he couldn't get his way with me, he quit to a church where he was immediately ordained a pastor. Few weeks later, I was inundated with cases of people he had defrauded. In one bizarre case he claimed he was pursuing a second degree and needed money for fees.

Truth is, he has no tertiary education and was only brought into our team with a view to helping him upgrade himself and hopefully learn to live in integrity, which he never did. He loved the pastoral collar and what he considered to be an easy path to popularity and making money. Not in my backyard. As a child of God, your life should be lived around Biblical principles and values such as truth, honesty, sacrifice, love, and reverence for God and His Word. You cannot call anyone a true friend who lives a life of promiscuity, dishonesty, fraud, and unbridled immorality.

It will rub off on you. It will attract you to sinful living. In Jn.15:15b, Jesus told his disciples, "I have called you friends, for all the things that I heard from the Father I have made known to you." Friendship is a relationship of mutual trust and confidence. It is deep, deliberate, and intentional. That is why friends must be chosen carefully. A friend occupies part of your space and life.

It was not for nothing that Paul wrote to the Corinthian church and warned them that "bad company corrupt good manners." Don't be a people-pleaser. Be careful who you call friend. Your friends can make or mar your destiny. Love everyone but commit yourself in friendship to people you can TRUST to add value to your Christian life, not those who will lead you away from God.

Choose your friends carefully and wisely, and always remember friends are a treasure. Don't take them for granted. Be a friend worth the name and continue to make as many friends as you can, but choose carefully. God help you in Jesus' precious Name.

God bless you.

Safety in the Word

Prov.19:16, MSG

Keep the rules and keep your life; careless living kills.

God gives us rules by which to live productive, prosperous, and peaceful lives. The Bible is like a manual that comes with a product. The manufacturer's idea for providing the manual is to guide the buyer in how to make maximum use of the product for his own benefit.

It is not an imposition. If the buyer decides to ignore the manual or operate the item in a way contrary to the manufacturer's direction, he might end up wasting his money. The God who 'manufactured' us, knows what is good for us, and what is not. He knows the things that if we do or do not do, can make or unmake us.

To protect us from self-destruction, he has provided us with a manual called the Bible. In this Holy Book, God shows us how to live in victory. It tells us all we need to know to navigate our way through every challenging terrain in our journey of life.

For those who commit to loving and living by the principles of the Bible, there is protection and safety; but for those who care less what God says or directs, they stand the risk of failure and untimely death. Obey what God says and live in the joy his Spirit provides.

God bless you.

Hidden Treasures

Matt.13:44, NIV

The kingdom of God is like a treasure hidden in a field. When a man found it, he hid it again, and then in his joy went and sold all he had and bought that field

---

Treasures are substances of value, so they are not exposed unnecessarily. The most precious minerals are buried in deep recesses of the earth. This parable in particular highlights the reaction of one who finds treasure and underpins the sacrifices one should be willing to make for a better future. The man who found the treasure could have stolen it, sold it, and lived on the proceeds.

In that case, he would have sinned against God and violated the laws of the land with impunity. He would also have forfeited possession of the land. Wisdom, diligence, and patience worked together in his favor, and in the end, he did not only possess the hidden treasure, but the land in which the treasure was hidden. The first lesson we can learn from this parable is that life is full of hidden treasures.

Some of these treasures may come to us through grace; without effort, while others must be sought. God may lead us in paths, places, and projects where unexpected doors may open. Some of these opportunities may need realignment and re-engineering with other things and people. You should not be running around with your breakthrough without thinking through what you should do to add value to it. Secondly, sometimes we have to lose the old in order to gain the new, the least for the best.

The reason the man went and sold "all he had" was because their value was far below the treasure he just found. If you value your relationship with God and his kingdom, you will not withhold anything the Lord requires of you. If you value your health, you will have no problem avoiding junk food. If you care about your family, you are not afraid to walk out on friends who want you to spend all your time and resources on them. And if you love your church and pastor, you can never be part of any group or activity that stands opposed to them. Impossible!!

Your value system is revealed by what gets your attention and interest. The third lesson is the joy of anticipation for a glorious future. It is sad when you talk to believers who think their joy is limited to this life, or in heaven only. God want you to have eternal joy, and eternity begins from today till forever, not when you die. The man in the parable began rejoicing at a time he didn't own the treasure physically.

He saw the possibility, embraced it and celebrated it, so before he came to possess it, he already considered himself rich and blessed. He saw a glorious ending to his life. What do you see about yourself? The Bible is the land with hidden treasures, and you should be rejoicing in its great promises. Deploy your God-given abilities in anticipation of coming to the place of hidden treasures. Whatever you do, you've got to do it joyfully. It is the way to get your gold, both spiritually, physically, and emotionally.

God bless you.

Praise God in All Things

Lu.1:47,49, NKJV

And my spirit rejoices in God my Savior...for the Mighty One has done great things for me - holy is his name

---

Mary praised God at a time the circumstances surrounding her pregnancy appeared embarrassing and shameful. In a world that demands proof for every product, she should have questioned God's wisdom in making her carry a pregnancy she could not explain with any tangible proof.

She chose not to do that. She was more concerned about God's favor, and less obsessed with man's opinion. Mary saw everything that happened to her from God's perspective; and was therefore able to rejoice in something that seemed to undermine her set goals and plans for the future.

In the end, she was glorified, and today she is celebrated as mother of the Savior of mankind. The shame and embarrassment she might have suffered from those who doubted the source of her pregnancy, cannot take the shine from her place in history. Give God praise, even if you don't understand the twists and turns of your present circumstances.

You haven't prayed until you have praised. Take a good look at yourself and bless your God for all he allows in your life, and for all he is worth. Some of the negative comments people make about you, are born out of ignorance of what God is up to with your life. Forgive their ignorance and stay hopeful and joyful. Praise the Lord and bless his holy name. It is well.

God bless you

Accept Your Strengths

1 Sam. 17:38-39, NIV

Then Saul dressed David in his own tunic. He put a coat of armor on him and a bronze helmet on his head. David fastened on his sword over the tunic and tried walking around, because he was not used to them. "I cannot go in these," he said to Saul, "because I am not used to them." So he took them off.

When David volunteered to fight Goliath, King Saul's initial response was, "You are not able to go out against this Philistine and fight him; you are only a boy, and he has been a fighting man since his youth (17:33). The king had enough information about Goliath to fear him, but no knowledge of David to respect him. As far as Saul was concerned, David could challenge any other fighter, but not "this Philistine."

How sad, that in our genuine effort to protect our own, we oftentimes end up stifling their dreams and visions. Even though I spent twelve years of my early life growing up along the beach, I never learned how to swim because my mother feared I might get drowned in the sea. When Saul saw he was unable to talk David out his dream, he gave David his war dress and equipment, an old formula that did not fit the young man's style of fighting. What was meant to equip David, became a hindrance and source of confusion.

It is not only bad folks who can hinder you from taking radical steps of faith, sometimes well-meaning family and friends can offer you "tunics" (counsel, or help) that are not cut to fit your vision. What you need to do is to graciously thank them for the offer and explain that it won't work for you. In an age of computers, typewriters are irrelevant. They are not dangerous instruments but are archaic machines that served a past generation and are of no use for the present. If you are a parent, you should be careful not to impose a profession on your child. Our children definitely need our impute, not our imposition.

When David tried to walk in King Saul's tunic, he realized he was wearing oversized clothes and shoes, which made him an easy target for the giant. Thank God, he maintained his boldness and told Saul he could not fight in his dress because "I am not used to them" (v.39). You've got to take a second look at what you are "wearing." Did you put it on yourself or it was imposed on you? Don't marry someone you don't love because someone you respect says he or she will be good for you. Check the person out for yourself and be convinced he/she fits your bill.

Don't pursue a career you don't like; you will be frustrated, no matter how much salary you take home. It is important to seek counsel, but unwise to live a lie. You have capabilities that are peculiar to you and aligned to your destiny. Your experience informs your expectation, so you don't have to run anywhere and everywhere. The legendary Jamaican athlete, Usain Bolt, was a great short distance runner, but he never tried competing in a marathon race, because he knew it was not his area of expertise.

So, what did David do next? He took off Saul's dress, and put on his own shepherd dress which worked for him. You may be trapped in someone else's tunic, and you are wondering why you are not getting any results. Time up for you to take it off and wear your own familiar clothes. Do what you've got to do in your own space and style. Stop trying to be what you are not. Nothing will work for you until you accept yourself and walk in your own shoe-size.

God bless you.

God's Work Over Factionalism

Mk.9:38-40, GNB

"Teacher, we saw a man who was driving out demons in your name, and we told him to stop, because he doesn't belong to our group." "Don't try to stop him," Jesus told them, "because no one who performs a miracle in my name will be able soon afterward to say evil things about me. For whoever is not against us is for us."

God want us to relate to people everywhere on the principles of his Word, and not on their personality. We should define people more in the context of what they do, rather than their caste, class, color, education etc. There are "bad" people everywhere in the world. Evil has no race or color. No community is immune to hatred, jealousy, stealing, or murder; these are all legacies of Adam's sin, and every human community has its fair share of it, depending on so many factors we cannot discuss here.

Jesus Christ told the disciples to encourage anyone who stood for the ideals they were pursuing. What's the point in opposing someone who is promoting an idea we believe in, because "he doesn't belong to our group?" When we put up walls in the face of people who believe the same God we believe in because they are not like us, we are doing the kingdom of God a serious disservice. It appears some believers will have to stay out of heaven because they cannot tolerate certain classes of people. The issue of factionalism, which was manifested by the disciples in this passage, is still a problem we are grappling with, and which we must confront in all honesty. Sometimes the underlying factors for these infractions are jealousy, hatred, and prejudice.

Take a second look at the reason John gave to justify the proposal to stop the itinerant preacher: "he doesn't belong to our group." Beloved, everyone doesn't have to belong to your group to be able to talk, breath, or fulfill his calling. No matter how huge your impact, you are not the only one with the right to live on earth or assigned to do the work of God. As long as you are working towards achieving goals that benefit humanity, you deserve to have my support and encouragement. Jesus' disciples might have been peeved because the preacher who did not belong to their group was gaining popularity and becoming a threat to the attention they were getting as close associates of the Master.

Come to think of it, even though they were closer to Jesus, they had not mustered enough faith and courage at the time to preach and cast out demons like the preacher who did not belong to their group was doing. So, the idea was, "if we cannot do it, nobody else should do it; at least not in the name of Our Master." They were so jealous of someone's performance, they cared less how it was positively impacting the lives of people and the kingdom of God. Their opposition was clearly wrong, and Jesus had to bring them to order.

If you are opposing someone simply because he or she doesn't belong to your race, class, or group of any kind, you may be sabotaging the work of God. Judge people by what they do, not who you think they should be, or what they should do. Everyone cannot belong to your group. Eagles fly alone, and you must accept their preference, or you might hate their performance. There is enough space in the skies for every bird to fly. Chart your own path, and let others operate as freely as they want.

God bless you.

Healing for Broken Relationships

Mal. 4:5-6, NIV

See, I will send you the prophet Elijah before that great and dreadful day of the LORD comes. He will turn the hearts of the fathers to their children, and the hearts of the children to their fathers; or else I will come and strike the land with a curse.

Malachi told Israel about the coming and ministry of John the Baptist. One of the key points of John's ministry had to do with repentance and restoration. There was going to be a turning of hearts. The turning of "the hearts of the fathers to their children, and the hearts of the children to their fathers," in order to avert the pronouncement of a curse on the land. God loves family, and wherever his children meet or live, he wants love, unity, and cohesion to prevail.

The figurative use of the father's relationship with his children is informative. Mothers, under normal circumstances, have better relationship with their children than fathers, and so God used father-son relationship as point of reference. Indeed, the difference between the annual celebration of Mother's Day and Father's Day confirms that fact. A father can disconnect from his child much easier than a mother, because the emotions of most mothers run deeper than that of fathers.

God, however, promises to do the impossible; he is going to turn our hearts to where it ought to be. Each of us will know and acknowledge the importance of having healthy family relationships. God can only bless where righteousness reigns, and we cannot have it if he does not give it to us. Grace is the answer to our redemption, and God through Christ has made it available to all. Repentance is the door to restoration, and what God requires of us is to co-operate with the Holy Spirit to fulfill God's desire to bless us, by repenting of our sins.

The Lord is not turning our heads but our hearts; it is a spiritual surgery with eternal results. Our "Elijah" is the Holy Spirit. He is here to heal our broken and hurting relationships. You can believe it for your family, church, and community. God is showing us that he hurts when our hearts are turned against each other. The only winner in a game of strife and confusion in a family is the devil. Give God your heart, and he will get the job done, bringing peace and blessing to you and yours.

God bless you.

A Solid Foundation

Ps.78:5-7, NKJV

For He established a testimony in Jacob, and appointed a law in Israel, which He commanded our fathers, that they should make them known to their children; that the generation to come might know them, the children who would be born, that they may arise and declare them to their children, that they may set their hope in God, and not forget the works of God, but keep His commandments.

At the beginning of every school year, majority of parents identify with the slogan, "Back to school." Money is spent to ensure the children are well equipped to face the challenges they will meet in school. New uniforms/dresses, new shoes, bags, books, and all they need to put them in good stead to learn and acquire the knowledge that would supposedly prepare them for a good future. While upholding this aspect of parenting as very important, there is a flip side that should not be ignored, and it has to do with "spiritual education."

The children God has given us are like wet clay in the hands of a traditional potter. Every day that passes by, they are losing their softness and flexibility. They are being influenced by what they hear, see, and feel. If we don't testify to them about what God has done in our lives, they will grow up being well "educated" in the ways of the world, without knowledge of the Word, Ways, and Will of God.

Children who would grow up to be well educated academically, and at the same time pursue Godliness, are those properly instructed in the ways of the Lord. The psalmist draws our attention to God's special interest in a generational transfer of faith. He expected the fathers (and mothers of course) to make known his testimony and law to their children, and the children were also expected to do same with their children. There was to be consistency in instructing every proceeding generation of the ways and works of God. This education was to be a priority, because it was the only way to ensure "that they may set their hope in God, and not forget the works of God, but keep his commandments."

For us as Christian parents, therefore, the beginning of every school year should not only be "Back to School," but also "Back to the Bible." Our children need more than head-knowledge; they need Jesus in their hearts, and you and I are responsible for getting that job done. Do not assume that they are just going to be fine, when you are not teaching them the principles of your faith in God and practically demonstrating it. The time to sow the seeds of Godliness is now.

Tomorrow may be too late. Think generationally and give the children the only thing that provides hope when their world is falling apart; that solid foundation is faith in Christ and obedience towards God's Word. Your past triumphs in Christ are a cushion to their future trials in life. Prepare them with what the classroom cannot give them, the unadulterated Word of God. May God's blessings be with you and overtake you as you do this in Jesus' Name.

God bless you.

Don't Lose Your Flavour

Mk.10:50, NKJV

Salt is good, but if the salt loses its flavor, how will you season it? Have salt in yourselves, and have peace with one another

---

Jesus used salt to drive home a spiritual truth. Like he usually did in his teachings, the Lord chose something very relevant and common to his hearers, which is salt. There is no doubt about the fact that "salt is good," but its relevance only depends on its ability to retain its flavor. If salt loses its flavor, it becomes useless and unprofitable. You, as a child of God, like salt, has flavor - a very dynamic, unique, and outstanding flavor.

God has imputed to you his goodness, through the indwelling Holy Spirit. When people relate to you, they should experience a taste of God's goodness. Salt has more than just flavor; it is a preservative. It has chemical contents that are preservative in nature, so beyond your good taste, God expects you to be one who works towards uniting family and friends. To lose your flavor means you are failing to play the role of preserving what God has given to you in terms of your human relationships.

It means you are not promoting a culture of peace and unity within your sphere of influence. Whether you are doing it deliberately or not is neither here nor there; it simply means you are not doing what God expects of you. You are just adding to the numbers, but not actively making any difference. Selfishness can be one of many reasons you have become tasteless. Anyone who builds life around himself alone, will definitely waste away without impacting anyone. Salt becomes profitable when it is applied or added to something else. Putting raw salt in your mouth is a recipe for disaster. The taste is horrible, and that is who you are if you choose to isolate and idolize yourself.

Connecting to people with right motives, and working to unite family and friends is honorable and worthy of pursuit. It is good, because it is Godly. Jesus commands us (he does not suggest to us), to "have salt in yourselves." We are to maintain the spirit of goodness, determining to move forward daily with deliberate intent to influence, protect, and preserve peace wherever we find ourselves. Part of this commission demands you stand up graciously but firmly against every form of action that undermines peace and cohesion. Remember that salt is not a neutral element.

If you cannot be tasted, you cannot be trusted. There is no neutral ground in spiritual warfare. You are either on the side of good, or on the side of evil. Take a stand for the good. Maintain your flavor. Let your stand on matters of principle be clear to everyone. Don't keep people guessing where you stand on issues that border on right and wrong. You are the salt of the earth. Don't lose the flavor, because your tastiness is the only reason peace can be maintained in your home, church, and community.

God bless you.

Honour Your God

Jer.35:5-6, NKJV

Then I set before the sons of the house of Rechabites bowls full of wine, and cups; and I said to them, "Drink wine." But they said, "We will drink no wine, for Jonadab the son of Rechab, our father, commanded us, saying, 'You shall drink no wine, you nor your sons, forever."

What an awesome testimony to dare to reject an invitation to do wrong because your dad told you not to do it? The sons of the house Rechab, gave Jeremiah only one reason why they would not drink wine: "We will drink no wine, for Jonadab the son of Rechab, our father, commanded us, saying, 'You shall drink no wine, you nor your sons, forever.'" Our Heavenly Father makes similar demands of us as his children. These instructions run counter to what the world proposes to us.

For example, God says marriage should be between a male and a female, but the world says that is not acceptable. It conjures a new and contrary concept that says people of same sex can marry; it is their "right." No limits to what you can do. If it feels good, then it must be right. The fatherhood of God is rejected, and his Word and Will, is bastardized. Modernity, driven by unbridled immorality, is seeing humanity which is supposed to be the crowning glory of God's creation, gradually destroying itself.

In the midst of all this moral depravity, God is looking for kingdom children who like the sons of Rechab in the days of Jeremiah, will stand up to be counted. Christians who walk the talk. God desires sons and daughters who will not bow to the pressures of this age, but insist on pursuing the path of truth and right as revealed in the Bible. Jesus warned us of the rot that will characterize the end times, which we are already witnessing. Beyond the grace that God provides, it will take determination and fortitude to withstand the pressure not to compromise.

No one is immune to temptation, but all of us can trust in the strength God supplies through the indwelling Holy Spirit, to say 'no' to every invitation to sin. Always weigh what the world is saying, against what your Father has said in his Word (the Bible) and base your decisions on His Word. If the world chooses not to obey him (and you are not forcing them to do so), it has no moral right to insist you agree with its line of thinking and modus operandi. Honor your God and Father by obeying his Word and following in His Way. This is the greatest and best testimony that identifies you as a child of God.

God bless you

Atmosphere for the Presence

2 Sam. 6:11, NKJV

The ark of the LORD remained in the house of Obed-Edom the Gittite three months. And the LORD blessed Obed-Edom and all his household.

When the Lord established David as king over the nation of Israel, David decided to bring the ark of God to Jerusalem, the new political capital of the kingdom. He mobilized 30,000 men to go with him to bring the ark, which represented the Presence of God to the people. Unfortunately, even though the idea of bringing the ark of God to Jerusalem was laudable, the method was lousy. Moses had made clear that anytime the ark was moved, it should be carried on poles at shoulder-level by the Levites.

David did otherwise and had them put the ark on a new cart. In the process, the cart tumbled, and when Uzzah tried to stop it from falling, he died on the spot. The king became upset and abandoned the ark in the home of Obed-Edom. It was not clear whether Obed-Edom requested to keep it or not; what is revealed is that "God blessed Obed-Edom and all his household" because he kept the ark in his home. There are three important lessons to learn here: Firstly, you don't worship God on your own terms. David's cart was obviously a beautiful, exotic, and expensive masterpiece, but it made no impression on God, because it was an act of disobedience.

God did not ask for a cart, he requested for carriers. God wanted the ark to be carried by human beings, for whom it was meant to impact, not a lifeless cart. Secondly, putting it on a cart meant shirking their responsibility and an unwillingness to sacrifice. They literally agreed to worship the Lord without the inconvenience of carrying the ark. They would rather pay for someone else to do what they've got to do for God, than do it themselves. Thirdly, it takes the Presence of God to enjoy the prosperity that comes from God. Obed-Edom and his household were blessed because of the ark (the Presence) of God in their home.

Where is the place of God's ark (presence) in your life today? You cannot have God's peace if you don't have God's presence, and you cannot have his presence if your walk, way, and worship is not according to divine order. Jesus told the woman at the well, "God is Spirit, and those who worship Him, must worship in spirit and in truth" (Jn.4:24), not on their own terms. The idea of relating to God on electronic gadgets, social media, and not committing to fellowship with the saints in a local church is alien to the scriptures.

It is similar to putting the ark on a cart; it doesn't fulfill the demands of scripture. You've got to worship God the way he wants to be worshipped, not according to your thinking and convenience. His Word says, "not forsaking the assembling of ourselves together" (Heb.10:25), and that simply means you've got to belong to a local church community. Beyond that, you've got to create the atmosphere for the Presence (ark) of God in your home through corporate prayer, Bible study, and worship. Tread this path, and the same blessing that impacted the household of Obed-Edom will surely come on you and your household.

God bless you.

Be Discerning

Ezra 4:4-5, NKJV

Then the people of the land tried to discourage the people of Judah. They troubled them in building, and hired counselors against them to frustrate their purpose all the days of Cyrus king of Persia, even until the reign of Darius king of Persia

Let's begin by looking at the phrase, "the people of the land" (v.4). They rose up in fierce opposition against Zerubbabel and the builders of God's temple. These were the same people who had earlier come to Zerubbabel, offering to help build the temple of the Lord (v.1-2). Thank God Zerubbabel was able to discern that they were adversaries and not sympathizers, and for rightly refusing to allow them to participate in the temple-building project.

Their immediate reaction to Zerubbabel was to hire "counselors to frustrate their purpose." They paid money to facilitate the destruction of the very work they had said they were prepared to assist in building. This is the experience of many of us in leadership position, and it is a very powerful tool the enemy uses to try break us down. Some of the people who offer to help you may have genuine intentions, but there are still others who know they can only frustrate you by pretending to be for you. They will say and do all it takes to win your confidence, and then deliver the killer-blow. Be careful you walk a fine line of caution and discernment when "the people" offer you help.

God's call to love all doesn't mean you relate to everyone at the same level. If you are dishonest, I can love you, but I am not mandated to trust you. I may joke and laugh with you, but I keep my censors on high alert. If you choose to believe the story everyone tells you and swallow every size of bait they throw at you, the possibility is that you may fall prey to the scheming of your detractors more often than you ought to. This is not to suggest you live in a closet, suspecting everyone who comes near you as a potential threat to your life and dreams; it is a time-tested warning not to go to sleep on projects you are personally committed to undertaking for God, family, or self.

No one can dream and fulfill your dreams for you than you, because you are the only one who carries the head that dream your dreams. It is better to have your detractors operating from a distance, than within your immediate circle. Don't be afraid to graciously ask those you know to be working against you to find something else doing. If you delay in dealing with "the people" who are against you, you are welcoming the day of trouble. They will breed "counselors" among those who genuinely support your course and mount a sustained opposition to whatever you set yourself to do.

Zerubbabel was opposed from the reign of Cyrus to the reign of Darius by the same people who had claimed to share his vision and offered to help in building the temple. Beware of "the people" who claim to share your vision; some are genuine, others are not. Pray for discernment; you need it to know at least some of "the people" who shouldn't be as close as they offer to be.

God bless you.

Don't Worry

Matt. 6:27, NKJV

Which of you by worrying can add one cubit to his stature?

The Good News Bible renders Matt.6:27, "Can any of you live a bit longer by worrying about it?" It then goes on to add a footnote, "or grow a bit taller" by worrying about it? The obvious answer to this question is "no," but the reality with all of us is that we get caught up in the cobweb of worrying ever so often. Sometimes we worry to the extent we cannot even tell what we are really worried about.

If we were to classify worrying as a disease, almost every one of us would be identified as carriers of its virus. Jesus is pointing us to a very basic fact about this chronic emotional poison called "worry." His point is that worry doesn't solve problems; it is a waste of time and energy. If there are issues you cannot resolve, problems you cannot solve, or situations you cannot change, your best option is not to worry about them.

Worrying will wear you out. It triggers chemical reactions in the body that affects your health negatively. Knowledge of its impact is not enough to take away worry. The Lord points us to the only way we can manage worry; it is by trusting in God's ability to meet our every need. The starting point is in admitting that we cannot always have answers to the challenges that come our way.

There are things that may happen to us, our spouses, our children, or in our careers that we may not be able to control, manage, or change. Instead of switching to worry-mode, we should turn them over to the Lord in prayer. You can trust him to extend help to you in the same way he is able to feed the birds and cloth the flowers.

Stop worrying and start singing. Life is too short to spend it in fruitless worry and endless anxiety. What will be will be. Keep the faith and liberate your soul from worry. This too shall pass way. God be your helper in Jesus' Name.

God bless you.

Your Plans, God's Direction

Prov.16:9, GNB

You may make your plans, but God directs your actions

Planning is important in achieving results in life. Anyone can have a goal or dream, but it takes planning and execution of the plan to reach set goals. It is wishful thinking to have a goal without a plan. God had a plan for our salvation, and in the fullness of time executed it to perfection by sending his Only Begotten Son, Jesus Christ, to die for us. Lack of planning is an endorsement to failure. As a child of God, your planning has to make room for God's sovereign will and ultimate direction.

You always have to make room for the Spirit's direction in your daily pursuits. It is possible to have a "good plan" today, that is outside the will of God for you. Do you quit on your plan because you don't know God's perfect will regarding it? No, you don't. You submit all your plans to God in prayer, trusting him to direct your steps. The important thing is the awareness of God's presence in the equation. It allows flexibility in the way you work towards your goals, and you are able to accept delays and accommodate disappointments.

Once you know God is part of your life's project, you are confident that whatever detours, delays, and disappointments your plans may encounter, you will make a safe landing at your final destination. It helps a lot to keep reminding ourselves that God works all things together for our good, including even those things we may perceive as failures and disasters. Our best intentions can never be as good as God's divine agenda for our lives, and that is why the scriptures insist we thank God always, no matter what our circumstances may be.

God is bigger than your plan and knows the end from the beginning. While you are trying to figure out how to achieve the desired results, he has already decided the path to your success. Don't be overly anxious about the goals you have set. You are not alone. Commit your plans into God's hands, and trust him to guide and help you, and he sure will.

God bless you.

Take Back Your Joy

Job 10:20-21a, NKJV

"Are not my days few? Cease! Leave me alone, that I may take a little comfort, Before I go to the place from which I shall not return..."

Uncle Job had no pleasure living under unnecessary pressure. The words of his friends, instead of bringing comfort, ended up compounding his pain and misery. When he could take it no more, he exclaimed, "Cease! Leave me alone, that I may take a little comfort, Before I go to the place from which I shall not return..." In context Job was addressing God, but in application we need to tell it to people who tear us apart with words of discouragement.

Beloved, you've got to shut some people up before they send you to an early grave. For all you may care to know, one of the certainties of life is death. A day is coming when we shall literally walk out of this earthly house called the human body and enter our heavenly home or glorified bodies. Between the present and that future, there are events and people that can spiral out of control, and enjoy making us feel hopeless, miserable, unhappy, guilty, bad and sad. Through judgmental pronouncements and hostile actions, they turn our lives into perpetual condemn cells.

At every twist and turn, they wear lenses that see our faults that never halts. Can I suggest to you that you are not the worst human species that ever walked this earth, and NOBODY has the right to sit in judgment over you? Free yourself from the suffocating grip of people whose words devalue, defame, and denigrate you on a daily basis. Nobody has the right to run you down. Take back your joy. A friend doesn't push you down the drain by amplifying your mistakes and pain. Say to them like Job, "Cease! Leave me alone, that I may take a little comfort before I go to the place from which I shall not return."

It is time to tell somebody who never sees anything positive about you - " Please accept me for who I am or shut up and leave me alone! I am no longer going to mortgage my joy and peace to your myopic opinions and self-righteous stance. I deserve some comfort before I die and am going to have it. Give me a break before you break me. Now!!" I pray the God of all comfort to restore to you the joy of His salvation in Jesus' Name.

God bless you.

You will Rise Again

Mic.4:11-12, MSG

"But for right now, they're ganged up against you, many godless people, saying, 'Kick her when she's down! Violate her! We want to see Zion grovel in the dirt.' These blasphemers have no idea what God is thinking and doing in this. They don't know that this is the making of God's people, that they are wheat being threshed, gold being refined."

Has it ever dawned on you that God sometimes allows persecution for our elevation? Gold in its raw form has no attraction or beauty. It needs the refiner's fire to get market value. As believers in Christ, we need refining too. The fire of the indwelling Holy Spirit does an internal cleansing work to conform us to the image of Christ. Beyond that, there are external pressures that God may allow, to teach, train, and prepare us for "palace" life. Moses needed a stubborn Pharaoh to showcase the power of God.

Joseph needed a family of jealous siblings, and a seductive and unrepentant liar like Potiphar's wife, to become Prime Minister of Egypt. Jesus needed a Judas Iscariot and a national council of spiritual leaders who hated him, opposed his ministry, and orchestrated his death, to fulfill His purpose on earth. Get ready for what is coming. You can never get to where God want to take you without encountering folks whose primary goal will be to see you fall and fail, but you must not fail.

Being human, you may fall. Even seven times! But God isn't relating to you on the terms of what others think, feel, or say about you. Far from that!! He loves you for who you are, and for what He called you to do. Always remember that whatever God allows in your life, whether good or bad, would ultimately turn out for your good.

Those who enjoy kicking you while you are on the ground will live to see you rise, seated on a dignified throne, and wearing a crown of glory. And trust me, some of them will come to you for "wheat" when starvation comes on their land, and you shall feed them in joy. Why? Because when that time comes, maturity and wisdom from God will instruct you to understand they did what they did because "these blasphemers have no idea what God is THINKING and DOING in this."

Your persecutor is God's elevator. Everything is going to work for your good. Keep moving forward. Victory awaits you. A glorious ending is your portion, and it shall come to pass. God bless and strengthen you in Jesus' awesome Name in whatever difficult situation you find yourself today. Peace be to you.

God bless you.

Confront the Darkness

Lu.12:49-52, MSG

"I've come to start a fire on this earth - how I wish it were blazing right now! I've come to change everything right-side up - how I long for it to be finished! Do you think I came to smooth things over and make everything nice? Not so. I've come to disrupt and confront! From now on, when you find five in a house, it will be - three against two, and two against three."

Disruption and confrontation are necessary for maintaining cohesion, stability and spiritual sanity. An ordered life sometimes calls for questioning the status quo. We cannot be so tolerant we allow the "...Father's house of worship to be turned into a den of thieves." Those are not my words. Those are words of Jesus Christ. They sound a bit abrasive and harsh, but they are not words of hatred or opinion, but of principle and position.

Compromising the truth of God's Word to gain popularity and acceptance with men, is as dangerous as jumping into a blazing fire with the hope that you will come out nice and unscathed like Shadrach, Meshach and Abednego. Sometimes we prolong our pain by simply shying away from "confronting" people and issues that need to be dealt with for clarity.

The only way confronting issues can become a problem is when it is devoid of tact or people are not prepared to accept their mistakes and reform or conform. What we need to remember, however, is that light and darkness can never dwell together. One must give way to the other. If you are not happy with something in your home, church, or society, pray about it and as you feel led by God, confront it in the right spirit and attitude.

If you have to excuse or remove yourself from that place or environment, do so graciously. Be careful you don't do it with a judgmental spirit, arrogance, disrespect, or "know it all" manner - especially when dealing with the elderly or people in leadership. Why? Because Biblical principle of confrontation is NOT a license to rebel against God's established order and authority in the home, church, or community.

Your faith in Christ will definitely upset your parents if they share another faith. The entrance of Jesus into any unbelieving family creates a disruption. Do you deny Christ? No. You "confront" your parents with the Light of God's Word if they should ask for the reason for your new-found faith in Christ. But you do so with respect.

The gospel of Jesus Christ will never be politically correct, so don't be afraid to confront the darkness. Compromising the truth of God's Word is not an option, even if the whole world should turn against you. This is not a popularity contest. It is a BATTLE for the redemption of lost souls.

God bless you.

Take a Stand

Phil.1:21, NKJV

For me, to live is Christ, and to die is gain.

What is your ultimate goal as a believer in Christ? There are two definitive choices; either to have a self-centered goal, which makes what satisfies your ego the basis for every decision you make, or you choose to focus on what pleases the Lord. Apostle Paul freed himself from fear, anxiety, and worry by taking a stand to the effect that, "to live is Christ, and to die is gain."

Given the circumstances in which he found himself at the time (he was in prison), he had every reason to complain and be fearful, but on the contrary, he showed absolute strength in the crisis. His statement portrays a picture of one who did not care less about what was happening or going to happen. He was relaxed and very confident in his predicament. This is a perfect example of one whose faith cannot be shaken by any change in his circumstances.

The worst that could happen to him was death, and he was ready for it; knowing that nothing could happen to him outside the will of God, and that death to him as a believer in Christ, is not a loss but gain. You may be hurting so bad, under stress, or going through a season of severe testing right now.

There seem to be so much negative events happening at such rapid succession that you have no desire to go any further. Take a cue from Paul and take your hands off the "steering wheel." Let Jesus take charge of the chaos. Live in his strength and hide under the shadow of his wings. If you don't know what else to do at this point, you don't lose anything telling him you want him to come and take over. Fear of the unknown will ruin your life, if you keep fighting battles you cannot win without God.

Let's keep this straight and simple; make up your mind that going forward, it's all about Jesus. You live or die at his pleasure; knowing that he has your best interest at heart, and "will not let you be tempted beyond what you can endure." You also know that nobody can take your life, and that in the worst scenario, even death is only a transition to a better tomorrow.

God bless you.

Wise as Serpents, Harmless as Doves

Matt.10:16, NKJV

Behold, I send you out as sheep in the midst of wolves. Therefore, be wise as serpents and harmless as doves. But beware of men, for they will deliver you up to councils and scourge you in their synagogues.

Anyone who decides to walk in the will of God should expect to run into walls of opposition and persecution. This goes especially for those of you dear friends who are involved in ministry work, both in the Church and outside of it. The super-hero minister-image you see on television and social media can be deceptive. If you want to live and work for Christ without compromise, then you've got to understand both the prospects and challenges.

Not everyone is going to like you, because you are a threat to Satan's kingdom and he is not going to sit down and pretend it's okay for you to operate freely. Jesus describes the kingdom worker as "sheep in the midst of wolves." That is quite extreme and frightening. It's like dousing your body with petrol and jumping into a blazing fire; you are dead before you land in the fire. It calls for great grace and wisdom to adapt to changing circumstances, and appropriate responses to different people.

The human factor (people) is what Jesus stressed on here; people are going to make it difficult for you to operate. It's not only about people you don't know, that is easy to manage. Most of your persecutors will be your benefactors; people you have blessed and have benefited from the sacrifice you made in laying down your life for ministry work. You cannot afford to be naive and assume that following Jesus is going to be easy.

The Lord warned: "Beware of men, for they will deliver you to councils and scourge you in their synagogues." Let me tell you that there are still "councils" and "synagogues" out there where men and women of God are being "scourged" daily. Some of these councils and synagogues are in the house of God itself. Many true servants of God live in a world of emotional torment, and carry wounds inflicted by "wolves" in their very congregations. It's always the people in whose midst you serve that the wound is deepest.

You are not to run and hide, because serving God's purpose is more important than any pain men may inflict on you. The mission must be accomplished. The warning signs are clear: (1) You are dealing with "wolves," and so you're at risk every day. Not my words; Jesus said so. (2) Be wise as a serpent. Move stealthily, and with extreme caution. Not everyone who smiles with you is happy with what you are doing, even when you have their best interest at heart. (3) Be harmless as a dove.

Operate in love and leave judgement to God. The ministry can be both exciting and exacting. It is a territory that makes you an endangered species, but at the same time gives God opportunity to touch lives through you. Continue giving yourself to the service of God. It is the reason you are still here.

God bless you.

Pray or Become Prey

Rev.12:7-8, NKJV

And war broke out in heaven: Michael and his angels fought with the dragon; and the dragon and his angels fought, but they did not prevail, nor was a place found for them in heaven any longer. So the great dragon was cast out, that serpent of old, called the Devil and Satan, who deceives the whole world; he was cast out to the earth, and his angels with him."

Can you imagine war breaking out at the very seat of God's government in heaven? The devil dared to launch a full-scale war right in heaven, where Almighty God manifests his limitless glory and power. This should serve notice to you that you are not beyond being attacked by Satan and his demons. When his plan to wrestle power in heaven failed and he was cast down to earth, the power vested in him as archangel was not taken away.

Indeed, the angels who fought under his command also came down with him, possessing the powers they had before the fall. We are therefore faced with a real battle against a rascally gang of wicked spirits, and God in his wisdom has provided us spiritual weapons for this battle. The most basic weapon aside of faith, is fasting and prayer. You either PRAY, or you become a PREY. Satan hates every child of God because we remind him of his lost glory.

He sees something about us that we cannot see with our natural eyes, so he is bent on attacking us and everything that belongs to us. Like the battle he launched in heaven, he hardly attacks from a distance; his demons and their human agents are always within close proximity of their targets. It is either in the family, church, workplace, or other similar settings. The crisis you see in your home as a parent, and the confusion you experience in your church as a pastor, are all part of the ongoing spiritual war.

You are fighting an enemy who you cannot see, but who sees you and monitors your every movement. If you don't commit to praying consistently, you cannot prevail against him. Satan stands opposed to every good thing God has planned for you. He hates to see you happy and excited about life. You have to stand up against him. You have God and the holy angels on your side. They will not impose themselves on you.

They are ready to answer to your call and respond to your prayer. Remember, God wants you to be a victor, not a victim. Begin this day and every day by praying for yourself, your family, your church, and your community. Resist, reject, and refuse the activities of evil spirits and wicked people from affecting your life. Insist on only God's will being done in your life, and his Spirit leading the way. Use every spiritual weapon in your arsenal. When it gets desperate, increase your firepower by fasting. You will win if you fast and pray.

God bless you.

Praise God in Trials

Ps.22:9-10, GNB

It was you who brought me safely through birth, and when I was a baby, you kept me safe. I have relied on you since the day I was born, and you have always been my God

---

It was a time of anguish for David, and yet he wouldn't forget the Unseen Hand of Almighty God that kept him from birth and continued to keep him even in distress. We usually have no foreknowledge of the kind of things that come to steal our joy and put us under stress. The more surprising the event, the more painful it becomes, and that is when you need some encouragement from your "memory file."

When you remember how far God has brought you, it becomes an incentive for staying the course. David was adept at looking back at what God did in the past, to face present danger and challenges. In his confrontation with Goliath, David recalled how God had delivered him from bears and lions, and boldly stood his ground against a veteran soldier who had intimidated Israel's national army for weeks.

This faith declaration of God's protection and provision over time, is repeated in this particular case when he was faced with extraordinary difficulties. He did not pretend he was in a very good mood. Everything that was tearing him apart was verbalized, but beyond all that, David still remembered God's sustaining grace in his life. This unmatched blessing dated back to the day he was born. He counted his blessings, while he was being choked by burdens, he could not offload by himself.

As far as he was concerned, without God's grace working in his life, he couldn't have survived so much hostility, pain, and betrayal. He may lose his sleep, but not his song. Beloved, your path may be strewn with similar thorns, and your face familiar to teardrops. You may be going through a cycle of painful experiences with no end in sight, but God!! He has your name written in the palm of his hands and saying to you that you are more than a conqueror through Christ our Savior.

Check your history and see what God has done since you were born, not what he is not doing now. It may not be as much as you expected, but where would you have been without God's little mercies in your life since birth till today? Come on!! Shake the devil off your back. You are not the worst case scenario. Stop weeping and begin thanking God for his blessings in your life. You are alive today by God's choice, not by chance. Praise him, not only one time, but all the days of your life.

God bless you.

The Right Time

Mk.1:14-15, GNB

After John had been put in prison, Jesus went to Galilee and preached the Good News from God. "The right time has come," he said, "and the Kingdom of God is near! Turn away from your sins and believe the Good News."

Time is of essence in fulfilling God's purpose for our lives, and discerning "the right time" to move into a new project is crucial to its success. Jesus knew he was on a higher mission than John the Baptist, but he did not do anything to shove John aside to prove he was more anointed than the prophet. Jesus could have begun working miracles to draw away the crowd that was going to John, but no, he rather went and submitted to John's baptism.

He added value to John's ministry by publicly associating with it. Two things are clear in this demonstration of solidarity; one, that the Lord's work is not a contest. It is not about human ingenuity or prowess. It has no place for self-promotion and personal aggrandizement. Secondly, it is a team effort, with each individual playing his part for the common good. Our emphasis, however, is on the time element. Jesus waited till John finished his ministry as forerunner, and then step into his own space and declared, "The right time has come...And the Kingdom of God is near."

He set us an example of waiting for God's appointed time to do what we have to do. It may be that you have more wisdom, knowledge, and understanding than everyone in your family, church, or community, but that gives you no right to impose yourself or ideas on anyone. You may have all the gifts of a leader, but as long as your "John the Baptist" is in active service, you have no choice than to wait till he is taken out of the way. When Jesus' right time came to launch his ministry, John was in prison, creating all the space the Lord needed to be effective. God is a God of timing and is never in a hurry.

When he calls you to do something, he trains you for the assignment, and part of that training involves teaching you to operate with time. David was anointed king, many years before he ascended the throne. He had to wait for Saul to die before moving into his call to the throne, and even that came progressively over a period; first becoming king of Judah, then after some years being accepted as King of a United Kingdom of Israel.

Every goal ahead of you is time-bound. Don't be discouraged by what you see as delays. There may be lessons you need to learn, and people you need to acknowledge. Ask God for wisdom to discern the right time, otherwise you may end up doing the right thing at the wrong time, and that will be recipe for discouragement and failure.

God bless you.

God Decides

Mk.10:41, GNB

When the other ten disciples heard about it, they became angry with James and John.

James and John had a burning desire to sit on the left and right of Jesus when he comes to reign as King of kings and Lord of lords of the whole universe. They managed for a time to contain their ambition, but when they couldn't hide it any longer, they openly presented their request before the Lord. Matthew's gospel added more detail to this account, indicating that they brought their mother to make the request on their behalf, applying the persuasive power of a woman, and a mother, for that matter.

There was nothing wrong with either the intent, approach, or request they made. James and John dared to believe what Peter and the other nine disciples might be wishing for, but never mustered the courage to ask. So why were they angry with those who asked to occupy vacant, uncontested seats? Why should a simple, harmless request to be closer to Jesus, offend people who have the opportunity to make the same request but were not bold enough to do so? This is a very common human failure; desiring what others are working for, without wanting to pay the price for what it is worth to possess it.

Isn't it interesting that the rest of the disciples got upset with the duo for making the request to sit on the left and right of Jesus in his Glory? They could just as well have made the same request and left it for Jesus to decide; but no, they'd rather kill someone's dream because they were unable sleep to dream same. Check the reason for your anger against the guy whose winning ways offends you. It may you can do better with what you have than he is doing, if you step out and act out your faith.

Nobody is the reason for your prison, and you only harm yourself being angry at people acting on their faith and achieving results. Instead of working hard at attacking my dreams and efforts, re-direct your energy to pursuing your own vision. There is enough space for all to realize our dreams, so locate your territory and get busy occupying it.

At the end of the day, it is God who decides how far we can go or how much we attain. Take your eyes off your "James and John." It is their God-given right to have their own goals and pursue their own dreams. If their confession upsets you, block your ears. And per chance you are on the receiving end of this anger, please don't stop believing for the best because someone got hurt or offended. The problem, if any, is not yours but theirs. Live your dreams and be at peace with God and yourself.

God bless you.

Eagle's Nest

Deut. 32:12-13, NKJV

As an eagle stirs its nest, hovers over its young, spreading out its wings, taking them up, carrying them on its wings, so the LORD alone led him, and there was no foreign god with him.

The training an eagle gives to its young ones, involve a lot of tough aerial maneuvering. The eaglet's comfortable nest is disturbed by its mother when it's time to learn to fly. However, this is done with careful precision, giving the eagle time and space to provide the needed guidance, direction, support, and protection in the air, until the eaglet is able to master the art of conquering storms. God draws a parallel between this high -altitude training of the eaglet, and how he led and trained the nation of Israel.

This model of training is applicable to every believer in Jesus Christ. The Holy Spirit will take you on diverse dimensions of high-altitude flights. God will not give you what he has not prepared you to be able to handle. If you want to be elevated in Christ, you should get ready for a little taste of Calvary. You cannot evade the cross and wear a crown. In God's School of Promotion, there is always a season of preparation.

What is heart-warming, however, is that like the training process of the eagle and its young ones, the Lord doesn't push us out of the nest and watch us do a free fall to destruction. He does a balancing act of spreading his wings under us, to provide a safe landing when the storm is stronger than we can handle. When God leads, he doesn't need any helper, because Yahweh is sufficient in himself to provide all the strength and support that you need.

Step out into your open heavens and dare to soar. You are taking a calculated risk if you acknowledge the presence of God in the trial. It is a step of faith, with the assurance that even if you should slip and fall, God's outstretched wings are beneath you to provide protection. When God disturbs your comfortable nest, it is because it is time for you to change location; time to enter a new dimension of life. You are being invited into a world of greater possibilities.

You do not gain the experience of a mother eagle by spending all your life in a nest. A little stirring of your nest is good enough for your going to the next level. Those with big testimonies are those who conquered massive storms. God takes a position where you do not see him; he spreads his wings under you, while he trains you to fly. Go for the sky, and let the storms come when they may, you are cut to conquer, and you will.

God bless you.

Thank God for His Work

Phil.1:1:3-6, NKJV

I thank my God upon every remembrance of you, always in every prayer of mine, making request for you all with joy, for your fellowship in the gospel from the first day until now, being confident of this very thing, that He who begun a good work in you will complete it until the day of Jesus Christ

---

The theme of our praise and thanksgiving should not always be our personal success stories and blessings. We should also thank God for the work he is doing in the lives of others. Paul told the saints in Philippi that he thanked God anytime he thought of them. He had birthed them in the faith and was grateful to God they were keeping the faith and growing in it. Paul says he prayed for them "with joy," and it was the outflowing of that joy that produced praise and thanks to God.

Is there someone you have helped in anyway to be able to stand in the faith? If you haven't, you are losing something that can be a reason for you to be thankful to God. Change your prayer format and begin to include your family and friends who share the faith with you; especially those who may be having serious challenges. Some of them may even have backslidden and no longer walking with the Lord, but you can trust God to restore them. Let your confidence be same as that of Paul.

Believe that the God who begun a good work in them is well able to complete it. Your child or children may not be where you want them to be with the Lord, but again, you can trust the Lord to finish the good work he began in them. Once you give of your best to whatever you do for God, praise God for the lives you have impacted. Be consistent in mentioning them in prayer and be confident and firm in your belief that God will bring restoration to those who need it, and indeed honor your work.

You will always have something to thank God for, if you stop centering the work of God around yourself alone. God wants you to have a world view, because he gave his Son Jesus, to the entire world (Jn.3:16). As you read this today, be assured that I count myself privileged to be your servant in the Lord, and to borrow the words of Apostle Paul, "I thank my God for every remembrance of you, always in every prayer of mine, making request for you all with joy, for your fellowship in the gospel from the first day until now, being confident of this very thing, that He who begun a good work in you will complete it until the day of Jesus Christ."

God bless you.

Praise the Lord in All Things

2 Sam. 7:22, NKJV

Therefore, you are great, O Lord GOD. For there is none like You, according to all that we have heard with our ears.

David had a plan to build a place of worship for God. In response to the blessing of God on his life, he called the prophet Nathan and shared with him the desire he had to build a temple for the worship of God. Nathan thought it was so good an idea they needed not to pray about it, but God later told him to tell David he was not the one divinely appointed to build the temple. That assignment was for his son, Solomon.

Beyond that, God made a covenant with David to maintain his dynasty through all generations to come, and in response, David sang this song of praise. The former shepherd boy looked back on his past, and with a heart full of gratitude, thanked God profusely for his loving mercies and kindness. He declared the greatness of God above all things, not only for what God had done in his life, but also for "all that we have heard with our ears."

The King praised God, not only for his person and performances, but also for his promises; what he had heard from the covenant promises. You are a covenant child of God, and one blessed beyond measure in Christ. The Son of God gave his life so you might have life. His Word has great promises for you, both in this life and in the hereafter. You are not helpless. You are not hopeless.

Look at yourself through God's divine lenses and begin to praise him like you never did before. Our God is indeed a great God, and there is none that can be compared with him. Declare his goodness in the face of the challenges. Praising God will create the atmosphere for your deliverance from fear and anxiety. It boosts your spiritual immune system and energizes you to soar like an eagle. Take your mind off the problems and stand on the promises.

Reflect on the grace of God that brought you this far. David praised even though he was denied the privilege of building the temple. You can praise the Lord despite the fact that he has withheld some things from you. If Jesus Christ is indeed the Lord of your life, then you owe him the love of your heart, and the praise of your lips. Praise the Lord, for He is good, and his Word will surely be performed in your life.

God bless you.

Strengthen Your Brothers

Lu. 22:31-32, GNB

Simon, Simon! Listen! Satan has received permission to test all of you, to separate the good from the bad, as a farmer separates the wheat from the chaff. But I have prayed for you, Simon, that your faith will not. And when you turn back to me, you must strengthen your brothers."

Before Jesus was tried and sentenced to death, he discerned in the Spirit that Satan "has received permission to test" all the disciples. There are three truths revealed in the statement he made in Lu.22:31-32. First, Jesus shows us that Satan cannot touch a true child of God without God's permission. Your life is too precious in the sight of God to be open to random demonic attacks. God has set boundary lines around you, and no power can penetrate those divine perimeters without his knowledge and permission. Why would God allow the devil to test us? He allows it to prove us, not to disprove us. A teacher subjects his students to tests to prove the depth of knowledge they have acquired from him. Even so does God make allowance for our testing to reveal what he has made of us.

God also allows the testing for the purposes of separating "the wheat from the chaff." There may be weaknesses in our lives that needed exposure to help us deal with them so we can be strengthened to help others. God is a Master tactician and exploits every demonic attack against us to improve us. This is re-stated in Rom.8:28; that all things (good and bad) work together to our good. Your trials are not meant to destroy you. They are meant to develop you. Stay strong. Stay stable. You will shine brighter when the battle is over. Second lesson is the assurance that you are not in the temptation alone. Jesus told Peter, "But I have prayed for you, Simon, that your faith may not fail." Nobody needed to tell Jesus that we don't have power in ourselves, and by ourselves, to overcome the vicious temptations and trials the enemy throws at us each day.

He lived through it, and knows exactly where each of us is, at any given moment. He knows what you are going through. Jesus stands with you through your trials, praying for you to prevail. Third lesson: Your deliverance and empowerment mean God has prepared you to be a channel of inspiration to those who go through similar struggles you went through. While celebrating the victory God has given you in your trials, remember there are others who are tottering under same weight and need a shoulder to cry on. You are the one who holds the key to their survival. It takes one who has fallen before, to teach how to get off the ground. Your experience is a textbook to all "fresh students" undergoing the same tests that you went through. If you don't use it to encourage others, you waste it.

There is something good in every bad situation you have had to deal with. Let God use your painful experiences to strengthen those who find themselves in similar trials. Don't only talk about your triumphs. Don't only display your trophies. Speak about the process, the disappointments, the fears, doubts, and tears. It will help others in that experience know that it is part of life, and not something strange and exclusive to them alone. It will inspire them to believe that they can pull through with the help of God, the same way you have been able to persevere and prevail. God is giving you an assignment: "when you turn back to me, you must strengthen your brothers." He did not say, "you MAY strengthen your brothers. He says, "you MUST strengthen your brothers," meaning it is not negotiable. It is something you MUST do because it is something you CAN do. So, do it.

God bless you.

Shake Off Gloom

Prov.17:22, GNB

Being cheerful keeps you healthy. It is slow death to be gloomy all the time.

Medical science has confirmed that our mood affects our health. Those who keep themselves happy despite their challenges, hardly experience depression and other forms of emotional breakdown. The mind is a powerful toolbox and is fashioned to tune and influence the body to stay healthy. Rom.12: 1 states thus, "Be transformed by renewing your mind." Clearly, the onus for our transformation lies to a large extent on us. If you will continue to live and not go to an early grave, then you must decide to be cheerful.

You cannot wait for a change in circumstances before being happy. Sometimes it takes a cheerful mood to attract the right people God want to use to help sort out your issues. I know how difficult it is to be cheerful when your world is falling apart, and your entire life looks like you are driving in reverse gear. It is not something you can just wish away. I did not read about it. I lived and walked through its times without number. It is an unseen internal struggle that has the capacity to hold and control your actions and inactions as long as it is allowed to fester.

You don't win over it by denying it. Pretending that you are not feeling stressful and unhappy doesn't help change your mood. If the doctor cannot diagnose the sickness or disease of his patient, how can he prescribe the appropriate medication? You are on your own, if you live in denial of your pain and struggles. Your first lifeline to reclaiming your cheerfulness is admitting that you lost it. You have drawn a blank, and that's it! Don't blame yourself for being unhappy but help yourself by agreeing that it is not God's will for you to live in frustration and so you are going to get out.

Knowing the price you pay in terms of your health when you allow yourself to live in gloom, should help you take the decision to ask for God's help. And please don't stop there but talk to confidantes; those who care enough to listen to you, pray for you and with you, and speak words of encouragement to pep you up, not pull you down. I find my wife a very powerful support base in my times of emotional distress. I believe God has put someone like my wife in your life to act in the capacity of encourager. If you look hard enough, you will find him, her, or them.

Do not bottle up, or the gloom will you blow up. Share your thoughts and feelings with God and the human support-systems God has put in your life. Avoid negative and judgmental folks; they will only add to your pain. Take the scriptures and read some inspirational passages like the psalms. Sing to the Lord, even though you don't feel like it. It's just like taking medicine; you don't take it because you like it, but because it holds the key to your healing.

And one more thing you can do is, go out! You are better off doing something than nothing. Get busy helping someone worse off than you. Be deliberate in your quest to be cheerful. Don't worry, be happy. Keep the faith and kick the fear. God is in absolute control of your life. May he continue to bless you and yours in Jesus' Name.

God bless you.

Value in Service

Lu. 22:25-26, GNB

Jesus said to them, "The kings of the pagans have power over their people, and the rulers claim the title, 'Friends of the people.' But this is not the way it is with you; rather, the greatest one among you must be like the youngest, and the leader must be like the servant."

The leadership style of Jesus was radically different from that of the society he grew up in and was one of the reasons his ministry was opposed by those who considered themselves spiritual heads of the Jews. The different Jewish sects, comprising the Pharisees, Sadducees, Herodians, Scribes etc., all believed in authoritarian leadership. Their position was that your importance in society is determined by your title, not necessarily your service. The unwritten law was that the leader should be served by the people. He was not accountable to anyone, but everyone is supposed to be accountable to him. The leader was the interpreter of the Law, but not to subject to its demands. Here comes Jesus, and he debunks this interpretation of Leadership as false.

The Jewish leaders saw immediately that their long-established privileges were under threat, so Jesus must be eliminated. Fast forward, the Lord saw his disciples display the same leadership tendency as the world around them, and so he had to teach them that Kingdom-concept and practice of Leadership is service-based, not self-centered pomposity and arrogance. It appears the Church has missed out on this all-important lesson for a long time since then and has gone back to the Pharisaic days of "Leadership is Power and Privilege." We love to be seen as being in charge; to be served, adored, and be the center of attraction. Our leadership style creates a distraction from God and establishes a platform for unhealthy competition and complacency. God's style of leadership is service.

As husband, father, mother, pastor, elder etc., you are in a lead-position as servant of the home and church. The Kingdom of God has only one Head, and everyone else (including you and I), is a servant in our different areas of calling. Can you imagine the amount of peace and sanity we shall enjoy in our homes and in the Church if everyone considers himself a servant, instead of a ruler? Jesus wants us to look at Leadership as opportunity to serve, not power to rule. If your marriage is in crisis, there is a possibility of lack of zeal to serve; selfishness has taken center-stage, and one or both of you are more concerned with what you can get out of the relationship than what you can give to it. As long as you insist on being served and never offering service, you cannot know the joy and peace that comes from ministering to others. We are not defined by titles and accolades.

Our true value is in our service. A true leader of God is a committed servant of people. Look for opportunities each day to be a true leader of Christ through service to your family, church, and community. Instead of sitting back and waiting for others to come to you, reach out and bless people with the gifts God has given you; call someone who lost a loved one and let him know you care, visit someone you heard is in the hospital, pray for someone in distress, and where possible bail someone out of financial crisis. You don't have to be called a bishop to be a blessing. Remember, our Savior is Servant personified. He has more titles than anyone else, yet dropped it all, that he might serve and save all. Beloved, let us seek to serve, and not be served. We can never get it wrong in serving others.

God bless you.

Accept God's Rest

Matt.11:28-29, GNB

Come to me, all of you who are tired from carrying heavy loads, and I will give you rest. Take my yoke and put it on you, and learn from me, because I am gentle and humble in spirit; and you will find rest.

The most common farewell message one can find on any tombstone in a cemetery is, "Rest in peace." Throughout the ages, and in diverse cultures, this simple but powerful parting wish, has been the expression of our desire for loved ones who pass away. Jesus, however, calls us into a peaceful rest that begins here and now, not one that will be inscribed on tombstones we may never see to read. Beloved, we all "carry loads," or "labor" (KJV), and there is nothing wrong with that, as long as it is not too heavy and making us restless. The point is that if the load you are carrying is too heavy and making you restless, you are going to end up depriving yourself of peace, which will ultimately destroy you.

This natural reality is same in the spirit; each of us are born into this world, completely burdened with the heavy load of sin. No matter how morally good a human being is, the soul carries a weight of sin that can be relieved by Jesus Christ alone. Religion tells us how to get rid of this heavy load of sin, but Jesus invites us to bring it to him. He neither commands, threatens, nor manipulates us; he invites us to "come." Jesus became like us, to make it easy for us to relate to him. He took away the scary image of a God who is so big and terrifying that no man can approach him and live and entered our world to help with our load. If you have not yet given your life to Jesus and are trying so hard to please God in your own strength and on your own terms, you are on a mission-impossible; religion cannot take away your load of sin. You need a PERSON, not a PROGRAM, and that person is Jesus the Christ. Stop wasting your time practicing what does not profit.

Hear the voice of Christ, heed the call to come, and you will find rest for your soul. You may have received Christ as your Lord and personal Savior alright, but still be carrying heavy loads of care and worry, which have dulled your hearing to the call to come to his rest. The Lord wants to remind you that you can access his promised rest any day, if you will take a step of faith and come closer to him in prayer. He has a yoke/assignment for you, unlike the one you presently carry; his yoke is light, and he will not impose it on you. He says to you: "Take my yoke and put it on you and learn from me." Everything you do with him must come from a willing heart. As long as you feel forced or threatened to do what you do for God, you are dealing with a spirit that has nothing in common with Jesus Christ.

You know why? The answer is in the second part of the verse 29: "for I am gentle and humble in spirit;" You cannot associate violence, compulsion, control, and manipulation with Jesus. No. The benefits of responding to his call are enormous. You may have denied yourself his rest for so long because you have been running FROM him, instead of running TO him. Come to the Living Water. Drink to your fill, and you will find rest in every storm of life. The rest you seek is found in the Savior; accept his offer and enter his rest. God grant you peace, as you respond to his call.

God bless you.

More Than Conquerors

Rom.8:35,37-NKJV

Who shall separate us from the love of Christ? Shall tribulation, or distress, or persecution, or famine, or nakedness, or peril, or sword? Yet in all these things we are more than conquerors.

A careful look at the challenges Paul lists here as potential threats to our union with Christ, should be enough to prepare any serious-minded disciple for the worst in this life. Tribulation, distress, persecution, famine, nakedness, peril, and sword; these are instruments the enemy can use, and indeed uses, to attack believers. We have the protection of God alright, but like Job and Jesus, and everybody else who lived and lives in this cosmic system corrupted by sin, God sometimes ALLOWS these things to touch us.

His purposes are not always clear to us in our times of distress, but we can be certain that God will not let us "be tempted beyond what we can endure." That is his promise. No matter how terrible your pain, distressing your situation, confusing your path, or intense your persecution, you can trust Christ to stand with you in the crisis. Remember that your enemy, the devil, has an agenda for pushing you so hard against the wall; his primary goal is to separate you from Christ so he can destroy you. Satan and his demons know that once you are connected to the Lord in faith, they may be able to hurt you, but they can NEVER destroy you.

They can touch your body, which is only your temporary house, but they cannot touch your soul, which is your real being and eternal personality. Paul was in total agreement with Job, who in the midst of extreme suffering and pain said, "though he (God) slays me, yet will I serve him." Those who acknowledge God only in the good times, do not have roots to withstand the storms of adversity. Any gospel that presents the Christian life as one devoid of the things Paul speaks about here, is a gospel of deception and falsehood. The Church of Christ is not a bless-me-club; it is a battlefield, that demands unwavering faith, tenacity, and commitment.

Jesus himself said, "in this world, you shall have tribulation;" which means there is no way we can escape bad times. What we can do, and should do, is to pray continually, holding fast to the promises of God, praising in the midst of pain, declaring in the face of the enemy that "nothing (including all the bad stuff he is throwing at us) shall separate us from the love of Christ." We are hooked on it, addicted to it, and intoxicated by it, and there is no going back.

I pray for you today that no matter what you are going through, the Lord by his Spirit, will strengthen and empower you to stand and prevail. You are more than a conqueror, and so keep standing, because no condition is permanent. This one thing I know for sure, that our God is in control, and we shall always have the last laugh, either here or in heaven.

God bless you.

Pursue Knowledge of God

Hos.6:3, NKJV

Let us know, let us pursue the knowledge of the LORD. His going forth is established as the morning; He will come to us like the rain, like the latter and former rain on the earth.

Hosea was called into the prophetic ministry to show God's people how far they had drifted from him, and what they needed to do to reconcile with the Lord. He stressed the need to know God as the only way out of Israel's dilemma. Some of us know more about our church and its history, than we know about Christ and Basic doctrines of the Bible. Others place more emphasis on knowing the man behind the pulpit, than the God upon the throne, who is the God of their salvation. That is why we sometimes see people give their lives to Christ, and after years in church, still will be calling the pastor to pray for them because they have a toothache.

We do not grow, because we refuse to KNOW. No doubt the Lord concluded, "My people are destroyed for lack of knowledge" (Hos.4;6). Our destruction does not come because our God cannot protect or provide for us, but "for lack of knowledge" of our God. The good news, however, is that God never tells us what to do without showing us how to do it. The prophet Hosea points to us the way forward by saying, "let us pursue the knowledge of God." The word "pursue" means we must continue seeking the knowledge of God. You don't relate to God on the basis of feeling; praying when you feel like or reading the scriptures when you feel like reading it.

Think about this; how well can you know someone by talking to him only when you feel like talking to him? God wants to relate to you and me at the level of friendship not acquaintanceship. He wants us to follow him, not to run from him. Even though he is unchanging, he always has something new up his sleeves to show those who make time to KNOW him by bonding with him in intimate relationship. The scripture says, "His going forth is established as the morning;" meaning he neither changes nor gets tired in doing what needs to be done.

There is beauty, consistency, and freshness about each and every morning. That is why the verse under consideration here closes with the assurance that God will come to those who pursue after knowing him "like rain, like the former and latter rain to water the earth." The solution to the dryness in every human soul is in the knowledge of God. Knowing God creates the right spiritual and emotional atmosphere to meet your physical and material needs. It is impossible to know God and not know yourself, and you cannot know yourself in the context of who God's Word says you are, and still live in fear, jealousy, worry, and discontent.

Those who "pursue the knowledge of the LORD," get our Father's attention, and are given the right amount of "rain" or grace they need every morning of their lives. The moment you stop seeking him, you will start blaming him; Satan will make sure of that, so keep on keeping on, and may the good Lord reveal himself to you always in all ways.

God bless you.

The Light of His Face

Prov.16:15, NKJV

In the light of the king's face is life, and his favor is like a cloud of latter rain.

The context of this scripture speaks of the king of Israel. In his peculiar position as king, anyone privileged to have access to his presence, was guaranteed certain advantages in society. It was not possible to dwell in the courts of the king and go hungry or live in misery. Everyone who serves in the courts of the king is favored in the affairs of state. Even so are we called to serve in the courts of the King of Kings and enjoy the blessings of that privileged position. There is light that comes from the Presence of our King. Our lives revolve around this light.

Every other light has its source in the light that proceeds out of Christ, who is the Light of the world. Without the light of Christ, we have no life. To walk in this life, we have to see the King's face; we must be in his presence every day. This demands our time. It means spending quality time with God. You cannot be too busy chasing everything else and not have time to be alone with God. The Sunday morning service alone is not enough to bond you to the Spirit of Christ. Make time for God. There should be nothing out there preventing you from a daily intimate relationship with God. Set aside time to commune with the Lord.

Cut back on some of the time you spend on the internet or doing stuff that have no eternal value. In the midst of intense suffering, Job pleaded to be directed to the place where he could see God and present his case to him. He knew who was responsible for restoring life-giving light into his life and was prepared to reach out to him in whatever way possible. Job cried out for light from the face of the King of glory to shine on his dark world, and was heard, delivered, and restored. Those who seek Jesus Christ, do not only receive "the light of the king's face," but also experience unusual favor.

This favor is described as being like a "cloud of latter rain." What difference does that make? There are clouds that point to destruction. Clouds that point to floods and storms that scares everyone, but benefits no one. It is not so with the cloud of the latter rain. It promises sufficiency and freshness. God's desire for you is to enjoy the light of his face, and favor like the cloud of the latter rain. May that be your portion always and in all ways in Jesus' Name.

God bless you.

Strength to Deliver

Acts 8:29-30, NKJV

Then the Spirit said to Philip, "Go near and overtake his chariot." So, Philip ran to him, and asked him, "Do you understand what you are reading?"

Those who want to walk with God, must brace themselves for instructions and assignments that sometimes does not make sense, in terms of our human understanding. The Holy Spirit doesn't always lead us beside still waters and to green pastures. He led Jesus to the wilderness to be tempted by the devil. Yes dear, sometimes his plan and purpose require that he leads us through storms and deserts; and that is what happened to Philip.

Right in the middle of a revival, where he was ministering to thousands in a city, the Holy Spirit led him to the desert to minister to an individual who he never met. This assignment was made even worse by the question he was instructed to ask the Ethiopian eunuch: "Do you understand what you are reading?" Come to think of it, it doesn't sound right to just interrupt someone you don't know, who is engrossed in reading, and ask whether he understood what he was reading. That might sound rude and disrespectful to the average person, but not when the instruction is coming from the Father of all flesh.

The task is made even more challenging by the fact that Philip had to ran and overtake the eunuch's chariot. How about that; Running and overtaking chariots to fulfill an assignment for God? How far are you prepared to go for Jesus? What distance are you prepared to cover for the salvation of a soul? And who is the Holy Spirit directing you to reach out to, who seem too far away from you, and doesn't share anything in common with you?

The assignment may not be convenient because it demands a sacrifice you may not be willing to make but remember the God of the city is also the God of the desert. The God of the multitudes is same as the God of the individual. When he directs, he gives strength to deliver. Stand up and ran towards the goal of your calling. Confront the challenges and refuse to be controlled by logic. Be led by the Spirit. Remember that if God commands you to run with chariots, he will give you all it takes to "overtake" and overcome them.

God bless you.

God's Provision

1 Ki.17:2-4, NKJV

Then the word of the LORD came to him, saying, "Get away from here and turn eastward, and hide by the Brook Cherith, which flows in the Jordan. And it will be that you shall drink from the brook, and I have commanded the ravens to feed you there."

Elijah pronounced judgment of drought on Israel in the days of King Ahab, because the king had promoted idol worship in the land. The interesting thing about the judgment was that it affected the servant of God too. Like everyone else, he didn't have food to eat, and that is sometimes what happens when you choose to obey God. Obedience doesn't always make you immune to the challenges that others go through. Jesus Christ learnt obedience at the human level through suffering (Heb.5:8).

What makes the difference between your suffering or challenges as a child of God, and that of the unbeliever is in the word "direction." God gives you direction as to what to do to survive. Elijah was given clear instructions on where to go, and what to expect. In fact, the direction wasn't something most modern-day prophets would easily embrace. The first thing he was told was to "turn eastward;" to face the place of the rising sun. Life comes from light, and God is both the Lord, and light of our lives. He who walks in the light of Christ, has the life of God.

If Elijah had stayed in the midst of the darkness with the idol worshippers, he wouldn't have had what God had prepared for him at the Brook Cherith. The second instruction was to "hide," and that is something very contrary to what we love to do in today's church. Today's saint is alien to God's hiding place. We want to be seen, applauded, and acclaimed, so we compete with each other instead of complimenting each other's ministry. Those who will feed from God's abundant grace, must learn to dwell in his hiding place. It is the only source of divine sufficiency in life's seasons of drought.

There is water for you in God's hiding place, and God will meet your every need in very unusual circumstances. It will take only God for ravens to carry food to a human being in a specific location. Birds feed their young only, and they do that only within a certain timeframe, after which time they expect the young ones to fly out of their nests and go fend for themselves. The raven, as a matter of fact, eats a lot, and cannot be trusted to share its food; but when God who created man and the bird commands a word, his will prevails.

If you turn where he tells you, and hides where he shows you, provision will come to you from unexpected sources. Yes, he will. Turn to the light. Hide under the shadow of his wings. Look to him for grace to meet your every need. He who fed Elijah in the midst of famine, will feed you good.

God bless you.

Be Rich Towards God

2 Chron.31:20-21, NKJV

Thus Hezekiah did throughout all Judah, and he did what was good and right and true before the LORD his God. And in every work that he began in the service of the house of God, he did it with all his heart. So he prospered.

The Bible clearly teaches God's desire for his people to prosper. David, for instance, speaks a lot about God's provision and prosperity in his psalms. The first verse of what perhaps is his most popular psalm (23), reads: "The Lord is my Shepherd, I shall not want." Apostle Paul says, "my God shall supply all your needs according to his riches in Christ Jesus." The Lord himself indicated how important our material well-being is, when he told the devil during his temptation that "man shall not live by bread alone."

Jesus never said bread is not important, no; he said man's total welfare is not dependent on meeting man's material need alone. His explanation was that there is more to life than the acquisition of material wealth (bread). If it were not so, and man can live by bread alone, how do we explain the fact that some billionaires and millionaires get so disillusioned with life that they commit suicide? Preaching a message that turns the gospel into a money-making machine, is an act of deception. Following Christ, without submitting to the cross, is a delusion.

God wants to bless us, but he also expects us to reflect him. No one who commits to honoring God with his life, ever lives all his life in shame and disgrace. The Word of God reveals the secret of Hezekiah's prosperity: "in every work that he began in the house of God, he did it with all his heart. So, he prospered." It was not just a matter of doing something for the Lord, but he did everything he did, "with all his heart." We can all claim to be doing something for God, but when we do the things we do without a heart-commitment, we may end up missing out on the blessings that come with it.

Three words marked the attitude of Hezekiah towards his work; first he did what was good, then what was right, and finally, he did what was true. Hezekiah did it all "before the Lord." There was no selfishness, no self-centeredness, and no desire to impress anyone. Beloved, it is important that when we claim the blessings of the Bible for ourselves, we also pray for grace to live God-honoring lives.

You can have all the wealth and health in the world, and still be the poorest human being on planet earth, if you are not rich towards God; and to be rich towards God, you must serve the Lord in a way that is "good and right and true." That way, you will not need to BEG God to bless you; the blessings will overtake you.

God bless you.

Wait on the Lord

Ps. 37:34, NKJV

Wait on the LORD and keep His way, and he will exalt you to inherit the land; when the wicked are cut off, you shall see it.

Waiting on the Lord is not being passive and inactive; it is activity and service. When you walk into a restaurant, those who serve you the meal, literally "wait on" you through the service they provide. They don't rush you, because you are the one who keeps them in business by patronizing their service. Likewise, we also wait on God because he is our provider and protector. In our waiting, we serve in worship, prayer, and work. The life we live and work we do for God, become steppingstones to our spiritual growth and elevation.

Each of us have a land we must inherit, and God's position is that if we serve him, and "keep his way," we come into that place and space of divine elevation and promotion. It is important to remind ourselves that God is a rewarder, and that even though salvation is free, works of obedience comes both with a price and a prize. The one who waits on you in the restaurant, knows that if he gives you a good service, he will not only get you to pay for his service, but also give him a good tip. He is patient with you, because waiting on someone demands patience from the waiter.

If you will be a good waiter on God, then you need to be patient with God; and the Lord by his Spirit will give you that patience if you ask him. If for one reason or the other, you are trapped in a vicious cycle of "wickedness" in any form, there is assurance for you: an unfailing, unchanging, irreversible promise of deliverance. Whatever constitutes the wickedness (setbacks and hindrances) will be cut off, and God's Word says when that happens, "you will see it."

The Lord will let you see the deliverance you have prayed and believed for, happen in your life. Keep waiting on him. Keep keeping his way. Faithful is he who has promised; he will elevate you, because you are meant to reign with Christ, not to run and hide. Your shame will be lifted, and his glory shall be revealed in you and through you.

God bless you.

God's Grace

Zech.4:7, NKJV

Who are you, O great mountain? Before Zerubbabel you shall become a plain! And he shall bring forth the capstone with shouts of "Grace, grace to it!"

The context in which the word "mountain" is used here does not imply a real physical mountain; it means a challenge, hindrance, problem, or something that stands between you and your set goal or objective. It means a very strong, stable, well-established, and impossible-to-change negative situation. In Zerubbabel's case, he was not dealing with an ordinary mountain, but a "great mountain." That exactly may be what you are confronted with right now.

You are faced with a situation that cannot be wished away; you may have had a bad report concerning your health, or that of a loved one, or maybe you failed an exam, lost a job or relationship, or your business may be nose-diving, and you appear to be heading towards bankruptcy. You can literally feel the pressure of fear and worry rise within you with the speed of lightening, and intensity of heat. This has nothing to do with faith, because you still believe in God, but the mountain before you pose a challenge that is too overwhelming and intimidating.

That fact feeds the fear and frustration, but thanks be to the Lord for his grace and mercy; for he who promised not to let us be tempted beyond what we can endure, but with the temptation make a way of escape, will keep his word to you. When your mountain defies human effort, knowledge, and ingenuity, then you have reached a point of depending on nothing else but the grace of God. Grace is a higher principle than faith, because your faith can fail, but His grace abides. When the angel told Abraham's wife, Sarah, that she would conceive and give birth to a son in her old age, she laughed.

It was not a laughter of joy borne out of faith; it was a laughter of contempt produced by doubt, but grace brought into manifestation what lack of faith threatened to wipe out. It was God performing to move a mountain where faith had collapsed, because of his unfailing love, grace, and mercy. The Spirit of the Lord is giving you a "lifeline to your deadline." It is called "grace." If the great mountains you are facing are creating fear and panic, don't pretend any longer; ask God for the grace that worked in the lives of many doubting and fearful saints like Sarah, Gideon, Zerubbabel, and Zechariah the father of John the Baptist.

Where God's grace abounds, great mountains become a plain. It cuts through the mountains like hot knife cutting through butter, making a way where there is no way. I pray for you today, that this grace will locate you and your entire family now and always, in all your ways in Jesus' name.

God bless you.

God's Comforting Arm

Is.66:13-14, NKJV

As one whom his mother comforts, so will I comfort you; and you shall be comforted in Jerusalem. When you see this, and your bones shall flourish like grass; the hand of the LORD shall be known to his servants, and His indignation to His enemies.

We serve a good God; one who does not distance himself from our pain and struggles. His word to you this morning is a word of assurance to stand with you in all your challenges. God uses the figure of a mother comforting his child to reveal the depth of his commitment to see you receive help in your times of need. Reflect for a moment on how a typical mother comforts a weeping child, and you can understand how much grace and mercy God has made available for you.

I guess nobody want to go through bad times, and Jesus Christ is no stranger to pain and sorrow, so it is important to keep reminding yourself that dark days are part of the life we are called to live here on earth. How one wishes there would be nothing to disturb our peace and give us anxious moments; but alas, that can only remain a wish. What God offers is his comfort.

He is challenging you through his Word to look beyond the bad stuff happening to you right now and begin to see the motherly comfort he provided in the past and will continue to provide. The scripture says it is "when you see this" that "your bones shall flourish like grass." The bone is the structure that holds your entire body in place. Weak and deteriorating bones cannot sustain health, and so the Lord zeros in on the life-sustaining Spirit within you (the bone of your being) and promises to make it flourish like grass.

Paul says even though the outer man is wasting away, the inner man is being strengthened. This can only be seen with the eye of faith. When feeling grabs the mind and points to the pain, faith sees the God of all comfort giving grace to smile through the storm. This is how "the hand of the Lord" is made known to his servants. His ways are made known to us even in the midst of our frustrating circumstances. God may be angry with his enemies; but for you, his comforting arm will always be stretched out to protect you.

God bless you.

Seek God's Will

1Ki.18:36, NKJV

And it came to pass, at the time of the offering of the evening sacrifice, that Elijah the prophet came near and said, "LORD God of Abraham, Isaac, and Israel, let it be known this day that You are God in Israel, and I am your servant, and that I have done all these things at Your word.

During the reign of King Ahab, idolatry thrived so much in Israel because of the influence of his pagan wife, Jezebel. It was obvious in the way the people of Israel behaved towards the God of their fathers, that they were not sure of the difference between Jehovah and the foreign gods introduced by Jezebel. If the God of Israel had priests and prophets, the foreign gods also had priests and prophets. If God worked miracles, the idols also appeared to put up similar performances.

It was at the height of this spiritual confusion and prostitution, that Elijah called for a contest of clarity on mount Carmel, with a view to helping the people make an informed decision on who was the one true God. When the prophets of Baal had had their fair share of chanting, dancing, and cutting themselves without any response from their gods, Elijah stepped up and prayed this simple prayer. First, he asked God to "let it be known this day that You are God in Israel."

Elijah's position was that God can only be known by divine revelation. Jesus said if the Father has not called you, you cannot come to him. You cannot know God through the accumulation of academic knowledge, or by subjecting him to a laboratory test. True knowledge of God comes through revelation by his Spirit. The second plea Elijah made to God was, "let it be known that I am your servant. For all of us who stand as ministers of the gospel, this should be a caution to us; never to try and PROVE anything to the world.

Let the Holy Spirit endorse your ministry. Don't try to do anything with the intention to prove that you are a man of God; let it be all about Jesus. The final part of his prayer re-echoes the point already made here. He prayed, "I have done all these things at your word." Elijah did not force God to send fire from heaven. He was not in the business of performing magic.

He needed a miracle, and he had to be sure about what God intended to do, in order to preach and act in accordance with God's revealed word and will. The prophet did not call a contest that demanded God's personal involvement without first seeking God's will. That would have been presumptuous. He did what he did because God told him to do it. Here is the final lesson: Do not force the hand of God in matters of signs and miracles.

Ministry is not about impressing people; it is about expressing God's revealed will. Let God lead and use you the way he wants, and his glory will be seen, when and where it must be seen.

God bless you.

Prepared Receptacles

Deut.28:8, NKJV

The LORD will command the blessing on you in your storehouses and in all to which you set your hand, and He will bless you in the land which the LORD your God is giving you.

Moses assured Israel of God's preparedness to bless them in a very special way if they walked in obedience to His Word. He spoke to them of "the blessing"; meaning it was specific and defined. It was not just any blessing, but "the blessing." The exciting news for you and I is that we are candidates of this blessing and need to understand how it works. First, "the blessing" is in Christ Jesus (Eph.1:3), and not in any other being or person. As a child of God, you carry within you the blessing of God, and God has given you the divine mandate to bless others.

Secondly, the practical application of the promise is targeted. Moses says the Lord will command the blessing on two specific areas of your life, "your storehouses and in all to which you set your hand." That means you should have "storehouses." God will not build the storehouses for you; that is your responsibility. You should have goals, dreams, ideas etc. to do something with your life. God cannot bless a visionless life. You cannot wake up every morning saying you don't know what to do. That lack of knowledge will destroy you. It means you don't have "storehouses" and so the blessing cannot locate and impact your life.

The storehouses may be empty. You may lack the resources, but not dreams, vision, and plans. The blessing of the Lord will bring the needed resources if you have a plan for your life. The blessing also demands of you to set your hand to do something. God will bless what you do, not what you complain about. Only few people start life and have an already laid foundation for a smooth take off. In general, people have to work their way up through sweat, toil, sleepless nights, and tears. Between Jesus and the throne, was a cross full of shame, pain, tears, and death. He had to endure the cross to ascend the throne.

God commands the blessing, but we must be prepared receptacles for the blessing. We must have our storehouses ready to be filled, and our hands ready to be blessed. If you come to God without a storehouse, and are unwilling to apply yourself to work, you joined the wrong bus and will not make it to your destination. Build storehouses and prepare to work towards a goal, and the blessing is yours for the taking.

God bless you.

Draw Your Satisfaction from God

Eccl.2:10-11, NKJV

Whatever my eyes desired I did not keep from them. I did not withhold my heart from any pleasure. For my heart rejoiced in all my labor. Then I looked on all the works that my hands had done and on the labor in which I have toiled; and indeed, all was vanity and grasping for the wind. There was no profit under the sun.

The book of Ecclesiastes is accredited to King Solomon, Israel's wisest king. The content reflects his personal experiences and observations, some of which do not line up properly with the mind of God. Solomon confesses here his lack of restraint when it came to earthly pleasures. In his own words he says, "Whatever my eyes desired I did not keep from them. I did not withhold my heart from any pleasure." No doubt he had 300 wives and 700 concubines.

It is not a sin to have fun. Having fun helps us maintain a life of sanity, joy, and peace. I wonder what life would be like, if we never have opportunity to talk, laugh, sleep, fellowship, sing etc. These are the real fundamental freedoms of life. A healthy soul cannot thrive without these things, but there is danger when pleasure has no boundaries. The fact that you have the means to do everything, doesn't mean you should do anything or live anyhow. Sometimes legitimate rights can be offensive and hurtful to others.

Apostle Paul told the church in Corinth that even though he had the right to eat anything, he would refrain from eating anything that would hurt someone else's faith. If everyone around you is starving, and you consistently display wealth and opulence without regard to their plight, you are not acting wisely, and may be exposing yourself to danger. God want us to enjoy life, not to abuse it. You must draw the line between what you can take and what you should not touch. Solomon, as king, had the advantage of accessing anything he wanted in Israel, but only within the perimeters set by God; he was not supposed to marry foreign women, but because his eyes desired them, he did not keep from them.

God wants you to prosper and be adequately resourced so you can live in joy and peace, but God doesn't expect you to be a victim of the challenges that prosperity brings with it; challenges such as pride, arrogance, insensitivity, and rejection of limitations set by God's Word to protect you. Free yourself from the trap of wanting to have EVERYTHING your eyes desires, because some of it may lead to your fall. You can have everything and still feel like having nothing, if you don't draw your satisfaction from God.

Following the desires of your eyes without restraint is a mistake you should avoid. Solomon, after feeding his fleshly nature with all the desires of his eyes, came to this conclusion: "indeed all was vanity, and grasping for the wind." Why? Because material wealth is not the answer to spiritual health. There must be a balance between the two; never neglecting the spiritual in pursuit of the physical.

God bless you.

Live for Christ

Rev.3:1, NKJV

And to the angel of the church of Sardis write, These things says He who has the seven Spirits of God and the seven stars: "I know your works, that you have a name that you are alive, but you are dead."

This very tough statement was made by Jesus when he spoke to John from heaven, during the apostle's incarceration on the Island of Patmos. The Lord's message to the church of Sardis was that the name they called themselves did not reflect the way they lived their lives. There was an issue of double-standards, or perhaps self-deception that the church needed to deal with immediately. Jesus Christ, as head of the church, was responsible for pointing out the wrong, and so he made the diagnosis and gave the prescription for cure.

He was quick to point out that he was unhappy with their hypocrisy. Our lives are like an open book before God. He does not need to google information on who we are, where we are, or what we may be doing, have done, or likely to do. What Jesus said emphatically to the church in Sardis yesterday, he is saying to us today: "I know your works." No one may know about you cheating on your spouse, but Jesus knows. No one may know about your abuse of children, but Jesus knows. No one may know how you manipulate figures in the account books of your church or organization, but Jesus knows for sure.

When all is said and done, Jesus is saying to us, "you don't tell me your name, or teach me what to call you, because I KNOW YOUR WORKS, and your works tell me who you are." You may call yourself a pastor, but if all you do is FLEECE the sheep instead of FEEDING them, you are a butcher, not a shepherd; and butchers and shepherds are not the same. The book of James (2:14-26) speaks extensively about the necessity to combine faith with works. In Revelation 3:1, the Lord takes the teaching on works a notch higher; it is not about doing without being. The early believers did not call themselves Christians; it was outsiders observing their "works" who named them Christians because they saw the Christ-like nature in them.

Friend, you are not a father because you impregnated a woman and produced children. Fatherhood is in responsibility; loving, providing, protecting, leading, and much more. And of course, you are not a mother just because you carried a baby in your womb for nine months and gave birth at the end of that nine-month period. What you and I call ourselves must be in agreement with what we do. We can't call ourselves children of God and live like cousins of the devil. Remember, if nobody knows, Jesus is saying "I know", so let's put our act together. There is a difference between a cop and a corpse; one is alive, the other is dead. You can't be both, you are either one or the other. Live for Christ because he knows you by name.

God bless you.

Live within Your Means

Phil.4:12, NKJV

I know how to be abased, and I know how to abound. Everywhere and in all things I have learned both to be full and to be hungry, both to abound and to suffer need.

Lack of knowledge is always a disadvantage. The things we don't know are the things that surprise us most when they do happen. Apostle Paul knew two things, and those two things helped him to live without wavering in faith. First, he learnt how to live when he didn't have enough, and then he learnt how to enjoy the bountiful blessing of God when they come. This flexibility is something we must all learn. Life is unpredictable, and we cannot always have a full supply of the things we need or want.

Jesus had needs when he hanged on the cross in the hot afternoon sun; he cried for water, and he cried for his Father's presence. There may be times in our lives when by the grace of God, we can have more than enough of the things we need; whether it be money, relationships, good health, peace of mind etc. In those times, the lights come on wherever you turn, and you have to enjoy the blessings of God's bountiful provision. However, the story doesn't end there for a child of God who is willing to be schooled in living a balanced life of contentment.

It continues with learning how to live when your well dries up; when you "suffer need." Anything can happen and change the circumstances of your life today, tomorrow, or next year. The change may bring joy or otherwise. God want you to know how to navigate through each and every storm. In the days of "hunger", you must show tenacity. When your health is failing, your finances are dwindling, and your relationships are disappointing, make your way to the throne of God in prayer, and there you will find grace enough to help you in your time of need. Learn what Paul learnt; "both to abound and to suffer need."

Always remember that no condition is permanent. Indeed, even our journey here on earth is not permanent. No one is going to be around here forever, and there is nothing we can hold or possess forever. Enjoy the blessings God gives you today, and where there is lack, live in hope and positive anticipation that the Lord is able to sustain you and supply your every need.

The 24 hours called "today" is already on the run, and so if you are stuck in what you don't have or cannot do, you are losing more than you ought to. Take what you have and enjoy it the best you can. Learn to live with what you have, and without what you don't have.

God bless you.

Set God at Your Right Hand

Ps.16:8, NKJV

I have set the LORD always before me; Because He is at my right hand I shall not be moved.

Security is mandatory for peace, joy, and prosperity. Companies and individuals invest lots of money to ensure security for themselves. Jesus Christ describes the devil as security- breaker; The Lord said Satan comes to "steal, kill, and destroy"(Jn.10:10a). This simply means the devil has a penchant for undermining human security. He can "shake" you if you let him. In Ps.16:8, David sings about the one thing that forms the basis of his security, which is the place God occupies in his life. He said, "I have set the LORD always before me," and so he was sure of his security.

The first thing to note is that David took a personal decision to "set the LORD always" before him. Nobody talked him into doing it. It was a personal conviction put into application without intimidation. Second is, David was not pliable and inconsistent. He said "I have set the LORD ALWAYS;" not sometimes. His mind was made up, and with deliberate intent, he was totally relying on the Lord to keep him. His first choice for protection and provision was God. His second choice was God, and forever it was God. Whether it was times of war or seasons of peace, David had God as his sustainer and provider.

The "right hand" is figurative and speaks of position or source of power. David used this figure of speech to emphasize the point of God being his all in all. Beloved, the Holy Spirit is in our lives to do what we can never do for us. If you woke this morning feeling lost and empty, you may be looking in the wrong direction. You may have set something or someone other than Jesus at your "right hand" and that is why you are being shaken.

Take a few moments to reflect on how big, powerful, and awesome our God is; the One "immortal, invincible, God only wise." Ask yourself, "where have I set God in my life today?" Begin to consciously retrace your steps back to the corridor of faith. Declare right now, " I have set the LORD always before me; Because He is at my right hand, I shall not be moved." May that be portion today and ALWAYS in Jesus' name.

God bless you.

Your Light Will Shine Again

Ps112:4, NKJV

Unto the upright there arises light in the darkness; He is gracious, and full of compassion, and righteousness.

"Darkness" as used in this scripture speaks to us of everything negative one can think of or imagine. Every one of us experience our dark days; and it wouldn't be a surprise if you just experienced one or are going through one. Those are times you are overwhelmed and feel like nothing is working for you. Everywhere you turn, you hit a wall; nobody knows what you are going through but you, and even those who know and have the best of intentions are unable to offer the solution or help you urgently require. It can get so dark that your passion for living collapses under the storm, and all you see is darkness, darkness, and more darkness.

Here is good news: Jesus Christ is your Light. He has imputed righteousness to you, and because of your new position in him, you have His sure promises that when darkness assails you, his light will shine for you. The light may come in as a shaft of ray. It may not be a sudden flood of light, but God in his own wisdom will throw in enough light to sustain you as long as the darkness lasts. Being knocked DOWN, is not the same as being knocked OUT. We all go down many times in many ways, but it takes those who trust in the unfailing goodness of Christ to pick themselves up and keep moving forward.

It takes those who have survived the ravages of "darkness" to understand the workings of God's grace, and to extend same to others. The redeemed of the Lord have no issues with showing kindness to others, because he acknowledges God's grace that brings light into his darkness. The Word of God says, "he is gracious, and full of compassion, and righteousness." That is the level of maturity God want to bring you. Don't let your dark circumstances overwhelm you. The darkness has an expiry date on it.

Your light will shine again. It will come when God has used what was meant for your shame, to shape you into a vessel that will dispense grace, compassion, and righteousness wherever you go. Keep hope alive, even if you are in a hole. Your light will shine again.

God bless you.

Cherish God's Presence

Hos.3:4-5, NKJV

For the children of Israel shall abide many days without king or prince, without sacrifice or sacred pillar, without ephod or teraphim. Afterward the children of Israel shall return and seek the LORD and His goodness in the latter days.

King, prince, sacrifice, sacred pillar, ephod, and teraphim, were all representations of God's presence in the life of Israel. When these things were withdrawn, it meant the people of Israel lost the presence, protection, and provision of God. They no longer enjoyed the rulership and direction of God; they were left on their own, and everyone became a law unto himself. God withdrew from them so they could see the difference between their being under his leadership, and their living without him. The wise have aptly said that "familiarity breeds contempt," and that was what was playing out here.

Israel had walked away from God, thinking they could be better off without him. After encountering the difficulties associated with the bad choice they had made, Hosea prophesied that they were going to return to the Lord, which they eventually did. Beloved, there is a void in every human heart that only the Spirit of God can fill. If money holds the key to joyful living, millionaires would never commit suicide; but it happens, and is happening. The gods of wealth, sex, fame, and power are deceptive. Anyone who replaces God with any of these things stand in danger of self-destruction.

The reason being that man is a spirit-being, and as one crafted and created in the image of God, any disconnection from his creator is a recipe for disaster. Many great men have fallen in the quest for inner satisfaction because they looked for it outside of God. Some acted inappropriately towards women and children and had to endure shame and jail sentences because their "inside" was devoid of the light and life of God's Spirit, who alone is capable of keeping the flesh under control.

When you drive a car and run out of gas, you don't go to a coffee shop. No, you check in at a gas filling station. It is same with God; he is the fuel we need to run the engine of our lives effectively and efficiently. He has to fill the inner space (our hearts), and the outer man (fleshly nature) will be able to handle material issues of wealth, sex, popularity, and power appropriately. When depression hits, you are powerless without the help of the Holy Spirit. Medication may offer temporary relief, but only the peace of God can give you permanent solution. So then, how do you keep this all-important relationship with God intact? The answer is in giving priority to this relationship itself, making God the reason for your being.

When nobody's word is more important to you than doing God's will, you are covered. Don't take the presence of God in your life for granted. Exercise yourself in the things of the Spirit daily; you don't only worship, pray, or read your Bible when you are in a crisis. Samson messed up with the presence of God, spending more time on the lap of Delilah than in fellowship with God, and the result was the loss of his ministry forever. God had it all written down so we can learn from it and avoid making the same mistake. Keep the faith, and you will be protected by the Spirit of grace.

God bless you.

Be A Chanel of Liberation

Eze.11:24-25, NKJV

Then the Spirit took me up and brought me in a vision by the Spirit of God to Chaldea, to those in captivity. And the vision I had seen went up from me. So, I spoke to those in captivity of all things the Lord had shown me.

There are people in "captivity" waiting to be informed, empowered, and liberated by your testimony. What you have been through, and how God brought you out, add up as invaluable treasures of wisdom that can bless someone caught up in a similar situation, and struggling to survive. Ezekiel had an encounter with the Lord and had information that could benefit his people who were not privy to his vision. The prophet did what needed to be done; he shared the vision with those who would benefit from it.

Note here that it was not a personal vision, but a national one. Your position as a child of God imposes the same obligation on you; to go tell the "captives" what God is showing you in His Word and in your walk with Him. Your constituency is bigger and larger than that of Ezekiel. He was sent to A NATION; you have been sent to THE NATIONS. There are many who interact with you on a daily basis who are in various kinds of captivity. Some are in spiritual captivity, without any relationship with Christ.

Others are in emotional captivity, hurting and silently dying without getting the help and direction they so desperately need to survive. Your assignment, and my assignment, is to be channels of encouragement and liberation for people in this category. It may be that you have your own "captivity" to deal with (and who doesn't have?), and so you don't feel adequate enough to be God's "freedom fighter". You got it wrong. Ezekiel was in captivity too, but God still used him to communicate to His people.

It is not about you. It's all about Him. Sometimes it is in seeking to set others free by sharing in their burdens, that we gain our own freedom. Your life's experiences can save lives. Someone going through a crisis that you've been through, needs you to tell him how you overcame and assure him he can overcome. Someone addicted to a destructive habit needs no judgment or condemnation.

He needs counseling and encouragement from God's Ezekiel, and you are the one chosen "for a time like this", within your circle of influence. If you haven't had an encounter with God, your impact will be minimal. Spend time in His Presence and He will give you the vision for the mission to go set the "captives" free.

God bless you.

Sow in Tears, Reap in Joy

Ps.126:5-6, NKJV

Those who sow in tears shall reap in joy. He who continually goes forth weeping, bearing seed for sowing, shall doubtless come again rejoicing, bringing sheaves with him.

The beginning of many things in life can be exciting. The energy and verve we need to work towards a defined goal is easy to find when we start a project. What usually cripples us on our journey towards our goals is lack of "staying power". The routine and rigorous demands of the process is not for the faint-hearted. Truth is, nothing good comes easy. If you want to achieve tangible results in any pursuit in life, you've got to commit to making long-term sacrifices. You don't go to work for only a day and look forward to a month's salary.

You don't sleep all day and believe God for money to pay your bills. God's Word says, "those who sow in tears shall reap in joy." If you don't want to shed a tear, it may cost you a cup of tea. The verse 6 of our scripture under reference here reads, and I quote: "He who CONTINUALLY goes forth weeping, shall doubtless come again with rejoicing bringing his sheaves with him." The word "CONTINUALLY" (emphasis mine) should engage our attention, because it holds the key to the ultimate result of a joyful harvest.

First thing to note is the classification. Not everyone will experience the joy of bringing sheaves. That joy is only for those who "continually goes forth weeping" - those willing to sacrifice continuously for the goal they set themselves. For such, God is giving you the assurance that your sacrifice will not be in vain. Look beyond the pain associated with the process.

There is joy awaiting you. God will help you reach your goal, no matter how long it takes. You (and I mean YOU!) "Shall doubtless come again with rejoicing." You will bring fruitful results of your labour, as a testimony. Go until you get there. Go until you get it.

God bless you.

Wait for Your Elevation

Dan. 2:20-22, NKJV

Daniel answered and said: Blessed is the name of God forever and ever, for wisdom and might are His. And He changes the times and seasons; He removes kings and raises up kings; He gives wisdom to the wise and knowledge to those who have understanding. He reveals deep and secret things; He knows what is in the darkness, and light is with him.

Disappointment with the past, frustration with the present, and fear of the future, are three major factors that fuel the practice of occultism, unhealthy competition, and lack of faith in God's promises. Daniel found himself a captive in Babylon; not a good place to keep trusting God. Some of his compatriots would rather sing and question God: "how can we sing the Lord's song in a strange land?"(Ps.137:1-2). But for Daniel, the "strange land" did nothing to affect his faith in God. He was committed to praising his God forever and ever.

The challenges he faced did not change his God, because all wisdom and might belonged to him. You can change your gloomy day into a glorious dance right now, if you embrace a few potent truths Daniel is sharing with us in this passage of scripture. First, you have to know your limitations. We all have dreams, but when it comes to change in fulfilment of our dreams, the God-factor is very important. When the 2018 World Cup kicked off in Russia, all the participating teams aimed at winning the cup. They prepared very well, and played each game with high hopes of winning, but at the end of it all one team realised that dream; only France went home with the coveted trophy.

Learning to accept the sovereignty of God will help you accept the things you cannot change; and accepting what you cannot change, frees you from disappointment, frustration, and fear. God is faithful in all he does; unfortunately, he doesn't always do what we want him to do, and even sometimes allows what we would rather not want to experience. But that is exactly what makes him God; accountable only to himself. The second lesson is that God is absolutely in control of who gets promoted and who gets demoted; "he removes kings and raises up kings."

You may not like your pastor or his wife and may even feel you are better qualified to lead the church than he is; but friend, if God really called him to that position, stay a safe distance away from him. My best advice for you is to go ahead and start your own ministry, and let God use you to do what he has called you to do. If you pull down what God is raising up, you will end up sinking in quicksand. Don't turn your ambition into a weapon against what God seeks to do with anyone.

You cannot relegate what God is elevating and cannot demote the one God is promoting; that is impossible. God doesn't use man's criteria to determine who gets what. Relax, and wait for your time and season. When your time is ripe, the Lord will raise you up, and nothing and no one can bring you down. The peace of Christ be with you.

God bless you.

Safety in Authority

Judges 21:10, NKJV

In those days there was no king in Israel; everyone did what was right in his own eyes.

There is a lot to learn from children who grow up without parental mentorship. When you have not been in their shoes, you can easily be tempted to condemn and reject them, because the missing link of parental love and guidance make most of them behave in ways that do not conform to societal expectation. The reality is that when a human being lives in a "borderless" environment, his behavior and that of an ordinary animal in the forest, are not far apart. Anyone who has "no king" in his life can be reckless and foolish without feeling any sense of regret or remorse.

Indeed, when it comes to people who fall within this category, anything is possible. The scripture says when Israel had no king, "everyone did what was right in his own eyes." This brings to the fore, the need for every one of us to have authority figures in our lives.

Can you imagine what it would be like to have a society without any law enforcement agency, or governing structure? If you are not accountable to anyone and you are a king unto yourself, you are standing on very slippery ground, and need to do a quick realignment. It doesn't matter who you are, or the amount of knowledge you have accumulated, you are not safe without being accountable to someone, especially to God. No family, church, society can survive without checks and balances. God created the family with a defined leadership structure. It is the collapse of this divine arrangement that is creating most of the chaos we see in our communities today. Every day we see a push towards so-called rights and freedoms that break down leadership and accountability, we need to be reminded that we are creating an environment for lawless and chaos.

We are already becoming lawless to the extent that children are being encouraged to take decisions that need adult input and direction, without recourse to such counselling. The same is the case in the lives of those who do not have Jesus Christ as King of their lives. Anyone who is not subject to the kingship of Christ can do anything without restraint. Fact is, you cannot accept Jesus as your Lord and continue to live a reckless, sin-filled life; his indwelling Spirit will not give you that space. He will convict and bring you to order; gently, lovingly, and with a firm resolve to establish you in disciplined living. It is not a matter of punishment, but an issue of protection. When everyone in the home, church, and society subscribes to a set of governmental authority, there is safety for everyone, and that is what God desires for every one of us.

Accountability creates accessibility to true freedom, peace, and prosperity. Count yourself blessed to have the King of kings (Jesus Christ) in your life; you cannot miss out on his protection, because he will not let you mess up with his grace. He will guide and counsel you through his Word and Spirit. All you need to do is submit to his leadership, and you are there. Thank God for the privilege and blessing of belonging to his kingdom and be sure to bring others to this wonderful family of God where there is order and life for all.

God bless you.

Loyalty

2 Sam. 9:1,6-7, NIV

Now David said, "Is there still anyone who is left of the house of Saul, that I may show kindness...Now when Mephibosheth the son of Jonathan, the son of Saul, had come to David, he fell on his face and prostrated himself. Then David said, "Mephibosheth?" And he answered, "Here is your servant!" So David said to him, "Do not fear, for I will surely show you kindness for Jonathan your father's sake, and will restore to you all the land of Saul your grandfather; and you shall eat bread at my table continually."

What an extraordinary show of love and loyalty? David and Jonathan made a commitment of love and friendship to each other. When Jonathan's father, King Saul, went after David to kill him, the young man Jonathan protested and helped David to escape. For many years, David lived a miserable life because of just one man - King Saul. The continuous persecution could easily have turned David against the entire family of the king and neutralized his pledge of loyalty to Jonathan.

When he ascended the throne as king, David could have chosen to be bitter and vindictive, chasing everyone belonging to King Saul's bloodline out of town. Instead, he revisited his pledge to Jonathan, who at that time had died, and sought to show "kindness" to anyone belonging to King Saul's family. This is the man described in the Bible as a man after God's own heart. He had a heart we should all covet; a loyal heart that would not succumb to pressure or persecution. Such hearts are very difficult to find, even among professing Christians.

They are gifts from God that reflect the nature of God. They are hearts of gold full of goodness and mercy. We are God's workmanship and candidates of divine grace. We can manifest this kindness if we commit to be loyal like David. If we look for who we can bless, instead searching for who we can hurt, we can find this ministry that comes with great reward of joy, peace, and satisfaction. Oh, that the Spirit of Christ will circumcise our hearts, and give all of us this heart of the "man after God's own heart."

God bless you as you say a big amen to this prayer, and may he give you a peaceful day as you commit to being a loyal worker, spouse, pastor, child, friend, and partner.

God bless you.

Let Your Yes be Yes

Lu.6:46, NKJV

But why do you call me Me ' Lord, Lord,' and not do the things which I say?

When I was growing up as a child, my late dad used to say to me, "every liar is a thief, so always try as much as possible to say what you mean and mean what you say." That admonishing came when he suspected I was being economical with the truth. I used to wonder how he was able to figure out I was not telling the truth, but now I know better; age and experience gave him discernment more effective than a lie-detector.

The issue with saying one thing and doing something else is that it portrays you as a deceiver; one who is dishonest, disloyal, and dangerous to count on in any kind or form of relationship. When you call someone a friend and damages his reputation when his back is turned, you are more dangerous than one who tells him straight in the face, "I don't like you."

At least once you know someone doesn't like you, it gives you a correct perspective on how he sees you and what you can do to make amends, or the amount of space you must allow in that relationship. Jesus was appalled by the hypocrisy of his audience, because while professing to love God, they never obeyed his Word. Their worship was full of performance without power. It was lifeless religion devoid of spiritual reality. Beloved, it is easy to say, "I love you," than to manifest or walk the talk.

Relationships based only on our thoughts and emotions, have a very short lifespan. God demands total submission to his will from all who profess to serve him. He wants to be who you call him; either you call him "Lord" and let him be Lord or wait till you are ready before you make that confession. There is a measure of frustration in the question Jesus asked: "But why do you call Me 'Lord, Lord,' and do not do the things I say?" It shows a sense of frustration with that kind of behaviour.

The conclusion of the matter is that God expects us not only to confess him as Lord, but relate to him as such, no double-talk. Either he is your Lord, or he is not; the pass mark is in the doing, so say it and show it by your obedience. Let it permeate all your relationships. Don't surprise people by telling them they are nice and then run around telling everyone how nasty those same people are. That is a sign of integrity deficiency, and when you are known to be such a person, it will be difficult for others to trust you. Let your yes be yes, and your no be no.

God bless you.

Stay Away

Ps.106:34-35, NKJV

They did not destroy the peoples, concerning whom the LORD had commanded them, but they mingled with the gentiles and learned their works; They served their idols, which became a snare for them.

This narrative of Israel's disobedience to God's instruction not to mess with the Gentiles, reminds me of two important Bible personalities who took the same route and produced very unpleasant consequences - i.e., Samson and King Solomon. Samson thought the anointing on his life would be there no matter what he did or did not do, so he allowed his insatiable lust for women to drive him beyond the defined borders of his love-life.

He married the power of God with the passion of a playboy; and in the end, Samson the deliverer needed deliverance, and had to pray to die with his enemies. King Solomon "married many foreign wives" (1Ki.11:1) in complete disregard to God's law (Deut.1:15-17). At the time of his death, King Solomon had become a victim of his romantic adventures. His foreign wives made mincemeat of his wisdom and led him into worshipping their idols. Solomon, through his disobedience, laid the foundation for the division of the kingdom of Israel. Let's take warning from the lives of these otherwise great men of God; whenever God restricts us from doing something, it is not meant to deny us legitimate pleasure or fun. He knows what we don't know.

What appears to us on the surface as harmless, may have within it seeds of destruction that we may not be aware of. That is why it is necessary to pray about everything. How many times have you not met people and thought they would be good company, only to see them take advantage of you? The easiest way to avoid being swayed to the path of disobedience is to keep reminding yourself that God's law is not meant to punish you, but to protect you.

A nice guy may not necessarily be a good guy, and a beautiful lady may not necessarily be a God-fearing woman. If the God who created "the Gentiles" commands you to stay away from them, don't ask him why; just keep your distance from them. God does not owe you any explanation for what he tells you to do or not to do. If you trust in his goodness, you can walk in obedience. Saying yes to his Word, opens the door to grace and empowerment. The things you tolerate in contradiction to divine order, can become a snare of sin. Reject and avoid them.

God bless you.

Run in His Strength

Jer.12:5, NKJV

If you have run with the footmen, and they have wearied you, then how can you contend with horses? And if in the land of peace, in which you trusted, they have wearied you, then how will you do in the floodplain of the Jordan?

If you want to walk with God and enjoy it, then you have to get ready for some bumpy rides along the way. The prophet Jeremiah was becoming disillusioned with the experiences he was having in ministry and questioned why God was not sorting things out as quickly as he expected. God's response to Jeremiah revealed that the situation Jeremiah was complaining about, was going to get worse: "If you have run with the footmen, and they have wearied you, then how can you contend with horses?" You don't need to run with horses to know the difference in running with men, so the application here needs no clarification.

Sometimes we go through challenges we think are the worse, only to come out and face even bigger ones. What God is saying to us is that we should not concentrate on the intensity or depth of the bad times, but his power and grace that keeps us going whether we run with men or horses. There is nothing wrong with expressing our feelings and emotions when we hit rock bottom and don't know what to do with ourselves. God does understand our weaknesses and limitations. What he won't do is deceive us into believing that things are going to get better, when that is not what the future holds. Jesus said, "in this world you shall have tribulation."

The truth is that the world cannot deliver on what it promises, because it did not evolve. It was created, and as long as it is out of order with its creator, it will continue to experience "tribulation," which unfortunately will impact both believer and unbeliever. The good news, however, is that Jesus did not only warn about the tribulation but showed us how we can win over it. It all boils down to running in his strength because he overcame the world for us.

Be prepared to run your race, whether it is against men or horses. God will give you the strength to go through what you need to go through. Some things cannot be explained today, but as you trust and keep moving forward, "you will understand it better, by and by."

God bless you.

Walk Circumspectly

Eph.5:8,15-16, NKJV

For you were once darkness, but now you are light in the world...See then that you walk circumspectly, not as fools, but wise, redeeming the time, because the days are evil."

A report on a recent gay parade in London showed a picture of lesbians blocking transgender females from participating in the celebration. Their reason was that transgender was a threat to their homosexuality. Pedophiles are now asking for their "rights" to be respected, because it is their sexual orientation to fall in love with children. This is just the beginning of interesting times to come, if they are not already here. What went round is coming round. The lion society raised as a pet, is beginning to devour its master. For too long, we have chosen to call evil good, and defined wrong as right.

The key word for keeping the floodgates of seduction and immorality open is "tolerance." Anyone who takes a stand for the Word of God, relative to righteousness, is branded as "intolerant." In an attempt to avoid this tag, you can compromise your faith to the extent of not being able to show any difference between your past and your present. The truth, however, is that you cannot claim to be a child of the Light and live in sin. Light and darkness have nothing in common. Indeed, they are like parallel lines; they do not meet.

To live in sin and feel good about it, is evidence of an unregenerate mind. It is like walking naked and claiming you are wearing clothes. The claim doesn't change the fact of your nakedness. As a child of God, you must have made a deliberate, conscious, and conscientious decision to reject your old way of life and receive the new life Christ offers. You have been moved out of Satan's darkness into God's marvelous light and owe no one apology for living a God-honouring life.

The Word of God says you have a choice between walking "circumspectly" (carefully and wisdom) or as a fool. This simply means, you either live out your faith in holiness according to God's Word, or you fool yourself by living in sin and thinking it's alright with God. There is no middle ground between heaven and hell, so declare your stand by producing fruit that befit repentance, "because "the days are evil."

God bless you.

He Hears

1 Jn.5:14, NKJV

Now this is the confidence that we have in Him, that if we ask anything according to His will, He hears us.

The scripture says that "if we ask anything according to His (God's) will, He hears us." Literally speaking, God hears every prayer we pray. Whatever we ask him to do for us, gets his immediate attention. However, for God to ACT on our requests, demand our asking "according to His will." There is an "if" clause to contend with; we can be sure of God's positive response "if we ask anything according to His will."

This presupposes that you cannot have answers to your prayers just because you are a child of God, or are involved in church activities etc. No. You must pray according to the will of God; and the only way to know the will of God regarding what you are asking of him, is knowledge of the Word of God and leading of the Holy Spirit. There is no subject under the sun that the Bible does not address directly or indirectly, and there is nothing concerning you that the Holy Spirit does not know.

It is therefore your responsibility to study the Word of God concerning the need you want to pray about. Let's figure out an example: If you want to know whether it is okay for you to pray and ask God to give you a partner of the same sex to marry, check from the Bible. If the Bible says God approves of same-sex marriage, go ahead and ask him. The Bible is not a textbook. It is God's Word. It is a revelation of the Will of God. If you know His Word, you know His Will, and can go ahead and ask accordingly. Remember, when you are dealing with God, you don't set the rules.

The reason is simple: He is the boss, and you are his subordinate. If you don't submit to his Word, then you can never know His Will. God loves you, but that love has no room for giving you anything and everything you ask, even when it runs counter to His revealed Will for your life. Jesus prayed in Gethsemane and asked that "if it were possible" the suffering he was going to face be lifted. The request was outside the Will of the Father so there was no response.

The Father heard, but did not "hear" (by way of response). When Jesus eventually yielded and added "thy Will be done" to the prayer, scripture says God sent an angel to strengthen him. That is what happens when the Will of God is "hurting" us, and we somehow submit to him; he empowers us to endure. Pray according to God's Will, and you can be assured that if he doesn't give you the answer immediately, he will give you grace to survive the long night.

God bless you.

Have Faith in God

Mk.11:22, NKJV

Jesus said to them, "Have faith in God."

Misplaced faith will always lead to disappointment. It makes a world of difference who we choose to believe. David observed how some trust in chariots and others in horses, but he chose to put his trust in the Lord. His position was that when he went to war, the ultimate decider of the outcome was not the weapons, but the God of Israel. Jesus admonishes is to do same; to have faith IN GOD. It is easy to think we are trusting God, when in fact our faith may be in men. Early in my walk with the Lord, his Spirit taught me how to depend on him, and trust him to meet my daily needs.

It was a whole school in itself. I faltered and failed many times, but through the help of the Holy Spirit I have come very far and am so grateful for the lessons learnt. When your faith is in God, you save yourself a lot of the crisis that comes with disappointment from fellow men. I have learnt that when someone promises to do something for me, that promise is subject to divine help, supply, and approval. God has to give to the person the resources, and also the will to fulfill the promise made. If the promise fails, I don't get upset with the person. I find an opportunity to pray for him or her. Maybe he genuinely does not have to give, or his lips run ahead of his thoughts. Both ways, he needs my prayer, not my chastisement.

You may be very bitter about something relating to a failed promise. That bitterness will not do you any good. Refocus your faith on God, because he alone has the power to promise and fulfill without fail. When you don't see any light at the end of the tunnel, there is still a God who you can trust to work things out. Have faith in God. Learn all the lessons you need to learn while you go through the disappointments. There is a positive side to every negative experience, and your faith in God can be strengthened through the failed promises of men.

Nothing good or bad can come to you as a child of God, without his endorsement. The devil could not touch Job without God's permission; even so shall his purpose for your life find expression and fulfillment in whoever he chooses. Have faith in God, because he is good, and his mercies endures forever.

God bless you.

Don't Live in Fear

Job 3:25, NKJV

For the thing I greatly feared has come upon me, and what I dreaded has happened to me.

Take a few minutes and ask yourself the question, "what do I fear the most?" The answer to this question can inform the rest of your life, depending on how willing you are to confront the fear and deal with it. Job confessed that he had harbored the fear of losing everything long before he had that experience. In context, we know what Job did not know at the time; that Satan was the real reason for his suffering. However, we want to examine Job's statement here in isolation and apply it to our lives. Look into the history of your past, and you will be amazed how many negative events you triggered through fear.

Someone might say, "everyone in my family suffered this fate, and so I know it's just a matter of time and I will go through the same experience." That is faith in reverse gear. You have faith in that which you know as a fact and have no room to believe in God's truth that with him all things are possible. The facts you accumulate cannot nullify or change the truth of God's Word. Fear, like faith, is a seed; if you sow it, you will reap it. Fear has power to drive you where you are not destined to be. Those who achieve great feats, are those who refuse to be dominated by fear. They don't wait for their fears to go away.

They move on despite their fears. The things we greatly fear come to pass because we end up believing in our fears, and so it becomes a matter of "as your faith so be it unto you." You are not going to sink because everyone is sinking. No, don't believe that lie. See yourself a survivor, and one destined to change the status quo. Act out your faith. When fear says, "sit down," you don't sit, you stand up. Praise God and stop pleading with the devil.

That is what will eventually break the yoke of fear. God is not dead. The things you greatly fear are not realities. Enjoy today, and allow the Lord who knows tomorrow, to take care of tomorrow.

God bless you.

Gratitude

Esther 4:4, NKJV

So Esther's maids and eunuchs came and told her, and the queen was deeply distressed. Then she sent garments to clothe Mordecai and take his sackcloth away from him...

Gratitude is a virtue that proceeds from loyal hearts. Esther would never have come anywhere near royalty without the mentoring, guidance, inspiration, and counsel of Mordecai. When she heard from her privileged position that the man who God used to make her queen was wearing sackcloth, "she sent garments to cloth Mordecai". Think about this act of gratitude for a moment. What other option did Esther have? She could have conveniently ignored Mordecai and pretended no one told her anything about Mordecai's state. Esther could have chosen the path of ingratitude and declared, "each man for himself and God for us all."

It would be choosing not to do what only she could do to bring relief to the old man's dilemma. There are people living with pain in their hearts due to the negative response they have had from friends and family they sacrificed for, and who in their own times of need turned their backs on them. It must be said here that some of these attitudes of ingratitude are without excuse. How can you call yourself a child of God and aim verbal "bullets" at someone God used once to help you? It gets murkier when instead of providing appropriate "garment" to cover the shame of our benefactors, we not only turn a blind eye to their "sackcloth" but go on the rampage telling everyone and anyone who cares to give us audience, all the bad things we claim to know about them.

You need to be at the receiving end of ingratitude to grasp the depth of the emotional pain it leaves on its victims. It is much easier getting a physical wound to heal than an emotional pain to subside. Esther is pointing us to a positive direction. She is telling us to remember those who have impacted our lives positively when it lies in our power to help them in their times of need. Showing gratitude should not cost us a fortune. Just a phone call, a written note, a visit, and you fulfill an obligation that can remove the "sackcloth" of your Mordecai. For those of us whose stock-in-trade is stripping people who helped us in the past naked, the principle of sowing and reaping stares us in the face. This is not a game of lottery.

It is a fact of life; you reap what you sow, and sometimes you do so with interest. Esther's show of gratitude to Mordecai initiated a process that did not only strengthen her relationship with her mentor but saved a whole nation. Please if you don't provide a garment for your Mordecai, don't take away his sackcloth (destroy his reputation). Be grateful to those who God has used to help you in your journey of life. You know the "bad" things you know about them because they gave you space you did not deserve in their lives.

Remember those same "bad" people were once instruments and channels God used to help you. Be grateful, and it will command unusual blessings on your life.

God bless you.

Move on to Where You are Accepted

Acts 6:1, NIV

In those days when the number of disciples was increasing, the Grecian Jews among them complained against the Hebraic Jews because their widows were being overlooked in the daily distribution of food.

Growth and prosperity have their peculiar challenges. Wherever people gather, there is always bound to be complaints. Discrimination is one of the products of our carnal nature. Many parents (if not all) have favorites among their children, even though they try so hard not to admit that failure. Jacob's mother showed partiality towards Esau and helped Jacob to steal his brother's blessing. One of the reasons for the persecution of Joseph by his brothers was the result of the preferential treatment they saw their father give to Joseph.

Here is the truth we have to contend with: It is unrealistic to expect everyone to accept you the same way they accept others. Fallen human nature does not guarantee that you will be treated fairly, respectfully, and with dignity by everyone. You must learn how to live above being dragged into unnecessary arguments and fights. Walk away from those who demonize and demoralize you; they are not worth your time and attention. If by some necessity you must be where they are, then you have to train your mind to concentrate on who God says you are, not what they think or say about you.

You are your own worst enemy if you keep trying to live to meet the standards set by others. It can get worse when your circle of relationship grows. The disciples never had that kind of sectional crisis until the Church began to grow. It was then that the differences began to show; "tribal" issues surfaced, and discrimination became the order of the day. How did the apostles resolve the problem? Bible says they delegated responsibility to others who were "full of the Spirit and wisdom" (v.3).

You cannot get it any other way. Unless you are dealing with people who are "full of the Spirit and wisdom," you must forget about being treated with fairness and dignity. And don't stretch it too far by assuming that church folks cannot treat you as bad as unbelievers do. What is recorded in Acts 6:1 took place in a Spirit-filled Church. There is no place on earth that you can find acceptance from every single person you meet, but the good news is that there will always be those who will identify with you in every way.

Jesus once told his disciples that when they go to a place to preach the gospel and they are not received by the people, they should walk away. If you are not being accepted where you are, stop trying to be accepted. Move on.

God bless you.

Commit to being Faithful

1Chron. 10:13, NKJV

So Saul died for his unfaithfulness which he had committed against the LORD, because he did not keep the word of the LORD, and also because he consulted a medium for guidance.

This scripture suggests to me that King Saul died when he should not have died. Israel's first king was a man of self will. Saul offered sacrifices when he knew it was not his assignment to offer sacrifices. His kingship was marked with a comedy of errors, and when God rejected him and will not answer him, Saul sought the services of a medium in complete disregard to God's instructions to the nation of Israel not to dabble in occultism.

In the end, he died for these two reasons (according to 1Chron.10:13); first for his unfaithfulness, and secondly for consulting a medium for guidance. These are the same issues confronting all of us today. We do things we wouldn't do if God were to be physically present with us. We have dual personalities; one that shows up when we know there is someone watching or listening, and the other comes of the bench when we are in a "safe corner" where nobody knows who we are, or where we are coming from. Faithfulness does not begin in another person's presence. Faithfulness is an internal state.

If it is on the inside, it will manifest on the outside. If you are not faithful to yourself, you cannot be faithful to anyone else. You do what you do because of who you are. Those who are faithful to God, their spouses, families, friends, and other associates are faithful because they commit to be faithful. If Saul had stayed faithful to God despite the challenges he faced, there would have been no need to go consulting mediums. Anytime we feel empty and alienated from the Lord, we should begin with some self-examination and repentance.

Sometimes our feelings can deceive us into thinking we have gone too far for God to forgive us. That is a lie from the pit of hell. God cherishes his relationship with you so much he has given you his Spirit to guide you "into all truth." Consulting mediums, who parade themselves in the garb of prophets, is a denial of Christ. Be faithful to God and be careful who you allow to speak into your life, so you don't die for all the wrong reasons like Saul.

God bless you.

Your life is in the hands of God

Jn.19:10-11, GNB

Pilate said to him, "You will not speak to me? Remember, I have authority to set you free and also to have you crucified." Jesus answered, "You have authority over me only because it was given to you by God. So the man who handed me over to you is guilty of a worse sin."

What a difference it will make in our lives if we can believe that no human being has power to interfere with our divine destiny if we live within the confines of grace and obedience. Pilate did not understand the dynamics of the authority vested in him by God. His claim of having the authority to either set the Lord free or crucify Him was an empty boast. Jesus was quick to correct him by pointing to the real source of authority, who is the Everlasting God.

Indeed, when Pilate's so-called authority was tested by the crowd who threatened to report him to Rome as enemy of the emperor for not handling over Jesus to be crucified, he caved in and yielded to their request, even though he had earlier pronounced a "not guilty" verdict on Jesus. In all of this, we, as children of God should learn that no one has authority to change, undermine, reverse, or stop what God has purposed for our lives. The people God sets over us as governing authorities in the home, church, government, work place etc., exercise authority delegated to them by God, and are accountable to God.

The reason we respect them is because we have committed to obeying God. When any of these delegated authorities use their position to threaten, intimidate, dominate, manipulate, exploit, abuse, or cheat those under their authority, they have set themselves at loggerheads with God. What you and I need to understand is that our very lives are under the watchful eyes of Christ. Even when Satan and his demons attack us and are able to inflict wounds and pain, God's Presence in our lives will not let them go beyond defined limits. The story of Job is a typical example. Satan was given "permission" to do the things he did to Job. He couldn't have done it without divine permission.

It may well be that something or someone has held you in "captivity" for so long and driven you to a point where you are beginning to believe you are at his or her mercy. It may be some spiritual, physical, emotional, or financial crisis that has become a Pilate sitting in judgment over you, and releasing a daily dose of pain, fear, and worry into your brain. You are so worn out believing for change, you now consider that thing or person the decider of your fate. The Lord wants you to know you are not a victim of circumstances beyond your control. The one who decides whether you breakthrough or breakdown is God.

All power belongs to Jesus. You can have peace in the midst of all the threats you face from men and circumstances, if you have the Jesus-perspective that God has the final say. Don't allow yourself to be frustrated any longer by a Pilate. Your life is in the hands of God, and only he decides whether you live or die; and even if he allows them to crucify you, it is only because he wants to glorify you through resurrection into a better life. Block your ears to the jeers of the crowd, and the boastful threats of Pilate. Keep your eyes on Jesus, and he will see you through the storm.

God bless you.

Preparation Precedes Manifestation

Lu. 22:14, GNB

When the hour came, Jesus took his place at the table with the apostles.

Our God is a God of timing. You may not be where you want to be, but that does not mean you are a failure. You are not. You are who God says you are. David said in Psalm 23:5 that God has laid a table before you in "the presence of your enemies."

The challenge is how to reconcile your present predicament with David's confession of faith. The answer is here in Lu.22:14, "When the hour came, Jesus took his place at the table with his apostles." You don't take your "place" before your hour comes. You take your seat when your hour comes.

Preparation always must precede manifestation. Don't yield to the devil's lies about your situation being hopeless, because even if it is hopeless, thank God you are not helpless. Bible says the Lord himself is our helper in times of trouble.

You have an empty seat prepared for you; and like Jesus, when your hour comes, all things will work together to bring you to your seat. The seating position is a restful place, where your pain, struggles, burdens, fears and lack, are effectively neutralized.

It is a position of anticipation and expectations of divine provision. This is the confidence that you should have henceforth; your standing alone is not a finality. You have a chair at the table of God's feast, and your hour is coming when you will be counted among those seated.

God bless you.

God's Ministry is About Service

Jn. 4:34, GNB

My food, Jesus said to them, is to obey the will of the one who sent me and to finish the work he gave me to do.

We pay attention to food when we are hungry, so the truth Jesus is putting across using food as analogy is very simple; the Master is saying that nothing satisfies his hunger more than doing what the Father wanted him to accomplish at any given moment of his life on earth. His entire earthly life hinged on striving "to obey the will of the one who sent" him, and to "finish the work he gave" him to do.

Three things stand out here: first is his acknowledgment of being sent by a higher authority (his Father). He was in a position of utter submission to that authority, and never in contention for recognition. That is where many of us called into God's work fall flat; we clamor for "respect" and applause, and when we don't get it, we DEMAND it by fair or foul means. We interpret leadership to mean ownership and rulership, so when God gives us space to lead his flock, we believe wrongly that we are in that privileged position because we earned it and deserve it, and so everyone should bow to us. You Got it wrong!!

A leader in God's kingdom is a MESSENGER not a MANAGER; so if you are in it, that is who you are. You are no bigger than your assignment, and your assignment is to serve, not to be served. Check the Holy Book and you find Jesus stating clearly that he did not come to be served, but to serve and LAY DOWN HIS LIFE for the flock. If you cannot lay it down for his sheep, he cannot lift you up for his glory. Indeed, you have no business being in ministry until you come to accept the reality that it is all about serving and not being served.

God wants shepherds, not butchers. The second essential truth is that Jesus was fully committed to obeying the Father. There was no way he was going to question what was demanded of him. He may not like it, but he was going to do it anyway. He may not enjoy it, but he was going to endure it anyway. He may not approve of it, but he was going to accept it anyway. If the Father commands it, he was going to obey him. This, beloved, is what it means to be a follower of Christ, obeying his Word, and submitting to his will.

The third on his menu card was "to finish the work he gave me to do." It is better not to run in this race, than to run and quit. One of my favorite scriptures is in 2 Tim.4:7 where Apostle Paul penned these words to his young disciple Timothy: "I have done my best in the race, I have run the full distance, and I have kept the faith" (GNB).

The good news is that we are not running forever. Each of us will end our race someday. Let us run with the goal in view. Let us run according to the rules set by God. Let us stay committed, humble, and faithful to the end; and may the grace of our Lord Jesus Christ help us all.

God bless you.

Jesus' Love Never Fails

Is. 49:15, KJV

Can a woman forget her sucking child, that she should not have compassion on the son of her womb? Yea, they may forget, yet will I not forget thee.

I cannot tell exactly why the celebration of Father's Day is comparatively so drab and lacks the excitement and euphoria of Mother's Day. All I know is that the difference between the two celebrations is huge. Is.49:15 seems to suggest an answer. The woman is credited with a unique kind of love for her children. Here the Bible put a rhetorical question as to whether it is possible for a woman to forget a child she bears after going through the painful experience of pregnancy and childbirth.

The idea is that the bond between children and their mothers is generally stronger because of an attachment that begins right from conception. While this is true with most women, God points to a limitation to this seemingly extraordinary love a woman has for her child; declaring that sometimes they "forget" their own children, but He (Jehovah) ALWAYS has us in mind. Our ministry cares for destitute children and I know women who do not care a hoot what happens to their own children. They may not hate them, but they do not want them either.

If the woman, therefore, is the ultimate expression of human love, then we see how much our best falls short of God's least. If you desire love that is unwavering, unshakable, unchanging, and unlimited, look beyond every human love. It doesn't have what it takes to be consistent in providing spiritual, emotional, psychological, and physical satisfaction. Expecting too much from any human relationship can make room for you to be hurt and become resentful. Go for the agape love of Christ. He is the only One you can trust to understand you and do something about you and your situation.

Someone may have promised to marry you, support you in school, or help you out of a crisis and suddenly walked out on you. You thought it shouldn't have happened because he/she "loved" you so much - maybe even too much to cheat on you or lie to you. Well, it did happen, and the lesson must be learnt; that there is no human promise that is 100 percent full proof. Your life doesn't have to stop at the junction of disappointment. Take the "right turn" towards God. He is the greatest dad and mum, and every day is His day because He alone remembers you 24/7. Live a life of trusting Him always in all ways. You will never regret it. Jesus Christ never fails.

God bless you.

Have Realistic Expectations of Your Relationships

1Chron. 27:32-34, GNB

Jonathan, King David's uncle, was a skillful adviser and scholar. He and Jehiel son of Hachmoni were in charge of the education of the king's sons. Ahitophel was adviser to the king, and Hushai the Architect was the king's friend and counselor. After Ahitophel died, Abiathar and Jehoada son of Benaiah became advisers. Joab was commander of the royal army.

You cannot be everything to everyone, and everyone cannot relate to you at all levels at one and the same time. King David began his ascension to the throne under very challenging circumstances. In the process, he learnt to deal with different classes of people. When he eventually became king, he knew by experiential knowledge who to allow into his circle of friends, who to appoint as counselor, who was competent to educate his children, who should be his army commander and so on and so forth.

It takes careful observation, knowledge, discernment, and diligence, to raise a competent team like David did. For those of us in leadership, this is something vital to our success. Parents should know the abilities and capabilities of each of their children to avoid making equal demands on all of them. Your eldest child may excel in Mathematics, the youngest may not do so well in Math, but that does not make him less intelligent than his elder sibling. Where one is weak, the other may be strong. Prejudice does not allow us to see the gifts and talents of our children. Sometimes as a parent you want all your children to pursue a profession of your preferred choice, forgetting that each has his own peculiar and divinely ordained gifts.

Let people do what they enjoy doing, what they are gifted in, and put them in areas where they are trained. We all perform at our maximum best when we do what we love to do. It is unfair to lump everyone in your team together and expect all of them to be good at everything. If you want good results, prayerfully seek for God's leading to know your personal strengths and weaknesses. Do not accept any position or assignment you are not comfortable doing, unless you are sure God wants to use it to prepare you for the next level.

Jealousy, pride, and egocentrism sometimes push us to try and do what we are simply not called to do. The fact that you have been in King David's circle for a long time doesn't mean you have to be counted among his friends and confidants. If your role is to educate his children, that's what you must do. The fact that you have been in a church since its establishment doesn't qualify you to preach. Manage your relationships with diligence, intelligence, discernment, and consideration for each person's God-given abilities and training.

Unrealistic expectations create distractions, delays, and confusion. David set us a good example of orderliness at all levels of relationship. Let us manage our expectations within the context of our own abilities, that of those we have the privilege to serve, and most especially those who look up to us as parents and leaders.

God bless you.

Thank God for Each Day

Ps. 3:6-7, NKJV

I lay down and slept; I awoke, for the LORD sustained me. I will not be afraid of ten thousands of people who have set themselves against me all around.

The dawn of each new day is an opportunity to thank God for his goodness. Sleep is a rehearsal of death. Not everyone who went to bed last night like we all did, had the privilege to wake up. It is not because they were more evil than anyone else. It is because God decided it was time for them to exit this life. One day you and I will also sleep and not wake up; but that day is not here yet, and so we have to acknowledge with joy the grace given us to live to see today. We can get so used to going to bed at night and waking up in the morning that we forget the Person and Power that sustains us through that cycle.

We all go to bed with our minds set on waking up in the morning as if it is a matter of course. David wrote this psalm when he fled from his son Absalom, who had overthrown his father in a palace coup. Sleeping every night without knowing whether Absalom had planned to attack him or not was not easy. However, the deposed king had to trust God and sleep without fear of what was likely to happen in the night. Reviewing his circumstances, and how he had been able to survive in the wilderness, David attributed his survival to Jehovah. His conclusion was that if the Lord had sustained him each night, then there was nothing and no one who could harm him.

He turned what was meant to torment him into a song of praise. He saw what God was doing in his frustrating circumstances and was not going to allow the devil to cage him in fear. Deal with your fears by reflecting on how far God has brought you. If you don't live a life of trusting God , you are going to be miserable and unhappy forever and ever. God wants you to trust him. The gift of life he has given you today is priceless. What you lack in health and wealth, God is able to provide in due time and season. Your starting point is to smile at the storm.

The Holy Spirit's power is unlocked in you when you begin to thank God for the gift of each new day. If God has finished with you and has no use for you here today, you wouldn't have lived to see this moment. There may be "thousands of people" who have set themselves against you, but let them continue to rage and rant, you are covered. Instead of looking at the "thousands," focus on Jesus. Let thousands of setbacks bring it on; your back is covered. Your life is an unfinished business. No one can stop what God has purposed to do with you and through you. Whether in the palace or in the wilderness, God is there for you, and will be with you. Confront your fears by confessing your faith.

God bless you.

The Spirit is Poured out on You

Joel 2:28-29, NKJV

And it shall come to pass afterward that I will pour out My Spirit on all flesh; your sons and your daughters shall prophesy, your old men shall dream dreams, your young men shall see visions. And also on My men servants and on My maidservants I will pour out My Spirit in those days.

God is a promise keeper. Many years before the outpouring of the Holy Spirit on the day of Pentecost, God promised through the prophet Joel that he was going to phase out the practice of putting his Spirit in a selected minority, and "pour out" on all flesh instead. It might hurt the Lord to see some of us still believing that God has favorites, and that unless we kowtow to them, we cannot do anything about our lives and challenges. When you receive Jesus Christ as your Lord and personal Saviour, the same Holy Spirit who convicted you to repent, is released in all his fullness to empower you to live a victorious Christian life.

You have no excuse to walk in defeat and hopelessness. God takes you to a "garden of Eden" experience where he communicates with you at a personal level. If he should speak to you through another person, it should be an exception not the rule; and what comes to you as prophesy from another person is most likely to confirm something God has already told you about or to provide clarity regarding his purpose for your life. Let me share with you my personal convictions about some of the things God is not likely to say or do outside of his indwelling Spirit.

God will not send someone else to come and tell you the man or woman you should marry or should have married. God will never tell your pastor, bishop, or prophet to tell you to buy him a car before he blesses you, when you don't have enough money in your pocket for your bus ticket. Don't get me wrong; you can give whatever you desire to give to whoever is your spiritual mentor, but the reason and condition should not be because it is conditional to your blessing. Yes, God promises to bless our giving, but the giving should be out of your freewill. If God wants you to give to your pastor or prophet, the Holy Spirit will prompt you to do it without threats or pressure.

You honour God by paying attention to the leading of his Spirit, and that is the way to experiencing more of his presence and power. God wants to have deep, intimate relationship with you. He is Spirit and can best connect to you at a spiritual level, and that is why he has not "'sprinkled" his Spirit but "poured out" himself into us. It is your time to prophesy (speak forth the Word of God) into your life, your family, your ministry, and the world at large. Nobody can say anything more prophetic and positive about your life than the Holy Spirit.

Spend time listening to his voice inside of you. Do not run around looking for prophets to tell you what to eat and where to go. If God wants to speak to you through a prophet, nothing can stop him from doing so. This is the day of fulfilment of Joel's prophecy; the Spirit is poured out on ALL FLESH, including you. Rise up and live in the now, believing what God has said, and flowing in his power and anointing.

God bless you.

Live Like You're Saved

1Jn. 4:7-8, NKJV

Little children let no one deceive you. He who practices righteousness is righteous, just as He is righteous. He who sins is of the devil, for the devil has sinned from the beginning. For this purpose the Son of God was manifested, that He might destroy the works of the devil.

Deception is when you are tricked into believing someone or something is what it is not. Here is a warning that suggests to us the possibility of being deceived, and the intention of the deceiver to make us believe there is no difference between one who lives in sin, and one who pursues righteousness. If anyone can get you to believe that it doesn't matter how you live because you are saved and already on your way to heaven, there will be no incentive for you to live a righteous life. He has taken away from you any appetite to live a God-honoring life.

The truth we glimpse from this admonition is that our spiritual rebirth creates in us a fountain of life that is supposed to overflow in right attitude, right words, right actions. You are born-again, yes; but what you manifest, by way of deeds and words, define whether you belong to God or the devil. Jesus said a tree can only produce its kind. The fruit identifies the tree. Don't buy into the lie that you can live anyhow because we are in a dispensation of grace. You have a responsibility to show the world that it is possible to live a life of godliness despite the temptations, pressures, and challenges.

It is not in your own strength that you stand and overcome the things that constantly seek to distract you from committing to pursue righteousness. The same grace that brought you to a saving knowledge of Christ, is still available to help you every day and every hour. Falling into sin should be an exception, not the rule. You cannot abide in Christ and continue living in sin. It defiles you, weakens your relationship with the Holy Spirit, and destroys your testimony.

God is not surprised because you fell into sin, but he is not pleased when you do not repent and come out of it because you believe his grace will take care of you. That's where deception comes into play. God's purpose for sending Christ is to "destroy the works of the devil"; which is nothing else but sin. Live for Christ. Live for truth. Live as light; never consciously doing anything to devalue the value God has placed on you. If ever you fall into sin, repent, and get out of it.

God bless you.

Contend for the Truth

Jude 1:3-4, NIV

Dear friends, although I was very eager to write to you about the salvation we share, I felt I had to write and urge you to contend for the faith that was once for all entrusted to the saints. For certain men whose condemnation was written about long ago have secretly slipped in among you. They are godless men, who change the grace of our God into a license for immorality and deny Jesus Christ our only Savior and Lord.

A lot is happening around us today that calls for every true believing Christian to rise up and "contend for the faith." The greatest disservice and damage you and I can do to the course of Christ and his kingdom is to remain silent and allow "wolves in sheep-skin" to devour God's flock. The Word of God doesn't teach that, and for those who think serving God is minding your own business and being politically correct, you need to revisit the ministry of Jesus Christ on earth.

He was never popular with governing authorities and the clergy. Indeed, Jesus never tried to impress them or "improve" his doctrine to get their approval. When long-robed Pharisees, Sadducees, Scribes, and their ilk came to his meetings and crossed the line, Jesus was not slow at all in calling them "fools and hypocrites." He never meant to insult them, he only meant to instruct them. When truth is not told, the lie gains prominence and acceptance. God is expecting us to be bold and courageous in denouncing those bent on trampling on the salvation message for their personal gain.

Someone has rightly said that when good men decide to do nothing, evil will rule and dominate. The Church must purge itself of charlatans, and not only pray and preach prosperity, but in the same vociferous voice preach against immorality in both pulpit and pew. There is a Middle Eastern country financing the growth of a particular religion in our country today. Their places of worship are being planted in our schools, police stations, offices, and gas filling stations. Meanwhile, the so-called leaders of the Church feel greatly honored to be at table with them and celebrate their god and enjoy their goodies.

On the flip side, we are seeing too many self-appointed prophets turning the House of God into a place of comedy and merchandise. I wish there were no scripture commanding us to "contend for the faith," then I would have kept a safe distance from tackling this issue; but as long as God's Word commands it, I will comply. If the apostles and martyrs of our faith had not stood up for what they believed, we would not have come to know anything about the wonderful grace God offers in Christ.

Let us be deliberate in speaking against anything, everything, and anyone "who change the grace of our God into a license for immorality and deny Jesus Christ our only Sovereign Lord." It is not hate speech. It is a healing balm. Preach it in love, without fear or malice. We are called OUT of the WORLD, into GOD'S WORD. Contend for truth, and you be fulfilling the course of Christ.

God bless you.

Jesus Christ, the Only Way

Col. 1:15,17, GNB

Christ is the visible likeness of the invisible God. He is the first-born Son, superior to all created things...Christ existed before all things, and in union with him all things have their proper place.

For the fear of being tagged intolerant or arrogant, or both, we see a certain trend developing in our country which clearly contradicts and compromises the Great Commission of Christ to the Church. Why would one called by God to preach the saving grace of Christ, stand on the platform of another religious faith and applaud their worship? Beloved, this is not an invitation to condemn another person's belief; that is not right and fair, it is a caution not to condone error and mislead innocent souls to hell.

Let's think about this for a moment: What would the apostle Paul have done, given the same platform and opportunity? If we continue to pamper the whims and caprices of politicians at the expense of the gospel, we will wake up one day to find the Church confined to silence. Jesus Christ is the only Saviour of the world. He has no equal because he is God. Bible says, "he existed before all things." If that is not okay with some people, it is squarely within their right, but that should not infringe on your right to also announce your faith.

For a professed believer in Christ to go public and confess the name of another person's god, is a betrayal of the course and call of Christ. Friends, it hurts me to say this, but such behaviour by the clergy is plain spiritual prostitution. We are muddying the waters and confusing our children. Why have we become so obsessed with power, money, and popularity, that we have become virtually insensitive to the rate at which souls are dying without knowledge of Christ?

Those who are not prepared to obey the Bible and exalt Christ as Lord and Saviour before unbelieving politicians, be they presidents or paupers, have no business portraying themselves as ministers of the gospel, and preachers of its truth. You cannot demean Christ to promote your ego. He did not die for us to do politics with his blood. Please, please, please, let's get serious and stand up for the truth. Jesus Christ is God, not an ordinary prophet. Paul writing to the Corinthian church declared, "we preach Christ, and him crucified." That's a complete summary of the assignment we have been given. Nothing more, nothing less.

Let us stop the confusion, pollution, and deception. Jesus Christ is not a way: He is THE ONLY WAY. Preach it, and you will save some lost souls. Of course, some might take offence, but who cares? It is their choice, and we can pray for them to come to a knowledge of the truth. It does not change the truth, because Jesus Christ is THE TRUTH, THE WAY, AND THE LIFE.

God bless you.

Honest Fathers

Prov. 19:7, GNB

Children are fortunate if they have a father who is honest and does what is right.

King David is touted as the greatest of the kings of Israel. He loved God and was loved by God. The Lord blessed him and made him a point of reference and measuring rod for every single king that reigned after him, in terms of his devotion and commitment to God. However, David showed gross dishonesty when he seduced the wife of one of his soldiers and plotted his death, after he saw that he had impregnated Uriah's wife.

God at that point was so disappointed with David that he pronounced a curse which impacted his family negatively. David's children had a father who loved the Lord so much, but whose dishonesty in his dealings with one who had sacrificed to go to war to defend the nation cost them dearly. David's lack of self-control when it came to issues of women was evident in his son Solomon. Solomon took his love for women beyond the borders of Israel, marrying 300 wives and having 700 concubines, effectively watering the seed of disintegration sown by his father David.

There is a lot we can learn from this particular mistake David made, but the one relevant to today's scripture is the impact we can have on children as adults, fathers, mothers, pastors, teachers et al. The prospects and problems of tomorrow's world are in today's adult behavior. That is why you have to make quality time with your children a priority. Children learn by imitation. They are open receptacles with little or no resistance. The one who spends most time with your kids, influences them the most. It will be in your own interest to give them more of yourself and less material stuff, than vice versa.

Beware of the power of technology, and don't allow it to steal away your social life as a family. When you are around your children, encourage them to put off the phone and computer and talk and laugh with you. Let your house be a home; and while away from home, act responsibly, being careful to do right and be honest. Remember the spiritual and emotional harm you visit on your innocent children if you are publicly exposed for inappropriate behavior.

It is a blessing to have "a father who is honest and does what is right." Every parent, pastor, teacher, and all others in leadership position should consider this a challenge, and work towards making it a reality in our lives.

God bless you.

Our Glory is in our Unity

Jn. 17:22-23, NIV

I have given them the glory that you gave me, that they may one as we are one: I in them and you in me. May they be brought to complete unity to let the world know that you sent me and have loved them as you have loved me.

Do we as THE CHURCH (Christ's Body) recognize how unique we are as individuals and as a corporate body? If we really do, then we should be rejoicing all the time and not be in doubt and fear. In this scripture, Jesus speaks of having given us "the glory" that the Father gave him. And he has done that for a purpose; "that they may be one has we are one." The goal of the glory is to unite us as One Body in Christ. Jesus has not given us his glory for self-aggrandizement. His glory should not divide us, but rather unite us.

The power-struggle and lack of submission to each other in our homes and churches is a bad advertisement of who we are in Christ. God wants you to know that you are a Container of Divine Glory. You may not have the best physical appearance, but your spiritual statistics are wonderful and perfect in beauty. You did not buy any factory manufactured makeup to attain that glory. Jesus Christ decided he wanted you to have it at his expense. He paid with his blood so you can possess the same measure of glory the Father gave him.

Take up the burden that comes with the blessing. Be a unifier. Avail yourself to be used as a channel to unite the family of God (the church) and your home. In Acts 4 we see how powerful the Church proved to be as a result of unity among the believers. Jesus made clear that "a house divided against itself cannot stand" (Mk.3:25). If you've been wondering why the Church of Jesus Christ is not walking in the same power and anointing of the first century saints, the answer to me, is in mainly due to our unbridled desire for individual popularity.

We are too obsessed with the world than obeying God's Word. Instead of keeping our eyes on "the ball" (God's purpose), we are looking at our "jerseys" and clapping for ourselves. We can grow bigger and do better as families and churches by restraining ourselves from unnecessary competition with each other. God will cause his glory to manifest when we work towards promoting unity.

Selfishness, covetousness, intolerance, greed, and unforgiveness are some of the negative attitudes we must eliminate to open the door to unity. The family and the Church can only be as strong and glorious as its unity. Let's hold hands together in unity; for therein lies our glory and prosperity.

God bless you.

Do What God Says

Jn. 2:5, NIV

His mother said to the servants, "Whatever he says to you, do it."

Jesus' mother was at a wedding with him when the wine got finished, and embarrassment was staring the host in the face. Under normal circumstances, Mary should not have shown any concern about it because they were there only as guests. She however made a request to Jesus to help solve the problem. It looks obvious though, that Mary had seen Jesus work miracles, and given her knowledge of who her son really was (God incarnate), she was believing for a miracle.

Even though Jesus' answer did not appear to address her request in a positive way, her simple instruction to the servants was, "Whatever he says to you, do it." I find this to be one of the most powerful instructions in the entire Bible. Indeed, it summarises all that can be said to every child of God about what he needs to do to please the Lord; "whatever he says to you, do it." Don't look for another word from God when you haven't obeyed what the Bible is demanding of you presently. For example, God says forgive your enemies, and you say "no, I can't do that." You shut the door to your receiving the miracle for a "better wine."

If you should ask me how many times I have had to struggle with the scriptures, I'd honestly tell you it's been more times than I can count. But as much as I have found grace to do what God says, I have never had reason to regret. You see, God's Word normally "doesn't make sense," because it is above our limited senses. It is wisdom personified, and those who choose to relate to it on the basis of common-sense, will always find themselves walking in disobedience. The Bible doesn't have to make sense to you before you obey it.

We are servants of God, not masters of our lives. As servants, our response to instruction should always be obedience. Mary's instruction to the servants at the wedding feast is a timeless message to every one of us who desires to serve Christ and the course of his kingdom. You may be struggling with something God has told you to do. It is no co-incidence that you are reading this piece; God wants you to get up and do what you've got to do.

The Holy Spirit strategically placed this before you today because the day to do right is today. Pray and ask God for grace to obey. If you claim Jesus Christ is your Lord and personal Savior, then quit fighting his Word: "Whatever he says to you, do it." God give you a "better wine" miracle in Jesus' name.

God bless you.

Hold Your Peace

Prov. 17:28, NIV

Even a fool is thought wise if he keeps silent, and discerning if he holds his tongue.

When attacked and vilified, it comes as a matter of course to try and tell your side of the story. It has been proven in many instances, however, that sometimes the best answer to people who are hostile towards you is a big, loud SILENCE. It is sheer waste of time trying to get people who are determined to nail you to a cross to understand your point of view. Your best option is to discern their motive and keep quiet.

Jesus Christ knew during his trial that there was no way he could assuage public sentiment and opinion against himself, so he refused to answer their queries. The verdict of his trial was already concluded, not subject to any review or compromise. Sometimes that is the situation we face or are likely to face. People who may not even have any intimate relationship with us, can take entrenched positions against us based on false information. The way forward is to pray for such people. Guard your spirit against hating them, because if you do, you are headed towards undermining your spiritual wellbeing.

Reflect a moment on Jesus on the cross. He set us a perfect example of how to deal with issues of persecution. He only spoke when he must, and for the greater part, Jesus spoke (prayed) to the Father. He never cursed any of his accusers, and persecutors. On the contrary he asked the Father to forgive them. The other day someone sent me a picture with what appeared to be fire burning the tongue of a guy. The inscription (prayer?) under the picture read, and I quote: "fire will burn the tongue of anyone who speaks against you". I wish to state categorically that I do not subscribe to cursing human beings. I totally reject that dogma. It is absolutely out of context with the letter and spirit of the gospel of Christ. It belongs to another religious faith, not the Christian faith.

If you are being persecuted and there doesn't seem to be space for you to get a fair hearing, ask God for grace to keep quiet. When Jesus breathed His last on the cross, a soldier standing by, finally confessed that He was the Son of God. If you will hold your peace and maintain your poise, a day will come when you may not be there to hear or see, but SOMEONE among your persecutors will wake up from his slumber and agree that you are better than who they said you were. Stop fighting your own battles and leave judgement to God. Keep quiet, for even a fool is counted among the wise when he holds his peace.

God bless you.

Praise God amidst Challenges

Dan. 2:20-21, NIV

Praise be to the name of God for ever and ever; wisdom and power are his. He changes times and seasons; he sets up kings and deposes them. He gives wisdom to the wise and knowledge to the discerning. He reveals deep and hidden things; he knows what lies in darkness, and light dwells with him.

Our God can never be controlled or confused by anything that happens in his universe. When Daniel and his three Hebrew friends were confronted with possible execution as captives in Babylon, he knew where to turn for help. Even though he was yet to see the answer to his prayer, he began by praising God. Daniel gives us a lesson in praising God when we are confronted with difficult challenges. He had confidence in the God who "changes times and seasons" and yet remains unchanging and unchangeable.

You can rest assured in Christ that your disappointments are not going to remain with you forever. God will bring about a change. You cannot die where you fell. Remember the revelation Daniel gives us in this passage: "he (God) sets up kings and deposes them...he knows what lies in darkness." As long as you are committed to trusting and obeying him, you will not fail. God never promised us a life without difficulties and setbacks. Jesus said, "in this world you shall have tribulations." He did not stop there; he gave us a winning formula when the challenges come. He said, "be of good cheer, for I have overcome the world."

You can't win by whining and throwing a pity-party because things aren't going the way you expect. Praising while you wait for a better tomorrow, opens the heavens in your favor. Nothing concerning you is hidden from God. No one standing against you is beyond the reach of God. When you are tired, he knows it. When you are at your wits end, he understands it. If you trust him to change your situation and praise him in anticipation, God will respond with love, and lighten your path.

Daniel did not need to be lectured on who his God was, and what he was capable of doing. He took hold of his personal testimony of God's goodness in his life and made that the theme of his praise. He touched heaven, and God answered. You share the same privilege with Daniel; if he praised and had an encounter with divinity, you can also praise and experience the love of God in higher dimensions of glory. May the God and Father of our Lord Jesus Christ, receive your praise and remove every plague in your life.

God bless you.

Be Slow to Judge

Job 39:19-20, GNB

Was it you, Job, who made horses so strong and gave them their flowing manes. Did you make them leap like locusts and frighten men with their snorting?

Job was going through a very difficult time in his life. He was sick and suffering from horrible wounds inflicted by the devil. God allowed the attack on Job to prove to Satan that Job's integrity and commitment in serving the Lord was no fluke. Interesting enough, Job himself didn't know the reason for his suffering. When pushed by his wife to "curse God and die," Job refused to yield to that temptation. When the suffering became unbearable, he raised issues about it, and began to question why he had to endure so much pain, knowing how well he had served his God.

This was perfectly in order with God. He knows our hearts and understands our once-in-a-while doubts and fears. Unfortunately, Job's friends took on a holier-than-thou attitude; questioning and rebuking Job for protesting his suffering. That is where we always get it wrong, misunderstanding the challenges people go through, and judging them wrongly. When a man has toothache, that is not the time to tell him why he shouldn't eat ice cream. Even when people go through problems that are self-inflicted, the least you can do is cheer them up, not to tear them down.

People in crisis do not need us to shut them up. They need those who will show up and share their pain. When you have someone going through a "Job crisis," sometimes the best you can do for them is to keep them company. You don't have to say anything. Your presence in itself is a healing balm. Job's friends had the right theology but manifested a wrong attitude. We may not know all the facts about a person's situation and therefore should be slow to judge.

God bless you.

Apply the Word to Your Life

James. 1:22-23, NIV

Do not merely listen to the word, and so deceive yourselves. Do what it says. Anyone who listens to the word but does not do what it says is like a man who looks at his face in a mirror and, after looking at himself, goes away and immediately forgets what he looks like.

God has given us his Word to teach us his ways, reveal to us his will, and help us to live in the joy that obedience brings. There is a world of difference between listening to God's Word and obeying it. Apostle James likened the attitude of merely listening without obeying, to "a man who looks at his face in a mirror and, after looking at himself, goes away and immediately forgets what he looks like." The obvious question is, "why and how would someone look in a mirror and IMMEDIATELY he walks away forget how he looks?"

The answer is not far-fetched; what the eye sees at any given moment is what IMMEDIATELY occupies the mind. To ensure we walk in the Word without forgetting what it says to us, there are a few things we have to consider. First, you must develop the habit of meditating on the Word. It's either the Word or the world; there is no middle ground. God told Joshua the pathway to success is not only hearing the Word but MEDITATING on it (Jos.1:8). If you don't discipline the mind to think about the Word you hear, the brain will relegate it to the archives "immediately" you are done with hearing it and begin to record the rhythms of the world.

What goes into the head should sift into the heart, and then we can be sure we will act it out in our lives. Secondly, you should try to put the Word into practice. Measure your thoughts, words, and actions against what the Word of God says, and that will make you more conscious of God's leading. The third important step is to prayerfully ask the Holy Spirit to help you remember the Word and apply it in your life. Jesus told the disciples not to worry what they would have to say when brought before kings because the Holy Spirit would bring to remembrance what he had taught them. The multiplicity of issues we deal with on a daily basis, and issues like aging, make it difficult to remember everything we hear, that is why reliance on the Holy Spirit is crucial.

To listen to the Word and not do what it says, according to Apostle James, amounts to self-deception. It doesn't benefit or bless you the way it should. Don't go to church just to add to the numbers. Don't read the Bible or listen to its preaching without putting it into practice. Transformation begins with obedience. The "sweetness of the pudding is in the eating," so eat and walk in the Word, and you will experience the fullness of God's blessing.

God bless you.

Your Armor-Bearers

1Sam. 14:6-7, NIV

Jonathan said to his young armor-bearer, "Come, let's go over to the outpost of those uncircumcised fellows. Perhaps the LORD will act in our behalf. Nothing can hinder the LORD from saving, whether by many or by few." "Do all that you have in mind," his armor-bearer said. "Go ahead; I am with you heart and soul."

Jonathan had a conviction that he could rout the Philistine army and break their siege on Israel if he got God's blessing on his plan. He did not tell his father about his plan because the king was very much dependent on the people, but nothing tangible had come out of his reliance on them. He affirmed that numbers do not matter with God. Jonathan believed that "nothing can hinder the LORD from saving, whether by many or by few." We all feel comfortable when we have lots of people endorsing our plans and offering to help out or be part of a project we are undertaking. A very good friend of mine would always say, "the bigger the better." Fortunately for some of us, that is not always true. We have seen God do "big things" with little boys and girls like us.

Beloved, the numbers help, but the crowd without the Christ is a non-starter. Whether fat or thin, big, or small, you need God to win your race. Sometimes the big numbers can turn out to slow you down, especially when they are not as loyal as Jonathan's armor-bearer. When his boss shared the vision, the armor-bearer responded by saying, "Go ahead; I am with you heart and soul." Anybody who finds such support from family, friends, team, or workforce is bound to succeed; and so, it was no surprise that Jonathan achieved his goal of defeating the Philistines. The two things that worked for Jonathan are, first his faith in God, and secondly the support and loyalty of his armor-bearer. If you lack these two support systems, you must ask God for it.

You should rise above the fear of not being able to achieve your goals because of limited resources and having only few people on your side. Many times than I can tell, God has taken our ministry on a wilderness journey that lasted for years instead of days, weeks, or months, just to teach us to trust him. God, for these 30-plus years of ministry never gave us a mega church, but he has given us grace to do what we never thought possible. When the going is tough, pray and ask the Lord for "armor-bearers" who will be loyal to the core. Your principal armor-bearer may be your spouse, friend, or even sometimes your children. These are people who love and trust you with "heart and soul," not just head and body.

When you share your vision, they don't get jealous of you; they join you. They encourage you and strengthen your hand to push for success. They love to see you happy and successful. They will never betray or blackmail you. You don't necessarily need many people to achieve your goal. The God of the sea is also the God of the lake. No matter the size of the challenge, all you need is faith in God and a loyal partner or partners who will support you in prayer and with words and deeds of encouragement.

Be very careful not to indulge someone you know is disloyal to you. It is impossible to convert a Judas, and there are too many out there. Save yourself unnecessary stress and emotional torment. If you look well enough, you will see those God has appointed to be armor-bearers for the fight against the "Philistines" in your life.

God bless you.

Godly Leadership involves Giving

2Chron. 35:7-8, NKJV

Then Josiah gave the lay people lambs and young goats from the flock, all for Passover offerings for all who were present...and his leaders gave willingly to the people, to the priests for the Passover offerings two thousand six hundred from the flock, and three hundred cattle.

Giving is the highest form of living; "for God so loved the world that HE GAVE..." (Jn. 3:16a). Everyone who seeks to lead, must be prepared to give. Can you imagine a world in which every creature decides to keep all that he possesses? The heavens will not release rain, the ground holds the seed and will not support its growth etc. The cycle of life will be broken, and all living things will go extinct. In some instances, what kills us is what we don't give out; we hold on to it until it becomes toxic waste and poisons our system and environment. This was what Jesus was implying when he said, "he who wants to keep his life will lose it."

When the Bible speaks of leadership, it is more than position of headship, rights, and privileges. Being head of the family as husband is not an opportunity to establish a kingdom where you eat the best and leave the rest for your wife and children. You got it wrong. It is your responsibility to make sure they are okay before you think about yourself. The pastor is a shepherd, and not a butcher. He is responsible for feeding the flock spiritually, but when he has a sheep whose situation calls for material assistance, it is his responsibility to help if he can. Jesus fed 5,000 congregants when the situation called for it. King Josiah and his leaders contributed towards the Passover celebration. They GAVE willingly!!!

Leadership is about giving. Anyone who is uncomfortable with giving, should not be in leadership position. It saddens my heart to see young people coming into ministry with the view that the congregants are there to provide for their every need. They want to live a lifestyle that is not within the means of the flock, and when they are unable to get it by fair means, they choose to play it foul; saying what God has not said and doing what they should not do. Let me make this humble submission to anyone out there, looking at the call to ministry as a call to make money, that God's work is not a goldmine. It DEMANDS selflessness, hard work, and sacrifice. It is eternally rewarding, not self-serving.

If you desire to lead, you desire a good thing; but always remember that God's call to leadership is a call to GIVE yourself to serve, not to be served. Godly leadership is love in motion. It is giving, and giving, and giving, and giving...from start to finish, from beginning to end. Those who give, get people to follow without asking them to do so. If you want to lead, begin by giving. If you want your family to accept your leadership, GIVE them your love. Let it show in the giving of your time and resources. Give them what they want, not what you think they should want.

If you want your church to respect your leadership, avoid doing or saying anything that gives the impression you are only interested in what they do for you. Show genuine interest in their spiritual and physical wellbeing, and God will bless you for it. He is able and will meet your every need "according to his riches in glory in Christ Jesus."

God bless you

Embrace Your Calling

1Cor. 12:29-30, NKJV

Are all apostles? Are all prophets? Are all teachers? Are all workers of miracles? Do all have gifts of healings? Do all speak with tongues? Do all interpret?

Apostle Paul asked these questions to stress the point that it is God who "appointed" ministers into office in his Body (the Church). All believers are connected to each other spiritually to form "the body of Christ" (v.27). For proper functioning of the Church, each individual is given different gifts as determined by God. Those in the five-fold ministry of Apostle, Prophet, Pastor, Teacher, and Evangelist, are equally "appointed" by God. They are neither expected to appoint themselves nor be appointed by men.

The Church in Corinth was facing challenges similar to what today's Church is experiencing; there is unbridled competition for position, power, and popularity. Everyone is laying claim to the title of "prophet," which obviously cannot be justified by the teachings of Paul. You can only be what God has "appointed" you to be. This mindset of being what we want to be (not what God has called us to be), is often carried over into our homes. Parents want every single child in the family to perform at the same academic level, without realizing that each child has his own God-given gifts and interests. We destroy ourselves and our children when we compete for what we are not equipped for.

It is possible to function in more than one gift, yes. It is even possible to have someone being multi-talented and who can score 'A' in every subject and excel in every endeavor; but those are the ones we call legends. If you don't have what they have, you don't have it. Get busy fulfilling your appointment, not living in disappointment. God's idea for giving each of us different gifts is so that we complement each other, not compete with each other. When you see a man trying too hard to be something he is not appointed to be, you see a perfect example of someone who is bent on denying himself peace and contentment in life.

The nurse is as important as the doctor, and the pharmacist is as important as the lab technician. Together they form a solid team that provides a health care system for the benefit of society. What if all were doctors? What if all were nurses? What if all were pharmacists? And what if all were laboratory technicians? The benefit will not be the same.You must know yourself. Know your strengths and weaknesses. See where you can make a difference, not where someone is making an impact. You can draw inspiration from others, without wanting to be them.

Your gifts and talents are as good and important as anybody else's. When you know who God has "appointed" you to be, and embrace your appointment with destiny, you are on your way to living a fulfilled life. Anything short of that is bound to set you on a journey without a destination, and which in effect is "a meaningless ramble." Embrace your calling in life. Stay focused, and you will experience satisfaction to the fullest.

God bless you.

From Rejected to Cornerstone

Mk.12:10-11, NKJV

"Have you not read this Scripture: 'The stone which the builders rejected has become the chief cornerstone. This was the LORD'S doing, and it is marvelous in our eyes'?"

In making reference to the scripture in Ps.118:22-23, Jesus was predicting his own rejection and the subsequent outcome. The process was going to be painful, but the product will outshine all the shame and embarrassment. He never expected acceptance from the people because what he had to offer was not what they were looking for. He was not bothered by the rejection because he knew God was going to turn things around, and the end was going to be glorious. That is the way it is going to turn out for you, if you are at the receiving end of rejection presently.

The immediate impact of rejection can be very devastating. Many have suffered mental and emotional breakdown from which they never recovered, while others have gone to an early grave as a result of rejection. Perhaps the safest ground on which you can stand against the negative effects of rejection is the consciousness that you cannot have everyone accept you for who you are or what you stand for. More importantly however, you have to believe God to work out what is intended for your destruction towards your elevation.

In the traditional building setting, the cornerstone is usually ignored at the initial stages of construction. It becomes a focus of attention when it comes to stabilizing the main structure with corner pillars. People will reject you for varied reasons, but your concern should be how to rise above it and trust God to bring you to "cornerstone" position. Life is so unpredictable, and so are the people you relate to. The same man or woman who proposed love to you yesteryears and wouldn't sleep without seeing you, can walk away from you without a second thought of how you feel; he/she care less whether you fall or faint.

Jeremiah warns us that "the heart of man is desperately wicked" (Jer.17:9). Those you least expect to reject you, might be the ones who strike the first blow. People you trust and have shared intimate relationship with can 'beat you down,' but you don't have to let them take you out. You have a life ahead of you to live. It holds problems, but it also has prospects.

If you only look at today's pain, you might lose out on tomorrow's joy. God will pick you up from where they dropped you, and they will come back to see you transformed from stone to cornerstone. Keep praying. Keep trusting. Even if everyone leaves you, remember God is always there for you, and he is more than enough for all the rough twists and turns that come your way.

God bless you.

God will Reward

Rev. 22:12, NKJV

And behold, I am coming quickly, and My reward is with Me, to give to everyone according to His work.

If you are not doing anything for God, then you are not going to get anything from God at Christ's second coming. This is a wake-up call. When you are saved, there are gifts God gives you to be used for the good of his kingdom. That means every born-again child of God is assigned specific tasks in accordance with the gifts, time, talents, and resources given by God. As explained by Jesus in the Parable of Talents, it is not the quantum of your work that God is going to look at, but the faithfulness with which you applied yourself to the assignment.

The Lord will not ask you to give account for ten souls, when he gave you only two. The clock is ticking, and prophecies pointing to Christ's second coming are being fulfilled in rapid succession. We do not know the actual time of his coming, but we know the SIGNS of his advent, and we do know our present assignment. Let us not be slack and careless in pursuing the heavenly agenda. The enemy knows his time is very short, so he is pulling every trick under his sleeve to keep us from putting priority on God's kingdom-building work.

Some of us are fast asleep on the job, relative to sharing our faith. Our attention is more on the rewards we get for what we do here and now, minus what God has promised to give us in the hereafter. The Lord is a rewarder, and everything we do for him is noted for reward. Encourage yourself in the things you are called to do for God. Serve the Lord. Delight yourself in being a blessing wherever he leads. Live in anticipation of what lies beyond the present. Sometimes you might have to endure hardship, as you submit to what the Lord is demanding of you. Keep your head up and remember the path to glory is often strewn with thorns.

Jesus is coming "quickly," so let's stop wasting time on things that distract us and concentrate on things that are positive and encouraging. Let's continue the work of bringing lost souls to a saving knowledge of Christ. Let's be all that God means us to be and do all that we are assigned to do; there is a reward for all who obey. God reward your service for his kingdom, both now and through all eternity.

God bless you.

All Power Belongs to God

Ps. 62:11, NKJV

God has spoken once, twice I have heard this: that power belongs to God.

Power, to some extent, is a neutral force; if it is applied graciously, it becomes a blessing. If it is used inappropriately it can kill, decimate, and destroy. There is a wise saying that "power corrupts, and absolute power corrupts absolutely." The truism in this adage is the reason democratic governance demand checks and balances at every level of government. History is replete with numerous dictators who under the influence of unlimited power, brought untold hardships to humanity.

Today, there is still evidence of abuse of power by parents, pastors, teachers, politicians, corporate managers, coaches et al. This situation can only change when we realize the source of all power is God. Whenever you find yourself in any position of power, remember you are exercising that power on behalf of God. You are never an authority to yourself. The power you hold in the home, church, workplace etc., is not a mandate to bully and abuse. It is an instrument to provide leadership, guidance, protection, inspiration, correction, and direction. Anything short of these, can spell disaster.

God wants you to acknowledge that all power belongs to him alone, and what is given to you is for the common good, not for controlling, manipulating, humiliating, and kicking your fellow men. You can gain power over a person or group of people based on your having more than what they have in terms of wealth and social status; being more knowledgeable, or through "accident of history." Whichever way it comes, its primary source is still God. As a child of God's kingdom, be conscious of what God expects you to do with his delegated authority.

If you are a parent, be mindful of the fact that you are accountable to God for your use of the position of power he has given you over your children. If you are a pastor, prophet, or in any leadership position in the Church, you are not a god unto yourself. The people God has placed in your care are to be fed, not milked. Don't make demands on them that are unscriptural, unreasonable and that they are unable to meet. And if you are a manager in the corporate world, please the ladies working under you are not there to satisfy your lust. Respect their dignity and exercise restraint in the way you relate to them. Don't threaten them with demotion because you cannot control your emotions.

What have you heard so far today? Here's a reminder: All power belongs to God. The little power he has given you should be used with discretion, responsibly, and with the view to being a blessing, not a bully.

God bless you.

God will Restore Your Praise

Amos 9:11, NKJV

On that day I will raise up the tabernacle of David, which has fallen down, and repair its damages; I will raise up its ruins, and rebuild it as in the days of old.

Every day comes with its own challenges, and yesterday was no exception. I was standing in the compound of our school when I heard a loud noise behind me, only to turn and see that a big truck loaded with sand had rammed into the school wall collapsing a portion instantly. A few minutes earlier, we had started work on the side of the school that is not walled. Before I could figure out what to do next, a contractor who supplies building materials to the school came from nowhere and offered to repair the damage for free. My relief was beyond description.

God "raised the tabernacle of David that had fallen down" in my circumstances because of the damage caused to the wall. My heart was filled with praise and gratitude to God. This was something very peculiar to the "tabernacle of David," which was radically different from the tabernacle of Moses, which had no music, no singing, no dancing, no rejoicing, and no celebration. Maybe a wall in your life has collapsed without warning. The pain, uncertainty, fear, and frustration have ganged up to put you on silent mode. God has a word of hope for you; Yahweh will raise up the tabernacle of David (praise and celebration) "that has fallen down" in your life.

He will walk you through the fiery furnace and it will not consume you, because he will be right there with you each step of the way. Beyond raising up the tabernacle of David in your life, God is promising a three-dimensional move that will restore your joy and give you hope for the future. Firstly, he promises to "repair" the damages caused. All you have to do is trust him to do it. I never expected someone who did not damage the school wall to step forward and offer to repair it for free. It didn't make sense to me, but that's how God sometimes chooses to work. God must be the reason for the offer.

Secondly, the Lord says he "raise up its ruins." Some of the challenges you are facing are a state of "ruin," so you are wondering how anything good can come out of same. The God who created light out of darkness is well able to do it. Keep holding tight to the promise. Thirdly, God is going to "rebuild it as in the days of old." Whatever has stolen your peace and joy will have to make way for God's healing to come back to you.

That "tabernacle of David" which serves as a focal point in giving you the impetus to praise God, and which the enemy has torn down in ruins is going to be restored. Begin the praise, and you will release the presence to manifest God's power. You may be down, but you are not out. Praise the Lord, and see his glory unfold.

God bless you.

A life of Balance

Matt. 24:1-2, CEV

After Jesus left the temple, his disciples came over and said, "Look at all these buildings!" Jesus replied, "Do you see these buildings? They will certainly be torn down! Not one stone will be left in place."

Watching massive buildings being washed away by tsunami tidal waves in Japan and Indonesia on television some years ago reminded me of the temporal nature of life here on earth. The disciples of Jesus might have been disappointed with Jesus' response to their discourse. Life in a typical Jewish community was centered around synagogues, but the temple in Jerusalem was the national spiritual rallying point. The disciples loved the sheer beauty of the architecture of the temple and had hoped Jesus was going to endorse what they were seeing.

That was not to be. The Lord was living in the future while they were hooked to the present. Jesus always focused on the future and still does. If you spend all your time and energy working for what will give you material comfort without recourse to your spiritual growth and maturity, you will wake up one day to find your "temple" gone. There must be balance to the things you do and the way you live. God put our feet on the ground and our heads in the air for a reason; to create perfect balance between the spiritual and the physical.

Be careful you don't get so excited about your present achievements that you care little or nothing about the life beyond the now. You cannot get so busy with your business and career pursuits you have no time to read the Bible, pray, and attend church services. Beloved, that is committing spiritual suicide. The "temple" (physical and material achievements) you have built will one day be "torn down". No one goes to the grave with his house, car, or bank account; and even if you are buried in your house or car, you cannot get up and claim ownership. It will only be an exercise in futility.

Whatever blessing the good Lord gives you, by all means enjoy it, but do so always remembering that it will not be there forever. Either it will leave you or you will leave it. Taking a Life Insurance policy is good, but the greatest and most important policy for your life is one vested in Jesus Christ. Live your life in such a way that when the "temple" is torn down, you will stay up.

God bless you.

Die to Sin

Col. 3:5-6, NKJV

Therefore, put to death your members which are on the earth: fornication, uncleanness, passion, evil desire, and covetousness, which is idolatry. Because of these things the wrath of God is coming upon the sons of disobedience.

Grace does not take away responsibility. The grace of God does not endorse reckless and sinful living. It empowers us to overpower sin and Satan. We have been set free from sin. What God gives to us, he expects us to keep and maintain with due diligence and reverence. Holiness is a gift from God, and we must maintain it. The fleshly nature which rules us before we receive Christ will always seek to re-assert itself and drive us into living in sin. God wants us to take responsibility to "put to death" the old sinful nature.

This is not a one-time shoot-to-kill exercise; it is a lifelong battle. Apostle Paul says, "I beat my body daily." The day you fail to put the old nature to death, it will resurrect with vengeance and cause you to say or do what you normally might not say or do. Don't make excuses for your sin, repent and come out of it. Here are some suggestions on how you can put the cravings of the flesh to death daily. First, you must make a conscious effort not to feed your senses with sights and sounds that are likely to influence you to sin. If you watch pornographic material, you are most likely to fornicate or commit adultery. You cannot sow mangoes and reap apples.

Secondly, you have to avoid places and persons that motivate you to sin. This is because your environment can influence your behavior. Third tip is to depend on the Holy Spirit to help you; and this calls for a disciplined and consistent prayer life, coupled with meditating on the Word of God and obeying its teachings and admonitions. The decision to stand or fall is in your hands. The grace of God has moved you from a position of helplessness to a place of power, from hopelessness to holiness.

You are now a new creature in Christ and should reflect the new light and life God has deposited in you. Walk in the freedom of God's Spirit, as you seek to live to please him. You don't need to impose any set of rules on yourself. The more you fall in love with Jesus, the more you will die to self and sin. If you cannot remember anything about how to live to glorify God, just remember to love him. Once your heart goes after him, your body will have no choice but to follow suit.

God bless you.

Intercede for One Another

Rom.1:9-10, NKJV

First, I thank God through Jesus Christ for you all, that your faith is spoken of throughout the whole world. For God is my witness, whom I serve with my spirit in the gospel of His Son, that without ceasing I make mention of you always in my prayers.

No prayer is ever wasted. The writer of the book of Romans was excited about reports that came to him that the believers in Rome he had been praying for, were holding on to the faith despite the ruthless persecution they were facing. They stood tall and strong at the peril of their lives, and this became topic of the day in the entire Roman empire. The writer was not surprised about that development because "without ceasing I make mention of you always in my prayers." He consistently prayed for them, and he had cause to thank God that his prayers were answered.

God has not changed. If we commit to praying for each other, we shall see similar results. The Church thrives on prayer, and our survival depends very much on interceding for each other. When the going is tough, and the road is rough, there is no power greater than the power of prayer. When your brother is sick and tired from the ravages and pressures of life, and gets to the point of giving up, your prayer is a necessary lifeline for his revival. Many of us can testify that we have come this far because of the continued prayers of family, friends and loved ones.

Some of us have experienced low points in our lives when even the prospect of opening our mouths to pray went completely caput. Somehow, somewhere, someone remembered us in his prayers, and God answered and strengthened us to stand. Upholding each other in prayer is very important. The prayer door should remain open 24/7; and we must be humble enough to ask for prayer support whenever necessary. Find a prayer partner who you can trust to keep faith with you and commit to praying for each other. Begin with your immediate family.

Each day pray for God's grace to be on each and every member of your family. Ask for God's divine presence, protection, and provision for each child and adult. Extend your borders of intercessory prayer to include the saints and those in political and ecclesiastical leadership. Prayer does what complaints can never do. Someone needs your prayers every day for heaven to perform in his life. Pray, and the good Lord will give you a testimony and theme of praise. And always remember to pray for me too, as I pray for you. May God always answer you speedily in Jesus Name.

God bless you.

God Will not Abandon You

Ps.94:9,14, ESV

> *He who planted the ear, does he not hear? He who formed the eye, does he not seem. For the LORD will not forsake his people; he will not abandon his heritage.*

I woke up one day to place a call to one of my darling daughters who was celebrating her birthday, only to hear her complain about experiencing unusual pain in her hands and legs throughout the night. She said she prayed all the prayer she knew to pray but did not get the relief she wanted. The obvious question one might be tempted to ask is, "where was God?" "Was God hearing and seeing the pain and suffering of one of his own?"

The psalmist gives us a word of assurance and encouragement that God hears and sees everything that happens to us. It is unimaginable that the one who created the ears and eyes can neither hear nor see. Like Job's crisis, God may allow (note the word 'allow') some bad stuff to happen in our lives not because we sinned or did something to deserve the pain, or that he enjoys seeing us go through suffering. Indeed, we only live by his grace and mercy, and not for any good works in ourselves.

It is not in his nature to bring suffering to his people, but when he allows it, he shares in our suffering. Remember, God is not only our healer, but also our Comforter; where he may not heal, he will definitely comfort. Change and decay are permanent features of life here on earth, and some of the changes are associated with aches and heartaches. Let this be your consolation, that the Lord is never a mile away from where you are; he is ever-present with you in your wilderness. The unseen presence of the Holy Spirit is right where you are. He is the 'Paracletos;' one who stands with you and by you.

There are strong assurances for you in the verse 14; first assurance is that "God will not forsake" you. It cost God the liFebruarylood of his beloved and only begotten Son to own you, therefore it will be a huge loss for him to disown you. You are too precious to be left to your fate. Second truth: He will not "abandon" you. Even if he doesn't take away what has become a thorn in your life, he will be with you in it, and give you a daily dose of grace to keep hope alive. Don't allow discouragement to demoralize you; his grace is sufficient for you. May the good Lord help you through all of your crises and crown you with victory in Jesus' name.

God bless you.

Stay in Your Lane

Gal. 2:6, NKJV

But from those who seemed to be something-whatever they were, it makes no difference to me; God shows personal favoritism to no man-for those who seemed to be something added nothing to me.

It should never be our business what God does in someone else's life. There are no duplicates in the kingdom of God. The grace on your life is radically different from the grace on any other person's life. You are only a small part of God's picture. You fit a specific space in the divine puzzle, and any attempt to occupy another person's space is likely to create distortion and confusion. Apostle Paul was not among the primary apostolic team the Lord chose while on earth; but he did not let that influence or intimidate him in any way.

Indeed, he tells us in no uncertain terms that "it makes no difference to me." How the Church today need this Pauline approach to life and ministry. Too many of us are out of our life's calling because we are too preoccupied with what is happening in the lives, ministry and career of others than what God wants to do with our lives. The fact that you call yourself a prophet doesn't make you a prophet. God has a good plan for your life, and you must prayerfully seek and walk in that plan. If you force yourself to compete where you are meant to compliment, you might end up being consumed by your own covetousness.

Take a second look at the goals you are pursuing and ask yourself if they are what God wants for you, or if you are taking that route because it has made someone you know successful and popular. You are created and called for effect and impact. Your real success is in accomplishing your own goals and targets as led and empowered by the grace of God. You are wired and equipped for what you are created to achieve. The other brother or sister may have a different call and assignment for his life, and likely is appropriately gifted to accomplish such. You should not concern yourself with how he/she is running his race, and the trophies and applause he/she is getting.

Stay in your lane. Stay focused on your goals. Mark your own script. Remember what the apostle is telling us, that "God shows personal favoritism to no man." In other words, God is no respecter of persons; what he did for others he can do for you if same is meant for you. What he desires of you is to accept yourself and walk in his purpose for your life. That is where you will have the peace and joy that comes through real success.

God bless you.

Dirt and Death

Jn.12:24, NKJV

Most assuredly, I say to you, unless a grain of wheat falls into the ground and dies, it remains alone; but if it dies, it produces much grain.

Jesus introduces us to two important conditions necessary for "a grain of wheat" to become productive. First, it must fall to the ground. The natural habitat for grain to grow is the ground, not the air. The grain that rejects the ground because it doesn't like the dirt, will forever remain an island to itself; it cannot experience the joys of growth, maturity, expansion, and multiplication. The truth applicable to us is this; the ground is the lowest point anyone can get to and speaks to us of humility.

Like the grain of wheat, you cannot make much impact in people's lives unless you hit ground-level (humble yourself). Jesus Christ had to come down to our level to raise us to God's level. The second condition necessary for a grain of wheat to multiply itself is death; it has to be subject to death. Jesus did not just come on earth to preach and work miracles. He "humbled himself and became obedient to the point of death, even the death of the cross" (Phil.2:8). There is a death you must die before you can experience a multiplying effect in your personal life, family, career etc.

Life is about making sacrifices. Dying to self is one of the highest forms of spiritual sacrifices, and it pays great dividends in what is accomplished. The one death Jesus died, continues to provide salvation for lost souls each passing day. In Jn.15:8, Jesus spoke about how we can bring glory to our Heavenly Father: "By this My Father is glorified, that you bear much fruit; so you will be My disciples." This demand to bear "much fruit" can only be fulfilled by those who, like a grain of wheat, are willing to go through the two-fold process of falling on the ground and dying to self.

Count yourself blessed to be given the opportunity to multiply and bear much fruit. Don't be afraid of the dirt and the death; both are positive means to godly goals. Let God use you as an instrument of blessing, and you will soon see others imitating and manifesting you; a reproduction of yourself. They are the fruit of your labour.

God bless you.

Answer Herod with Silence

Lu. 23:8-9, NKJV

Now when Herod saw Jesus, he was exceedingly glad; for he had desired for a long time to see Him, because he had heard many things about Him, and he hoped to see some miracle done by Him. Then he questioned Him with many words, but He answered Him nothing.

A child of God should know when to talk and when to keep silent. Jesus Christ set us a perfect example of how to use silence to answer questions we should not answer; because no number of rational arguments and explanations we put forward can change the status quo. Folks may hear things about you and come to conclusions you can neither change nor influence, no matter what you say or how good you are to them. If you insist on talking them out of their negative perceptions, you might end up hurting yourself and entertaining them.

Scripture tells us that when "Herod saw Jesus he was exceedingly glad." Herod wasn't glad like Zacchaeus who saw his need of salvation, but he saw his meeting with Jesus as an opportunity to satisfy his curiosity and make fun of the Lord. To Herod, Jesus was a local magician not a universal Messiah. There was no way Herod's mindset could be changed, so the most befitting answer to his questions was dead silence. As a discerning child of God, you should know by the help of the indwelling Holy Spirit when it is unprofitable for you to respond to your accusers and detractors.

If you are dreaming of the day everyone is going to love you, understand you, or accept you, I'm afraid you are having a bad dream and need to wake up to reality. Those who consistently "desire" that all men love and accept them, only subject themselves to avoidable emotional torment. Bible records that Jesus did good wherever he went (Acts 10:38), and yet it was within the same geographical area that he was hated, chastised, and crucified. If you have not come to grips with the fickleness of humanity yet, then you are miles away from catching the flight to what will give you peace.

I have been here on earth long enough to know that the Word of God is eternally true that says, "cursed is the man who puts his trust in another man." I have seen "believers" come before the altar of God, vowing to love and cherish each other "till death do us part," only to turn their backs on their vows at the least opportunity. Mark my words; not everyone deserves your answer to their questions about you, your family, your ministry, or your career. Nothing you say or do can make "Herod" love, appreciate, or accept you.

Luke 23:11 records the end of Jesus' encounter with Herod: "Then Herod, with his men of war, treated him with contempt and mocked him..." The hatred and rejection were deep. It soon spilled over and manifested itself in contempt and mockery. To try and change the mind of a "Herod" in your life is an exercise in futility. Your best answer to his, her, or their questions is, and should always be, a loud SILENCE!

God bless you.

Do Right, Give Justice, Be Honest

Jer. 22:15-16, CEV

"More cedar in your palace doesn't make you a better king than your father Josiah. He always did right - he gave justice to the poor and was honest. That's what it means to truly know me. So he lived a comfortable life and always had enough to eat and drink."

Having inner peace has more to do with building healthy human relationships and doing right towards all people, than accumulating material wealth. If it were not so, we could safely conclude that our joy and peace is dependent on purse and power. When we don't have enough to eat and pay our bills, it is nothing to cheer about. God's plan, as revealed by my Bible, is for us to have more than enough so we can help others.

In this regard, understanding God's purpose for prosperity becomes crucial. God does not give wealth to prove you are "a better king than your father..." Beyond the blessing is an assignment to bless others. Two things are mentioned as being of priority. King Josiah was identified as one who knew God because he covered these grounds. First, "he always did right". He intended it and acted it. You don't struggle with something you are settled on doing.

Second thing King Josiah did was give justice to the poor. Do you realize how the system goes easy on the rich and people of influence? In my part of the world, justice can be bought by the highest bidder. The justice system is so corrupt and unjust that the supposed peace officer is more part of the problem than the solution. We need a paradigm shift. If we pretend it's not there, we shall live in the rot till Jesus comes again. The starting point is God's people. A little standing up for the poor and vulnerable in society will make a big difference.

Finally, Josiah was honest. If you to ask me, I would say finding honest people today (even in the Church) is like searching for a needle in a stack of hay. Beloved, I am saying what I am saying based on personal experience. You are free to disagree. Truth has only one name. Bible tells us King Josiah's posture, ensured him "a comfortable life and he always had enough to eat and drink." May we do right towards all men - especially the poor and underprivileged, and be honest in all our dealings, so we can live in comfort like King Josiah, having "enough to eat and drink" every day of our lives in Jesus Name.

God bless you.

Love Your Enemies

Lu.6:27-28, NKJV

"But I say to you who hear: Love your enemies, do good to those who hate you, bless those who curse you, and pray for those who spitefully use you."

Something is not right with a lot of the language format I see believers put out on social media. We curse those who Jesus says we must bless. Unfortunately, this rampant craze of cursing "enemies" is mostly spearheaded by preachers. Frustration is making us do and say things that completely contradict the Word of God. Jesus made some strong statements here that we need to examine against the backdrop of what we are practicing today in His name.

First, he said, "But I say to your who HEAR..." He is speaking to a specific audience. Not everyone who LISTENS to you HEARS you. Jesus is addressing those who are open to instruction and do not give excuses why they cannot do what He commands. I know for a fact that the moment we identify someone as "enemy" we develop a certain mindset towards the person, making it impossible to tolerate him, much more to bless him. The problem however is that it is the price we pay as disciples of Christ. We don't claim to be followers of Christ and contradict His orders. So, to all of you out there busy cursing human beings, you are walking in disobedience to divine order.

I found out many years ago that the one person I could not love was my "enemy". I found it very easy hating those I knew were against me, until I took it to God in prayer. The Holy Spirit showed me I was "right" in failing to love my enemies, because it was beyond human nature and capability to love our enemies. I had to ask Him to love the people I couldn't love, for whatever reasons, through me. It worked, and always works. When you find yourself in that tight corner where it is much easier to hate and curse than to bless, do good, and pray for your enemies, invite the Holy Spirit to do the job of loving them through you.

Our natural "fruit" is not love. It is anger, bitterness, vengeance, cursing etc. It is both Adamic and endemic, a part of our DNA. On the contrary, the fruit of the Spirit of God is LOVE. When you have the Spirit dwelling within you, His fruit of Love manifests through you as you yield to His Word. You obey Christ not your emotions. God is not happy about the death of your "enemy" so stop calling down fire to destroy your human enemies. By all means, attack Satan and his demons; that's where the battle is fought - in the realm of the Spirit. So, from today decide to do these four things the God you worship is COMMANDING (not suggesting) you to do - (1) LOVE your enemies (2) DO GOOD to those who hate you (3) BLESS those who curse you (4) PRAY for those who spitefully use you.

Beloved, I will not be surprised if this message doesn't appeal to you (especially if you are among my African readers). This is because of the present craze to curse perceived enemies. Once again, I appeal to those who have "ears" (willing hearts), to HEAR what the Spirit of Christ is demanding and obey it, despite the cost. No bishop, archbishop, or pope is above the Word of God. No race, creed, situation, or circumstance can justify hatred, vengeance, and any form of evil. By your fruit you shall be known. If you are of the Jesus stock, your words and works will show. Stop cursing and be a blesser.

God bless you

Give Your All

Lu. 21:3-4, NKJV

So He said, "Truly I say to you that this poor widow has put in more than all; for all these out of their abundance have put in offerings for God; but she out of her poverty put in all the livelihood that she had."

God is interested in what you GIVE to him vis-a-vis what you KEEP from him. It is quite interesting that when we ask from God, we know no limits, but when it comes to giving to him, then we begin to raise questions like "how much do I have to give? Is it necessary to pay tithe on my salary etc.?" Sometimes I meet believers who know God is calling them into full-time ministry, or a specific mission field but would prefer staying in business and supporting God's work financially. Instead of paying the prize to fulfill their calling, they prefer to "bribe" the Lord and stay out of the battlefield.

Let me caution that when it comes to what people do with what God has given them, we should not force anyone to do or give beyond their convictions. Pastors should teach the Word as clearly as they understand and leave application and implementation to the individual. No coercion, no criticism, and no condemnation. Jesus was so much interested in what each individual put in the offering bowl that he sat close enough to see every single individual's offering; otherwise, how did he come to the conclusion that the widow gave more than all? Yet, he never tried to influence anyone's giving.

He shared his observation only with his disciples, and he had a reason for doing so. He did not want to make anyone feel bad about his giving, and that should be our attitude towards how far people are willing to go in their giving. Bible says God loves a CHEERFUL giver, not a TEARFUL giver. Give to God according to your faith and conviction not out of force and condemnation. If God is asking you to give him more of your time by stepping into full time ministry and you are not ready for it, be honest with yourself and tell him exactly how you feel. God may be disappointed but will not kill you or withdraw his love from you.

You will never be happy giving what you don't want to give. And as much as I wish to encourage you to give what God requires of you without delay or argument, let me stress that God will not kill you because you withhold time, talent, money etc., from him. He has more than enough "poor widows" out there, willing to give their all to fulfill his purpose on earth. Your giving is an opportunity for you to tap into his principle of Sowing and Reaping, so give him your best. It is a door of grace to take you into greater blessings.

Give with a heart of gratitude. Jesus is saying that you may give a lot, but when the account books are checked in heaven, it is what you could have given which you did not give that makes the difference. You can be so used to giving a certain amount in church as offering that for the past many years even though your salary has quadrupled your offering remains the same. Think about what you are giving and doing for God presently, and as you are led by the Spirit of God, take it a notch higher. This is the right time and place to do what you've got to do for God. Tomorrow may be too late.

God bless you.

Be Your Brother's Keeper

Gen. 37:28, NIV

So when the Midianite merchants came by, his brothers pulled Joseph up out of the cistern and sold him for twenty shekels of silver to the Ishmaelites, who took him to Egypt.

One memorable place I had the privilege of visiting with my wife about twelve years ago was the Tanzanian island of Zanzibar in East Africa. The beauty of its beaches, the culture of its people, and the unique features of its history, gave us a wonderful never-to-be-forgotten experience. The one thing I personally never get excited about (but which I was compelled to see on the island) was what used to be a slave market.

Coming from a country with unpleasant landmarks of slave trade, I thought there was nothing else to see that could shock me about the dehumanizing nature of slavery. I was wrong; the stench from the dungeons where the slaves were kept before being shipped out by Arab slave traders, images of where and how they were chained and tortured, made everything I had seen and known about slavery back home seem like child's play.

Turning the pages of the Bible the subject of slavery is re-visited with very important lessons. It is interesting to note that the one who sells the slave is the one supposed to protect him - his own kith and kin. This is what happened to young Joseph. He was sold into slavery by his own brothers. Before you pass judgment, let's do a little reality check and you'll find that on a daily basis, we are equally guilty of "selling" each other into slavery.

We sell our spouses, families, and friends into spiritual and emotional slavery. Our self-centeredness drives us into a state of insensitivity towards them. Sometimes we say things we know we should not say because it's going to hurt. We walk away when family and friends are hurting, and they need us the most. We pull our "Joseph out of the cistern," only to sell him to the "Midianites." It is no surprise therefore, that one of the biggest challenges our world (including the Church) faces today is the issue of trust.

Words no longer mean what they used to mean. When someone says, "I love you," you want to be sure what his real intentions are, and what exactly he hopes to gain from you. Professed believers stand before the altar of God and vow to keep the marriage bond "till death do us part," only to walk away from their vows at the least opportunity. God's desire for you is to take responsibility for the 'Josephs' in your life; serve them, don't sell them.

Let Christ be seen in you by being trustworthy, protective, kind, and generous towards all men. Do not be influenced by anyone's "coat of many colors." Neither should you be jealous of the dreams and ambitions of others. Wish the best for everyone and rejoice in their victory. Be your brother's keeper. It is good, and it is Godly.

God bless you.

Foundations are Important

1 Ki.7:10, NKJV

The foundation was of costly stones, large stones, some ten cubits and some eight cubits.

The stability of every building depends on its foundation. Jesus once used the example of two buildings with different foundations to explain why it is important to pay attention to the kind of "foundations" we lay in life. When King Solomon built the temple in Jerusalem, scripture records that "the foundation was of costly stones." He had a choice between cheap stones and costly stones, and he chose the latter because of the difference it will make in the outcome.

He did not only choose costly stones, but chose different sizes, which in essence means he was flexible and diligent. Dear one, your life is full of foundation-laying projects, and the durability of everything you build will largely depend on each foundation. If you live on lies and deception, you may come up with some impressive "achievements," but they will not be able to stand the test of time. Jesus said the man who built on sand saw his house tumbling down when the storm hit; that is what happens when you build your life on cheap foundations. That is what happens when you are not selective, diligent, and positively discriminatory in the things you do and how you do it.

Every act of omission and commission is a stone you are adding in building your future, the future of your business, family, ministry et al. If you allow complacency to influence you into settling in a comfort zone instead of sacrificing for the future good, then you should not be surprised if you run into a future with a 'collapsed building.' If you live above your means today, you will live in need and lack tomorrow. It has nothing to do with the devil; it has everything to do with poor foundations built with cheap stones. God needs you to lay some expensive foundation-stones in the hearts and minds of everyone in your sphere of influence.

The mess we are seeing in our society today, is a direct result of the cheap "foundation stones" being used in our school system, on our media landscape, and in political discourse to train our children. We have allowed our children to be indoctrinated with everything and anything that is against the Word of God. Our silence in the face of moral rottenness has already become a death sentence against spiritual growth and godliness. Check the quality of the stones you are using to lay your foundations.

Remember that when you are finished with the foundations, no one can see them because they will be hidden in the ground, but there are storms in your future that will test them. When that time comes and you have used "costly stones," there will be no cause to worry; but if you have compromised the foundation, you will have to contend with failure. Carefully choose the stones (deeds and words) you use, to ensure you build for yourself and others, a future that can stand the test of time.

God bless you

Give God some Praise

Ps. 67:5-7, NKJV

Let the peoples praise you, O God; Let all the peoples praise You. Then the earth shall yield her increase; God, our own God shall bless us. God shall bless us, and all the ends of the earth shall fear Him.

Praising God is an eternal exercise. One day all praying, preaching, healing, and prophesying will cease; but praise unto God will continue through all eternity. The psalmist presents praise as spiritual rain that causes the earth to "yield her increase." This means a "Praiser" will always stand in an atmosphere of freshness. Whenever you praise the Lord, you trigger divine response. God's presence and peace saturates your whole being. You come to know and have a foretaste of heaven. You may not have immediate physical healing, but even while you hurt, there is assurance of divine help.

Today is the beginning of a new phase of life for all of us. It's a day that has never been and will never be. You have come this far only because God's grace located and kept you. Show some gratitude. Give God some praise. Don't wait till tomorrow. Your praise has the potential of breaking every yoke in your life.

God delights in your praise. Give God the praise. You have the power to change whatever is happening in your life; especially to bring freshness to your dryness. Give God a celebration of praise, and a harvest of blessings shall be yours for the taking.

God bless you.

Dealing with Rejection

Jn.6:65-67, NKJV

And he added, "This is the very reason I told you that no one can come to me unless the Father makes it possible for him to do so." Because of this, many of Jesus' followers turned back and would not go with him anymore. So he asked his disciples, "And you— would you also like to leave?"

Not too long ago, I had the privilege of ministering to a pastor who was going through extremely painful marriage crisis. He was so devastated he became suicidal. While on the plane to meet him, I asked the Holy Spirit to give me a direct word of wisdom for the pastor's particular situation, and this was exactly what the Lord ministered to me; you cannot keep what you cannot keep. You don't die because someone you love and care about, rejects your love. That amounts to worshipping that person.

There are situations you can never change, and you do yourself a world of good by learning to live with it and above it. Jesus saw that the people he cared about were only following him because of the free bread they ate the previous day, so he had to tell them in plain language that he was more concerned about the destiny of their souls than the demands of their flesh. Unfortunately, but not surprisingly, his "congregation" took offense and they all walked out of "church" leaving only the leadership team of twelve disciples. Note carefully Jesus' reaction to that mass-walkout and obvious rejection; he allowed them to go.

He may not have been happy about it, but he was not going to beg them to accept the truth of the gospel. He was clear in his mind that his role was to preach, and the Father decides the results. Jesus set us an example to accept the things we cannot change and move on with our lives. This is not to suggest that you do nothing to try and restore broken-down relationships, no! It is to lay bare the fact that it is possible in this life to sometimes come to a dead-end with people who simply don't want to have anything to do with you.

God expects you to allow such people to walk away. Don't cry over spilt milk. You have a whole life ahead of you with its own joys and challenges. Holding on to a past you cannot control or change and blaming yourself for the cause of rejection is not necessary; indeed, it is very unhealthy and counterproductive. Jesus wants you to understand that the people God has divinely ordained to be with you cannot leave you. Even when you are in different geographical locations you still feel the connection.

On the reverse side, there may be some you trust to be with you "till death do you part" because they swore to it, but who walked away when you least expected and in such a manner that caused you maximum emotional pain. Don't hate them for it. Pray for strength to move on. There is more to life than those who left you. At least there will always be some people who will forever love you for you. Connect to them and continue your journey with joy and gladness. Smile through the storm, for this too shall pass.

God bless you.

Sin Must Not Rule

Rom.6:11-14, GNB

And so because he died, sin has no power over him; and now he lives his life in fellowship with God. In the same way you are to think of yourselves as dead, so far as sin is concerned, but living in fellowship with Christ Jesus. Sin must no longer rule in your mortal bodies, so that you obey the desires of your natural self. Nor must you surrender any part of yourselves to sin to be used for wicked purposes. Instead, give yourselves to God, as those who have been brought from death to life, and surrender your whole being to him to be used for righteous purposes. SIN MUST NOT BE YOUR MASTER (caps mine); for you do not live under law but under God's grace.

When I accepted Jesus Christ as my Lord and personal Savior some thirty-seven years ago, I initially lived under the false impression that since the scripture says in 2 Cor.5:17 that when one is in Christ, old things are passed away and everything is become new, I was beyond temptation. Soon I was to find out that I was misinterpreting scripture, and that I was into fighting more battles against the sinful nature than I ever bargained for.

The Holy Spirit was not going to turn me into a remotely controlled human machine. No. God makes available the power to live a victorious life and overcome the trappings of sin, but it was forever going to be my responsibility to choose how to live my life. If I choose to live in sin, I make sin my MASTER; and if I choose to live in accordance with God's Word, God becomes my MASTER. No two ways about that. Jesus said you cannot serve two masters, and that is applicable to the choices we make as to whether we live for God or in sin.

Sin cannot impose itself on you, so you can always excuse yourself from sin by choice. At best it will "pinch" and excite your flesh and wait for your response. Whether you stand or fall is your choice. The new birth in Christ does not give us immunity from sin. Indeed, you become more sensitive to the cravings of the sinful nature. The scripture offers two solutions here. First, "you are to think of yourselves as dead to sin." You must die to sin. A dead body is not aware of anything happening around him. That's the first thing you must do to yourself to gain power over sin; die to it. Don't entertainment it, or it will enslave you.

The second is to "live in fellowship with Christ Jesus." In John 15:5c Jesus said, "for you can do nothing without me." Overcoming sin is not simply a matter of will-power; it is a matter of tapping into God's power. It is a battle that is fought and won by yielding to the leadership of the Holy Spirit. These are evil days, and sin is the official language of almost every society, but you should not bend to the whims and caprices of men. Draw on the strength which Christ supplies through the Holy Spirit and pursue righteousness.

You owe no one apology for standing up for God. If society says it is its human right to live in sin, it is your divine right to live for God. Be holy, because it is healthy - spiritually, physically, emotionally, psychologically et al. Have a wonderful day, and God empower and bless you to live for him and not in sin.

God bless you.

Live Each Moment Like It's Your Last

2 Pet.3:8-9, NKJV

But, beloved, do not forget this one thing, that with the Lord one day is as a thousand years, and a thousand years as a day. The Lord is not slack concerning His promise, as some count slackness, but is longsuffering toward us, not willing that any should perish but that all should come to repentance.

The Second Coming of Christ was very highly expected in the early church than it is today. Some of the saints, in their anxiety were beginning to wonder if the Lord was ever going to return in their lifetime. Peter, writing to address these concerns, asked them to be mindful of the fact that God operates outside the framework of human timing. Heaven does not use a 24-hour day clock or 12-month year calendar. What we may regard as a very long time, may be just a split of a second in God's sight.

God's "delay" is always for our good, but when we narrow down his promises to our programs and timing, we are bound to have problems. God is in eternity and want us to think in terms of eternity. Some of his promises will find fulfillment in this life, others will roll over into the hereafter. Whether it's now or then, here, or there, the Lord will do what he says he will do. Jesus Christ is coming again, and we must get ready. The signs are clear, with the world basking in wickedness and celebrating sin. The world has diluted moral sanity in the name of "human rights." That should not be so with us. We should be clear in our minds about the limits of our liberties, because "it won't be long, we'll be going home."

Let us live each moment as if that is the final moment. If you are living in sin, don't make any excuses; repent and come out of it. God is willing and able to give you grace to live in righteousness and truth. Do not do what everyone is doing. You are not everybody; you are God's royal priest, chosen vessel, apple of his eye, and bride of Christ. Do what is right towards God and all men, keeping in mind that your King is coming any second from now. Leave the arrival date of the Lord's coming in his hands. Your worry will have no impact on his timing. Live in the fullness of his joy as long as he keeps you here. Live a life that glorifies God. Endure to the end, until we see him face to face.

God bless you.

God wants a Shobi

2 Sam.17:27-29, NKJV

Now it happened, when David had come to Mahanaim, that Shobi the son of Nahash from Rabah...brought beds and basins, earthen vessels and wheat, barley and flour, parched grain and beans, lentils and parched seeds, honey and curds, sheep and cheese of the herd, for David and the people who were with him to eat. For they said, "The people are hungry and weary and thirsty in the wilderness."

Wilderness experience is a terrible experience; especially for a king like David, who for forty years had lived in the comfort of a palace. Absalom chased his father out into the wild, after cunningly undermining confidence in his dad, and stealing "the hearts of the men of Israel" (2 Sam.15:6). He executed his palace coup so well that the mass of the people fell for his treachery. It was in that gloomy and hopeless situation that a man named Shobi showed up.

He risked his life to bring relief to the king. In this singular act of love, reverence, and loyalty, we catch a glimpse of God's faithfulness to his anointed. Our focus however is on Shobi, the man God used to help the king in one of the most difficult seasons in his life. Shobi is a symbol of the people God has used and continues to use to help you in times of need. In every facet of life, you have to be careful not to lose sight of the "Shobi's" God brings along to encourage and strengthen you.

Some may come with material support, while others will come with words of encouragement. Do not take them for granted. They must be in your prayers every day. Ask God's blessing on their lives. You should also seek to be a Shobi to others -your spouse, children, friends, and even strangers. Sacrifice something for the good of everyone who needs your help without demanding an applause. When Shobi had done what needed to be done to bring relief to the king and his entourage, he walked away. That page of his history was closed. His mission was accomplished, and his joy was made complete.

When you get offended for not being recognized for your role in helping others, you are not a giver; you are a creditor. God wants you to be a Shobi. Give help without any strings attached to your giving. And if you are out there in a wilderness-experience presently, running from some Absalom (sickness, financial, job or family crisis etc.), trust God for a Shobi.

Sometimes the person may be there, but you are so pre-occupied with the crisis that you are not aware of the help you are receiving from him. Your advantage as a blood-bought child of God is that even when there is no human help in your wilderness, God's very Presence is with you. The Holy Spirit is your ever-present Shobi. You are not alone. Peace be to you.

God bless you.

Time will Tell

Gen. 42:29-31, NKJV

Then they went to Jacob their father in the land of Canaan and told him all that had happened to them saying; "The man who is lord of the land spoke roughly to us and took us for spies of the country. But we said to him, 'we are honest men...'"

This was part of the report Joseph's brothers brought to their father about their experience in Egypt. Of course, at that point in time, they had not recognized Joseph and simply referred to the brother they had sold into slavery, as "the man who is lord of the land." What they failed to realize then was that the lord of Egypt was the same lad they rejected as God's chosen savior of their family. Learn this in good time; being jealous about someone's gifts, position, or achievement, will do nothing to change what God has ordained for that person.

Now here comes Joseph's brothers describing themselves as "honest men." They deceived their earthly father, but not our Heavenly Father. This is the second lesson: God's opinion about you should matter most to you than the impression you create before men. The sons of Jacob were very successful in deceiving their father and for many years lived in the comfort of the old man accepting them as honest men. There was no question of repentance because there was no exposure of any wrongdoing on their part. Living with a lie, and saying you are what you know you are not, is one of the highest forms of self-deception.

An honest person does not need to go shouting from the rooftop about his honesty. If you are honest, time will tell. People will know you by your fruit. Let God be judge, and time will confirm it. Sometimes your good intentions may be misconstrued, and men may use very defamatory words to describe you. You need to explain your position as and when you have the opportunity; beyond that, you have to wait, for "time will tell" who you really are. Joseph's brothers lived for many years under the illusion that their true colors would never be seen. The "plane" finally landed, and they were exposed for who they really were.

Beloved, if "honest men" are selling you into "Egypt," keep a cool head. Do not be distracted by the attacks and accusations. A day is coming when God will vindicate you. Those who sold you will come to you for food. Give it to them. They will no longer call you negative names, but rather, "lord of the land." Stay blessed, honest, and truthful. It pays good dividends.

God bless you.

Productivity is Key to Prosperity

2 Thess.3:6-10, GNB

Our brothers, we command you in the name of our Lord Jesus Christ to keep away from all brothers who are living a lazy life and who do not follow the instructions that we gave you, and we are sure that you are doing and will continue to do what we tell you. You yourselves know very well that we did not accept anyone's support without paying for it. Instead we worked and toiled; we kept working day and night so as not to be an expense to any of you. We did it to be an example for you to follow. While we were with you, we told you, "Whoever refuses to work is not allowed to eat."

One of my personal weaknesses is lack of patience with lazy people; especially when they claim to be Christians. It is interesting how such folks tend to think they have a right to what everyone has worked for, when all they love to do is sit and stare. Everybody within our circle of friends complains about the rate at which my wife works, and sometimes I have cause to complain too. But truth is, knowing where we have come from, and where we believe God wants to take our ministry, laziness is not an option.

The God who gives grace expects hard work, long-term commitment, prudent management, and integrity. All of these are components of hard work. Thank God for what Apostle Paul wrote to the church in Thessalonica; Christianity is not for idlers. The God of the Bible is a worker, not an idler. Our entire body is fashioned for work, and that is the reason why even without hands and limbs, some have been able to impact the world. The believer's worship cannot be separated from his work, so whatever opportunity comes your way to do something positive, take it.

Activity brings productivity, and productivity is the pathway to prosperity. The scripture clearly says that if someone has the opportunity to work but doesn't want to work, you have no business sharing your food with him. He has made a decision that should not be encouraged, because of the long-term consequences on himself and society at large. No pain, no gain. May the good Lord bless the work of your hands in Jesus Name.

God bless you.

Embrace Change

Jn.16:7, NKJV

"Nevertheless, I tell you the truth. It is to your advantage that I go away; for if I do not go away, the Helper will not come to you; but if I depart, I will send Him to you."

Life in Christ is premised on losing to gain. Those who want to grow in Christ must learn to constantly release past experiences for fresh revelation of His glory. The disciples at this point in time were so comfortable with the physical presence of the Lord that when He hinted His departure from them, no one was prepared to discuss the topic. They simply were not interested because they did not want that to happen. They had enjoyed walking, talking, eating, and doing so much stuff with Jesus, they were unwilling to let go.

It was too dangerous experimenting with "another comforter". They were okay with familiar territory so any discussion about going to the next level was out of the question. Jesus saw He had some explaining to do, to bring the disciples on board; He pointed out to them the necessity for change so God's purpose could be advanced. You may be enjoying something that God has taken away, or is about to take away, and you may be feeling like it is the end of your world. Beloved, it is not. The "good" must give way to the "better", and the "better" must give way to the "best".

When God initiates change (be it spiritual or physical), it always comes with a better alternative, although it may contain an element of temporary bitterness, disappointment, emptiness, and pain. Apostle Paul says even when our physical bodies grow weak, our inner man grows stronger. Something must go for something to come. If God is initiating a change in your life, seek His strength to embrace it. Some blessings will never come to you until and unless some people and some things get out of your life.

Don't be afraid of the change. Embrace it. Jesus Christ in physical manifestation was limited to a geographical location. But when He left, the Holy Spirit who came manifested Him everywhere, unlimited by time, substance, or space. Let God move you out of limited experience to a higher level of revelation and impartation. You are wired for continued growth and unlimited possibilities.

Go for it!

God bless you.

Let the Children Come to Jesus Now

Joel 1:3, NKJV

Tell your children about it, let your children tell their children, and their children another generation.

Joel prophesied at a time of great distress in Judah. The invasion of locusts was something the people had never witnessed in their lives. All that happened as a result of sin, but despite the judgement, God promised restoration. In order for the people not to forget what brought them so low and brought the judgment, the prophet admonished them to "tell their children" and proceeding generations about it. If there is one area in which the Church continues to fail God, it is in Children's Ministry.

Sometimes I am tempted to believe most pastors and parents don't see it as a serious calling to teach the children the things we have learnt from God's Word, and the experiential knowledge we have gained in serving him. Much of what we teach and share about Christ with our children, are mere tokens of scripture without depth and impact. Perhaps because they don't bring in tithes and tangible offerings, the Church (generally speaking), does not give them as much attention as we give the adults. This mistake is what is breeding empty chapels and moral decadence the world over.

Our healthy "traditions" have been taken over by unhealthy technology. Religions that are experiencing phenomenal growth have one thing in common; they don't take chances with their children. They make conscious effort to teach their beliefs to their children. Indeed, with some it is an imposition, which of course is to the extreme and not recommended by our faith. One major Orthodox Church used to go by the precept, "give me a child before he or she is six years old, and he/she will forever remain a part of the faithful".

Children are raw materials ready to be fashioned into any product by the hand willing to hold, mold, and lead them in love. Attending Sunday morning service with your child is good, but not enough to give him the foundation he needs to make a life-long commitment to Christ. Your first and most vibrant church should be your home. That is where you have all the time and space to teach by word, and show by example, the truths of the gospel.

The battle to reach this generation for Christ is not easy, due to the things our children are exposed to on social media and other media platforms like television etc. But thank God for grace; we still have hope that the Spirit of God is able to break through the iron curtain of moral perversion in this present age, if we take the time and make the effort to TEACH them the way of God. They may not always get it right, but the seed you sow in them will never die. Let the children come to Jesus NOW, before it is too late.

God bless you.

Stay Humble

2 Sam.7:29, NKJV

"Now therefore, let it please You to bless the house of Your servant, that it may continue before You forever; for You, O LORD GOD, have spoken it, and with Your blessing let the house of Your servant be blessed forever."

David never allowed his elevation from shepherd boy to statesman, get in the way of his reverence and submission to the Lord. The difference between him and King Saul is so loud and clear. Whereas Saul moved away from God after he became king of Israel, David was very consistent in his humility and obedience towards God throughout his life. Whenever he sinned against God, he was always quick to repent. He never made excuses for his blunders. His humility towards God was phenomenal.

2 Sam. 7:18 reads, "Then King David went in and sat before the LORD; and said, 'Who am I, O LORD GOD? And what is my house, that You have brought me this far?'" This statement alone is a reflection of a man who does not only know where he was coming from, but also acknowledges WHO was the source of his success and victory. He was not complacent and would not take the blessings on his life for granted. David was grateful for all God had done, but he would not live on yesterday's manna. He prayed for the blessings to continue. He prayed God's promises back to him. He said, "let it please you to bless the house of Your servant, that it may continue before you forever; for you, O LORD, have spoken it."

The fact that God had said it, gave David a blank check to cash the blessings. Three lessons stand out here; the first is that no matter how high God lifts you, the glory must always go back to him. Always remember you cannot ascend any higher than the God who lifted you up to where you are presently. You must continue to humble yourself enough to be willing to "sit" before him like David everyday of your life. Secondly, you've got to avoid the temptation of taking God's promises for granted. Pray back the Word to God, showing you trust him for its fulfillment, and are prepared to wait for as long as it takes.

Thirdly, the blessings on your life can be truncated; that was the reason David prayed, "let the house of your servant be blessed FOREVER." He saw what happened to King Saul, who was also chosen and blessed by God, but in the end lost his throne, family, and life, in a very undignified manner. While you rejoice in your past achievements and success stories, do not forget the God who made it possible for you to come this far.

Deepen your relationship with him by constantly confessing his goodness and asking for his continued grace on your life. "Sit" before him every day in prayer, worship, and studying of the Word. Pride cannot penetrate a posture of humility, and as long as you "sit" in God's Presence, his grace will empower you to "withstand in the evil day and having done all to stand." (Eph.6:13b, NKJV).

God bless you

You will Overcome

Job 3:11-13, NKJV

Why did I not die at birth? Why did I not perish when I came from the womb? Why did the knees receive? Or why the breast that I should nurse? For then I would have lain still and been quiet, I would have been asleep; Then I would have been at rest.

Why? This is a simple, unassuming word, loaded with messages and mysteries. It is a word that everyone of us have asked, may be asking, and will continue to ask God, ourselves, and others, several times in this life. Even Jesus, in his moment of excruciating pain on the cross, asked "why" the Father had forsaken him. The interesting thing about the word "why" is that sometimes we ask when (like Jesus), we already know the reason. It comes as a spontaneous response to unbearable pain and frustrating events.

We normally don't ask "why" when life is good and everything around us is going as planned and makes a lot of sense. Job had no idea about the confidence God had in his ability to keep the faith in the face of adversity. Satan had argued that Job's love for God was a result of God's blessing on his life; that if things turn against Job, he will denounce the Lord (Job 1&2). When Satan was given permission to assault Job, God did not tell Job about what was taking place in the spirit-realm. In his extraordinary suffering, Job came to a point where he felt his very birth was a mistake. He asked the one question every human being would have asked and will continue to ask "until Shiloh comes;" that powerful word, "why".

The sick are asking, "why is God not healing me?" The jilted spouse is asking, why is he/she doing this to me? The frustrated parent is asking, "why is my child making these bad choices?" There are too many "why's" that we cannot have answers to, because as in Job's case, we don't have any way of accessing every activity in the spirit realm that impacts our lives. It is impossible to know all the reasons for all we have to contend with.

Difficult challenges should remind us of the need to live by faith, because sometimes they are sanctioned by God and we cannot change them. Job wished he had not been born, but he could not reverse the fact of his existence. To do so would have meant to cut short his life and miss out on the greater blessing awaiting him at the end of the tunnel. You may have a lot of unanswered why's on your mind right now. They are legitimate because you are in pain, frustrated, confused, and feeling hopeless.

You want answers to your anguish, and you want them now. Calm down. Look at the cross of Christ with an eye of faith and pray the question (why) to our Father in heaven. Trust him to sustain you, even if he does not remove the "thorn in your flesh." A day came when Job's "why" was answered with restoration of everything he had lost and more. A day came when Jesus' "why" was answered with resurrection. Your day will come when God will answer the "why" of your life. He is the same God, yesterday, today, and forever. Keep the faith and kick the fear. You will overcome.

God bless you.

Sharing is Caring

Lu.22:14,17, NKJV

When the hour had come, He sat down, and the twelve apostles with Him...Then he took the cup, and gave thanks, and said, "Take this and divide it among yourselves;"

Jesus gives us a picture of consistently sharing what he has with those who do not have. On more than one occasion in the scriptures, we see him giving instructions to his disciples to share or distribute something to meet the need of people. When the wine run out at the wedding in Cana (Jn.2:1-11), his first reaction was to do a miracle that would benefit everyone. In the feeding of the 5,000 with five loaves of bread and two fish, the same scenario was played out.

By these positive examples, Jesus is showing us that those who care, are those who share. There was no better place to re-echo this principle of caring and sharing, than at the communion table. The body of Christ was not broken for one person. It was broken for all humanity, irrespective of color, gender, age, or social status; "for all have sinned and fallen short of the glory of God." His blood was shed for all because God's gift of salvation is meant for all. The Christian life is a life of caring and sharing, not getting, and keeping.

When was the last time you shared "the wine and the bread of life" with a lost soul? Every time you have the opportunity to minister salvation to an unbeliever and you don't take your chances, you are violating the principle of caring and sharing. It doesn't matter what spin you put on it; failure to share, is admission that you don't care. You can do better than that. God has entrusted you with an assignment he knows you are capable of carrying out.

You are empowered by the Holy Spirit for great exploits, but you cannot rise to the level of manifesting great works until you begin to release and give out. Remember that the Dead Sea remains dead because it receives water without giving out any. Be part of what God is doing in the earth today by sharing your faith in Christ, and you will never run dry of God's Presence, Power, and peace.

God bless you.

Lamp of the Lord

Prov.20:27, NKJV

The spirit of a man is the lamp of the LORD, searching all the inner depths of his heart.

Anyone not born-again of the Spirit of God, has a spirit that is in utter darkness. Jesus put it this way: "If therefore the light in you is darkness, how great is that darkness" (Matt.6:23b). The "spirit of a man is THE LAMP (or candle) of the LORD." An unlighted lamp or candle is as good as poisonous water to a thirsty traveler. Every one of us has God's Spirit dwelling in us, but that spirit or lamp only comes alive when it is ignited by the Holy Spirit.

As long as a man rejects Christ, he carries an unlighted lamp (spirit). He is dead, and that makes him completely insensitive to the things of God. It takes the entrance of the Holy Spirit into a man's heart to lighten or quicken his spirit (which is "the lamp of the Lord") to come alive and respond to God. Like attracts like; and so, a dead soul full of darkness, cannot interact with the light of the Living God. Note that "the spirit of a man is the lamp of the Lord;" meaning it is God's bona fide property.

In Rev.2:5, the Risen Lord served notice to the Ephesian church that if they don't repent, "I will come to you quickly and remove your lamp-stand from its place." Is your lamp lighted or filled with darkness? Remember God began his creative work with light. You need that light to live your life, and THE ONLY TRUE LIGHT OF THE WORLD IS JESUS CHRIST; nothing added, nothing subtracted. If you haven't given your life to Jesus, your spirit is like a beautiful lamp decorating a dark room. It is of no use to the owner until it is lighted.

Receive Jesus Christ into your life today, and the entrance of his Spirit will inflame your spirit with power and passion for God. He will bring clarity to the confusion in your life. Are you born-again and yet living in sin? Is your light dim or completely gone out? The Holy Spirit wants to give you fresh fire. All you need to do is repent. Embrace the love of Christ and you will receive the light of God.

God bless you

God Will not Let you Down

Hos.11:3-4, NKJV

> *I taught Ephraim to walk, taking them by their arms; but they did not know that I healed them. I drew them with gentle cords, with bands of love, and I was to them as those who take the yoke from their neck. I stooped and fed them.*

Those who take a stand against the Lord have one thing in common: ignorance of his unfeigned love towards us. When God does not do everything we want, it still boils down to love. There are some things God does for us without asking for our participation or contribution. That does not mean God has to do everything for us. Many times, he teaches us "to walk." He knows we don't know how to walk, so he takes it upon himself to teach us how to do it. He is aware that if he leaves us on our own to run our lives, we will mess up our destiny; so, in teaching us to walk, God takes us by the "arms."

He does not drag or pull us along, but gently moves at a pace he knows we can endure. Like toddlers trying their first few steps, we often want to hit the road running. We ignore our Teacher's outstretched arm, and even after we've hurt ourselves and He has graciously healed our wounds, we fail to acknowledge him. This grieves the Holy Spirit. Our obsession with unmet needs often blind us to the moves God is already making to better our lot. What a privilege for the Creator of the entire universe to "stoop and feed" us.

You may be lacking something materially, but as far as your spiritual supply is concerned, the Lord has your back covered. King David confirmed this awesome leading of God and wrote for our instruction in Ps.23:2b, "He leads me beside the still waters." The king of Israel could not for once imagine his God leading him into destruction, so even when he found himself in very uncomfortable situations, he had no problem declaring his continued faith and trust in God. Wake up to the truth of God's unfailing love for you. Any attack on your peace and joy is a weapon the enemy is using to create doubt about God's love but let me tell you this; if it had not been for the Lord, you would not be here today.

If you are "fed up" with God and have walked away from him, his Spirit is waiting for you to come back to his arms of love. If your hand is in His hands and you are contemplating removing it and having your own way, don't do it. Trust God through the trial. He will lead you with his gentle arm. When you think he is being slow, it is because that is the speed he has determined for you to go. If God says he stooped to feed Israel, he will do same for you. He will not let you down. Thank him for being there for you always.

God bless you

Miracles are only Signposts

Jn.6:25-27, NKJV

And when they found Him on the other side of the sea, they said to Him, "Rabbi, when did you come here?" Jesus answered them and said, "Most assuredly, I say to you, you seek Me, not because you saw the signs, but because you ate of the loaves and were filled. Do not labor for food which perishes, but for the food which endures to everlasting life, which the Son of Man will give you, because God the Father has set his seal of approval on Him."

Jesus never seems to me to be ever concerned about being diplomatic or politically correct. His love for humanity wouldn't allow him to pretend it's okay and look away from addressing issues of deception, hypocrisy, and selfishness. When he fed the 5,000 men in the wilderness, his purpose was to get them to commit themselves to God and serve him. Unfortunately, that was not to be; when they came looking for him the following day, it was to get more free bread.

They may have invited many families and friends to come along for the easy life that the ministry-work of Jesus Christ appeared to offer. My guess is that many of today's church leaders would have applauded them for coming back with such high expectations for more miracles, and more importantly for inviting cousins, uncles, boyfriends, and girlfriends, to the 'Jesus Free Bread Miracle Service.' The Lord was not enthused with the sheer numbers; he was more concerned about the motive, and he was not diplomatic about it. This is what he said to them: "I say to you, you seek Me not because you saw the signs, but BECAUSE YOU ATE OF THE LOAVES AND ARE FILLED."

Beloved, God's miracles are meant to be sign-posts directing us to him, not away from him. The Church is dead wrong in using "the loaves" as bait to fill the pews. We are turning our backs on God's purpose by ordaining men and women who look on ministry as a means to earn an easy living, not a call to serve Christ. In my part of the world, it is getting worse by the day, as we witness the rise in the number of false prophets, self-appointed apostles, pastors, and teachers; some of whom demand payment for prayer. We are seeing young people who are not prepared to face the challenges of life, suddenly pronouncing themselves bishops and prophets.

When they preach, it is motivation to make wealth, devoid of repentance and reaching out to lost souls. They set goals to have houses they never worked to build, cars they never worked to buy; all at the expense of a gullible flock. And if you are unfortunate to have them as friends, you can be sure you are wearing shoes without soles. Get ready to be pricked by thorns if you don't want to face the truth of what you are dealing with. Jesus refused to feed the greed and laziness of people who did not have any spiritual thirst, love for God, and integrity. The lesson is this; there must be a willingness to seek the Kingdom first, and the "loaves" will be added; not by man, but by God.

God bless you

God Accepts You

Ps.139:3-4, NKJV

You comprehend my path and my lying down, and are acquainted with all my ways.
For there is not a word on my tongue, but behold, O LORD, You know it altogether

---

Having a close relationship with someone, gives you insight into what they are likely to say or do in any given situation. Parents, spouses, and friends can rightly predict the body language of their children, partners, and colleagues because of years of association. We can admit however that in all our human relationships, our knowledge and understanding of each other is limited; that is why we often surprise each other with the things we say and do. That also explains why we sometimes hurt each other.

God, however, does not need to google any information about us. Indeed, he knows us more than we know ourselves. The scripture says he understands "my path and my lying down and is acquainted with all my ways." There is no other person in your life who can claim such absolute knowledge and understanding of the 'why' and 'how' of your life. Knowing the full extent of your strengths and weaknesses, God has chosen to accept you where men reject you. He alone understands your pain and challenges, and gives consolation where men are quick to judge and place you under condemnation.

The depth of God's knowledge and acceptance of who you are, where you are, and precisely how you are feeling right now, should inspire you to want to keep moving on with your life. You cannot get everyone to understand what you do, or how you feel, but you can be sure God knows everything about you and is ready to help you. Your best is yet to come.

God bless you

Don't Show Partiality

Jam.2:2-3, NKJV

For if there should come into your assembly a man with gold rings, in fine apparel, and there should also come in a poor man in filthy clothes, and you pay attention to the one wearing the fine clothes and say to him, "You sit here in a good place," or, "Sit here at my footstool," have you not shown partiality among yourselves, and become judges with evil thoughts?

Anytime I read the history of the early Church, I see a world of difference between their concept and practice of Christianity, and our present perspective of the faith. The scripture shows that when they identified a wrong, they did not brush it under the carpet, but addressed it. This was one of the reasons the Church grew stronger and faster, despite the vicious hate-campaign and unprecedented persecution mounted against her.

Relational issues were of paramount importance to leadership of the early Church. Nobody was made to feel inferior or out of place. In Acts 6:1-7, when 'tribalism' tried to rear its ugly head in the Church, the apostles were quick to nip it in the bud. Our weakness today is what Apostle James was complaining about; discrimination in the Church on the basis of who a person is, or what a person has. If you have a lot of bucks, we give you a padded seat at the front, no matter your moral ineptitude. If your tithe is the main cushion to the budget, you are beyond being corrected. Sometimes I wonder if we believe we are all heading towards the SAME heaven.

Our confusion is a creation of our carnality. Most things are interpreted in terms of wealth and influence. I have heard preachers say they want "quality people" in their churches. Since when did God create a human being who has no "quality" (value)? Christ died for all; both rich and poor. What you must never forget is that every human being you meet is first and foremost a spirit being, living in a human body. No matter the color of his skin, the state of his health or wealth, God loves him because he created him. Whether he is responsible for his poor state or not, does not justify any discrimination against him. Why? Because while we were still sinners Christ died for us, and that message must be preached to the world, not only in words but also in works of kindness and love.

Shabby treatment of the poor and disadvantaged, is an indication of spiritual immaturity and lack of understanding of what faith in Christ is all about. Thank God for the "robes of righteousness" prepared for us in glory; it will effectively neutralize the class and club mentality of the Church. You are either part of the Bride of Christ, or out on your own forever. Look at people through the love-lenses of God, not the myopic concept of discrimination. Let the poor feel equally welcome and accepted among God's people. The kingdom of God is not for a selected group of people; for as many as believed him, he gave them power to become children of God (Jn.1:12).

God bless you.

No Longer Afraid of Death

Eze. 37:11-12, NKJV

Then He said to me, "Son of man, these bones are the whole house of Israel. They indeed say, 'Our bones are dry, our hope is lost, and we ourselves are cut off!' "Therefore prophesy and say to them, 'Thus says the Lord GOD: "Behold, O My people, I will open your graves and cause you to come up from your graves, and bring you into the land of Israel."

In Rev.1:18 Jesus made an extraordinary declaration that no one else can make except God. The import of that statement is that he is the ultimate decision-maker in matters of life and death. Apostle Paul, having a deep understanding of this revelation wrote: "whether I live or die, I live or die for Jesus." Knowledge of this truth is key to freedom from fear of death. It gives you all the peace you need to live in the liberty that the Holy Spirit gives. Shakespeare's Julius Caesar said, "cowards die many times before their death," and that is very true with people who live in constant fear of death.

God wants you to know that where He is in charge of affairs, death does not have the final say, because it is subject to a higher authority called Jesus, the Christ. God has the power to reverse every adversity. When asked about the fate of the dry bones, Ezekiel told the Lord it all depended him. The prophet was not confused about his limitations as a servant of God. That humble response opened the door for the next level of divine assignment; to proclaim a message of hope and restoration. He became God's partner in restoring life to a "dead" nation.

What are the issues overwhelming you, and how hopeless and helpless are you feeling today? You are looking at some situations that are not showing any signs of changing or coming back to life. They are not only dead, but dead and dry. It is time to step out of the pressure and enter God's peace. Ezekiel's position on the matter should be your stand in times of stress; the final outcome of every challenge is in God's hands, and so let him lead the way. If God doesn't raise the dead, no one can. You can have peace in every difficult situation, knowing that nothing affecting your life happens on the blind side of our God.

The Savior of your soul takes no pleasure in seeing "dry bones" in your life. Prayerfully seek his face, while you "prophesy to the dry bones." It May take longer than you wish, but he will come through for you. When Ezekiel spoke the prophetic Word, everything didn't happen at once. There was a process of spiritual formation before the physical manifestation. That is the way you will get to your level of liberation. God will never leave you in shame and disgrace. He loves you too much to do that to you. Your dry bones will surely come back to life in Jesus' Name.

God bless you.

God will Speak for You and through You

Matt.10:19-20, GNB

When they bring you to trial, do not worry about what you are going to say or how you will say it; when the time comes, you will be given what you will say. For the words you will speak will not be yours; they will come from the Spirit of your Father speaking through you

---

Life is full of times and seasons of trials. Many of the trials we face put pressure on us, causing much anxiety, stress, and worry. In the context of today's scripture, Jesus was preparing his disciples for the persecution they were going to face because of the gospel. He reckoned that being arrested and brought to trial for their faith, was not going to be easy for his followers; especially when it came to how to provide appropriate answers to the questions they were going to be asked.

The solution he provides is what you need to overcome every single trial that you face today; let the Holy Spirit take over your response. Don't struggle, and don't worry about what you ought to say or do. Stop trying to cross the bridge before you get to it. Let God speak to the situation. If worry could ever solve a problem, many of us would be better off than we are today. Worrying about something beyond your capability, only drains your strength and wears you out. Jesus Christ is showing us that God is not going to tell us everything before it happens. We've got to learn to live by faith.

When we find ourselves in situations where we don't know what to say or do, there is one thing we must remember to do; we must keep trusting God for "fair trial." He is both our advocate and judge, and always has a way or word to address whatever trials we face. It is important as a child of God to realize your limitations. You can do "all things through Christ who strengthens you," but you cannot do those things that only God can do.

What Christ has not strengthened you to do, you simply cannot do it. If you don't yield to him when you should, you may compound your problem by saying what you shouldn't say or doing what you shouldn't do. Be confident that God is with you, and will "speak" for you, and through you, in every trial you go through.

God bless you.

Preservation in God

Ps.145:20a,21

The Lord preserves all who love Him...My mouth shall speak the praise of the LORD. And all flesh shall bless His holy name forever and ever

The things we preserve, are things we value; and the things we value most, are the things we preserve longest. When you don't love something, or someone is not related to you in any meaningful way, you don't waste time trying to keep them. You only keep what you value, and that is why you don't keep every food item in your refrigerator. Some of your leftover foods are only good enough for the trash can.

The pain and disappointment you feel in losing someone or something precious to you, is vested in the truth that we all love to "preserve" what we love. God has loved us with immeasurable love, and his Word says our positive response to the love he showed us at Calvary triggers his protection. If you love the Lord, he will preserve you; this is God's unchanging and unfailing promise. Put your fears to rest. There is no principality, or power of darkness that can snatch you from the hands of God.

Instead of trumpeting the works of Satan and demons, confess the Word of God and praise his wonderful work of grace in your life. There is no surer Word of prophecy than the Holy Bible. Apostle Paul says our vision and prophecy is not perfect (1Cor.13:9) and will pass away, but not so with the Word of God; it is a solid database of truth and life. You only have to believe what it says, and you will experience the manifestation of the promise in your life. Today, the Lord is saying to you that as long as you maintain a love-relationship with him, he will preserve you. Nothing can touch you without his permission, and whatever he allows will work out to your ultimate good.

You may be going through some very difficult times presently, and how you wish you could hear God speak some words of comfort to you. This is His Word of assurance to you; God is saying, "I will preserve you, because you love me." Let your mouth speak a different "language;" speak the language of praise. The sights and sounds around you may be ruthlessly unpleasant and discordant, but it has no power to change who our God is, or what he has purposed to accomplish in your life. Keep the faith and kick the fear. Let anthems of praise and thanksgiving fill your mouth, and His joy shall be your strength.

God bless you

Go, Preach, Teach

Matt.28:18-20, NIV

Then Jesus came to them and said, "All Authority in heaven and on earth has been given to me. Therefore go and make disciples of all nations, baptizing them in the name of the Father and of the Son and of the Holy Spirit, and teaching them to obey everything I have commanded you. And surely I am with you always, to the very end of the age."

When Jesus Christ rose from the dead, He gave all of us who claim to be His disciples an assignment. He said we are to go into all the world, not as mere tourists, and ordinary visitors, but as preachers and teachers of the gospel. And because there are many kinds of "gospels" being churned out there, I want to be specific about the Jesus-gospel. It is THE GOSPEL OF SALVATION that calls sinners to REPENTANCE.

My personal view is that if there is one area the Church universal is failing the Lord, it is in the area of sharing "the gospel of salvation". Our voices are low when it comes to telling the world it is sinking in sin and needs to repent. Today's preaching is not meant to "offend" the sinner; it is mostly about self-improvement, wealth creation, and the niceties of temporal stuff. For sure, there is nothing wrong with that. It is all in the Bible. God does not trade in poverty; but whatever a man acquires or possesses, he is still very poor without an assurance of salvation.

We cannot exchange salvation with salad, coffee, gold, or silver. Jesus also tells us to 'TEACH ALL THINGS I have commanded you". The problem is, how can you teach what you don't know? It surprises me how many Christians have been in church for years and cannot understand or explain very basic doctrines of the faith they profess. A teacher is supposed to know something the student does not know, so if we don't know what we should know, how can we teach what we are supposed to teach to those we lead to Christ? It is time we get serious in obeying the command of Jesus to (1) go (2) preach and (3) teach.

There are no specialists with special anointing for this simple assignment. If you are born-again, you have all it takes to reach out to all the world with all the Gospel. When I was growing up as a young Christian, we used to sing songs like, "Go tell it on the mountain, over the hills, and everywhere..." We don't hear these songs anymore because the burden for lost souls is gone. Let's stop playing church and start obeying Christ in these three areas of ministry - going, preaching, and teaching.

Paul told Timothy to "study to show yourself approved unto God". If you don't study the Word for yourself, you cannot win the world for Christ. Remember, "he who waters will himself be watered". The blood shed on Calvary is God's highest investment, and the returns on that investment is salvation of souls. Not winning souls to Christ amounts to wasting God's investment. We dare not fail Him. Let's spread the message. The lost sinner must be saved.

God bless you.

God will Prove Himself

Is.30:18, NIV

Yet the Lord longs to be gracious to you...Blessed are all who wait for him.

Our faith is put to test when we are challenged to wait for God. King Saul had a lot of problems with God because he was never able to pass the test of waiting. He placed his faith, fate, and security in the people, so when the people threatened to leave him, he moved when he did not have to move. The prophet Samuel gave a line in what should be his priority - "to obey is better than to sacrifice".

Today you might have so many things that you may be waiting on God for that are still stuck on the drawing board. Perhaps you have taken the lead role and you are expecting God to follow. He will not, but He will wait for you to handle it until you agree to hand it over to Him. God is so merciful and gracious and will prove Himself if you will deny yourself.

Bring Him out of the "exile" to which you have banished Him in your plans. Exalt Him, and your reward for waiting will amaze you. I bear witness that our God is good, gracious, and merciful, and I know your day is coming. God will glorify you...much sooner than you think.

God bless you.

Do it Now

Mk.16:1, NKJV

Now when the Sabbath was past, Mary the mother of James, and Salome brought spices, that they might come and anoint Him

---

In Jn.12:1-7, there is a story about Jesus being anointed by Mary with "very costly oil of spikenard" (v.6, NKJV). This provoked criticism from Judas Iscariot who posited that the fragrant oil poured on Jesus' feet should have been sold, and the money given to the poor. In response, Jesus said Mary had anointed his body "for the day of My burial." The only opportunity anyone could have had to anoint Jesus' body was whilst he was alive. Three days after his death was too late to benefit his glorified body.

Indeed, on resurrection morning, we see the well-meaning mother of James and Salome, coming to anoint the body of Jesus and meeting an empty tomb. The oil (gift) should have been given or poured on Jesus' body before his death. What is that saying to us? Whatever good lies in your hands to do, go ahead and do it NOW! Tomorrow may be too late. If you must visit someone in the hospital, why procrastinate? Our lives are not in our hands, so fulfill that obligation today. If you've got to witness to a lost soul, do it now. If you need to apologize to someone you've hurt or wronged in any way, don't wait; crucify your pride, and do it now. The women loved Jesus and sacrificed a lot to produce the oil to embalm his body, but their good intentions came to nothing, because the timing was wrong.

I prefer you showing me how much you love me in word and deed, while I am alive, rather than hating me all my life and bringing a truckload of flowers to my grave when I am dead and gone. It will be of no use to me because I will not be there to see and enjoy its beauty and fragrance. If there is anything God is prompting you to do, he wants you to do it today; so, lace your shoes and go do it. If you wait till "resurrection morning," you might meet an empty tomb, and would have wasted time and resources to no one's benefit.

God bless you

A "Little" Disobedience

Lu.17:32

Remember Lot's wife

One act of disobedience was all it took to cost Lot's wife her life. There are some things that we may do and get away with. The immediate consequences may not be as grave and swift as is usually the case and this can lead us into thinking we are succeeding. Lot's wife had a great deliverance from the judgement of fire and brimstone that fell on Sodom and Gomorrah. God gave a very simple instruction not to look back. He owes them no explanation for that instruction, in the same way that He owes us no apology for His words and acts of omission and commission.

When God says don't cheat on your spouse, you don't do it; simply because God said so. Period! When God says forgive everyone who offends you, you forgive; not because you are stupid, but simply because He is your Lord, and Master of your life. He says it, you do it. Remember Lot's wife. She was saved, yet she died an untimely, undeserved, and unnecessary death. Indeed, it was a very foolish death. Why did she look back? Was it to test God? Was it to outsmart God and get information she was not supposed to get? Was it curiosity or misdemeanor?

Whatever be her reason, Lot's wife paid a heavy price for disobeying God's instruction. This is written for our information and instruction. Let us reflect on this one "little" act of disobedience and what it cost Mrs. Lot and resolve never to look back when God says not to look back. Friends, I'd rather obey the Lord than die a foolish death through disobedience. The things you left behind in "Sodom and Gomorrah" should vacate your heart. Keep your eyes fixed on where the Lord is leading you, not the world you left behind. Rise with Christ from thoughts and things that hinder your growth and peace. Take your eyes off Sodom and Gomorrah. It belongs to your past, let it remain in your past. May you live and not die.

God bless you.

You are God's Property

Rom.14: 7-9, NKJV

For none of us lives to himself, and no one dies to himself. For if we live, we live to the LORD; and if we die, we die to the LORD. Therefore, whether we live or die, we are Lord's. For this end Christ died and rose and lived again, that He might be Lord of both the dead and the living.

God created us to "dominate" and take care of all his creation. This delegated authority appears to have been interpreted to mean we are lords of all we survey. We confuse the role of stewards and custodians with that of ownership. This scripture reminds us that we are God's property. Once you accept Jesus Christ as your Lord and personal Savior, there is a paradigm shift; the life you live from that moment onwards is totally subject to God's sovereign will. It is a call to absolute surrender of your will, so that it no longer matters whether you live or die; Jesus takes the first and last place in your life.

There are no borders or limitations to what God can do or allow in your life. Whether you live or die, you live or die for Jesus. Some of the things you planned for, may not turn out exactly the way you want, but you accept the result and move on with your life, because you know you don't have the final say. God is your boss, and he knows the terrain more than you do. You have no reason fighting his will for your life. You might end up struggling over pig-feed like the Prodigal Son. We are on a journey that is full of uncertainties, unpleasantries, and unresolved mysteries. God is the One you can trust and entrust yourself to and be eternally secure.

Nothing worse can happen to you than death, and even when that happens, your connection to God remains intact through all eternity. The reason Jesus died and did not remain dead but rose from dead, is to be "Lord of both the living and the dead." Whatever situation you find yourself in today, know that the One who owns you is aware, and stands with you and by you; supplying all the grace you need to keep running the race to the end. And even when nothing seems to be working for you, His unseen presence is silently maintaining a steady flow of life in your soul.

God bless you.

You are Who God says You are

Lu.4:3, NIV

The devil said to him, "If you are the Son of God, tell this stone to become bread."

In the most challenging times of our lives, the voice we hear loudest is the voice of the enemy. When we are sick or have lost a loved one; when we face financial challenges, or we are struggling with family relationships that are in crisis, that is when we hear the devil say, "if you are who God says you are, then prove it. If God can fix it, why are you still in this mess?" He did not start this game of attacking the very foundation of our faith today.

In the garden of Eden, he used the same tactic on Eve to create doubt about God's integrity. Satan knew that if he took a straight shot at God's integrity it wasn't going to work, so he just laid a trap with the simple question: "has God said you should not eat?" (Gen.3:1) When Eve made the mistake of engaging him in conversation, she opened the door for the fall of creation. In Lu.4:3, the devil came at Jesus (the Second Adam) with the same glass of juice, laced with the poison of pride. This time around he was dealing with his creator, and even though Satan knew he could not win, he was not deterred. He asked Jesus to PROVE his deity.

If the Lord had done what Satan suggested, he would have indirectly obeyed him, and fallen like the first Adam. Friend, you have nothing to prove to the devil, or anyone for that matter, when it comes to your faith, calling, or gifts. Any attempt to prove something God has said about you without recourse to his will and timing, can only make you a victim of demonic manipulation. It is even more dangerous when you try to be something God has not called you to be. Save yourself embarrassment and frustration by letting God be God.

Sometimes you may pray to God about issues troubling your mind and get an instant response. At other times, you get no response. What do you do? Invent your own solution? No. You leave matters in the hands of God. If you are a pastor, evangelist, prophet, Apostle, teacher, or all of it put together, please be mindful of the fact that the ultimate result of your ministry is not determined by you. Restrain yourself from the pressure to prove something God has not approved.

When you pray for the sick and healing comes, give God the glory. If healing is delayed, don't take it as personal failure, and try to do anything beyond what God's Word commands. It may lead you into the enemy's trap of pride. Refuse to "turn stones into bread" just to prove who you are, or what you have in God. You are who God says you are, whether in sickness or in health, in sorrow or in joy, in poverty or in plenty. The blessing always abides, despite the weight of the burden.

God bless you.

Home in God

Lam.3:58, NKJV

O Lord, you have pleaded the case for my soul; you have redeemed my life.

When Bible speaks of a lost soul, it is referring to someone who is disconnected from God as a result of sin. Before Jesus Christ came on earth to die for us, we were all held captive in sin, and were lost souls. The sin of Adam and Eve introduced us into a world of spiritual darkness called "death." We lost our original DNA and fell victim to spiritual disorientation, emotional confusion, and physical decay.

There was nothing in us, or in all creation that could re-engineer our fallen nature to become what the creator had meant it to be. We became selfish and self-centered, instead of selfless and God-centered. We tried to satisfy the void in our souls with our own "good" intentions and inventions, but the spiritual and material "gods" we created for ourselves couldn't quench our thirsts. It was in this state of hopelessness, with our souls roaming in careless abandon, that Jesus Christ stood up, stepped in, and brought us salvation.

The Lord "pleaded the case for my soul." That is why no one else deserves my praise and worship than the Lamb of God, Jesus Christ the Son of God. David said in Ps.23:3, "he restores my soul." The redemption of a soul is beyond the performance of any human being. Only God can bring you to himself, and that is the difference Christianity makes; while all other religions teach things to DO to be acceptable to God, our faith says the death of Christ has already DONE what needed to be done, and so we are acceptable to God.

Jesus Christ paid for our sins on the cross, and so our salvation is secured. We are no longer victims of dead religious performances, but victors through the finished work of Christ on Calvary. We don't need a "religion." We have a relationship with God. Our lost souls are now at home IN GOD through Christ. This is the source of our strength and peace. Give glory to the Lamb; in him you live, and move, and have your being.

God bless you

The Stones will Cry Out

Lu.19:39-40, NKJV

And some of the Pharisees called to Him from the crowd, "Teacher, rebuke your disciples." But He answered, "I tell you that if these should keep silent, the stones would immediately cry out."

I wonder what the Pharisees were doing among the crowd they themselves described as "disciples." This was a man they hated to the hilt, so why would they leave their homes to join a crowd celebrating him as Savior? The answer is very simple; they were looking for an opportunity to destroy him. They were not there to acknowledge him; they planted themselves where they could find fault with him. Forget about them calling him "teacher." They had earlier accused him of using Satanic power to cast out demons.

Remember this: when the enemy wants to frustrate and take you out, the weapons he uses against you will not be too far from your immediate environment. If you are a pastor, your testing ground will be in your own church, and most often within your leadership. Failure to accept this truism has led many servants of God down the path of burnout, from which they never recovered. Satan will not put your temptation two hundred miles away from you, so stay vigilant. Judas was very effective in playing the role of betraying Jesus because he was very close to his Master. And if you care to look well enough, you will realize that the end-result of everything thrown against you by your enemies (whether spirits or humans), is to deny you any glory.

The Pharisees were offended by the praise Jesus was receiving, and it has not changed and will not change. Today, an innocent schoolgirl is in the grip of Islamic terrorists in Nigeria simply because she is a Christian, and the only condition they have set for her release is to deny Jesus Christ and embrace Islam. She is standing up for her faith and not yielding, despite being denied her freedom and despite the continued threat to her life. This is one of the "stones" Jesus was referring to, in his response to the Pharisees. At a time when Christians, including church leaders, will only show up where it is politically-correct, God has a "stone" in that small girl shouting hallelujah in the face of demonized terrorists.

Such unconditional praise to God is like a tsunami; it is simply unstoppable. For those of you who have lost your songs of praise to the Lord Most High, remember the cross and renew your love for Christ. Stand up and let the "Pharisees" hear your praise. You cannot love him and not praise him. Praise the Lamb of God! He is worthy of our worship.

God bless you.

Enslaved by Blessings?

Mk.10:21-22, NKJV

Then Jesus, looking at him, loved him, and said to him, "One thing you lack: Go your way, sell whatever you have and give to the poor, and you will have treasure in heaven; and come, take up the cross, and follow Me." But he was sad at this word, and went away sorrowful, for he had great possessions.

A man came and knelt before Jesus, asking what he could do to attain eternal life. The Lord referred him to the Law and asked him to obey them because that was the dispensation in which he was living. The man responded that he had kept the Law from his youthful days. Bible says, "Then Jesus, looking at him, loved him." Jesus' love for the man, would not allow him to keep quiet over the self-deception in which he was living. The man interpreted the Law only in the context of what he was called to DO, nothing relative to what he had to GIVE. His claim of having obeyed all the Law of God since his youth, did not stand the test to give away everything for the course of God.

Truth is, his walking away from the call to surrender his wealth for God's work, is violation of the first law: "You shall love the Lord your God with ALL your heart..." He loved his God, but only to the extent that it didn't affect his goods. His possessions possessed him, and he was not willing to be separated from them. Beloved, Jesus loves you too much not to make a similar demand of you. Whatever is in your life that takes precedence over your allegiance to Christ, has become an object of worship, and before you go to the next level in God, you will have to surrender it. You must be willing to trade earthly possessions for heavenly treasures. Nothing you have right now, should have such a hold over you that you will not be able to let go if God so demands.

The man who came to Jesus, appeared to be very religious. He knelt before the Lord, which in itself shows his sense of reverence; and when he talked about his spiritual track-record, it was quite impressive. Only Jesus could see the loophole; that it was all ACT without HEART. The Lord asked him to do three simple things: (1) come (2) take up the cross (3) follow me. These were going to radically change his lifestyle and circumstances. It involved sacrifices he was not prepared to make. In the end, he walked away from it all. Any lessons learnt?

Well, let's take note that God does not use our individual marking-schemes to measure our love and commitment to him. As long as there is something we are not willing to give up for his sake, and something we are unwilling to take up for his service, we are turning our backs on his love. Nothing we acquire in this life, is worth exchanging with our love-relationship with Christ. Enjoy the blessings of God without making them enslave you; for the One who blesses is greater than the blessing.

God bless you.

Outshine the Darkness

Matt.5:14-16, NKJV

You are the light of the world. A city that is set on a hill cannot be hidden. Nor do they light a lamp and put it under a basket, but on a lamp stand, and it gives light to all who are in the house. Let your light so shine before men, that they may see your good works and glorify your Father in heaven.

When I was growing up as a child, many of our communities had no access to electricity, so the easiest way to lighten up your environment in the night was the use of a lantern, lamp, or candle. In the countryside, it was the gathering of wood and setting it on fire to provide the needed light. Today all that has changed so it may be difficult for some of us to understand what our Lord means when he speaks of lighting a lamp and putting it under a bed.

However, the import of the lesson cannot be lost on anyone, as he connects the light to "good works." Jesus is using the impact of light on darkness to indicate to us the necessity to make a difference in this dark world of sin. In a world where people are finding it difficult to walk in love, but are prone to hatred, unforgiveness, jealousy, blackmail, discrimination and the like, the Master is asking us to lighten up the societal darkness by our good works. He is asking us to walk in love, refusing to be drawn into the darkness of ungodly living.

We should be a people so Kingdom-minded that we are not moved by how the world sees us, what it says about us, or how it defines us. When we do "good works," it is not to impress the world, but to express His Word. When you have God's Word dwelling in you, the Word lightens you up and keeps you on the path of "good works." Bible testifies about Jesus that in his days on earth, "he went about doing good" (Acts 10:38). It is not the Pharisee-type goodness where you announce to everyone to come and see how good you are; no, your work will speak for itself, because like light in the darkness, it cannot be hidden.

Sometimes I meet believers who tell me they cannot continue doing good because people took advantage of them, and the wounds from the pain caused them are refusing to heal. If you feel that way, let me help you out. My reason? I have worn those size of shoes you are wearing many times before. They hurt, but God has a cure for it. First you must understand that you are dealing with "darkness," and that includes a whole world of ungrateful people. Some might even bite your fingers while you are feeding them. Secondly, the reason you do good is not to get appreciated. That's why scripture says "whatever you do, do it as unto the Lord."

The reason you MUST do good is because your God is good. He indwells you and wants to express himself through you for this one reason: "that men may SEE your good works and GLORIFY your Father in heaven." Of course, not all men will "see and glorify." Some may refuse to see, but that should not put out your light. Shine wherever you find yourself, till you outshine the darkness.

God bless you.

Do Justly, Love Mercy, Walk Humbly

Mic.6:7-8, NKJV

Will the LORD be pleased with thousand rams, ten thousand rivers of oil? Shall I give my first born for my transgression, the fruit of my body for the sin of my soul? He has shown you, O man, what is good; and what does the LORD require of you but to do justly, to love mercy, and to walk humbly with your God?

Jesus criticized the religious leaders of his day for placing more emphasis on RELIGION than RELATIONSHIP. Here we see a similar picture, and that attitude prompted the prophet to question the priorities of his people. You can easily live with an inflated ego of your own goodness, because of what you do or give to the Church. That is another name for "self-righteousness." We cannot give God enough to meet his righteous demands. It is important to understand that whatever we have, was acquired from God; He gave to us, so there is no room for boasting.

Indeed, there is nothing God lacks that when we give to Him, we score "A" in His class. There are three things we are asked to consider as being of prime importance to God in this scripture. All three can be practiced by anyone willing to die to self and be submissive to the Holy Spirit. The first is acting justly. You don't mistreat people because of their gender, race, color, or educational background. Right and wrong are the same, no matter who you are relating to.

The second thing God demands of us is to "love mercy." This seems to suggest to me that if you don't love mercy, you can't have mercy; and if you don't have mercy, you cannot give mercy. You cannot give what you don't have, and of course you cannot have what you don't love. The third is to "walk humbly with your God." I personally believe this goes more to those of us the Lord is using in his vineyard. A life of purity and purpose has nothing to do with power, position, and titles. Thank God for the life and work of Billy Graham. He gave us a wonderful example of how to serve God in humility; never tagged himself with any big titles but made an impact that all the modern-day "major prophets, archbishops, Apostle-generals" etc. can never match.

The only thing it will cost us to practice living these three simple spiritual principles is our pride. Let's sacrifice our pride, and do justice to all manner of men, love mercy, and walk humbly with our God, and the Christ within us will manifest for all to see.

God bless you.

Continue to Trust God in the Darkness

Is.50:10

Who among you fears the LORD? Who obeys the voice of His Servant? Who walks in darkness and has no light? Let him trust in the name of the LORD and rely upon his God.

The Bible shows us how we can live to please God. David calls the Word of God, "a lamp to my feet, and a light to my path" (Ps.119:105). However, we can all testify of times when we are simply overwhelmed by challenges of physical, emotional, and mental exhaustion and do not know what to do with ourselves. We don't lose our faith, we don't doubt our God, but cannot tell his location in our dislocation. That is what the prophet Isaiah is talking about here.

Many times in the past, I have gone down that route; my wife would be asking what was wrong with me. The problem with the problem was that I did not know what the problem was, except that the challenges within those particular 24 hours had knocked me out emotionally and was beginning to tell on me physically. I doubt if you never walked in that world of "darkness." You may even be in the middle of that river at this very moment and may be wondering how you can survive it.

The prophet's counsel, is the best lifeline; he says if anyone has kept faith with God and found himself in the darkness of pain, setbacks, and other challenges, "let him trust in the name of the LORD and rely upon his God." It's not trusting for a period of time and giving up. It means trusting in his name and relying on him even if that means death. You have no second choice; it's either the Lord or no one else.

Be strong and be encouraged, because God is standing with you in all your trials and tribulations. He is faithful and will let his light shine and dispel your darkness. I don't know His time, but I acknowledge the truth of his Word; "faithful is he who has promised, and he will also do it" for you.

God bless you.

When Jesus Owns You

Lu.21:3-4, NKJV

So He said, "Truly I say to you that this poor widow has put in more than all; for all these out of their abundance have put in offerings for God, but she out of her poverty put in all the livelihood that she had."

It sounds a bit odd that Jesus would position himself at a place in "church" where he would observe how much money each person gave as offering to the Lord; but that was exactly what he did, and when the service was over, he shared his conclusion on what he saw with his disciples. He was not impressed with the mere amount of money given by each worshipper. He weighed the giving against the backdrop of what they had left. A millionaire can impress a congregation of poor laborers with an offering that may amount to their total annual income, but which only accounts for the amount he spends on his dog on any given day.

Jesus' analysis of the real value God attaches to our giving, shows that the millionaire's thousands is comparatively lower than that of a poor widow with only a coin, who gives it all to God. The reason Jesus used the widow as his point of reference was because widows in his days were generally classified among the poor in society. For the widow to give all she had to live on to the Lord, was very unusual. Jesus commended her act of faith and gratitude. It is interesting that today when we talk about giving our "widow's mite" (referring to this widow's giving), we mean giving a small portion of our big earnings to God.

A believer should have no struggle at all with what amount of time or money he needs to give to God. God does not compel us to give. He loves a "cheerful giver," and that means if you don't have peace about it, don't do it. God is not going to kill you because you don't give. Giving is an expression of love. I am completely sold out to the course of Christ, because I love my Jesus like crazy. Yes, I do; and am sorry, but I owe no one apology for that. I have sacrificed my personal ambitions in life for the sake of his kingdom and the people for whom he died. I have done it all because I love him.

I have no other choice because he first loved me. When I buy stuff for my family and friends, I don't fret about "wasting" the money spent, because I love them. Be careful you don't feel compelled against your will in your ministry to the Lord; and never discount the value of what you do or give to him. God is excited about your giving to him out of love. When the heart is grateful, the amount is beautiful in his eyes, even if it is a coin. The most important thing you can give to Jesus is YOURSELF. When he owns you, you will know by his indwelling Spirit, how much you owe him.

God bless you

Love the Lord's Presence

Ps. 26:8, GNB

I love the house where you live, O LORD, the place where your glory dwells

---

Anytime we have been in a worship service where the message draws our hearts and minds to the goodness of God, and the need for us to be grateful despite the challenges we face, the Presence of the Lord manifests in awesome measure. Last night we experienced a very spectacular wave of the "house where God lives," as my son Frank, challenged us to drop the complaining and murmuring and thank the Lord for whatever little mercies he has blessed us with. The worship turned out to be one of my greatest experiences with divinity. Jesus Christ was in his house. Awesome! What amazed me was that there were no instruments accompanying the worship (like we were used to), but thank God the instrumentalists were not in the "house;"

His glory came down. David, the great psalmist of Israel said, "I love the house where you live, O LORD." Yes, the difference is really great, when the King is in the house. Do you know we can worship in the biggest cathedral with the largest orchestra and still miss the Presence of the Lord? The house where God lives, is the place where hearts of gratitude celebrate his majesty! I have come to realize that sometimes our order of worship is so rigid and regulated the Holy Spirit is only allowed to WATCH, not to WORK.

We have everything set in perfect order and are just happy to go through the rudiments and rituals without any spiritual content. Chapels are being sold and turned into mosques in the U.K and other places in the Western world today because those buildings no longer experience the glory of God. Like Israel in the days of Eli, it is "ichabod" (they have lost the glory). Let us give the Lord space to manifest his glory in our midst. You cannot go to "the house" or place where God lives and not love it, because his glory dwells there, and wherever God's glory dwells, his goodness manifests.

In a more personal way, you can project and protect the presence of the Lord always, by focusing more on what God has done, and less on what he hasn't done. That way, you can be grateful, and his presence will make you joyful. I praise God for your life and ask that you "love the house" where God lives; that the first house you shall offer him is a grateful heart. May you forever dwell in the glory, and never lose his Presence.

God bless you.

Choose to Serve

Gen.18:6-8, NKJV

So Abraham hurried into the tent to Sarah and said, "Quickly, make ready three measures of fine meal; knead it and make cakes." And Abraham ran to the herd, took a tender and good calf, gave it to a young man, and he hastened to prepare it. So he took butter and milk and the calf which he had prepared, and set it before them; and he stood by them under the tree as they ate

---

In Abraham we see a perfect picture of a servant-leader. One day he had three men visiting, while he was resting under a tree. Abraham discerned immediately that these were no ordinary men, but an unusual encounter with divinity. As a man of wealth, and head of a family which had so many servants, Abraham could have sat back and ordered whatever he wanted for his august guests to be prepared for them, without lifting a finger. Of course, that was the norm in the Eastern culture at the time; but Abraham gave us an example of the servant-spirit of a man who knows God. The movement of Abraham within these verses (6-8) should inspire us to do our best for God, family, and community without grumbling. His first reaction on seeing the men was that he "hurried" to Sarah. If you sincerely enjoy serving others, you do it with joy and expediency.

Slowing the process of service breeds corruption. Sometimes people deliberately go slow on providing a service because they expect a bribe. It is wrong. The second thing Abraham did was to ask his wife's help and input. He asked Sarah to keep pace with him by acting "quickly." It is important to have your family or leadership team moving with you at the same pace, otherwise you may not be able to achieve the desired results. Thirdly, the scripture says, "Abraham ran" (v.7). He kept the momentum, and so when he delegated a role to one of the young men in his home, the young man "hastened to prepare it." This is the domino-effect that a servant-leader can have on his/her family, church etc. If you behave like a military commander who never fires a shot, but insists on others fighting, you will wake up one day to find your troop gone "AWOL."

You've got to be involved in the lives of your wife and children. You've got to show members of your congregation you can do anything and everything you ask them to do in the House of God. Don't sit and say, stand and share. If you feel too big to help sort things out in your own home or church, then you must be big indeed! Let's take a look at Abraham in the verse 8: "So he (Abraham) took butter and milk and the calf which he had prepared and set it before them; and he stood by them under the tree as they ate." No doubt the next verse says they immediately asked Abraham to call his wife and gave Abraham and Sarah a definite timeline they would receive the greatest desire of their hearts - a child in an unusual season of their lives. Humble service to the Lord, executed with joy and speed, bring unusual blessings.

Do not let complacency and pride rob you of God's unusual blessings. Do what you've got to do and do it with passion and joy. Be an inspiration to your family and leadership team. Those who serve have no room for sorrow; they are too busy to be bothered with cares and burdens. If you want to soar in the spirit, find space to serve in the natural. The beauty and sanctity of service is that while it benefits the one being served, it blesses the one who serves. Be a servant. It's a healthy spiritual lifestyle; rewarding and refreshing.

God bless you

Love, Forgiveness and Restoration

Gal. 5:14-15, GNB

For the whole Law is summed up in one commandment: "Love your neighbor as you love yourself." But if you act like wild animals, hurting and harming each other, then watch out, or you will completely destroy one another

---

Our worth as God's children, and our walk with Christ, is devalued when we show little love for each other. We may not want to admit it, but all of us sometimes do "act like wild animals, hurting and harming each other." The message here was based on what was happening among believers, and was appropriately addressed to believers, not unbelievers. It is applicable to all generations of Christians. If we never acted like "wild animals," there would never have been divorce cases among Christian couples, no church splits, strained relationships etc.

For me, the issue is not that we sometimes "act like wild animals, hurting and harming each other." No, as long as we live in this flesh, we are bound to commit such blunders, because of the constant battle between flesh and spirit. The challenge is what we do when we realize that we have not acted properly towards a brother or sister. It is sad that many times we fail to take full responsibility for our folly and are quick to go the way of Adam: "the woman made me do it." Someone or something is always the reason for "hurting and harming each other." There is no repentance, and therefore no forgiveness, and consequently no restoration.

When this animalistic behavior begins to take its toll on us, the ultimate culprit who is blamed is the devil and his demons. How often we act wrong is not as important as how willing we are to humbly seek forgiveness and maintain right relationship in the home, church, and the larger community. Saying sorry is not a sign of weakness, but of maturity. I remember a particular instance when one of our daughters told me her mum was not happy with something I had said. She waited for my response. I told her I was going to apologize, and I did for her to see that I was not beyond being corrected.

The smile on her face as she looked at me walk away to apologize, was worth more than all the money in the world to me. I knew I had imprinted an indelible message on her mind and spirit for the rest of her life. It is good to pray, but prayer alone does not create a conducive atmosphere for peace and prosperity in the family, church etc. It takes a consistent effort in dealing with issues of abuse, hurt feelings, misunderstanding etc. to get there.

He who loves, is he who is willing to work towards forgiveness and restoration, not one whose ego makes him feel you either do it his way, or he goes on a rampage. Apostle Paul says when you take that position, the destruction you cause will impact everybody - including you, so "watch out!"

God bless you.

Recount the Goodness of God

Ps.40:5, NKJV

Many, O LORD my God, are your wonderful works which you have done; and your thoughts towards us cannot be recounted to you in order; if I would declare and speak of them, they are more than can be numbered

---

When pressure mounts on us, the flesh in its weakness blinds us to the continued grace and mercy the Lord has dispensed towards us. There is a hymn I love so much that amplifies the scripture we are considering today. One of its stanzas I remember so well says, "When upon life's billows you are tempest tossed. When you are discouraged thinking, all is lost; count your many blessings, name them one by one, and it will surprise you what the Lord has done." Yes, counting your blessings makes you more conscious of what God has done, and less concerned with what he hasn't done.

One thing is sure; there will always be an unmet need in your life. It is not always because God doesn't want to meet your need. When Paul was desperate for divine intervention, God pointed him to his grace and said, "my grace is sufficient for you." Nobody living in the grace of Christ can deny the blessings of God on his life. While you are believing for greater works of grace, stop cursing your stars and begin counting your blessings, "and it will surprise you what the Lord has done."

On your sick bed, you can recount the goodness of God that still sustains you. In the midst of your marital crisis, you can recount the favor God has shown you; making it possible for you to smile despite the heartache. There is no bad day without a broad smile from God's presence. Even when he doesn't seem to care, he takes care. "Count your blessings, name them one by one, and it will surprise you what the Lord has done.

God bless you.

He Will Surely Help You

Deut. 33:26, NKJV

There is no one like the God of Jeshurun, who rides the heavens to help you, and in His excellency on the clouds

---

We have all needed help in varying degrees at different times in our lives and will continue to need help as long as we live. God made us to be interdependent. The sick person needs a medical doctor to diagnose his condition and prescribe the necessary medication, and the medical doctor needs a mechanic to fix his car. Everybody needs somebody.

However, the one we need most is the "God of Jeshurun" (Word "Jeshurun" used here refers to Israel). Without the help of God, every human help comes to nothing. The human being is limited, but God is limitless. The human being has SOME of the answers to your challenges, God has ALL of the solutions to your problems.

You may be getting desperate and frustrated because the human friend you trusted to bail you out, has fizzled out. You are not finished yet. Don't believe the devil's lie. Greater help is available to you from the God of Jeshurun. Call to him and he answer you.

There is no lack in him. He may seem slow in coming, but this God who rides upon the clouds will surely come through for you. He is the help you need, and you will get it, if you keep asking him for it.

God bless you

Put on the Armor of Light

Rom.13:12-14, NKJV

The night is far spent, the day is at hand. Therefore let us cast off the works of darkness, and let us put on the armor of light. Let us walk properly, as in the day, not in revelry and drunkenness, not in lewdness and lust, not in strife and envy. But put on the Lord Jesus Christ, and make no provision for the flesh, to fulfill its lusts

---

In almost all elections held in our country over the past few years, the opposition parties always promise one thing - change! I call it "the change that never really changes anything apart from the pilot and his crew." But they do promise us change that would change our lives for the better. Whether anything better happens or not, my opinion is that the promise and the performance is always a mismatch. The promise is always bigger and larger than they ever deliver to us.

Interesting enough, once the politicians get into office, their reason for not delivering on their "change" promises is attributed to something the previous government did wrong or didn't do right. Thank God for real change; the reign of sin is coming to an end, and real PERMANENT, POSITIVE CHANGE is coming. The "night" of sickness, pain, frustration, depression, and death is phasing out. This is no political hot air; it is change initiated by the only One who cannot lie, because there is no lie in him. He has no desire for power, for he is the source of all power. No one can summon or contest him in an election because he is sovereign over all.

He is God, and he is challenging us to respond to the new order that is coming, by aligning ourselves to his taste and style, a life of holiness. God is asking us to "put off the works of darkness and put on the armor of light." The responsibility lies on us to reject sinful living, and deliberately "walk properly, as in the day, not in revelry and drunkenness, not in lewdness and lust, not in strife and envy."

Let me make this point that the grace of God does not glorify sin. It deals with it and empowers us to overcome it. It is a shame that sometimes the Church does not reflect enough light for the world to see the difference. We celebrate people who promote promiscuity. We tell the world they are okay to "come to church" (not Christ), and as long as they give money gained from "lewdness" to the preacher and the church, grace will take care of the rest.

This is plain deception and is leading many souls to hell. It's like telling a student who is going to write an exam that there is no reason he should study; all he needs to do is show up in the exam room and God's grace will be enough for him to pass. You and I know that won't work for him, and yet we want to believe that we can continue living in disobedience to God's Word and produce fruits of righteousness.

God is calling us to prepare for the dawning of a new day, the arrival of a permanent, peaceful, and glorious change. He is calling us to do our part by putting off the old sinful nature and putting on the new man of the Spirit of righteousness, because he has done his part by imputing righteousness to us and empowering us to pursue same. Live for God because he died for you.

God bless you

Your Reward in Due Season

Eze.33:31-32, NKJV

So they come to you as people do, they sit before you as My people, and they hear your words, but they do not do them; for with their mouth they show much love, but their hearts pursue their own gain. Indeed, you are to them as a very lovely song of one who has a pleasant voice and can play well on an instrument; for they hear your words, but they do not do them

---

When you expect too much from people you sacrifice your life for, you can become vulnerable to undue pressure and disillusionment. A doctor friend sent me a news item about a pastor who committed suicide because he was frustrated with the lack of appreciation and love from his congregation. They pestered, pressured, and persecuted him until he could take it no more. Instead of pouring out his frustration, he bottled it up until it exploded in his face. We have no right judging him, but we can learn to avoid being pushed into taking that route.

Every parent, pastor, coach, counselor, and all other persons in leadership ought to know for a fact that we cannot always get people to respond the way we desire, relative to what we teach them. You can put in the best of efforts and resources to raise a child, and he may grow up to live a life contrary to all the values you taught him. That is never a parent's wish or dream, but it can happen, and indeed, it does happen. As a shepherd of God's flock, it is dangerous to be overly concerned with the attitudes they show towards you. It is not your responsibility to change anybody. You don't make decisions for your children when they are grown enough to rationalize.

God told Ezekiel that the people who came to sit before him were only pretending to be interested in his counseling, but each of them was going to walk away and do whatever they deemed fit. As a parent, pastor, or counselor, you must learn to leave your children, members of your congregation etc., in the hands of God. Do your best for them but be careful not to raise the bar of your expectation so high that when they don't respond appropriately your entire world crumbles. When you have done your best for those you mentor, you know it, and so should not take the negative response too personal. You have a life to live, and mentorship is only a part of it, not all of it.

If you are hurting, make no pretense about it. Talk about it with those who identify with your pain and despair. It is better to seek help than pretend you can handle it alone. God's Word provides you a wonderful resource base. Encourage yourself in this one thing; that you did your best and cannot be held responsible for the rest. Let God be judge and interpreter of your actions and inactions. You are not and will not be the first or last to sow seeds that fall on unproductive soil. Your reward is in the hands of God, and it will surely come to you in due season. I pray for every hurting pastor and parent for God's grace and presence to keep and protect you always in all ways. May the good Lord give you His peace and joy in Jesus Name.

God bless you

Numbers Do Not Guarantee Success

Judg.7, NKJV

Then the LORD said to Gideon, "With the three hundred men that lapped I will save you, and deliver the Midianites into your hand. Let all the others go home.

Many of us get psychological satisfaction from having lots of people getting involved in our life's project, but sometimes bigness can become a hindrance, rather than a blessing.

Gideon was going to fight a very difficult battle, and God told him to ask for volunteers to form an army. Initially 32,000 men answered the call, but when the Lord told Gideon to tell his macho men to be honest with themselves and quit his contingent if you were afraid, a whopping 22,000 went home immediately. What a shocker!!

These 22,000 had volunteered with their head, minus their heart. Indeed, when God demanded that the remaining 10,000 should be further scrutinized because it included more 'babies in military uniform', the number reduced to 300. Those three hundred men became the powerful instruments God used to deliver Israel from the Midianites.

Think about that for a moment; you are about to fight enemies who have subjected you to consistent bashing for years. You get 32,000 men standing up to the call to join your army. Here comes God and he says, "Hello, cut the army to 300 men." What?! Oh, yes, my brothers and sisters, that's the ways of God; defying logic and common sense, focusing on content and intentions.

The truth revealed is that you don't win in life by virtue of the numbers, whether in terms of people or treasures. You win with the PRESENCE of God. When you have the PRESENCE of God, even prison can become an opportunity that opens doors to palace for you, check Joseph's experience in Egypt.

It's a new year with great opportunities. Covet the Presence of God, and every battle or challenge will be within reach of victory. You don't necessarily need many people or huge resources to make an impact where God has placed you. Use the little that you have, and you will get what you deserve.

God bless you.

All Power Belongs to God

Jn.19:10-11, NIV

"Do you refuse to talk to me?" Pilate said, "Don't you realize I have power either to free you or crucify you?" Jesus answered, "You would have no power over me, if it were not given to you from above..."

Destinies are not determined by human authorities, because ultimate power belongs to God alone. As long as you have truth on your side and holding on to your integrity, you should not be unduly intimidated by anyone.

When Jesus was arrested and brought before Pilate, his lack of resistance made him look hopeless and helpless. His detractors were having a field-day, abusing him with impunity. Jesus had power to overpower them, but restrained himself; showing strength in the face of stress.

Pilate knew that per the Roman legal system, the arrest and subsequent abuse of Jesus was against the law. He told the Jewish leaders that he found "no fault" in the man they were accusing and wanted executed, and yet he proceeded to ask questions irrelevant to the situation at hand.

Initially, Jesus chose to answer Pilate with a loud silence. This provoked the Roman governor and he issued a threat, suggesting that the fate of Jesus was in his hands. Pilate wrongly assumed he could use intimidation to force Jesus to submit to his whims and caprices, but he got it wrong. The answer he got was far from anything he had expected. He was made to understand that the power he claimed was delegated to him by God, and only temporal.

There are two major lessons here for us. Firstly, those of us who have some measure of "power" or "authority" over others, should be very circumspect in the way we exercise them. As a parent or boss in the work place, you have "power" over your children or workers, but it is not absolute. The moment you use it to intimidate, harass, and bully those under you, its legitimacy is undermined. Restrain yourself from reminding everyone of your position and power; it is only temporal.

Secondly, those under authority should know they also have rights. It is in your right not to allow yourself to be treated in a way that takes away your dignity as a human being. You ought to be assertive without being disrespectful or aggressive. Maintain a careful balance between Godly submission and autocratic suppression; upholding the former, and rejecting the latter.

As a child of God, no one can hold you to ransom in matters of life and death. Don't fear the threats of men. Any person or situation that is making you fearful can only do as much as God would allow. Keep the faith, and kick the fear. Your destiny is secure in the hands of the Lord. Brace yourself to bless the world, in humility and love.

God bless you

Jesus Is the Answer

Is.30:2-3&5, CEV

You trust Egypt for protection. So you refuse my advice and send messengers to Egypt to beg their king for help. You will be disappointed, completely disgraced for trusting Egypt...But Egypt can't protect you, and to trust that nation is useless and foolish.

A man called me on phone after one of my weekly radio Bible presentations. He said he was in extreme difficulty and needed immediate relief from the challenges he was facing. I asked if he had given his life to Jesus, and whether he was a practicing Christian. He said no.

I tried explaining to him why he needed to accept Jesus Christ as his Lord and personal Saviour, but he was not interested. All he wanted was someone to pray away his problems, and command miracles into his life. I graciously explained to him that it does not lie in my power to solve people's problems. God is the miracle-worker, not me.

If he wanted power-display outside of Christ, I guess that might be the job of occultists and magicians, and fortunately for me I am not one, and do not even have what it takes to be one. Indeed, am too intoxicated with love for Christ to be recruited by demons; so the long and short of it was that he ended the conversation.

He was obviously disappointed. He was angry. I called him back, and appealed to him to calm down and listen to the gospel of salvation. He would not budge, so I called it quits.

Beloved, if you think for once, that you can live without Christ and fulfill God's purpose for your life, it's like challenging God to a wrestling contest. You lose the fight before you enter the ring.

It helps to seek counsel from people because one of the ways God speaks to us is through human channels. Indeed, given the pressures we have to contend with on a daily basis, it will be suicidal to "walk alone" without help from others. The problem arises when we DEPEND on them to the extent we trust what they say than what God's Word admonishes.

The people we trust for miracles then become our "Egypt" and the Lord is showing us that making a god of our wisdom, a person, thing, or place, and attributing to it or them our source of blessing, brings unpleasant consequences. First, it brings disappointment. Nothing holds and gives constant satisfaction outside of Christ.

Second, depending on "Egypt" brings disgrace. Wherever grace is missing, dis-grace is bound to manifest. Third, we loose divine protection when we remove ourselves from trusting the Lord and seeking His direction for our lives.

There is no guaranteed protection outside the name and blood of Jesus Christ. The fourth consequence is hopelessness born out of foolishness. Not my word; that's exactly how God's Holy Word puts it in the Contemporary English Version of the Bible.

If there are issues you haven't committed to God in prayer, do so now. God is interested in every nitty gritty of our lives. He cares about all the details, both big and small. He is not enthused with us running on our own steam and tangent and turning to Him only when we mess up. Begin your day, week, month, and this new year with Jesus.

You cannot do any better than that, because no one loves and cares for you more than Jesus Christ does. With Christ, you always win, no matter how long you have to wait. Trust in the Lord, and he will do you good. Serve the Lord with passion, and great shall be your reward.

God bless you.

Rejoice in The Holy One

Is.29:19, NKJV

The humble also shall increase their joy in the LORD, and the poor among men shall rejoice in the Holy One of Israel

---

Despite the many challenges you face, it is important to maintain a joyful spirit "in the Holy One of Israel." God did not create you to EXIST; you are re-created in Christ to LIVE.

Allowing the pressures of everyday life to overwhelm you, throws the passion to live out of the window. Jesus announced the purpose of his coming in Jn.10:10b saying he came "that you might have life and have it in abundance."

Beloved, once you have received Jesus Christ as your Lord and personal Savior, there is a door of grace opened for you to access the joy of the Lord. The Holy Spirit dwells within you in full anticipation that you will enjoy, not only his peace and presence, but also his joy. You miss the mark when you look for joy in money, people, and things.

Nothing in this life can give us the kind of joy that saturates our spirit-man; joy that brings peace and inner satisfaction and has its source in Christ alone. People and things can make us happy, and that is helpful; but it doesn't last long enough to keep us joyful. It takes "joy" that is fruit borne by the Holy Spirit to keep the momentum going.

The scripture says, "and the poor men shall rejoice IN THE HOLY ONE OF ISRAEL." The "poor men" are not necessarily those who lack material possessions (ref. Matt.5:3). It refers essentially to those whose entire life is dependent on God's grace, goodness, and mercy. They shall "increase their joy IN THE LORD.

The increase in the joy of the Lord is solution to our frustration, anxiety, confusion, fear, rejection, and worry. We have to get past the cycle of being emotional pendulums; one moment we feel good, and the next we feel lost and dry. This has been going on forever. It's all about our feelings.

It's time to stop the wheel from spinning out of our control. We must create a joyful atmosphere by FAITH!! Living outside the borders of joy and gladness in the Lord equals to wasting our lives. Let's be grateful for what we have, and thankful for God's grace on our lives. Let's renew our minds and free our souls from the trenches of depression. If God's will for us is to live in his joy, why should we choose to live without it?

Look into the mirror. What image do you see? It is exact reflection of the state of the soul sitting inside of your body. "Rejoice in the Holy One of Israel;" not only for a season, but for every single moment God gives you in this life. Your life depends on it. Rejoice in the Lord, and you will receive power to endure the pain, and overcome the loss.

God Bless You.

Finish the Race

Jn. 20:3-6, GNB

Then Peter and the other disciple went to the tomb. The two of them were running, but the other disciple ran faster than Peter and reached the tomb first. He bent over and saw the linen wrappings, but he did not go in. Behind him came Simon Peter, and he went straight into the tomb. He saw the linen wrappings lying there

---

Peter and "the other apostle" (identified by Bible scholars as apostle John), were told by Mary Magdalene that the body of Jesus had been taken out of the tomb. Both men took off and began running towards the tomb.

John, who was much younger than Peter, outran his compatriot, but only stopped at the entrance of the tomb. He did not go inside. Peter was late in coming, but bypassed John and entered the tomb, only to be followed later by John. There are two immediate revelations to grasp in this episode. The first has to do with John. He had speed but lacked momentum. His failure to enter the tomb made him lost the "first" position. Peter, who came from behind, is recorded as being the first to enter the tomb.

We accomplish nothing, till we finish something. The race is not won till we cross the finish line. Every one of us has started something. Even for those of us who are not doing anything, we are doing something; it is called NOTHING! The results we achieve will be determined by the sacrifices we make. Every new year is a new season of life, with a race to be run to the end.

The second light from this scripture is relative to Peter. He shows us that in the race of life, there will always be people like John, who will run ahead of us. We may start with them in pursuit of a goal, and they may achieve more within a shorter period of time than us, but that should inspire us instead of discouraging us. We ought to concentrate on our race and rhythm, not their speed and success.

Sometimes, those ahead are positioned there to beef up our faith. Our energy and adrenaline level rises because we realize we are not in this alone, and like Peter, we push ourselves to go beyond where those who went ahead of us reached. Scripture records that when Peter bypassed John and entered the tomb, John followed; the leader became the follower. What changed the dynamics of the race was the individual's attitude and approach.

If you are not running, get up and join the race. If you are in the race, stay the course. Life is a long-distance race. Don't be distracted by the position and possession of others. Stay the course and cross every line you need to cross this year with regard to your spiritual, financial, educational, relational goals.

God bless you

Preparation Before Possession

Ex.23:28-30, NIV

> I will send the hornet ahead of you to drive the Hivites, Canaanites and Hittites out of your way. But I will not drive them out in a single year, because the land will become desolate and the wild animals too numerous for you. Little by little I will drive them out before you, until you have increased enough to take possession of the land.

God does his work in our lives with our best interest at heart. Every blessing we seek from the Lord Jesus Christ is already in stock and ready to be delivered. What he is not prepared to do, is to give us something we are not adequately prepared to handle. Evidence abounds of people who displayed such humility in their time of need to the point one would think it was part of their nature. When their needs were met, and their status changed, they became the very epitome of pride and arrogance.

Many of us can easily relate to such situations which was the reason God told Israel he was going to drive out their enemies alright, but he was not going to do in a single year. "Little by little," he said, "I will drive them out before you, until you have increased enough to take possession of the land." If you agree that our God does not change, then you should admit that his principles do not change. There are some things God will give to you immediately you ask for them, but there are others that may delay. This may not sound good, but it is true; the period of your preparation for certain things may go beyond a year, so you've got to brace yourself for the process.

Indeed, there are so many factors that come into play in determining what we get or do not get in answer to our prayers, but God is saying to us that "prepared blessings are for a prepared people." Apostle Paul prayed fervently for healing, but God's answer to him was, "My grace is sufficient for you." If you are going to be a strong believer in Christ, you will need to understand that answers to your prayers will not always come at the snap of a finger, and the fact that the answer to a particular prayer is not met is not a sign of God's denial.

There may be enemies lurking around you, posing as friends, who may attack you because of the blessing. You may have some innate weaknesses that may surface and destroy you if the Holy Spirit does not root them out. It is matters to God that he deals with these and other potential threats before he brings you to the place prepared for you. It is not wise to start a car in fifth gear, and so the Lord is taking you through a process to ensure the end will be glorious and peaceful.

We all get to the point where we think what we are asking the Lord to do is not something that requires any further delay; he has to do it here and now!! However, we have to take comfort in the fact that God knows what we do not know, and sees what we do not see, so it is in our best interest to allow the process of preparation to continue as long as God our Father desires.

Keep praising and praying. You are on God's mind, and He is preparing the way for your glorification. Rise up and live! All things are working together for your ultimate good.

God bless you.

God Has Your Back

1 Chron.28:20, KJV

And David said to Solomon his son, Be strong and of good courage, and do it: fear not, nor be dismayed: for the LORD God, even my God, will be with thee; he will not fail thee, nor forsake thee, until thou hast finished all the work for the service of the house of the LORD.

Taking on new responsibilities bring different reactions from different people, depending on the challenges involved. Some may be excited and joyful, while others may struggle with fear and anxiety. In the end, all will want to succeed.

As an old man conversant with this reality, King David had to impress on young Solomon the need to have a positive mindset as he stepped into his father's shoes as new king of Israel. Solomon could not afford to ascend and succeed with a confused mind, fearful heart, or timid spirit. If his father's personal experience as king was anything to go by, his successor was to understand that leadership is not a tea party, whether in the home, church, job place, or larger community.

Firstly, Solomon had to be strong. This is not physical strength; it is spiritual, mental and emotional stability. He was to be a leader who could take decisions and stand by them. As parents, pastors, business leaders etc. we ought to show "strength" to those who look to us for direction. The lives God has entrusted into our hands are too precious to be toyed with.

Secondly, the young man was advised to show "good courage." The challenges of leadership are overcome with courage. Leaders are endangered species, and those who are called into that privileged should know they have a price to pay, and should be courageous.

David's third advice to his son was not to be afraid. Indeed, it was a rehashing of the need to be courageous. It takes faith to lead effectively. Indeed, victorious living is only possible to those who live above fear, and the only way to get there is to live by faith. If you can believe for something, it gives you enough vim to face whatever fear it brings. Deal with your fears, and you are good to ascend to higher heights.

The assurance that cap all the above, was that success was guaranteed because God was going to be with Solomon. Our greatest and best guarantee as Christians is the presence of God in our lives. We dare not doubt the love of God and our heavenly Father's desire that we "prosper and be in good health."

Every day God gives you is another opportunity to arise and shine.

Go where he leads, face the challenges with faith and tenacity. You are not alone. Cheer up and believe that you can do anything that falls into your realm of influence. Your best bet is that God is with you.

God bless you

Celebrate Life

Eccl.3:12-13, NIV

I know that there is nothing better for men than to be happy and do good while they live. That everyone may eat and drink, - and find satisfaction in his toil - this is the gift of God

What does this writer identify as "the gift of God?" He pinpoints having enough to eat and finding satisfaction in one's toil or work as "gift of God." He sees poverty, or lack, as bondage with power to cripple one's ability to live joyfully. It was never part of God's original plan for man.

The creation story in the book of Genesis 1 & 2, makes clear how God made adequate provision for man's comfort before creating him. The same God will not let us live like paupers. Those who lack necessities of life, have a greater tendency to commit crime than those whose feed good and feel well.

Come to think of it, there are people who work so hard and yet get very little returns from their work. Others are not able to enjoy the fruits of their labor because of circumstances beyond their control. What a gift God has given to anyone reading this piece, who is able to work and generate enough income to be happy and content?

Consider the many innocent victims of war and violent crimes in many countries of the world today and pray for them. This scripture is saying that if you are in this privileged bracket, where you have peace and contentment, "there is nothing better to do than for men to be happy and do good while they live."

It's not advice that should be taken lightly, because the truth is that if we are not happy with ourselves, we can't do good to others. Indeed, it is necessary to do ourselves a favor by deliberately pursuing happiness. Don't ever feel guilty about having fun, as long as it is not sinful. Be excited about life.

Lighten the atmosphere in the home, and wherever possible, by choice. Be deliberate about how you want to live. There is only one life: be happy. Stop the constant argument and nagging and give love and laughter a chance.

Life is a gift, and the recipient of a gift is the one who decides what to do with the gift. You can earn the best income in the world and still live a miserable life. If you do, it is your choice, and a bad one at that, because it will stifle your ability to be a blessing to others.

Stand up for yourself. Identify the people and things that make you happy and stick to them. Remember you can do no good until you are happy with yourself. There is nothing better for you than to be "happy and do good." Be happy.

God bless you

Acknowledge Your Helpers

Neh.1:18, NKJV

And I told them of the hand of God which has been good upon me, and also of the king's words that he has spoken to me. So they said, Let us rise up and build." Then they set their hands to this good work.

For those who move in faith and obedience, God always opens doors for helpers. No matter your level of faith, commitment, and sacrifice, you cannot achieve much in life without helpers, and God has enough people standing by to stand with you in building your "wall of Jerusalem".

Nehemiah had a passion to rebuild the broken-down walls of Jerusalem. They were in captivity and it was almost suicidal to request to be allowed to go and rebuild a city wall that was destroyed by their captors. Jerusalem's fallen walls was symbolic of their subjection, and its reconstruction was not up for discussion.

Nehemiah fasted and prayed for God's favor from the king as he took the bold step of faith to request the king's permission to go and rebuild the wall. The door of grace opened, and the king granted his request. Like any other project or undertaking in life, Nehemiah saw the need for helpers in fulfilling the task. God drew the right people to him, and success crowned his efforts.

Beloved, your life's journey must have helpers. God gave you a mother who carried you in the womb, and he has appointed people to support you at every stage of your journey. Some may be older than you, some may be your peers, while others may be younger. The most important thing is to stay expectant and appreciative of the grace to have these uniquely divine relationships.

One of the many pleasant surprises in our ministry have been people coming around to offer help in very unusual times and ways. It is humbling to know that someone is thinking of helping you to succeed, especially when you have been used to encountering enemies and opposition at every twist and turn.

Do not take your divinely appointed helpers for granted. Pray for God's peace and prosperity on their lives and families. Remember the help they give you, and never for once forget to thank them. Nehemiah took note of the individuals and families who supported him, and consistently asked God to bless and protect them.He knew where each stood and the specific assistance they gave.

It is important to have faith for building your Jerusalem wall, but having faith and acting as a lone-ranger does not achieve much. Even Jesus needed people to support his ministry and push his agenda forward. His need of people was so urgent that Judas Iscariot found himself invited to participate.

Indeed, we have faith to be doing the work we believe God has called us to do, but we will be the first to acknowledge that God has used people to help us to come this far. And if you are among our helpers, I want to thank you on behalf of my wife and myself for your love, support, and encouragement.

Let me suggest that if perchance you are not seeing any helpers or cheerleaders in your life, make it a subject of prayer. Maybe you are ignoring your own call to be a help to someone worst off than you. If you sow it, you will reap it.

God bless you

Maintain the Momentum

Heb.10:35-36, NIV

So do not throw away your confidence; it will be richly rewarded. You need to persevere so that when you have done the will of God, you will receive what he has promised

---

Your confidence is what you need when you are confronted with delays, setbacks, and opposition. Count yourself blessed if you have started the year with some level of confidence in what you hope to achieve, otherwise pray for grace to receive this necessary empowerment for the race ahead.

Some things are going to turn out right, while others may not go the way you want or expect. No matter which direction the wind blows, you must muster the courage and confidence to soldier on. Flow in the determination to soar higher, no matter the odds and opposition. "Do not throw away your confidence" because something went wrong, or someone rejected or said something negative about you.

Confidence is the stabilizing force of every goal and objective you would want to achieve; without it you are out of balance. As long as you hold to it, you are sure to navigate through the challenges that are bound to come your way, and that is why the writer of the book of Hebrews strongly admonishes God's people in very clear language: "...do not throw away your confidence."

It means everyone of us can get to a point of feeling discouraged, disappointed, or disoriented; the tendency to give up on our dreams becoming stronger than the desire to soar higher. If you read John's account of the reaction of Peter and his friends immediately after the death and resurrection of Jesus, you see a classic example of that tendency to give up (Jn.21:1-13).

For three years, the disciples had Jesus with them everyday. Life was interesting and exciting, and they looked forward to each day with eager anticipation of miracles, signs, and wonders. The job description was well cut-out, and there was some level of predictability and security. Suddenly, the light went out; Jesus was absent much longer than they were used to, and they did not know exactly what to do next.

They literally threw away their confidence. Peter gave the cue to desert camp by saying, "I'm going out to fishing," and the rest responded, "we'll go with you." He was their inspiration, so the moment he threw away his confidence, the rest could not hold on to theirs.

As God's chosen people, no matter where we find ourselves, we have innate leadership roles because of the light of Christ within us. Being in that peculiar place means no matter how difficult our circumstances may be, there is one thing we can't afford to do. We cannot afford to throw away our confidence, because the Word of God says, "it will be richly rewarded."

If you are convinced that you are doing your best, and not consciously fighting God's will for your life, then keep on keeping on. Aim higher. You can do better!! The journey may be long, but the joy awaiting you at your destination will be worth the long march and wait. Hold on to your confidence.

Keep praying. Continue praising. Your miracle is on the way. Men may write you off, but God has already counted you in. Persevere, and your day of laughter will come, "after you have done the will of God."

I pray for you that the good Lord himself will strengthen and empower you to stand tall and strong through every storm and struggle; that in the end, you will come out like gold refined in fire. Don't throw away your confidence, it is carrying the seeds of great rewards.

God Bless You.

Remove the Grave Clothes

October 5

Jn.11:44, NIV

The dead man came out, his hands and feet wrapped with strips of linen, and a cloth around his face. Jesus said to them, "Take off the grave clothes and let him go

---

God will never do for you what you can, or ought to do for yourself. When Lazarus, Jesus's friend was sick, the sisters sent to call him. Jesus did not come as quickly as they had expected, and that resulted in Lazarus death.

Four days later, Jesus showed up, and after some words of hope and encouragement to the deceased's family, he went to the tomb and raised the dead man to life. But the Lord's instructions before and after this episode has a few lessons for us; key among them, once again, is that God will never do for us what we can do for ourselves.

The first thing the Lord did when he got to the tomb was to ask them to roll away the stone that sealed the tomb. God want to meet our needs, but he desires us to do first things first. You cannot build without a plan or raise a structure without foundation.

If you want God to bless your home with peace, it is your responsibility to remove attitudes and tendencies that hinder peace. You have to take responsibility to create the atmosphere for peace. Using unkind, demeaning, and abusive words in your home, will definitely produce "hell" that you will have to live with.

When Lazarus rose from the dead, his hands and feet were still wrapped in grave clothes. Jesus did not remove the grave clothes, because that did not require a miracle.

He asked the family to play their part in the miracle journey by doing what they could do; to remove the clothes hindering the resurrected man from moving about freely.

The truth revealed is that God works in partnership with us to fulfill his purposes for our lives. When you pray for something, you must step out in faith and work towards achieving it. Waiting ON God, is quite different from waiting FOR God.

In the first instance, you enter the sphere of prayer and seeking direction. Beyond that, you've got to hit the road running; doing whatever you can, while waiting (trusting) in expectation for God to give you what it takes to achieve your goal.

If you are looking at your resurrected Lazarus and at the same time expecting God to remove the grave clothes for you, it's not going to happen. Grace does not produce grapes for those who choose to do nothing. Heed the voice of the Spirit, and move your limbs and legs.

If you are a student and want to improve your academic performance, you do well to pray and ask God's help; but after the prayer, you have to dedicate quality time to your books and commit to studying. It is the only guaranteed path to scoring good grades.

Are you having problems in your marriage? God is willing to help you sort them out, but recognize that someone within the context of the marriage relationship has to do what God will not do for you; there must be compromises made to accommodate what cannot be changed; and changes made, where necessary and possible.

The lifeline is to do your part to help in solving the problem and resolving the issues. When God moves, you must move, or you miss the flow. It's never too late to make that move. My Latin lesson in school years ago taught me the proverb, "dum spiro spero" (while there is life, there is hope). You have life, so you can do it!

I pray that grace will abound to you to see all the "grave clothes" in your life and relationships, and to remove them so that you will experience peace, joy, and prosperity to the glory of God.

God Bless You

Your Defined Audience Will Accept You

Matt.10:13-14, NKJV

If the household is worthy, let your peace come upon it. But if it is not worthy, let your peace return to you

---

Jesus's first assignment to his disciples entailed going out on a house-to-house evangelistic mission. The Master did not want his students to have any illusions about the harvest field.

They needed to understand that not everyone was going to be receptive to their message; a lesson we must all learn and learn quickly to maintain our peace in the face of possible resistance, or even rejection, as we relate to different people at different levels of society.

The pain of rejection sometimes come because of the expectation of acceptance from people we see as friends or profess to like us. I learnt long ago that the blessings we carry as individuals are not meant for everyone. Even some of the "lips that suck from our breasts" can turn round to bite us till we bleed.

Jesus told the disciples that it was okay if they were not accepted by some people; they had to keep their "peace" and move on. There was no point for arguments, bitterness, regrets, or appeals. Those who were meant to receive them and accept their message would do so without pressure or coercion.

Your life will not attract everyone, because what God has given you is not meant for everyone. Some may be attracted to it for a season and walk away after they have had their fill. Others will slight you and dump you. Pick yourself up, and move on, being mindful that even

Jesus was not accepted by everyone. Don't waste time on those who have clearly indicated to you that they don't accept you. Standing and waiting for their acceptance can waste your time, diminish your impact, and undermine your peace. Take a detour and walk away in peace.

Remember this; there will always be someone who will appreciate you for you. The power of choice is the prerogative of every individual. Those who don't like you have not committed any sin. It is their legitimate right, choice, and prerogative, and you should be able and willing to accept it and live with it.

You should not be obsessed with their views and opinions. They are entitled to them. The issue is not about the rightness or wrongness of what they think and do, it is about your ability to grow beyond the negative actions and reactions and pursue the goals you have set to achieve with greater zeal. It's about you staying the course, and soaring higher.

If they don't like your "peace", take it back and walk on. That is Jesus's command, not my word. Don't pick a quarrel or go pity-partying. Move on!!

God Bless You.

Beyond the Pain

Jn.16:21-22, GNB

When a woman is about to give birth, she is sad because her hour of suffering has come; but when the baby is born, she forgets her suffering, because she is happy that a baby has been born into the world. That is how it is with you: now you are sad, but I will see you again, and your hearts will be filled with gladness that no one can take away from you

The normal term a woman carries pregnancy is nine months; but sometimes children are born before the scheduled nine-month term. However, the climax of the whole process is not so much with the time the baby is born, but the actual birth of the baby; when the baby is out of the womb and the woman relieved of the pain of childbirth.

Every woman who gives birth is subject to pain before introducing a new life into the world. Jesus, speaking about what the disciples were going to experience after his ascension, explained that it was going to be rough, tough, and painful. It was not a nice thing to say, but it was truth that needed to be told.

He gave them a graphic preview of the crisis of ministry awaiting them by using the analogy of a woman in labor; what she goes through during the process of giving birth, and her reaction after the child is born. It begins with labor pains and ends with joyful praise.

The pregnancy period is long and dreary, and such is our time here on earth. As a pregnant woman looks forward to the birth of her baby, even so should we as believers anticipate the joy of our reunion with Christ when he comes again in his glory. Meanwhile, there are birth pangs to endure before we enjoy the fruit of our labor on earth.

With some of the apostles and disciples of old, it was persecutions that ended in executions. Following Jesus comes at a cost for those who would wear the crown of victory. To narrow our worship of God to the temporary joys of this life is to miss the point of our salvation, which is to bring us into everlasting glory with Christ in His kingdom.

Our hope does not lie in what we get or hope to get here, and now; it hinges on something greater, bigger, better, and larger than this life. It is possible to suffer loses, experience pain, and setbacks in many ways in this life. They are the birth pangs preceding our entrance into God's eternal rest in Christ.

When that day comes, what joy we shall have. The process will end, and we will see our "baby"; the reward of our labour, faithfulness and endurance. Expand your horizon. Everything will not always go the way you planned, and some of the bad things that happen to you are not meant to be avoided; they are meant to be endured.

If you refuse to endure for Christ, you are on the road to causing spiritual abortion. It means you go through the pain without producing the life you are meant to produce.

Beloved, the Christian life involves a certain measure of pain, but always remember that there is joy beyond the birth pang. Be strong. Keep the faith, and kick the fear. "Soon and very soon, we are going to see the King."

I pray that the good Lord will give you all the grace you need to go through your full term of "pregnancy" (challenges), to endure the pain of delivery, and to bring forth triumphantly as you enter God's promised rest in Christ in every area of your life.

God Bless You.

Covet God's Presence

(Ps.51:11, NKJV

Do not cast me away from Your presence. And do not take your Holy Spirit from me.

A child of God who lacks the Presence of the Holy Spirit in his life can be likened to fish out of water. When Adam sinned, he lost the Presence. He began to run and hide from his Creator.

God did not walk away from Adam, and indeed does not remove himself from anyone who sins against him; it is sin itself that creates the barrier between us and Father-God.

Sin comes with consequences, and the first and most devastating consequence is separation from God; a break in fellowship, otherwise described as death.

David knew the negative effect of living "outside" the Presence of God. He saw King Saul struggle with mental derangement anytime the Lord's Presence left him. Saul would go into a frenzy, and would need the anointed music of David to recover from abnormality and regain calmness.

Nothing in life holds together in perfect harmony without the Presence of God.

Wherever God shows up becomes heaven, and wherever his Presence does not inhabit becomes hell.

We cannot exchange anything with the awesome Presence of the Lord. Many of us crave for power, peace, and prosperity, without realising that all of these are embedded in the PRESENCE of the Lord.

It's impossible to maintain an atmosphere of peace, power, and prosperity without God's abiding Presence.

Our joy should not only be in what God does for us, but in WHO he is to us. He is our Immanuel (God WITH us). The reason Jesus died on the cross is to redeem us from sin, and the reason he sent the Holy Spirit is to ensure his permanent Presence in our lives.

It's all a work of grace, but it is not a license to continue living in sin (Rom.6:1). Light and darkness cannot dwell together. To enjoy the continuous Presence of the Lord, we've got to honor him by living in His Word and Christ's world (holiness). Let your life without, reflect the light within.

When the Spirit convict you of any wrongdoing, restrain yourself from justifying it; go to God in repentance. It is our loving Father's joy to be a part of our lives. He grieves when we erect barriers between us and him by indulging in sinful living.

God's unchanging, unfailing, and unwavering love has made room for our continuous sanctification. It is our responsibility to appreciate and appropriate that provision in the blood of Jesus. Embrace his Presence, and you will enjoy his Peace, Power, and Prosperity.

Let us humbly come to a place of repentance anytime we sin against God; and like David, may we be consistent in praying, "Do not cast me away from your presence. And do not take your Holy Spirit from me." Without the Holy Spirit we cannot live in godliness.

Let all the saints say "Amen and glory to the Lamb of God, who lives and reigns forever and ever."

God Bless You.*

Discipline

Deut.8:5-7,9, GNB

Remember that the LORD your God corrects and punishes you just as a father disciplines his children. So then, do as the LORD has commanded you: live according to his laws and have reverence for him. The LORD your God is bringing you into a fertile land - a land that has rivers and springs, and underground streams gushing out into the valleys and hills...There you will never go hungry or ever be in need

---

This was a generational promise to Israel in the wilderness, which has relevant lessons on discipline to all who desire a deeper walk and relationship with the Lord.

Moses told Israel that disciplined and ordered life was necessary for the preservation of inheritance. He said there is a reason for maintaining discipline through correction and punishment.

God does not correct to intimidate, control, or embarrass us.

When God allow us to go through the "fires of affliction" without immediate intervention, he has the beneficial end-result in mind, not temporary relief that teaches nothing. Every wilderness experience we go through is not meant to break us down, but to build us up.

The Lord corrects us when he sees us take a route that would lead to our ultimate destruction. The discipline of God is neither bullish, nor selfish. It is targeted at building in us the CHARACTER we need to make a difference wherever he positions us.

King David did well (with the help of God) to subdue all the nations around him, and left for Solomon an inheritance of national cohesion, peace, and prosperity. Unfortunately, David's legacy did not survive the test of time. This was because the moral laxity in his own life, with regard to women, disoriented the family structure.

The domino effect of King David's unbridled lust for women was disappointing. His sons manifested the same traits of personal indiscipline. Amnon raped his half sister, Tamar; Absalom staged a palace coup, while Solomon married 300 wives and had 700 side-chicks called concubines, many of them from nations God had warned Israel not to marry from(1Ki.11:1).

Solomon's foreign wives eventually led him into idol worship which laid the foundation for the destruction of David's legacy of a United Kingdom of Israel. The issue with David's sons was lack of self-discipline, which was necessary requirement for successful living.

When we falter and don't adhere to discipline, then God, as a loving and responsible Father, exercises the right to discipline us in areas we may need to be disciplined. The discipline of God is part of the process to bring us to "an expected end".

Sometimes the discipline may confine us to the "wilderness." The "wilderness" confinement is only a period of transition. It is our submission to God's dealings that will determine how long or short the journey is going to take.

You are on your way into "a good land" (a good place, both here and in the life hereafter); a place of water and fountains - speaking to us of abundant life. Be of good cheer. You are in safe in God's hands. Even in times of His discipline, and seeming chastisement, God remains focused on your ultimate good.

Nobody loves and cares for you like Jesus does. Submit to his leading, and accept his rebuke and correction. God want you to enjoy his abundance without abusing it. May his peace be with you and yours today and always in Jesus' Name.

God Bless You

Endure the Waiting

Acts 1:4, NLT

Once when he was eating with them, he commanded them, "Do not leave Jerusalem until the Father sends you the gift he promised, as I told you before"

Every promise of God has a timeline for its fulfillment. Indeed, God has set times and seasons for "every activity under the sun." Impatience can bring you some pleasure but rob you of spiritual treasures. The instruction Jesus gave his disciples centered around the phrase, "Do not leave Jerusalem until..." It was a call to WAIT, and not to run ahead of God. Sometimes a little knowledge can trigger in us a desire to run a race not mapped out for us. Jesus is teaching us some vital lessons of life.

First, is the importance of letting God lead and equip us for the tasks assigned us. We ought to reckon with preparation before thinking of celebration. We should not leave our Jerusalem because of the little knowledge we have acquired or present challenges we face. Life is short, but its chapters can be very long. The place of preparation is as important as your final destination. If the preparation is not allowed to run its full course, the separation will not benefit you. Peter nearly missed his calling when he decided to go back to his fishing business after the death of Christ. Don't quit the place appointed for your preparation.

The second lesson is the time element. Jesus did not instruct them to stay in Jerusalem forever, but for a specific period; "until the Father sends you the gift he promised." The promised gift was key to their success, and so to leave without the gift was a nonstarter. God's Word says, "a man's gift makes way for him." That gift must be given before it can be owned.

Let's look at it this way; you are contemplating quitting your job because someone gave you a promise to get you a better job. Wouldn't it be better for you to hold on to your present job until the promise is fulfilled? What happens if you quit your job and the promise fails? Don't cross your bridges before you reach them.

There is a reason God has positioned you where you are right now. The prison wasn't an ideal place for Joseph at the time of his incarceration, but time came when the Father's promise was fulfilled, and he was moved from prison to palace. Until then, he had to contend with years of waiting. In the case of the disciples, they waited 40 days, and that may have been a long time because they did not know when the Father's promise was going to be fulfilled. Their obedience and patience became a blessing for all mankind for all eternity.

Don't be in a hurry to leave where God has placed you UNTIL the promise is fulfilled. There are things you need to know about God, yourself, and others that will only come to you during the times of sticking it out in your Jerusalem. Endure the waiting, and your end will be glorious.

God bless you.

Turn the Wanderer

Jms.5:19-20, NKJV

Brethren, if anyone among you wanders from the truth, and someone turns him back, let him know that he who turns a sinner from the error of his way will save a soul from death and cover a multitude of sins.

Wandering from the truth, otherwise referred to as backsliding, is no news to God therefore we should be careful not to sideline those who fall into sin. Our struggle against sin will last as long as we have breath. The body in which we live and move, responds more to the things of the world, than the dictates of the Word. Being equipped with this knowledge, begin to understand your responsibility towards a fallen brother as a special assignment from God that cannot be compromised.

It is very easy and tempting to turn away from a fallen brother or sister, but God's army is depleted of its strength when we turn our backs on a fellow saint who falls into sin. Indeed, if the person is involved in walking in rebellion against Christ and his Church, that is a different ball game altogether. The mode of restoring a lost sheep is not the same as that of a prodigal Son. You go after a Lost Sheep, because he is sheep ("animal") and is lost, but you wait, pray, and hope for the Prodigal Son (rational being) to come to his senses and return home.

Apostle James says to tell you that when you allow God to use you to restore a brother who "wanders from the truth," you have killed two birds with one stone. First, you have saved a soul from death. You become part of the reason that person is not going to end up in hell. Second, you play a major role in covering a multitude of sins. All that the brother would have continued to do by way of sin, comes to an end because of your intervention. If there is someone you know, who is wandering away from the truth, do not let him die in sin.

If he is a Lost Sheep (immature believer trapped by the carnal nature), go after him and do all you possibly can to help him trace his steps back to the path of truth, light, and life. If he is a Prodigal Son/Daughter who is living in open rebellion against the truth and will not listen to counsel, you can still pray for him and hope for the best. A true Spirit-filled and Spirit-led child of God should never be indifferent towards brethren who fall into error. Do your part, and let God take care of the outcome.

God bless you.

Lessons from the Transfiguration

Lu.9:28-32, NKJV

Now it came to pass, about eight days after these sayings, that He took Peter, John, and James and went up on the mountain to pray...But Peter and those with him were heavy with sleep; and when they were fully awake, they saw His glory and the two men who stood with Him

---

There are two lessons we grasp from today's devotional scripture. The first is in verse 28; Jesus selected three of his disciples to witness the transfiguration on the mountain. It raised a question why the Master would not take all the twelve apostles along, but chose only the three to experience this unique phenomenon?

The answer and message conveyed is clear; not everyone on your team or in your circle of friends should know everything about you. You've got to have different levels of relationships with individuals and different groups of people.

It is not wise to go out there telling anyone and everyone about matters relating to your marriage, family, children, business, finances etc. No, that is a suicide-mission in the making. No matter how people outside your home or family claim to love you, you will be better off not exposing your "nakedness" in public. God does not expect you to take everyone to your "mountain of transfiguration." The glory can offend some Judas you wrongly assume is a brother or sister. They might work against your vision. If it is a challenge, some may turn round to use it against you. Don't take anything for granted.

Remember no one out there is perfect. Many of the folks you are selling yourself to, may be dealing with issues worse than yours. They are smart enough not to let you in on their negative issues. This is not to suggest you don't seek help when you are in a crisis that is going beyond your immediate control. No, the emphasis is on defining the borders of your relationships. It is different when you are seeking counsel, but even with that, you must choose the "three" who climb the mountain with you carefully and prayerfully. Those who go with you to the mountain must be Spirit-filled matured Christians with integrity. Don't just go to anyone because you are sure he or she will tell you what you WANT to hear.

Choose the one who will tell you what you NEED to hear because it is what God want you to know, and who beyond that will not market your challenges in the public domain. Be very selective in the choice of people who go with you to your "mount of transfiguration." O ur second lesson is in the verse 32 which states that the disciples fell asleep, "but when they were FULLY AWAKE, THEY SAW HIS GLORY..." Beloved, could it be that we may be sleeping in the hour of prayer and that is the reason we are not seeing His glory?

We may be tired because climbing the mountain for so long a time has taken its toll on us, but enough of the sleep. We are redeemed to recover everything that the enemy has stolen, and we should not settle for anything less than that. Why sleep in the very presence of our Redeemer and at a time that we should be praying? Wake up and shave off that feeling of despondency. His glory is our goal and we must not only see it, but receive and possess it. Nobody is better qualified to see for you than yourself. Telling you what I see isn't the same as seeing it for yourself.

Christ has elevated you to mountain status. Stay awake and keep praying. You will see His glory and possess His goodness. God bless you and give you strength to keep up the good fight till you break through and possess the fullness of His glory.

God bless you

Don't be Like a Horse

Ps. 32:8-9, GNB

The LORD says, "I will teach you the way you should go; I will instruct you and advice you. Don't be stupid like a horse or a mule which must be controlled with a bit and bridle to make it submit

The language format used in communicating with a horse is radically different from that of a dog, or any other animal. My first experience in horse-riding was in Ethiopia in 2006, and one of the lessons I learnt was that horses on their own do not follow instructions like dogs generally do; horses have to be prompted, controlled and maneuvered. Lack of trust in the leading of God can push us into a corner where we behave like a horse who must be "controlled with a bit and brittle to make it submit." The scripture calls such posture and attitude "stupid."

Yes, it is stupid for us to ignore the direction of the God who created the world and all that is in it, and assume control of our own lives when we don't even know how we arrived here in the first place. Living without self-discipline and restraint is pushing us to the brink of moral disaster. My heart bleeds at the continued surge of immorality and our society's low esteem for preservation of human life. Sole dependence on human knowledge and wisdom is leading us daily on a path of self-destruction and obvious stupidity.

I watch the National Geographic documentaries on television and see animals protecting their babies, only to turn to the news the next moment to hear educated human beings, created in God's image, sign a document to approve the murder of full-term innocent babies in cold blood. No matter how hard we try to justify this and other evil practices, it still comes down to the fact that we are disconnected from our creator. We have rejected his Word and embraced the world.

The consequences of our actions stare us in the face; the greater our exploits in technological advancement, the weaker we become in terms of the true essence of morality and values of life. Beloved, God has a better option for you and I. He says, "I want to teach you the way you should go." He is not forcing, he is not pushing, and he is not imposing; he is deliberately appealing to our conscience.

God want our hearts before he acts. It is possible that the crisis we are going through right now is because we are not considering the God-factor in the way we are living our lives. This is not about praying, reading the Bible or going to "church." All that is good and an essential part of receiving teaching from the Lord; but we can do all that, and still do what we want to do without reference to what God is asking us to do.

In that circumstance, the only choice left for the Lord to bring us to order and prevent us from destroying ourselves is to apply "bit and bridle" to make us submit. That in itself is not how God want to relate to his children and is a far cry from the choice he might make.

When we reject his direction and refuse his correction, he respects our freedom of choice, and in the end, we harvest unpleasant consequences. May we become students of God's Word who read the scriptures to receive teaching and instruction, and not as a religious obligation to numb our conscience against guilt.

God Bless You.

Focus on Jesus

Mk.9:7-8, NIV

Then a cloud appeared and enveloped them, and a voice came from the cloud: "This is my Son, whom I love. Listen to him!" Suddenly, when they looked around, they no longer saw anyone with them except Jesus

---

It was a day like no other. Jesus asked Peter, James, and John to follow him as he climbed a mountain. When they finally reached a place the Lord felt was convenient, they stopped. Soon there was a strange phenomenon. A cloud suddenly appeared and overshadowed them. Then followed a voice from that unusual cloud addressing the three apostles, "This is my Son, whom I love. Listen to him!" This statement stands out as a very strong endorsement of the divinity of Christ. Given the fact that Moses (representing the Law) and Elijah (representing the prophets) were present, and were not even mentioned by the Father, means a lot.

Our Father and God is saying emphatically that no human or spiritual entity has the standing Jesus Christ has with him. The Son of God is a direct and total representation of who God is. Listening to him and obeying his commands supersedes anything attributable to Moses and Elijah put together. God wants us to relate to his Only Begotten Son the same way we relate to him. Jesus is the one we are to listen to, not Moses or Elijah. We are not to bring Christ to the level of an ordinary human being. He is more than a prophet and lawgiver; he is the fulfillment of the Law and the prophets. He is God incarnate.

When the dramatic event came to an end, scripture records that "when they (apostles) looked around, they longer saw anyone with them except Jesus." Yes! He will never leave us or forsake us. No relationship will last through eternity, apart from the one we have with Jesus. He is the true friend who sticks "closer than a brother." Focus on Jesus today, tomorrow, and forever. Whichever way we look at the "Moseses" and "Elijahs" of this world, they are sinners and need salvation like all of us. By contrast, Jesus Christ paid the price for our sins. He stood in a place neither Moses nor Elijah could stand.

Hear the heart-cry of our Father in heaven saying, "Listen to him!" Indeed, Jesus assures us that no one who follows and obeys him will ever suffer shame or damnation. There are many voices clamoring for our attention, but only the Master's voice deserves our respect. If we listen to the Christ, we can overcome our crisis. He is the source of life, and the repository of all wisdom and power. No man can do the things he does, and no one can take you any further than him. Do you know Jesus, the Christ? Whether you do, or don't, the creator of the universe is saying to you the same thing he said to Peter, James, and John: "Listen to him!" And you shall live.

Walk this month with determination, not only to listen to Jesus Christ, but also to obey what he says, and follow where he leads.

God bless you.

Thank God for Your Foundations

Ezra 3:11, NIV

With praise and thanksgiving they sang to the LORD: "He is good; his love to Israel endures forever." And all the people gave a great shout of praise to the LORD, because the foundation of the house of the LORD was laid.

Those of us addicted to building lives and physical structures like houses, know how important foundations are in the scheme of things. A foundation marks the beginning of what used to be a mental picture. It is the beginning of a journey that ignites hope and confidence in future possibilities. It is worth celebrating, even though we often ignore its importance.

Friend, every foundation you have laid in your life is an achievement. If you look too far into the future, you may not see so clearly enough to appreciate what is close to you right now. You may miss out on opportunities to be appreciative of your present triumphs. Be careful you don't cross your bridges before you get to them; worrying about tomorrow when you should be thankful for today. The nature of foundations is that they are usually buried under the ground. They are not seen with the natural eye, and that is exactly how your efforts and sacrifices may appear to be today. You've done a lot, worked your heart out, but seeing very little result.

You have trusted and waited, and now you are beginning to wonder if it was worth the while putting in the effort to come this far. The answer is a big, loud "yes!" There is absolutely nothing like wasted time and effort in the kingdom of God. Don't make the mistake of ignoring your "foundations." If you do, the picture you get about yourself will always be one of failure. Everyone who started building with you may have completed their life's project, but that should be none of your business. What should be your business, is YOUR business!!

Remember that Noah was called to build an ark, Moses was assigned to build a tabernacle, while Solomon was mandated to build a temple. All of these structures had different time frames for completion. If Noah had tried to build a temple, he would have been a failure. You are not called to imitate someone else's life and assignment. Drive in your defined lane. Stay the course. Praise the Lord for grace to grow in your role. Your foundation is evidence of a glorious future, not only in this life, but in the hereafter.

You have a beginning; foundations of what you have deposited in time, space, and people. That is where the party should begin, and that should be your anthem of praise. Give God some high praise and get ready to raise the structure to the next level. Peace and prosperity to you.

God Bless You.

Be a Blessing to the Burdened

Tit.1:8, NKJV

This is a faithful saying, and these things I want you to affirm constantly, that those who have believed in God should be careful to maintain good works. These things are good and profitable to men

---

One of the many testimonies regarding Jesus Christ in the scriptures is the act of goodness that he did. He did not only preach goodness but lived it in real time (Acts 10:38). The writer of the book of Titus is urging all of us who claim to be followers of Christ to "be careful to maintain good works." If we claim to be sons and daughters of God, then we have an obligation to DO and MAINTAIN good works.

Acts of goodness should be our modus operandi. Sharing and caring should be a common feature in our dealings with men, especially those who are vulnerable.

Compassion for the lost, those who are weak in faith, the lonely and vulnerable, demands our attention. Many are laughing with us every day, but who beyond that expression of joy are contending with emotional challenges that are eating them up like cancer. Mental health issues are rising on a daily basis, and it is possible some of the people closely associated with us may be in dire need of help to save them from the brink of emotional collapse.

Prayerfully consider becoming a channel of hope for someone worse off than you. Like Shakespeare rightly wrote, "there is not act to find the mind's construction in the face." In other words, it is impossible to know what someone is thinking or the struggles he may be going through by merely looking at his face. It takes the grace of God and a genuine desire to help to discern such situations, and it all begins with a mindset to do good. If you are ready to help others, God will show you the way forward. It's not always about money; sometimes all it takes is your presence and attention.

God will give you the ability to hear the unspoken words of a struggling soul, and you can save some lives and restore hope to the helpless. Expand your borders of influence. Jesus said out of your innermost being shall flow rivers of living water. He means every one of us has the capacity to do good and impart life. The Holy Spirit has deposited in us all we need to make a difference in people's lives. You may not be seeing evidence of this truth in your life because you are not taking the necessary steps of faith. God's marching orders to the Church is to "maintain good works." It is that simple, but it is loaded.

God's will for us is to be consistent in doing good. Let's put our hands to the plow and go on God's rescue mission. Wait no longer. Unlock the river of God's goodness within you, and while it flows to heal others, it will release blessings into your own life.

God bless you

You Can be Free

Ps.68:6a, NLT

God places the lonely in families; he sets the prisoners free and gives them joy

---

Being alone is not the same as being lonely. One has to do with isolation, while the other is purely a feeling of exclusion. You can be a a crowd and not feel a part of it at all; that means you are not alone, but lonely. Loneliness is an emotional state that far outweighs the effect of being alone. It sets an agenda for anxiety, worry, and possible depression. Some of us feel very much okay when we are by ourselves. It gives us time to reflect and strategize.

We are able to look into the mirrors of our lives through sober reflection and see what changes should be made, and how to make them. However, when it comes to being lonely, most of us need a lifeline to get over it. We can physically control our "aloneness", but not always so with our "loneliness". Today's scripture shows us another dimension of the love of God. He works behind the scenes to sort out our dreadful feelings of loneliness. God understands how the weight of loneliness oppresses the human soul and tackles it at its roots.

Indeed, distorted human relationships and a sense of isolation are conveyor-belts that often bring us to a state of loneliness. Rejection can also result in same. God's solution is to "locate" us where he can heal us. The reason the scripture connects loneliness to setting prisoners free is because that feeling in itself imprisons us. God's plan for us is to live a life devoid of stress. He is intent on ensuring that you and I are free to enjoy the life he has given us.

Some of your family and friends may have failed you, but that should not be the reason to live under the yoke of loneliness. God's position is that you can be alone without being lonely, because he has the capacity to create the right environment for your peace and pleasure. Where there is the need for company, he will work things for your good. Come out of any emotional prison that is holding you captive. The door of deliverance is open for you. God has done his part, and now it is your turn to remove the sack clothes and walk into the freedom set before you. Make the best out of your day. You deserve better than burdens.

Trust the process God is taking you through and refuse to dwell on issues that deepen your fears, anxieties, and worries. God is setting you up for a life of peace and joy. You can be free today. Yes, no longer a prisoner of loneliness, and forever free from depression.

God bless you.

Divine Determinations

Mk.10:40, NKJV

"But to sit at my right or left is not for me to grant. These places belong to those for whom they have been prepared."

There are limits to what we can do, and how far we can go in the quest for fulfillment in life. As children of God, we have to make room for things that have been determined by God, and not subject to change. Someone may not look as smart as you but may get something you may never get. Jesus's interaction with John and his brother James, regarding their desire to take the right and left seats closest to him in his kingdom, highlights possible limitations to our expectations, relative to the sovereignty of God.

The two brothers asked for what they considered very privileged positions when Jesus returns to establish his kingdom on earth. When the Lord drew their attention to the extreme suffering he was going to go through and asked if they could endure same, they answered in the affirmative. They were ready to die for what they wanted. Jesus saw their determination and applauded them for it but pointed out that performance was not enough for qualification to the positions they were seeking. God in his sovereignty had predetermined the persons who would occupy those seats.

Some things in life are not up for grasp through human wisdom, expertise, negotiation, imposition, or competition. They fit squarely into God's eternal plan for each person. Our prayers are answered in accordance with God's will for our lives. Some crowns are reserved for certain heads. Grace can propel someone to a height we may think he doesn't deserve, but then who are we to determine how God dispenses his blessings? He doesn't owe us explanation for giving someone more than he has given us or answering the other person's prayer quicker. Indeed, that is what makes him God!

Knowing this truth, that God is sovereign and so can do and undo as he pleases, is like a soothing balm to a terrible pain. When we make a request to the Lord, we should expect any one of these three answers; a "yes", a "no", or a "wait"! All three are legitimate answers. The answer Jesus gave to John and James was a firm "no"! No matter what sacrifices they make, it was not going to make any difference. Heaven has taken a stand and it cannot be reversed. Who knows, maybe you and I are the chosen ones for those seats. Very possible! We are all sinners saved by grace.

The crux of the matter is that whatever belongs to us by divine right will come to us if we keep the faith, do our best, and stay the course. The things we don't get after working so hard may disappoint but shouldn't destroy us. An unmet goal or unfulfilled dream is not necessarily a sign of failure. Pursue your dreams with an open mind; sensitive to God's sovereign right to redirect your steps into paths you never dreamt charting. God's "yes" is as good as his "no" or "wait". Its end is always glorious, and that's what your ending will be like.

We may not seat at his immediate right or left, but we surely will be there, sitting with him at the same table, enjoying the same meal. What is ours by divine will come to us. No shaking!! Love life, sing, laugh, and give yourself a break from worrying about things that God has not determined for you.

God bless you

Forgive and Let Go

Mk.11:25, NIV

And when you stand praying, if you hold anything against anyone, forgive him, so that your Father in heaven may forgive you your sins

---

Many times, when I have had the privilege to speak in Pastor's conferences and interact with younger ministers of the gospel, one major question most ask is how to make their marriage survive the test of time. I have always maintained that forgiveness is one of the major keys that unlock blessings of peace and prosperity into all relationships, especially marriages. Let me state emphatically that I don't, as a matter of principle, endorse abusive relationships.

I have zero tolerance for people who deliberately and consistently disregard decency and subject their spouses and children to verbal and physical abuse. I will pray for them and counsel them where necessary, but not make them feel their behavior is okay. It is not right or proper. The culture of forgiveness, however, should be prominent feature of our lives as Christians. First, because of what Jesus says in this passage of scripture; that it guarantees us God's forgiveness. Forgiving others produces a domino effect. We decide whether to forgive or not, and our decision gives us equal response from God.

A child of God ought to make choices that reflect his faith. Once we relate to people, we should expect that offenses will come. Those who are likely to "offend" us most are the people closest to us. It is that easy for your family and friends to get on your nerves because of the proximity of your relationship with them. Until you understand and appreciate that God expect you to love them as he has loved you, and forgive them as he has forgiven you, the place you call home that is supposed to be filled with love, may only be a house full of strife. You live there because you "tolerate" the folks you call family or friends.

Forgiveness becomes a big struggle, and you see people who should bring you joy, as enemies. You draw so many red lines around you that your spouse, children and friends are not allowed to cross because they have offended you, and you are not ready and willing to forgive them. Your mind virtually becomes a library filled with files of past and present offenses. It's time to break free from that self-imposed bondage. If (conditional clause) you forgive those who have offended you, God reciprocates the gesture by forgiving you. It creates room for your prayers to be heard and answered.

Until you learn to forgive those who offend you, there is very little you can do to build healthy relationships anywhere. Your prayers will not register with God. You will burden your soul and hurt your body. The deal is on the table, and you've got to sign it for your own good and peace of mind. Forgive, and you will be forgiven.

God bless you

Fulfill your Ministry

1 Sam.16:1, KJV

And the Lord said unto Samuel, how long wilt thou mourn for Saul, seeing that I have rejected him from reigning over Israel? Fill thy horn with oil, and go, I will send thee to Jesse, the Bethlehemite: for I have provided me a king among his sons

---

Nobody is indispensable in the kingdom of God. It is a privilege to be given opportunity to serve the Lord in any capacity whatsoever. Whether you are apostle, prophet, evangelist, pastor or usher in the House of God, your only qualification for that role is the grace of God - nothing more, nothing less. The moment you allow pride to inflate your ego and walk in disobedience to what God has for you to do, you are likely to lose that position to someone else.

Satan lost his place in heaven for that reason, and King Saul suffered the same fate when his allegiance to God was compromised. He departed completely from relying on God, and broke the heart of prophet Samuel, who scripture records grieved over Saul's intransigence for a long time. God eventually had to step in with assurance to prophet Samuel that He had already replaced the king and had someone standing by to step in at the right time. All the prophet needed to do was to locate God's chosen candidate and go for him.

In Acts Chapter 1 we see the same scenario played out, with Judas being replaced effectively. For three years he walked and worked with Jesus, but he lost his life and ministry because he loved gold more than God. Beloved, all scripture (including this one) is written for our learning. The truth revealed here is that God is counting on us to play our part in fulfilling his purpose on earth, being mindful that none of us is so special that God's work will come to a standstill if we decide to quit on our calling in the home, church, and community.

Souls are dying, and people are desperate. The wolves have arrived, devouring the flock of God. Lift your voice. Stretch your hands and pull someone out of hell. Tell someone about the love of Christ and the finished work of Calvary. Take your call to serve the Lord serious, because it is a privilege, and not a right. Remember, no one is indispensable in the Kingdom of God. King Saul walked away from God and was replaced by David. Judas Iscariot walked away from Jesus and was replaced by Matthias. Alexander walked away from apostle Paul, and Paul reached out to Timothy. Keep your place and fulfill your ministry.

God bless you.

Faithfulness

1 Chron.9:1, NKJV

So all Israel was recorded by genealogies, and indeed, they were inscribed in the book of the kings of Israel. But Judah was carried away captive to Babylon because of their unfaithfulness.

If your name is missing from God's records, the fault cannot be from God. The door of grace is still open and accessible to all. When God was making captains of his people, Judah became a captive, because Judah was unfaithful to the Lord. Judah's unfaithfulness denied her the safety and security available to the rest of her brethren.

Let's do a connect here and ask ourselves why the rate of divorce is on the upward surge, even among believers. In a majority of cases, the issues are related to unfaithfulness. Husbands are unfaithful to their wives, and vice versa. This creates an atmosphere of distrust. A dark cloud casts its influence over the home, and everyone becomes captive to lies and deception.

We go to church and go through all the spiritual motions without any conviction that will drive us to repentance. It is sad, but truth is, there is a lot that families and individuals go through, that is avoidable. Like Judah's captivity, some of the challenges we face in life, are self-imposed.

Most people will commit to you if they can be sure of your words and deeds. Avoid the snare of spiritual captivity. Be faithful, even if it means losing out.

God bless you.

Plan with God

2 Sam.5:22-26, NIV

Once more the Philistines came up and spread out in the Valley of Rephaim; so David inquired of the LORD, and he answered, "Do not go straight up, but circle around behind them and attack them in front of the balsam trees. As soon as you hear the sound of marching in the tops of the balsam trees, move quickly, because that will mean the LORD has gone out in front of you to strike the Philistine army. So David did as the LORD commanded him, and he struck down the Philistines all the way from Gibson to Gezer

---

It doesn't really matter how many battles and challenges confront you today; if you seek God's direction, you will see his power work on your behalf every time, and victory will be yours always. David's reliance on God was unquestionable; he would not take on any serious battle without seeking God's help and direction. Being someone scripture described as "a man after God's own heart," we should be very much interested in studying how he related to the Lord.

What are some of the things that might have excited God about David? One of them is his tendency to seek God's direction whenever he had to go to war. This attitude easily stands out as a major plus for David, and something worth our emulation. Right from his early days as a young man, he boasted about how he routed lions and bears through the help of God, and insisted he was going to win the fight against Goliath because he was confronting the giant, not in his own strength, but IN THE NAME OF THE LORD (1Sam.17:45-46).

The deciding factor, as far as David was concerned, had nothing to do with who you are, but rather who is your God. When your battle plan is crafted in the WAR ROOM of heaven, the enemy has lost the fight before the first shot is fired. You honor God when you plan with God. He knows what you do not know. Sometimes you may share dreams with people who may seem very excited about it, but whose deepest desire is to see you fail. That's the reason the prophet Jeremiah declared that "the heart of man is desperately wicked" (Jer.17:9).

There may even be people who sincerely wish you well, and whose counsel may be as good as that of Ahithophel; but trading their limited knowledge with God's unlimited wisdom and direction, is not a safe option. See how David's reliance on God's direction was richly rewarded. He defeated the Philistines because he depended very much on the Lord. Don't wait till you are caught in a tight corner after moving without God, before calling on him. Go to him for direction before you take off, and you cannot miss your target.

You have nothing to lose planning with God, trusting and depending on his leading. The path he leads may sometimes take a detour towards the Red Sea, but he has the power to open it up for you to walk through it. Keep praying. Keep trusting. You are in the safest place if your life is in his hands. May the good Lord give you total victory in all your battles against any "Philistine army" in your life. Shalom, and grace to you.

God bless you.

Appreciate the People in Your Life

Rom.16:3-4, GNB

> *I send greetings to Priscilla and Aquila, my fellow workers in the service of Christ Jesus; they risked their lives for me. I am grateful to them - not only I, but all the Gentile churches as well.*

It is good and right to take time to appreciate the people who have made impact on, and in our lives; wonderful people like our parents who invested love, time, and resources to give us a start in life. We have to remember and appreciate our teachers, our friends, pastors, and other mentors who help shape our lives. The wise have said that "Familiarity breeds contempt," and this is so often evident in the home. We take our spouses for granted, enjoying their company and hurting their feelings.

We take our children for granted. We are not mindful of the huge difference they make in our lives; not realizing that even the irritating things they say and do, help our growth and maturity. They are useful tools for testing our patience level, and how far we can go in offering unconditional love. The writer of the book of Romans devoted the whole of the 16th chapter, mentioning those who played key roles in his ministry.

He thanked and appreciated those who needed to be appreciated, while encouraging those not in right relationship to reconcile. When he mentioned Priscilla and Aquila, he said, "they risked their lives for me." When you think of how far God has brought you, can you identify some "Priscilla and Aquila" folks that God has used and maybe is still using, to do the work he has done, and still doing with your life. Such people are treasures.

Let them know you are grateful for their love. Show some gratitude to your mum, dad, wife, husband, son, daughter, and friend, for whatever little blessing they have been to you. Thank them for the joy and laughter they give you that money cannot buy. Thank them for upsetting you sometimes, because God uses them to show you the level of your maturity, and so that's okay. They are still a pleasure, because without them your life will lack momentum and color.

When I get unreasonably upset with my wife, that is always a wake-up call that this boy has a long way to go in the school of patience and long-suffering. So even in that situation, I see the uniqueness and blessing of her presence in my life. If she had not been there to trigger the lurking "monster" in me, I would be congratulating myself where I should be acknowledging a weakness. Whether they make you laugh or make you mad, the people who accept and love you for who you are, and stand by you and with you, deserve your thanks and appreciation.

Treat them as precious gifts from God, because that is what, and who they are. Indulge me this opportunity to thank my wife and family, and all of you friends and loved ones, for being part of my life. You make my joy complete, and I appreciate you for it. Now it is your turn to take time and say thanks to your Priscilla and Aquila. It is simple, but sufficient to put another layer of bonding in your relationship.

God bless you.

Things that Accompany Salvation

Heb.6:10, NKJV

But, beloved, we are confident of better things concerning you, yes, things that accompany salvation, though we speak in this manner

---

God has not saved us to suffocate or starve us. Salvation is a package, and that is what the writer of the book of Hebrews is referencing in this passage. Salvation does not only bring us out of sin and its consequences but guarantees us abundant life in Christ. Jesus brings us OUT to bring us IN. Apart from being reconciled with our Heavenly Father, we are given, among other things, power over Satan and all his demons. If you are a believer in Christ, and you are always obsessed with Satan, demons, witches etc., you are belittling your God.

By virtue of the things that accompany salvation, God has deposited in you ALL power and authority, and so the Word of God declares, "Greater is he that is IN YOU, than he that is IN THE WORLD." You can't overcome an opponent you think is stronger or better than you. Your fear will make you fall before him. You will bow without him bending you. Ignorance is the number one spiritual virus killing today's confessing Christians. We prefer listening to flamboyant "prophets" than accessing Biblical truth. So here comes a preacher who says you shouldn't eat pork meat because it will expose you to demonic attack. He gives you a scripture in Leviticus to buttress his point, and you swallow it hook, line, and clinker.

A careful study of the scriptures puts a death-nail on this distortion of scripture. First, the forbidding of certain foods was part of the ceremonial law given to natural Israel which has nothing to do with New Testament saints (spiritual Israel). In any case, it was not only pork that was forbidden. There are so many varieties of fish we are eating today that are also forbidden in that same scripture. Therefore in Rom.14:13ff, the Word of God states that food has nothing to do with faith, because "the kingdom of God is not a matter of eating and drinking." Think about this; if eating a particular food gives Satan and his demons power over us, then there is a limit to the power and protection God has promised us in his Word. "Things that accompany our salvation" include freedom from fear, liberty of the Spirit, victory over sin, Satan, demons, and all agents of the devil.

Our level of growth and maturity determines the extent to which we can appropriate these promises. We don't grow by drinking or bathing with olive oil and Holy water; we grow by meditating on God's Word and obedience to its demands, spending quality time with God in fasting and prayer, submission to the leadership of the Holy Spirit, and living by faith. Dearly beloved, no one can "mature" you. Sentimental rhetorics do not cast out demons, or bring prosperity and power. The "things that accompany salvation" include hard work. Check the life of the apostles. Paul said they were not "ignorant of the devices of the devil." Beyond that knowledge, he said, "we are MORE THAN CONQUERORS" through Christ who strengthens us. Are we saying eating a particular food can take away the strength Christ has given us? Impossible!!

This shallow thinking and faithlessness drove apostle Paul to write to the Galatian church stating: "Oh, foolish Galatians! Who has cast an evil spell on you? For the meaning of Jesus Christ's death was made as clear to you as if you had seen a picture of his death on the cross. Let me ask you this one question: Did you receive the Holy Spirit by obeying the law of Moses? Of course not! You received the Spirit because you believed the message you heard about Christ.

How foolish can you be? After starting your new lives in the Spirit, why are you now trying to become perfect by your own human effort?" (Gal.3:1-3, NLT)

You are a child of the King of kings, and you ought to live like one. Appropriate all the blessings that accompany salvation and stop living in fear and imposing on yourself yokes God has removed from your neck.

God bless you.

Service will Elevate You

Ex.33:11, NIV

The Lord would speak to Moses face to face, as one speaks to a friend. Then Moses would return to the camp, but his young aide Joshua did not leave the tent

There is always a price to pay for promotion and elevation. The most exciting revelation in our devotional scripture for today relates to a young diligent servant of Moses called Joshua. Joshua is described as "aide" or assistant to Moses. Other versions of the Holy Bible use the phrase "servant of Moses" in reference to him. The mere mention of being a servant might put some of us off, but it is in serving that unusual doors of blessing and opportunity open.

Our tendency is to be managers rather than the ministers; oblivious of the fact that it is impossible to be an effective manager without first being a committed servant. Service is key to the productive life that brings prosperity. Those who cannot serve, hardly succeed as good managers. Joshua did not serve Moses with a goal to inheriting his position. The young man loved the Lord, and his submission to Moses was an overspill of that love. He was not after power and position. Joshua was driven by passion for God.

It is the only way one can explain why he wouldn't leave the tent (chapel) when the "service" was over, and Moses had left. After all, he was there to serve Moses. Let me break down a few more of the things we can learn from Joshua in this particular scripture, aside his deep love for God. First, Joshua had the rare opportunity to be closer to the Presence of God and be part taker of Moses's experience than any other in the camp, because of his humility. He was humble enough to decide to SERVE Moses.

He could have could have chosen not to play that role, or even to have done so grudgingly. Indeed, if he wasn't doing it wholeheartedly, he wouldn't be hanging out there after Moses left. Joshua went the extra mile; serving beyond the "normal working hours." The second lesson is his willingness to sacrifice for the comfort of Moses, his mentor. Remember that Moses at this time was quite old and would be needing a lot of help and assistance, given the huge task of leading a whole nation in a wilderness, while dealing with his own family issues.

The assistance required would not have given room for the young man to focus much on his personal goals, but Joshua accepted the challenge and paid the price. He pushed himself to the front-burner, as the one Moses could trust to provide the moral and physical support he needed. Third lesson is that genuine and selfless service can never go without reward. Young Joshua never dreamt of inheriting the leadership mantle of Moses. Indeed, he did not give any indication of being interested in position or power.

What we do know, per this scripture, is that he was so passionate about his relationship with God that even when Moses, the man of God, for whose sake he was at the tent had left, he stayed behind, still reveling in the Presence of God. His heart was after God and wanted more than a relationship with the man of God. Last, but not least, Joshua was patient. He was willing to WAIT! He WAITED

ON Moses and WAITED FOR God. He is a classic example of elevation through seeming humiliation. In the short-term, his service to Moses appeared to hold no future prospect, but in the long-term, it elevated him to a position he never dreamt possible.

Selfless sacrifice brings great rewards. Deepen your relationship with God. Do your best, regardless of what you stand to lose or gain in the short-term. No sacrifice is ever wasted. "Humble yourself before the Lord, and he will lift you up."

God bless you

Draw the Line

Gen.19:14, NKJV

So Lot went out and spoke to his sons-in-law, who had married his daughters, and said, "Get up, get out of this place; for the LORD will destroy this city!" But to his sons-in-law he seemed to be joking

---

Once upon a time, angels who had visited Abraham, were hosted by his nephew, Lot. Before the angels left Lot, they warned him of the impending judgment on Sodom, where the young man had taken residence after separating from Abraham. Lot's first concern, and rightly so, was the safety of his immediate family. He had to relocate to a place of safety, and it was incumbent on him as head of the family to ensure he got everyone to come along with him. Indeed, that is what responsible fathers and mothers are expected to do; to provide a safety-net for their family; spiritually, physically, emotionally, financially, et all.

Unfortunately for Lot, the response to his advice was not what he expected. His "salvation message" was rejected because his sons-in-law thought he was "joking", and we can figure out probable reasons for that reaction. Firstly, Lot may have been known to them as someone who never took God and the things of God seriously. They came to the conclusion that he was joking, based on his past record as one who made fun of spiritual things. His history of leaving Abraham and choosing to live in a morally bankrupt city like Sodom did not make him a credible preacher of divine judgment.

Second probable reason his in-laws thought he was joking, might be his penchant for joking about anything and everything. Indeed, no one will take you seriously if you are never serious about anything in life. Some of the perceptions and opinions people may have about you, may come from how you present yourself most of the time. If you keep shouting "wolf! wolf!!" when there is no wolf, the day you see a wolf and ask your family and friends to run, they will stand, stare at you, and laugh. Healthy jokes have their place. A good laugh is necessary for our mental health and emotional well-being, but the problem arises when no one is sure whether we are joking or saying something that needs to be taken seriously. A lot depends on what we communicate and how we do it, and for the sake of the lives we impact, we should never be defined as "jokers" in times of crisis.

More importantly, our children and all who relate to us should be clear in their minds that God, and the things pertaining to his kingdom, do not form part of our jokes. When we declare the Word of God, we say what we mean, and mean what we say. The Holy Bible is not a comedy book; it is a life manual. Our jokes should stop where its pages start.

Draw the lines and indicate clearly where the jokes stop. If you fail to do so, you will endanger both yourself and those in your circle of relationship. Someone may be described as a jockey, while another person is referred to as a joker. It is about what people see them do continually. One is a profession, whilst the other is a pattern of behavior, but they both define a person. Let your world know the difference between your jokes and your principles.

God bless you

God Will Reward You

Heb.6:10, NIV

God is not unjust; he will not forget your work and the love you have shown him as you have helped his people and continue to help them

---

What is your perception of the God of the Holy Bible? The question is relevant to our relationship with him. If you perceive God as untrustworthy, it will undermine your faith in him. Today, we are reflecting on a scripture that unequivocally declares that "God is not unjust." In other words, God is just; he does what is right and proper in all situations and circumstances. He cannot be bribed or corrupted. God does not cheat on his creation. He is not only a giver, but also a rewarder.

Whatever you do in line with his will and principles comes with a reward. God's sense of justice holds in memory every act of goodness, especially "love you have shown him as you have helped his people." Those who receive the help you give may forget. They may even pay you back with ingratitude, but the God for whose sake you did the good NEVER forgets and will reward you for it. The scripture says God acknowledges the help you give to his people as an expression of your love for him. It invariably means that withholding help when it's in our power to do so, signals lack of love for God. The litmus test is this: How can you say you love the Lord when you find it difficult helping his people?

Love for God is the believer's primary identity. Everything we do or do not do should be motivated by this one thing - love for God. Whatever I give or do for my brother or sister should be motivated by my love for God. That way, I am not impacted by his or her attitude towards me. If he is appreciative, praise God! If he gives a thumbs down, amen!! Either way I am protected from being bitter because like the venerable Mother Theresa would say, "I did it for Jesus."

You may be grappling with some anger or pain because of the way someone you helped reacted towards you. This is the balm for your healing; you did it for God and he will reward you good. Be like Mother Theresa who would always say, "I did it for Jesus." Move on and enjoy your day, "God is not unjust; he will not forget your work and the love shown him as you have helped his people."

Get out there and give all the help you can to all you can, including that ungrateful friend, spouse, child, colleague etc., knowing that you are a channel of divine love, and a candidate for unusual blessings from a God who never forgets and surely rewards.

God bless you.

Contend for The Faith

Jer. 32:17-18, NKJV

They sacrificed to demons, not to God, to gods they did not know, to new gods, new arrivals that your fathers did not fear. Of the Rock who begot you, you are unmindful, and have forgotten the God who fathered you

---

These are words of a song composed and sang by Moses to the children of Israel in the wilderness. The words recounted the faithfulness of God to his people, and their response of ingratitude and rebellion. Before we pass judgement on them, we must first reflect on our own individual and collective attitudes relative to God's grace and mercy towards us. If Israel sacrificed to idols, it means they took the blessings they received from the Lord and used it to honor other gods.

What it is saying to us is that our stewardship of the blessings the Lord gives us is important to him. We should not use the money God gives us the strength to acquire to promote lewdness and ungodliness. Whatever God gives us should be used to promote people and programs that stand the test of righteousness.

The places we spend your time, and how we use our resources are indicators of our commitment to honoring the grace of God on our lives.

The world is aggressively pushing idols of sex, money, power, and fame in our faces each day, and if we are not careful, we may tacitly endorse practices and lifestyles that are contrary to the Word of God. We are redeemed from the CURSE of the LAW, to pursue the COURSE of God's LOVE and righteousness.

Satan has a way of drawing us away from God and making us worship the creation instead of the creator. When the world threatens us with sanctions and insists we bow to its dictates and follow its ungodly directions or face its wrath, we have to take a stand for Christ and truth. Indeed, following the path of righteousness is neither popular nor politically correct, but if you are given the choice between pleasing the Lord and becoming popular with the world, where would you cast your vote? You have to take a stand for righteousness to preserve the sanctity of life.

Remember, the applause of the world is only temporary, but your relationship with Christ is eternal. The "new" is always attractive and promises what it may never deliver. Do not trade anything the world offers for your relationship with God. Keep your eyes on Jesus Christ, the author and finisher of our faith. Anything and anyone that exalts itself to the status of deity and demands your worship must go down the drain of rejection and contempt. When they package evil and present it to you in the form of entertainment and modernity, refuse to yield to the deception.

Tell the world what Jesus told Satan, "You shall worship the LORD your God, and Him only you shall serve." This is the most appropriate response to the "new gods" that today's corrupt socio-political systems are churning out. Let your conviction be clear and your confession above board. As much as the world is free to believe and worship its own gods, you should have the audacity to contend for your faith in Christ and tell the world not to impose its standards on you. Their freedom ends where yours begin. Keep the faith and do the right.

God Bless You.

Clothed in Divine Glory

Rev.3:4, NKJV

You have a few names even in Sardis who have not defiled their garments; and they shall walk with Me in white, for they are worthy

---

Like attracts like; if you identify with Jesus, you will be with Jesus, become like Jesus, and behave like Jesus. As the good Lord rejoices over us, we have to respond appropriately TO him, and rejoice IN him. Our rejoicing should be with the deepest understanding of our privileged position in Christ Jesus.

God has clothed us with a very extraordinary spiritual garment, described in scripture as a robe.

Adam's sin de-robed us of our spiritual covering. Before the fall, man had no need of clothes. There was no "nakedness" to be covered because Adam and Eve wore robes of purity, righteousness, and absolute innocence. The glory of God enveloped them, and they glowed in divine glory. When sin entered their lives through disobedience, everything changed. They literally stripped themselves naked and exposed themselves to shame and embarrassment. They brought themselves so low that their self-imposed humiliation overshadowed their divinely ordained exaltation.

We can all understand the time and effort that goes into "covering our nakedness" (naturally speaking). All of us manifest our color and other preferences in the way we dress. Some of us like to dress simple, smart, and sharp; not enthused at all with gay and loud colours. Others find their taste in the latter. Whatever choices we make in the dress we wear; our confidence level goes up when we dress to taste and satisfaction. However, the best of our clothes never last for long. Change and decay is a constant part of our lives.

Here comes Jesus, who gives us new birth, and clothes us with just ONE spiritual garment in the form of a robe, and presto, the lost covering and glory is restored. The Father offered Adam and Eve animal skin to cover their nakedness, but gave us His Son, Jesus Christ, to cloth us in His own garment of righteousness. How blessed we are, to be wearing the best spiritual designer-clothes made by God Himself. This should be the basis for our joy. It's not about money, people, popularity, possessions or position. All of that may have their place in life, but none of them is a lasting "garment". We can and will lose all of those things one day.

When we stand before God, we either stand naked like Adam and Eve as unrepentant sinners, or we stand clothed in the righteousness of Christ as saints redeemed by his blood. There is no other dress to choose from. Friend, let us rejoice, for the Lord has done us good. He has clothed us with garments not made with human hands but woven out of His saving grace and mercy. Let's put it on anytime and every time. It is the difference between us and the world; that difference is clear, and it must show.

God Bless You

Ride the Storm

Prov.24:10, GNB

If you are weak in a crisis, you are weak indeed

The depth of our faith, and the strength of our character and commitment, are hardly seen when things are going well with us. Anyone of us can claim to have faith in God when things are going well. People can easily identify with you when they consider you as a "safe haven"; someone whose relationship doesn't pose challenges. Once you give them a treat, and do not pose a threat, you are forever their hero. The day your supply of milk and honey stops flowing, you are dropped from hero to zero.

Your true lovers are those who stick with you when the heat is on, and you don't have anything that benefits them. In the same vein, you are your own worst enemy if you cannot stand up to crisis, because many of the crisis you will have to deal with, are people related. Your being a parent or a child, employer or employee, teacher or student, pastor or lay person, married or single, young or old, does not exonerate you from one form of crisis or the other. As long as this life shall last, you will have many "crises rivers" to cross; some shallow, others deep, some exciting, others excruciating.

The interesting thing about crisis is that most of it come without warning; and even if you see it coming, you may not be able to stop or dodge it. The best you can do is to endure it, and that is where the grace factor comes into play, and prayer becomes crucial. Jesus Christ had many shades of crisis in his days on earth. Gethsemane was the doorway to what amounted to the mother of all his earthly crisis. The path he pursued and survived, is the way to our victory. Jesus prayed until sweat coming from his body looked like blood.

You cannot love life and wish away crisis. You can hope for it not to come but be prepared to stand and not sink if and when it comes. The writer of this proverb says clearly that "one who is weak in crisis is weak indeed." When you are tempted to do what you know you shouldn't do, it is crisis time for you, and you must win over it. When you have given of your best, and the result is worse than anticipated, emotional crisis is not far from your gate. You must master it!! There is no formula to escape crisis, whether in the home, church, workplace, or anywhere else; we all face diverse kinds of crisis. You have to learn to live with and overcome it.

Jesus taught us to pray not to be led into temptation. It is key to winning over the crisis even before it strikes. You don't wait for the crisis to come before asking God for help; you make it a subject of daily prayer, asking God to give you strength to stand and overcome any crisis that might come your way. It is my prayer that if you are contending with any crisis today, the good Lord will give you strength and tenacity to be able to stand and conquer.

God Bless You.

Closer Than You Can Imagine

Ps. 34:17-18, NIV

The righteous cry out, and the LORD hears them; he delivers them from all their troubles. The LORD is close to the broken-hearted and saves those who are crushed in spirit

---

The power of God's Word is embedded in its truthfulness. The Holy Bible tells it like it is, so that we don't get confused about the issues of life. God never said in his Word that we are not going to face any challenges because we are his children. If we read today's scripture carefully, the truth that stands out is that the righteous are not exonerated from "troubles" and being "broken-hearted." Indeed, bad things happen to good people too.

Our consolation is not in the fact that we don't face challenges. It is based on the truth that we have someone bigger to look up to, and a shoulder to cry on; "the righteous cry out, and the LORD hears them; he delivers them from all their troubles." The reason the righteous "cry out" is because of "their troubles." It is the multiple troubles that make us call out for multiple help. Without God's help, we would have no hope. His unconditional love for us provides a safety net for our deliverance and comfort.

The writer of this psalm, David, was a man who had a very difficult life as shepherd boy and Israel's king. He fought lions and bears, faced hostility from his own brothers, confronted a giant, messed with Uriah's wife, had his loyal soldier murdered in cold blood, and contended with rebellion from his beloved son, Absalom. He wrote this psalm with a rich experience of the faithfulness of God, God's unwavering commitment towards his children. David literally tasted of the goodness of God. The testimony he shares with us in this song should inspire us to continue praying in times of stress and need.

You may be down, but don't count yourself out. The God you serve is closer than the very cloth on your body. David says, "he (God) is close to the broken-hearted and saves those who are crushed in spirit." If that is you, here is your God; only a call away from the crisis you are facing.

This is your day of healing, deliverance, and breakthrough. Kick the fear, and trust in Christ. The yoke shall be broken. You will be free because Yahweh loves you.

God bless you

Let God Make You

Deut.28:13a, NKJV

And the Lord will make you the head and not the tail

God's promotion doesn't need explanation. Trying to make yourself THE HEAD, when it is clearly against God's timing can create problems for you. It is like Moses rushing to the defense of his fellow Hebrews, and being confronted with the question, "who made you a king and a ruler over us?" Beloved, I want to encourage you to allow God to MAKE YOU! It is good to put your best foot forward in whatever your dreams are; but you are better off doing so with the leading of God. God holds the key to who, and what you become.

When God speaks of making you the head, it doesn't necessarily mean you are going to become the head of your company or president of your country today or tomorrow. That is possible, but it goes further and deeper than that; it means he is going to make you RELEVANT in your space and beyond. God is saying to you that he has the power to make something out of your nothingness. Reference the life of Joseph. It doesn't matter whether you serve in a restaurant, are on a sick bed, or an average student struggling to make good grades in school, God is well able to "make you the head, and not the tail."

Your headship may come in the form of people seeking your advice before making weighty decisions, while others will see in their relationship with you a blessing you might not see yourself. When God "makes" a man, that man doesn't push for recognition. Indeed, he restrains himself from being "crowned king" by the crowd.

God's man or woman becomes like Joseph, whose light shone from prison to palace. That person becomes like Daniel, whose gifts could not be overshadowed by Babylonian captivity; and he or she becomes like Ruth, whose position as the last and the least known among the reapers in the field, could not stop her becoming part of the ancestry of David and Jesus.

Beloved, striving to make yourself what God has not made you, is a dangerous adventure. One of the ways you can discern your drift towards that direction, is when you begin to desire to be somebody else other than yourself. Remember all "heads" are not of the same size, shape, or color. God made them without asking our input or opinions.

If you don't accept yourself, nobody will accept or respect you. Untie the hands of God and let him MAKE YOU the "head" he wants you to be, and not the tail you are likely to become if you resist him.

God Bless You

Pursue Knowledge of God

Hos.6:3, NKJV

Let us know, let us pursue the knowledge of the Lord. His going forth is established as the morning; He will come to us like the rain, like the latter and former rain to the earth

---

Hosea is pleading with us to "know" and "pursue" the KNOWLEDGE of God. The immediate question arising from his call is, "Why should we strive to "know" God?

The answer is simple; ignorance is a very expensive commodity. You cannot own what you don't know, and you cannot know what you don't commit to studying. God's heart desire is to have a relationship with us based on love and knowledge.

This is not knowledge gained from mere hearsay. It is knowledge acquired through daily, progressive, intimate relationship with Jesus, as we spend time in prayer, meditating on His Word, following His Ways, and fulfilling His Will. It is knowledge gained in the prayer-closet, fueled by praise and worship, a life of love, discipline, sacrifice, integrity, and compassion.

Despite the rare miracles worked through him by the Lord, the apostle Paul still expressed the desire "to KNOW Him (Jesus) and the power of His resurrection" (Phil.3:10a). Paul was not referring to academic or head-knowledge. It's "full knowledge" (Greek "epignosis"); academics inclusive, not exclusive. When we don't feel like praying, that is when we should pray. When we don't feel like praising, that is when we should praise. When we don't feel like witnessing for Christ, that is the time to witness.

The LEARNING process should begin with a LEANING posture. You cannot learn anything from God if you are leaning on your own understanding. Lean on the Holy Spirit. He is our real Teacher in the School of God. Sometimes I find myself hard-pressed not to love some folks because they treated me real bad. The only way I come clean is to ask the Holy Spirit to love them through me, and He always does. He is so faithful, gracious, powerful, and consistent.

Beloved, Jesus Christ (our Bridegroom) is coming again. The signs of His coming are clearer than ever. His Bride (the Church) must get ready for the wedding. Ideally, you cannot marry someone you don't know, and the more you know your future spouse, the better. You can look into his or her eyes on the wedding day with a heart bubbling with joy and love because you know your beloved in a way that makes you feel safe and secure in his or her presence. Even so must we know our soon-coming King.

Let us "press on" to KNOW Him in a very personal and intimate way. Depending on the preacher to know God isn't good. It is not recommended for kingdom elevation. Therefore, wean yourself from spiritual baby-milk. Learn to pray for yourself. Talk to God as a child talking to his or her father, and He will reveal Himself to you. He will come to you "like the rain...that waters the earth."

God Bless You

Everybody Needs Somebody

Eccl.4:9-10, NKJV

Two are better than one, because they have a good reward for their labor. For if they fall, one will lift up his companion. But woe to him who is alone when he falls, for he has no one to help him up

---

There are experiences in life you never seem to forget and making reference to, no matter how hard you try. One day in the month of April 1989, I slipped and took a heavy fall on the street outside the Paris airport while trying to board a bus to the hotel I was lodging. It was Springtime, and the ice had made the ground very slippery. Within a split second of that fall, I began to feel the cold bite into my bones. Thankfully, I was with a beloved friend, Rev. Samuel Otu Pimpong, Senior Pastor of the University of Ghana Baptist Church.

He graciously extended a hand to help me get up on my feet; that was one of the many times I have experienced the value of having true and caring friends in my life. Someone to help me get up on my feet was all that mattered to me at that moment, and he proved a worthy solution to my dilemma. Indeed, "two are BETTER than one". We are created for relationship, not any kind of relationship, but meaningful, healthy, and mutually beneficial relationship. Genesis 2:18 records, "And the Lord said, 'It is not good that man should be alone; I will make him a helper comparable to him." This clearly points to the fact that relationship is God's idea.

Like everything else God loves and cherishes, Satan and his demons hate it with unrelenting passion and aggression. The devil attacked the first human relationship in the garden of Eden, and introduced fear, mistrust, and murder (Gen.4:1-20) and has since maintained notoriety for creating confusion in families and among friends. Some of us have been wounded and "damaged" too often and so badly that we prefer to keep to ourselves than commit to deep relationship. Too many people have taken advantage of us and so we no longer know who to trust. We cannot trust our pastors, friends, and even sometimes our own parents. You have been hurt too much, too often, and for far too long that you've locked yourself up in a world of seclusion and isolation. That may work for a time, but there is a BETTER way to live; it is the way God planned it to be from the beginning, and that is, for you to build and MAINTAIN healthy relationships.

Despite the past disappointments and hurt feelings, there are people God want to bring into your life to give you that fresh spiritual, emotional, and physical back-up you need. God will need your "permission" to do that. If you maintain an entrenched position that everybody is bad because all the people you related to in the past ended up taking advantage of you, and left you wounded and bleeding, you may never see the right folks God would want to introduce into your life.

You need someone to talk to. You need someone to be your "dung gate"; someone who is willing to be at the receiving end of all your stress and distress garbage. I call such true friends, "emotional detoxification agents." You need such to survive. By virtue of the work I do in the Lord's vineyard, I am almost always a victim of ministry "toxic wastes" of varying types, shapes, and degrees. I sincerely don't think I could have come this far without the extraordinary strength and support of my wife. She shares the pain and lightens the burden.

Your lifeline may not be your spouse (if he/she is abusive, and I hope not) but God has someone you can trust. Ask the Holy Spirit to open your eyes so you can see those assigned for your company. And while you wait, deepen your relationship with the One True Friend (Jesus, the Christ) who can never stop loving you.

May the Spirit of the Lord lead you into relationships that build you up, and not tear you down.

God Bless You.

The Presence of The Holy Spirit

Lu.1:35, NKJV

The angel said, "The Holy Spirit will come upon you, and the power of the Most High will overshadow you. So the Holy One to be born will be called the Son of God."

What makes the biggest difference between you (as a believer in Christ and child of God) and the unbeliever, is the presence of the Holy Spirit in your life. Mary received the promise of God that she was to be the mother of the Savior of the world. What she found intriguing, was the process of conception. She was a virgin, and the biological facts do not support the angelic declaration. In response, the angel explained that the impossible was going to become possible because of one person, the Holy Spirit.

First, the Holy Spirit would "come upon" her; another way of saying the Holy Spirit would envelop her. There was going to be a complete take-over of her entire life - body, soul, and spirit. Secondly, she was going to be empowered to execute the call upon her life to carry baby Jesus for nine months without miscarriage. This scenario had been played out many times in the Old Testament. The judges and prophets performed their tasks as the Holy Spirit empowered them. On the day of Pentecost, the Holy Spirit did the same job of overshadowing and empowering the 120 disciples in the Upper Room, and the result was phenomenal.

Here is the key lesson; you cannot give birth to God's 'baby' without the overshadowing presence and empowerment of His Spirit. God's assignment must be carried out in God's power, and you cannot get the power if you don't have his presence. Mary needed more than physical strength to carry the 'strange' baby for nine months. She needed mental toughness, and emotional stability to ignore the gossiping that the pregnancy was likely to ignite. She got it all sorted out by the presence of the Holy Spirit, who gave the power to overpower the challenges. The truth is that you and I, have need of the Holy Spirit as much as Mary.

We cannot be effective and productive in our various callings without the Holy Spirit. As you meditate on the Word, pray, praise, and celebrate the Lord's goodness in worship, you activate the grace for a fresh wave of his presence in your life. Let us welcome him with the song: "Come, Holy Spirit, we need you. Come, sweet Spirit we pray. Come in thy strength and thy power. Come in thine own special way." I pray him into your life; to come to you, to stay with you, to lead you, to comfort you, to heal you, to anoint you, and to glorify you. Receive him and overflow in him.

God bless you.

No Condition is Permanent

Eccl.7:14, GNB

When things are going well for you, be glad, and when trouble comes, just remember: God sends (allows) both happiness and trouble; you never know what is going to happen next

---

Anytime I hear a preacher or "prophet" claiming to have anointing to solve every problem, it makes me shudder. I have met many Christians whose faith has been undermined by being promised breakthroughs in the name of God that never materialized. For lack of knowledge of the Word, these brethren believed whatever they were told was from God, and sometimes turn the heat of their anger on God. Today we have quite a sizeable number of Christians who believe wrongly that adversity can never be a part of the believer's life.

Beloved, I hate to tell you this, but it is a Biblical truth I cannot hide from you - life has many days of adversity, no matter how many hours you pray, and how holy your life. The truth is that we are living in an imperfect world, full of imperfect people like you and I. The cosmic system is not in its original pure state. It is corrupted by sin and heading towards an inevitable dead-end. All of these add up to affect and impact our lives (especially our moods) in two ways. First, we have days of joy, when everything goes well according to plan. Our heads appear properly screwed on, the world seem bright and beautiful, and we don't want to stop singing and praising God.

Then there comes the flip side - a day of "adversity". We feel listless, bored, hopeless, and helpless. Our bodies hurt from sickness and pain, while friends and loved ones betray and upset us. Parents see their children become a thorn in their flesh, while to some the finances do not add up and your debt profile continue to go up. Like Israel in captivity, you sit by your own "rivers of Babylon" and wonder, "how can I sing the Lord's song in a strange land?"

Friend, let me tell you something I found out; the one thing that makes it difficult to survive "days of adversity" is denial and deception. When you have been brainwashed to believe that as a Christian you are never supposed to go through any difficult times, your chances of surviving such periods is minimized. But take it from me from today, that to expect to live a life without any "days of adversity" is like saying you can stop the weather from changing. It is a hopeless venture. You cannot do it. Brace yourself for whatever comes your way.

Continue trusting in the faithfulness of God, always remembering that NO CONDITION IS PERMANENT! One day this pain, disappointment, frustration, rejection, and humiliation you are experiencing shall pass away, and your star will shine again. All things (times of joy and days of adversity) will work together to your good. May the good Lord bless you plenty and give you the strength to survive your days of adversity and celebrate your seasons of joy in Jesus' Name!

God bless you.

Let God Lead

1Ki.18:36, NKJV

And it came to pass, at the time of the offering of the evening sacrifice, that Elijah the prophet came near and said, "LORD God of Abraham, Isaac, and Israel, let it be known this day that You are God in Israel, and I am your servant, and that I have done all these things at Your word

---

During the reign of King Ahab, idolatry thrived so much in Israel because of the influence of his pagan wife, Jezebel. It was obvious in the way the people of Israel behaved towards the God of their fathers, that they were not sure of the difference between Jehovah and the foreign gods introduced by Jezebel. If the God of Israel had priests and prophets, the foreign gods also had priests and prophets. If God worked miracles, the idols also appeared to put up similar performances. It was at the height of this spiritual confusion and prostitution, that Elijah called for a contest of clarity on mount Carmel, with a view to helping the people make an informed decision on who was the one true God.

When the prophets of baal had had their fair share of chanting, dancing, and cutting themselves without any response from their gods, Elijah stepped up and prayed this simple prayer. First, he asked God to "let it be known this day that You are God in Israel." Elijah's position was that God can only be known by divine revelation. Jesus said if the Father has not called you, you cannot come to him. You cannot know God through the accumulation of academic knowledge, or by subjecting him to a laboratory test. True knowledge of God comes through revelation by his Spirit. The second plea Elijah made to God was, "let it be known that I am your servant.

For all of us who stand as ministers of the gospel, this should be a caution to us; never to try and PROVE anything to the world. Let the Holy Spirit endorse your ministry. Don't try to do anything with the intention to prove that you are a man of God; let it be all about Jesus. The final part of his prayer re-echoes the point already made here. He prayed, "I have done all these things at your word." Elijah did not force God to send fire from heaven. He was not in the business of performing magic. He needed a miracle, and he had to be sure about what God intended to do, in order to preach and act in accordance to God's revealed word and will.

The prophet did not call a contest that demanded God's personal involvement without first seeking God's will. That would have been presumptuous. He did what he did because God told him to do it. Here is the final lesson: Do not force the hand of God in matters of signs and miracles. Ministry is not about impressing people; it is about expressing God's revealed will. Let God lead and use you the way he wants, and his glory will be seen, when and where it must be seen.

God bless you

Desperate Times Demand Focused Prayers

Ex.15:24-25a, NKJV

And the people complained against Moses, saying, "What shall we drink?" So he cried out to the LORD, and the LORD showed him a tree. When he cast it into the waters, the waters were made sweet

---

Crises time is crying time. Whenever we experience crisis, we hear voices inside us, and I simply can't stop stressing this truth; that inner voices, like the people who confronted Moses for water, always demand immediate attention and solutions to difficult circumstances. Moses showed us the way out of such a dilemma; he cried out to the LORD. When all hope is gone, because no help is available, it is the best of times to cry out to the Lord. Indeed, that is the time to remind ourselves that Christ is our only hope; "the solid rock on which I stand."

Beloved, crisis-prayer is no ordinary petition. Examine the phrase carefully; "Moses CRIED out to the LORD." It is not the kind of praying you do at the dinner table. No! It is a cry of desperation and a battle-ground stance. It is akin to Jesus's prayer at Gethsemane; no grass was left uncovered to get the attention of Father-God. When the answer came, Moses was directed to a tree he might have been seeing for days, weeks, or even months without paying much attention to. It may well be that you (like Moses), may be overlooking some present blessing that God has placed in your life to help you.

Moses' solution was not in another community or person. It was right within his reach. He did right by crying out to God, but I guess Moses would have been quite surprised to know that right within his immediate environs stood the solution to the problem that had brought so much pressure on him. Today, do not give up on God or yourself because of the "bitter waters" of your present circumstances. God has a "tree" for every trouble and turmoil you are facing in your life. Your part is to walk in obedience to His Word. His responsibility is to watch over you and make sure that at the end of each day, ALL THINGS (both the good and the bad) work together for your good.

Moses did not only pray, but also listened. You can be so emotionally deadbeat and detached from the Holy Spirit that you may not hear what he is asking you to do or follow where he is leading. Calm down. Sort out the confusion in your mind. Fix your mind on Christ. Untangling yourself from emotional confusion in a time like this can be a challenge, but with the help of God's Spirit, you can break through that stronghold, "bringing every thought captive to the obedience of Christ."

I pray that the good Lord help you maintain a sober mind, in order to hear his voice in the midst of the challenges that are casting shadows of fear, worry, pain, sorrow, and anxiety over your life today. May the Lord cause your "bitter waters of Marah" to become sweeter than honey. This too shall pass. It is a new day, look at the bright side of your life and make the best of what you have. It is well.

God Bless You.

Hosanna to The King of Kings

Lu.19:39-40, NKJV

And some of the Pharisees called to Him from the crowd, "Teacher, rebuke your disciples." But He answered, "I tell you that if these should keep silent, the stones would immediately cry out

---

I wonder what the Pharisees were doing among the crowd they described as disciples of Jesus. Here was a man they hated to the hilt, so why would they leave their jobs and homes to join a crowd celebrating him as Messiah? The answer is that simple; they were looking for an opportunity to eliminate him. They were not there to acknowledge him; they planted themselves where they could find fault with him and get rid of him. Forget about their calling him "teacher." They had earlier accused him of using Satanic power to cast out demons, so why the sudden change in describing him as "teacher"?

Remember this: when the enemy want to frustrate and take you out, the weapons he will use against you will not be too far from you. If you are a pastor, your testing ground will be in your own church, and most often within your own leadership. Failure to accept this truism has led many servants of God down the path of burnout, from which they never recovered. Satan will not put your temptation and haters two hundred miles away from you, so stay vigilant.

Judas was very effective in playing the role of betraying Jesus because he was very close to his Master. He was not just a member of the apostolic team, but the treasurer. The same scenario is playing out today and every day. If you care to look well enough, you will realize that the end-result of everything thrown at you by your enemies (whether spirits or humans) is meant to deny you peace and glory. The Pharisees were offended by the praise Jesus was receiving, and that opposition has not changed and will not change. History bears witness to millions of innocent Christians slaughtered for their faith. Thank God that in spite of the ruthless nature of the persecution they were subjected to, the saints stood, and still stand, for their faith in Christ.

This is one of the "stones" Jesus was referring to, in his response to the Pharisees. At a time when Christians, including church leaders, will only show up where it is politically correct, God has a "stone" in these martyrs, whose blood is shouting "hallelujah! and refusing to be intimated or silenced. Such unconditional praise to our living God, is like a tsunami or a dam that has broken its boundary; it is simply unstoppable. If you have lost your song of praise to the King of Zion because of the present challenges, remember the cross and renew your love for Christ. Stand up and let the "Pharisees" of your Jerusalem hear your praise. You cannot love him and not praise him. Praise the Lamb of God! He is worthy of our worship.

God Bless You.

Follow Where He Leads

Ex.13:21, NKJV

And the Lord went before them by day in a pillar of cloud to lead the way, and by night in a pillar of fire to give them light, so as to go by day and night

---

Leadership begins with God. Israel in the wilderness had Moses as their leader, but only as under-shepherd acting on behalf of God. God varied the style of His leadership depending on the time of day, but the important thing was that He was always there.

Jesus promises us in *Matt.28:19-20 of His abiding presence to the end of the ages. Let this assurance carry you through the day. Have a quiet time with God. Acknowledge His Presence and submit to the Spirit's leading.

The shape and form of His leading you may not be able to tell, but you can trust Him whether in prison like Joseph, in a pit like Jeremiah, or in a lion's den like Daniel. Jesus Christ never fails. He delivers on His promises. Dare to trust him like David who made the faith confession, "he leads me leads me beside the still and quiet waters, he restores my soul." (Ps.23:2b,AMP)

Peace comes to those who are sensitive to His leading. Wait when you are not sure where He is leading. It is always best to wait when you are in doubt. Give yourself to prayer and worship, and once the signs are clear and you are sure where He is leading, get up and follow in faith.

God Bless You.

Battles You Fight Alone

Matt. 26:36, NIV

Then Jesus went with his disciples to a place called Gethsemane, and he said to them, "Sit here while I go over there and pray

---

Some of the people God put in our lives, care enough to share our burdens and help us cope with challenges. What we glimpse from today's scripture, however, is that no one can do it all with us or for us. Sometimes we ought to leave our "helpers" behind and fight our battles alone. In preparation for his death, Jesus needed to strengthen himself with prayer. He desired the spiritual and moral support of his most trusted disciples. Having taken them to Gethsemane, he asked them to wait while "I go over and pray".

One might wonder why Jesus had to move a distance away from them when they had come there to do the same thing; to pray. The answer lies in the fact that the sympathizer cannot feel the pain and suffering in the same manner as the person who is suffering. It is the one who wears the shoes who knows where it pinches. Further reading of the scriptures show how Jesus came back to find his trusted friends sleeping their heads off. In the verse 40 we read, "Then he returned to his disciples and found them sleeping." They still loved him, but they did not have the capacity to endure beyond their limits.

Come on now and stop blaming people for not being there for you ALL the time. Your expectations of family and friends may be legitimate, but not necessarily realistic. No one can stick with you to the end of every race you run. There are battles you have to fight alone. If you insist on doing everything with everybody, you will lose battles you are supposed to win. When it gets to where it matters most, the "helpers" you are depending on will STARE at you, instead of STAND with you. They will sleep on the job because the assignment is too complicated for them. It's not their fault, that's your fate.

As a caring parent, you should not let others take decisions for you, regarding your children. They can advise (if asked) but should not arrogate to themselves the right to decide the career path of your child or children. It is in your right to draw boundaries for everyone. Jesus told his disciples exactly where to wait, and we ought to do same when the need arises.

Identify the battles you must fight alone, and deal with each prayerfully. Indeed, personal matters cannot be put in the public domain. It is not for nothing that eagles fly alone. Make room for helpers, because you need them, but be prepared to stand alone when you have to. God will give you victory if you pray like Jesus did.

God bless you

Chosen for A Purpose

Eph.3:7-9,13, CEV

God treated me with kindness. His power worked in me, and it became my job to spread the good news. I am the least important of all God's people. But God was kind and chose me to tell the Gentiles that because of Christ there are blessings that cannot be measured. God who created everything, wanted me to help everyone understand the mysterious plan that had been hidden in his mind...that is why you should not be discouraged when I suffer for you

---

Apostle Paul followed the example of Jesus's ministry. He had his job description cut out for him. He had no illusions about what God had called him to do, and as far as he was concerned, position, power, and prestige were irrelevant.

Paul publicly declared himself "the least important of God's people." This was a man credited with almost half of the New Testament writings. I can only imagine how many leaders in today's Church will "tolerate" being introduced in public with such words - "please let's welcome the least of God's people, Bishop..." Apologies would be required and demanded. We trade the approval of God for the applause of men. Our issues are many and complex, but God's solutions are simple. It takes knowing God's purpose for our lives, accepting who we are in Christ, and moving into God's plan for our lives to get our self-imposed complexities sorted out.

Paul was willing to accept "suffering" because he had a clear understanding of what was involved in pursuing the call on his life. He counted it a privilege to be used by God to preach the gospel to the gentile world. He wouldn't encourage anyone feeling sorry for him, because he was enjoying every bit of his ministry despite the suffering that came with it.

The apostle's life teaches us that we can never have peace about our state in life until and unless we acknowledge WHO we are in Christ and WHAT our assignment in Christ is. We are called to TOIL for souls to be won into God's kingdom. We are not called to chase TITLES which add no value to kingdom agenda. Jesus Christ "made Himself of no reputation", and Paul introduced himself as "least important of all God's people".

This posture of humble service takes the pressure of trying to keep up with the titleholders off your back.

There is a job for you to do for the Lord right where you are; to love, care, and share. You are called and anointed for it, so do it. It may be a "backstage" call where nobody sees or applauds you; just occupy that space and fulfill your assignment.

Every day offers an opportunity to show-case your love for Christ by pursuing his purpose for your life, no matter the cost to your personal comfort. Move into your space, and put your hands to the plough. You deserve an eternal crown, not a temporary crest.

God bless you

Look Beyond the Pharisees

Lu.15:1-2, NKJV

Now the tax collectors and sinners were all gathering around to hear Jesus. But the Pharisees and the teachers of the law muttered, "This man welcomes sinners and eats with them

---

Anyone who is well versed in communication knows that the primary objective of an effective communicator is reaching your "target audience." If you are not able to identify exactly who you want to reach with your message, it will derail your efforts, and produce minimal results.

Jesus was a great communicator; he clearly defined his "target audience" and took his message to them. According to the scriptures, "the Pharisees and teachers of the law" complained about his ministry saying, 'This man receives sinners and eats with them.'" Herein lies their confusion; the very people (sinners) they were complaining about were the reason Jesus Christ came.

His assignment was about sinners, not lawyers and prosecutors. If you take out the sin-factor, Jesus had no business coming on earth to die. Without sin, there obviously will be no sinners, and the Messiah will have no audience. Those the self-righteous Pharisees regarded as unworthy of their company, were embraced by the Lord as worthy of his love.

Beloved, it is not the prerogative of any one to determine what God has assigned you to do. Unless and until you stay focused on what you know God has called you to do, you might step out of your calling and communicate with an audience who may not understand your message. The language of your message may be semantic noise to those who are not destined to be part of your "target audience."

You might frustrate yourself unnecessarily by insisting on associating with, and ministering to, "Pharisees and teachers of the law" who have no value for your message and question your every move and motive. You will weary yourself insisting on helping someone whose body language and response to your good intentions is clearly saying, "you are not welcome to my world."

One important lesson we should learn is that we are called to love everyone, but we are not to expect everyone to accept us for who we are, or what we do. Your "Pharisees and teachers of the law" will always complain about your ministry to "sinners", but that shouldn't stop you from eating your bread and letting them enjoy their cake. Your ultimate goal should always be to please God, not men. Stay focused and keep moving forward in the things that give you joy and peace.

God bless you

Jesus Christ Paid It All

Is.53:5, NKJV

But He was wounded for our transgressions, He was bruised for our iniquities; the chastisement for our peace was upon Him, and by His stripes we are healed

---

Humanity was separated from divinity, courtesy the sin of Adam.

The decision to disobey God's order not to eat the forbidden fruit, separated Adam from his creator. In their quest to re-establish their lost dignity and glory, Adam and his beloved wife, Eve, sewed fig leaves to cover their nakedness. God's love for Man was immediately revealed when he replaced their fig leaves with animal skin.

God couldn't have gotten the skin of the animal without the animal dying. An innocent animal's blood was shed to provide a proper covering for Adam and Eve, so right in the garden of Eden we see a type and shadow of the redemptive work of Christ on Calvary. An innocent animal, who was not part of Adam's sin, had to die for Adam and Eve to get a reprieve from their nakedness which was a consequence of sin. On Easter Friday, Jesus Christ, who John the Baptist describes as " the lamb of God who takes away the sins of the world," stepped up as the animal that God was to sacrifice to away the "fig leaves" (man's unproductive effort) to redeem himself from the consequences of sin.

Jesus Christ the Son of God died a gruesome death, not only because of the stripes, thorns, nails, et al. Like the animal that had to die in the garden of Eden, the Son of God who died on the cross, died for a crime he did not commit, so that the real culprits (you and I) could be set free from the consequences of sin. This is what the prophet Isaiah capturers so explicitly in his writing: "But He was wounded for our transgressions, He was bruised for our iniquities; the chastisement for our peace was upon Him, and by His stripes we are healed." (Is.53:5, NKJV)

Jesus paid the ultimate price to reconcile us to our God and Father. His wounds dealt with our transgressions, the bruises our iniquities, the chastisement our peace, and by his stripes we are healed. What more could he have done? He gave up his life so that we might live. Today, if you don't have a relationship with this Jesus, I invite you to accept him as your Lord and personal Savior. He is the ONLY way to God, and ultimately to heaven. Every other way is a fig leaf. It may only cover the nakedness of sin for a season, but eventually dry up and expose your nakedness.

Jesus Christ is the Lamb of God who shed his blood, not just to cover sin, but take it away completely. He doesn't offer religion with rules and regulations; he desires relationship with his most treasured creation, man. This is the day of salvation. Tomorrow may be too late.

Confess your sins, ask Jesus to be the Lord of your life, join a Bible- believing church, and serve God and humanity the best you can, and with all you have. And to my brethren in the faith, let us reflect on where we were, and how far Christ has brought us. Let's live to reflect the faith we confess. His blood is our plea forever. Tell the world that redemption has come.

God bless you

Opposition Can Be the Ladder to Your Position

Acts 23:11, NKJV

But the following night the Lord stood by him and said, "Be of good cheer, Paul; for as you have testified for Me in Jerusalem, so you must also bear witness at Rome

---

It was a real "night" in the life of Paul. He had been arrested, insulted and assaulted by the Jewish religious leaders for preaching the gospel. He was in the perfect will of God, fulfilling God's perfect will for his life. The result of his obedience was beatings, persecution, and imprisonment.

This teaches us that obeying God or being in the perfect will of God doesn't guarantee freedom from pain and persecution. Indeed, walking in the perfect will of God can mean lots of unexplained inconveniences, pain, pressure, and even death. Check the lives of Joseph, Jeremiah, Jesus, and the apostles; it was not as easy and rosy as most of us have gotten it today.

We need to get this right, otherwise we might become frustrated in our walk with Christ when things don't go the way we expect. You don't have to measure God's approval or disapproval by the challenges you face. When people want to make you feel guilty on the basis of reverses in your life, do not buy into it. Lock it down in your spirit that sometimes terrible things happen to us exactly because we dare to obey God and do the right thing. Paradox? Yes, it is.

Paul could have chosen to walk away from preaching the gospel, and that would have spared him the beatings, suffering, times in prison, and losing his life the way he did. His faithfulness to the preaching of the gospel cost him his life. Good is not always rewarded in equal measure; many times, it goes unappreciated and attracts hostile backlash. God will not withdraw your assignment because you face opposition, failures, pain, or setbacks. He will not always come to take you out of it.

Sometimes when God shows up, he comes to encourage you, cheer you up, until you get up. Your focus then should be centered more on how to get to the next level, than the present problems and challenges. Nothing should stop you from going where you know God has ordained for you to go and doing what he has assigned you to do. The OPPOSITION is part of the process of bringing you to your POSITION. It took the trial of Paul to bring him to Rome, where God had planned to take him to the next level of his ministry. Don't let any negative word, deed, or circumstance stop you from pursuing your goal.

What God is doing with, and in your life can take you to the cross, before setting you up on the throne. Cheer up. Stand up. Stay strong. God is with you, and he will see you through.

God Bless You.

Close That Door

Eccl.7:21, NIV

Do not pay attention to every word people say, or you may hear your servant cursing you

---

Most of the things people say about us are based on mere perception, not facts. Unfortunately, perception can sometimes be so strong it becomes impossible to convince people it contains no element of truth. Wrong perception creates a situation that make people say things about you that doesn't reflect who you really are, or what you stand for. This is one of the reasons the writer of the book of Ecclesiastes is cautioning us "not to pay attention to every word people say."

If you get overly concerned with what others think or say about you, chances are you can get hurt more often than you should. Truth is, not everyone is going to admire your posture towards life, and those who don't like something about you (for whatever reason or reasons) may not speak kindly of you. What your non-admirers say about you, will definitely be influenced by their personal prejudices and perceptions. If you get fixated with their opinions about you, it is an invitation to self-crucifixion. You can't hear people say negative things about you and not be hurt, so heed the counsel of this scripture and avoid wanting to hear everyone's opinion about yourself.

Human beings created by God, walk this earth and denounce their creator. Some even deny the very existence of God (Ps.14:1). Jesus healed the sick and raised the dead, and yet when it suited them best, his benefactors become his detractors and asked for his crucifixion. Who are we then to imagine for a second that everyone is going to have a good opinion about us?

What you don't hear doesn't hurt, so quit paying attention to what everybody is saying about you. Unkind words can stick with you forever; don't pay attention to them. Discourage those who are bent on telling you whatever bad things are being said about you from continuing in that pursuit. It won't help you the least, it will hurt you the more.

There is more to life than what others think or feel about you. It's okay to make mistakes, as long as it's not deliberate. If people choose to dwell on what they see as your weaknesses, you also have the right to highlight your strengths, instead of being unnecessarily pre-occupied with their negative opinions and perceptions.

Hear again the good counsel of the Preacher; "Do not pay attention to every word people say, or you may hear your servant cursing you."

God bless you.

Peace to You

Lu.24:36, NKJV

> Now as they said these things, Jesus Himself stood in the midst of them, and said to them, "Peace to you.

When Jesus rose from the dead and his disciples were told that he had arisen, they were skeptical about the news. They were discussing the probabilities and possibilities when the Lord appeared and "stood in the midst of them." The first statement that came out of his mouth was, "peace to you." I have always maintained that the value of peace cannot be quantified in any way. Looking at the destruction that civil unrests and wars bring on people and properties can give us some idea of how precious peace is to our existence.

Indeed, the peace Jesus speaks into our lives through the Holy Spirit is uniquely different from the peace the world offers, and he tells us that in Jn.24:27 -"Peace I leave with you, My peace I give to you; not as the world gives do I give to you. Let not your heart be troubled, neither let it be afraid."

In order to enjoy His peace, we have to address our fears and worries. We ought to keep reminding ourselves we are not alone in our struggles. The same Jesus who gives us His peace, shows how we can enjoy and not lose it; he says to us, "Let not your heart be troubled, neither let it be afraid." These two things, (a) a troubled heart, and (b) fear.

A troubled heart is emotional disturbance that imprisons and paralyses us from daring to believe for better things and days. Fear is the master killer of initiative. It takes the driver's seat and put faith in the back. Jesus warns that if these two emotional elements are allowed to rule our lives, the peace he promises will always be an illusion.

It is in our power as children of God, to contain our fears and worries. Our desire to live in an atmosphere saturated with the peace of Christ should be a priority. It will take peace in our own lives to ensure peace in our homes and communities. Truth is, we cannot give what we don't have. Anyone who says or does something to hurt another person is manifesting his own emotional sickness.

You can get all you desire in this life, but that will not exonerate you from worry and fear. Jesus Christ, the Prince of Peace, is offering us His peace. It is part of the benefit we get from His death and resurrection. When we accept His Lordship, and allow His Spirit to indwell us, we experience and enjoy His peace.

Bring your challenges to the Lord and exchange your pain with His peace. He will take care of your fears as you step out in faith on the promises He has given; to give you His peace and be with you always.

God bless you.

Your Healing has Come

Is.535c, NKJV

And by His stripes we are healed

There is only one Jesus Christ who died on the cross of Calvary and obtained salvation for all mankind. He died a death that no one can ever imitate or replicate. This is so, not because of how he was murdered, but because of WHO he was and is, and WHAT was achieved through his death and resurrection.

One of the benefits of Christ's death as amplified by the prophet Isaiah is that "by his stripes, we are healed." The question that immediately arises is, "are we sick to require healing?" The answer is, "Yes, indeed we are sick unto death."

Our sickness goes beyond mere physical weakness or disability to spiritual impotence, blindness, and disconnection.

The wounds Jesus Christ sustained are open fountains for the healing of our spiritual, physical, and emotional wounds.

The Son of God presented his body as sin offering to save us from the continuous ravages of the consequences of sin.

Jesus Christ used physical healing during his earthly ministry to demonstrate lto us the greater healing of our souls and spirits. Indeed, he conquered death for us, and prepared another body (a glorious body) to replace this temporary "tent" in which we now live.

Today, God want you to remember that receiving Jesus Christ as your Lord and personal Savior is loaded with benefits of healing that covers your body, soul, and spirit. It spans from now to all eternity. Faith is the key to accessing these glorious benefits of the sufferings of Christ. If you believe it, you can possess it.

There is nothing God requires of you than to receive by faith His offer of salvation through His beloved Son Jesus Christ. It's by grace and grace alone that you can access this blessing. Do not look any further than the Man who died on Calvary's tree. The only life worth living is life lived in, and through Christ.

Whatever sickness you are contending with right now, you can trust Jesus to heal you. The same Jesus who healed the sick and raised the dead 2,000 years ago, is still in the miracle-working business. Are you lost in sin? Jesus Christ died that you might live.

Are you worried, frustrated, confused, and feeling like giving up on life? Hold it there!! You have a friend in Jesus. He will heal your emotional wounds if you will meditate on His Word and pray it back to Him.

Jesus Christ is a friend like no other; always loving, forgiving, and empowering; never condemning, berating, or judgmental. He is your healer, and today, I speak his blessing on your life, and declare that "by His stripes, you are healed."

God bless you

Maintain the Momentum

2 Chron.6:12, NKJV

Then Solomon stood before the altar of the LORD in the presence of all the assembly of Israel, and spread out his hands

---

I love Solomon's posture, as he stood before the altar of God with outstretched hands. This gives an impression of a man who was in absolute surrender to the will of God. In my mind's eye, I see a man who was deeply in love with his God. I see Solomon offering worship flowing out of intimate relationship with Yahweh. If Solomon had guarded his heart and stood firm in his convictions and commitment to his God, he would not have dropped the outstretched hands and lost his relationship with God. Unfortunately, this same man of worship, who we see here publicly showing so much reverence and faith in God, was later recorded as serving foreign gods.

King Solomon dropped the outstretched hands and bowed to the attractions of the sinful nature. He chose foreign women over faithful worship. The scripture reads in 1Ki.11:4, "For it was so, when Solomon was old, that his wives turned his heart after other gods; and his heart was not loyal to the LORD his God, as was the heart of his father David." When we violate God's Word and throw caution to the wind, we sow seeds of self-destruction and reap a huge harvest of "spiritual lockdown." At the time Solomon married the foreign women that God had clearly warned Israel not to marry, he was young, alert, and thought he knew better how to enjoy the romance and handle the pressure. It was only a matter of time, and his foolishness began to bear fruit. Lust for the "forbidden fruit" weakened the hands he used to lift up in worship.

The devil knows the right time to take us out, if we choose not to pursue righteousness but play around with sin. Grace does not glorify deliberate sinful living. Always remember that Satan and his demons have been here long before we entered this life, and they are better informed in the game of temptation. The hands you stretch out in worship to God today does not stop the enemy from coming at you, as long as you show a propensity to compromise the truth of God's Word. Satan and his demons will wait for you for as long as it takes, and when you have effectively disconnected yourself from the source of your strength, they will take you out.

Don't let anyone deceive you into thinking that the things you do for God today, guarantee your relationship with him tomorrow. Maintain the momentum; deliberately, consciously, and conscientiously. Keep your eyes on your goal. Avoid every appearance of sin. Live a holy life. This may no longer be a popular message, but it will forever remain a relevant call.

Go the extra mile to ensure that the hands you have stretched out in worship today will never be brought down by the lusts and attractions of this world. God gives grace and strength, but you bear the responsibility to appropriate it.

God Bless You.

Fleeting Glory

Ps.49:16-17, NKJV

Do not be afraid when one becomes rich, when the glory of his house is increased; for when he dies he shall carry nothing away; His glory shall not descend after him

---

In our part of the world where poverty is the rule, rather than the exception, those who command wealth, generally tend to intimidate the poor. A person's status in society change in accordance with his or her wealth, irrespective of how they come by it. Money, in a broad sense, becomes a tool of domination, oppression, discrimination, and attention; those who don't have enough, live at the mercy of those who have more than enough. One may be the dumbest person on the block, but once he has financial clout, he can talk louder and longer than the wisest.

The Bible clearly frowns on that kind of distorted relationship. It teaches us that the real value of a human being is in WHO he is as a living soul, not what he has to show in material terms. Everyone needs money to live the kind of decent, joyful, and fulfilling life God planned for us, but our lack of money at any given time should not make us feel intimidated in any way.

There is no point in looking at what others have, or are getting, and becoming fearful or jealous. The Bible speaks to this issue and says, "Do not be afraid when one becomes rich, when the glory of his house is increased." Feel free to celebrate the achievements of others without being intimidated by it. It is a sign of maturity and source of peace. Work towards your own set goals. What the scripture is saying to us is that nobody is going to be here forever, and nobody is taking anything out of here. When we are in our youthful years, we all love to accumulate as many things as possible, but as we grow older, we begin to throw some, or most of those "treasures"

As you grow older, you realize you can't hold on to too many things, and you will end up holding on to nothing at all. The real value of a human being is his soul; that unseen part of you that is destined to live forever. If there is something you need to be concerned about, it is the destiny of your soul. The sons of Korah, who wrote this psalm, encourage us not to be afraid because "God will redeem my soul from the power of the grave, for He shall receive me ((Ps.49:15). Your story is larger, bigger, and longer than the temporary treasures and pleasures of this life. As long as you keep the faith and do your best, you can trust God to help you through the difficult times.

The value Jesus places on you is the reason he redeemed you with his own precious blood. You are more than flesh and blood, and no amount of money or earthly treasure can be traded for your soul. God want you to look at WHO he has made you, not what he has given to others.

God Bless You.

Open Your Mouth

Prov.31:8-9, NKJV

Open your mouth for the speechless, in the course of all who are appointed to die. Open your mouth, judge righteously, and plead the cause of the poor and needy

To keep quiet in the face of injustice is to condone evil and sin to the detriment of the vulnerable in society. Your mouth is a very powerful communication tool. If you use it wrongly, the consequences can be very disastrous; but you can never go wrong in speaking out for what is right and proper. There is a school of thought that suggests that if speaking out against wrong will cost you your peace, then you've got to just keep quiet and walk out of the "kitchen." This may be acceptable if your walking away doesn't encourage or entrench evil and injustice. Otherwise, it is negligence of our Godly responsibility.

Each of us is challenged on a daily basis to take a stand for right or wrong. If we are not committed to the truth, then we are comfortable with the lie. Light and darkness have nothing in common; even so, you (as a born-again child of God) should have a radically different approach to life than an unbeliever, when it comes to issues of morality and justice. The principles by which you live your life should be in sync with the Word of God, and not the wisdom of men. You don't water down the demands of the Holy Scriptures to make it acceptable to the world. God's desire is to reach out to the world in love through you, but not at the cost of reducing him to a caricature of his deity and holiness.

Let's zero in on two specific issues our devotional scripture for today is challenging us to speak out for: First, is to "Open your mouth for the speechless... all who are appointed to die." Can you imagine where we would be today if Jesus Christ had taken the easy route of maintaining his position as God, refusing to sacrifice his life, and remaining insensitive to our plight? We have become what we have become because Jesus became who he became. Got the drift? He MADE HIMSELF OF NO REPUTATION so that he could lift us up from our DEGRADATION. He stepped DOWN, so he can lift us UP. He paid a PRICE so we can win the PRIZE.

Somebody's salvation is in your mouth, and unless you witness Christ to him, you are sending him to hell. Somebody's deliverance from depression is in your mouth; until and unless you pray for him or speak a word of hope and encouragement into his life, you are responsible for the consequences of his emotional trauma. Here's one of the many things you can do. Pick the phone and make that call to the "speechless...all who are appointed to die." Preach the message of salvation to them. Speak a word of encouragement to those who are frustrated and discouraged. Pray for them. Warm their hearts with words of hope. By all means do something about someone.

Let's move on to the second challenge (ref: verse 9) which says, "open your mouth, and plead the cause of the poor and needy." In other words, you are to intercede for those are worse off than you; it may be in their spiritual lives, health wise, financial, or emotional state. I count it a wonderful privilege for me to be sharing the Word of God with the world. Indeed, I love "opening my mouth" to tell of the love, grace, and mercy of my Lord and savior Jesus Christ. In such a time that true believers in Jesus Christ are exposed to so much hostility and persecution, it may seem prudent to stay mute; but such unholy silence is a death sentence against truth, life, light, freedom, and justice.

No matter what it may cost you, remember that God has assigned you to speak out for the lost, weak, poor, defenseless, sick, and lonely; and to "judge righteously." You have to be prepared to suffer some inconveniences as a result of "opening your mouth," so that others can benefit. Jesus died that we might live. Let's die a little for the good of others.

God Bless You.

You Are Your Brother's Keeper

Gen.4:9, NKJV

Then the Lord said to Cain, 'where is Abel your brother?' He said, 'I don't know. Am I my brother's keeper?'

This is the first instance in the Bible that we see a human being asking God a question. It was registered very early in the history of creation, when two brothers, namely Cain and Abel, each presented an offering to God. One was accepted, but the other rejected.

Cain, whose offering was rejected became very upset. God explained to him that if he did the right thing, his offering would be accepted; meaning he had a second chance to correct the mistake, and right the wrong. Cain, however, chose his innocent brother as target for his anger, and murdered him in cold blood.

God approached the young man and asked him to account for his brother Abel's whereabout. His answer began with a lie: "I don't know," and ended with a question which everyone of us must answer every day of our lives. The question is, "am I my brother's keeper?"

The answer to that question is, "Yes, you are your brother's keeper." It is the least God expects from every single one of us; to watch out for each other's interest. The Christian life cannot be lived in a world of isolation and self-centeredness. Today's technology is deepening the secular concept of "each for himself and God for us all."

When we take pictures, it is "SELFIE"; we don't need anybody to do it for us. It's all by SELF, to SELF, and for SELF, and thereby making it easy to be cocooned in SELFISHNESS. We share our IMAGES, not our LIVES. We spend more time relating to our phones than our folks at home.

The human touch is missing, and the bond is weakened. We are addicted to technology and are far from finding a cure to our addiction. The more educated we are, the more sophisticated we become in our discrimination and isolation. This ought to change. Every blood-bought child of God has a responsibility towards others.

If we are not our brother's KEEPER, then we are your brother's KILLER. We are accountable to God for the spiritually dead, the emotionally wounded, and physically sick. Let's help whoever we can in whichever way we can. Of course we don't have to let anyone take undue advantage of our generosity, but as much as God leads us to help others, we do not have to turn away from doing so.

Here is the million-dollar question, "Am I my brother's keeper?" God's definitive answer to that question is, "Yes, you are!!" That is what makes you different from all others - a child of God, full of grace and mercy.

God Bless You.

Deliverance is Assured

Nahum 1:13, NKJV

For now I will break off his yoke from you, and burst your bonds apart

---

If you need fresh assurance from God's own mouth to carry on with the challenges you face presently, here is a solid one: "For now I will break off his yoke from you, and burst your bonds apart," says the Lord. The name of the prophet who wrote this book itself speaks volumes of God's goodness towards you and his determination to give you relief from distress, pain, and everything that makes life a misery. The prophet's name, Nahum, means "Comforter", "full of comfort" or "one who comforts." It reveals God's unchanging goodwill towards us.

God positions himself to comfort us because that is what you and I need to survive the "yokes" of this life. No one is immune to disappointment, pain, frustration, and distress; they come without prior notice. I still remember one of those challenging times when I was called upon to minister to a mother who received information from the police that her 28-year-old daughter's dead body had been deposited in a morgue by some unknown persons.

Preliminary results showed that the young lady had been murdered through poisoning. The mother was so traumatized that despite the pain, shock, and confusion we were all going through, I had to muster the courage to be a strong pillar of comfort to her. Thank God for the grace to do just that.

It's not an easy role to play in this drama called life, but it is certainly something we cannot afford to shy away from, despite our own challenges.

To be honest, sometimes I just wish l could fly away like a bird to somewhere I simply don't know; but God... He gives comfort and removes yokes. When he chooses to allow the yoke to remain for a season, he guides, empowers and comforts us all the way through the process. While walking through the heat, you can trust him for grace to stay the course.

The tears you shed that no one sees, our God sees and interprets correctly the reason behind each drop. The psalmist put it aptly in Psalm 119:50, "This is my comfort in my affliction, for Your word has given me life." If the sun has set on your hopes and dreams, if sickness and pain is afflicting your body, if you have lost a loved one, facing crisis of betrayal from your friends, and the ground under your feet seems to be caving in, there is still hope for you.

Turn to Jesus! You might say, "well I turned to him long before this yoke came around my neck." You are right on, my beloved, but here is the next thing you've got to do and continue doing; KEEP TRUSTING AND OBEYING. It comes with great reward. If you must die, the best place to die is IN Jesus, the "author and finisher" of our faith.

You have come this far WITH him, and you should keep pressing on IN him. Someday, somehow, God will break the yokes and set your spirit free. Remember, no condition is permanent. God is already sustaining you, and will comfort you with his love.

God Bless You.

Love Your Enemies

Lu.6:27-28, NKJV

But I say to you who hear: Love your enemies, do good to those who hate you, bless those who curse you, and pray for those who spitefully use you

---

There are scriptures we need to keep going back to, in order to keep faith with Christ and the course of his kingdom. The admonition to literally "drive in reverse gear" when people do not treat us well is one of them (Lu.6:27-28). Loving our enemies, doing good to those who hate us, blessing those who curse us, and praying for those who spitefully use us. What a package of unusual demands!! It may be easy to preach it, but not as easy to practice it. The good news, however, is that DIFFICULTY is not IMPOSSIBILITY, so let us go to the substance of the message this scripture conveys, trusting God for grace to practice it.

Sometimes, we are too quick to judge and "curse" those Jesus says we should bless. The Lord made some strong statements in Lu.6:27-28 that we need to examine against the backdrop of what we are practicing today in His name. First, he said, "But I say to you who hear..." He is speaking to a specific audience; those who "hear." Not everyone who LISTENS to you HEARS to you. Jesus is addressing those who are open to instruction and do not give excuses why they cannot do what He commands them to do. Those humble enough to accept that they cannot claim to be his disciples and live by their own rules and standards.

Our natural tendency is that the moment we identify someone as "enemy", we develop a certain mindset towards that person; making it difficult to tolerate him, much less to bless him. The issue, however, is that blessing our enemies is a crucial part of the price we pay as disciples of Christ.

We can't claim to be followers of Christ and contradict His instructions; so if you get busy cursing human beings, you are walking in disobedience to divine order.

I found out many years ago that the one person I could not love was my "enemy". I found it very easy "hating" those I knew were against me than loving them. Anyone who stands in that space, gets a red card. The Holy Spirit showed me that at the human level, my inability to love my enemies was normal, because it is beyond human nature and capability to love our enemies.

It takes yielding and asking the Holy Spirit to love the people I couldn't love (for whatever reasons) through me. It worked, and always works. Whenever you find yourself in that tight corner where it is much easier to hate and curse than bless, do good, and pray for your enemies, invite the Holy Spirit to do the job of loving them THROUGH you.

Love is not part of the fruit of our fallen nature. The flesh is very comfortable with anger, bitterness, revenge, cursing etc. It is both Adamic and endemic. On the contrary, the fruit of the Spirit of God is LOVE. He gives us the capacity and joy to obey Christ, not our emotions.

Bible says God is not happy about the death of a sinner, and that definitely includes your enemies, so please stop calling down fire to destroy your human enemies. Their suffering or death will add nothing to your bank account. You are free to attack Satan and his demons in prayer, because that's where the battle is fought, in the realm of the Spirit.

The four things the God we worship as believers in Christ is COMMANDING (not suggesting) us to do are these: Firstly, to LOVE our enemies. It doesn't mean to go partying with them. It means guarding our hearts from hating them or going after their blood. (2) DO GOOD to those who hate us. Crazy? That's Christianity for you; if it's in your power to help someone who hates you, the command is for you to go ahead and do it.

The third is to BLESS those who curse you. That's a tough one, I guess; but this is Jesus Christ himself speaking. Fourth is to PRAY for those who spitefully use you. What a tall order?! By your fruit you shall be known. If you are of the Jesus-stock, your words and works will show. Stop cursing and be a blesser.

The atmosphere we create by cursing people is more attractive to demons than the Holy Spirit. Let's drop the curse and lift the cross. Love, forgiveness, turning the other cheek are the real testimonies of our Christian faith. We can resist evil without becoming evil. Love is light, and no darkness can withstand its impact.

Show some love. Give it out, especially to those who don't deserve it, and see God release immeasurable peace, joy, and prosperity in your life.

God Bless You.

Be Grateful

Jer.18:19-20, NIV

Listen to me, O LORD; hear what my accusers are saying! Should good be repaid for evil? Yet they have dug a pit for me. Remember that I stood before you and spoke in their behalf to turn your wrath away from them

---

One of the most common features of life is the canker of ingratitude. The prophet Jeremiah was surprised that the very people he had been praying and asking God to forgive and bless, turned on him so viciously. He asked a question that many of us have asked too many times: "Should good be paid for evil?" The obvious answer is "no", but the reality is the opposite; we easily forget the good that friends and family have done to us and become ungrateful to them.

Today, we want to remind ourselves of the good others have done to us in times past, and how important it is to refrain from attacking them in a heartless manner like the people did to Jeremiah, even if they offend us one way or the other. The proceeding verses of our devotional scripture indicates how Jeremiah responded to the ingratitude of the people; he prayed judgment on them, and these are scriptures we often hear believers quote in justifying the curses they invoke on those who offend them.

Fact is, Jeremiah is not our perfect example; Jesus Christ is the deal, so whenever we are confronted with issues like this, we should reflect on what Jesus said and did in similar circumstances. He blessed his enemies and asked us to do same. Those who specialize in cursing, become victims of bitterness and are unable to forgive. Ingratitude is product of our fallen nature, and we should be careful not to yield to it or react towards it in ways that do not conform to scripture. Every one of us should learn how to appreciate people for what they do for us. Even those who tend to irritate us can be God's instruments to mature us.

Pay special attention to your family and friends, because each of them is part of God's blessing package. Take time to tell those who help, comfort, and inspire you, how much you appreciate their love and support. If you are a husband who never made any comment about the meal your wife puts on the table, except when it doesn't taste good, you have a problem.

A gentle holding of the hand and saying, "thank you for the wonderful meal" will not kill you, it will boost your relationship. If you are a student, you have something to thank your parents for; you can tell them how grateful you are for the sacrifices they are making in taking care of you. The price we pay for being ungrateful is as big as the reward we get when we show a sense of gratitude to those who have been a blessing to us. We should not walk away from those who help us without appreciating them, and we should never target him with false accusations and blackmail. It is unfair and very much likely to sour our relationships.

Listen to Jeremiah declaring, "they dug a pit for me." If you won't thank me, why would you trash me? Let's be fair to each other and appreciate the blessing God meant us to be to each other. If we do, we shall be fulfilling God's divine law to be each other's keeper.

God Bless You.

Dare to Be Different

Jn.10:41-42, NKJV

Then many came to Him and said, "John performed no sign, but all the things that John spoke about this Man were true." And many believed in Him there

---

The portion for our consideration in this particular scripture is in the statement, "John performed no sign, but all things that John spoke about this Man (Jesus) were true." In essence, we are being told that John did not try to be someone he was not meant to be or do something he was not called to do. His assignment was to prophesy, and as long as he remained true to that calling, God confirmed his ministry, and people testified to the fact that "ALL THINGS THAT JOHN SPOKE ABOUT THIS MAN WERE TRUE" (caps mine).

This is one of the major keys and signs of success and effectiveness in life; knowing and operating within your space and calling, not trying to do what others are doing because it is more flamboyant or popular. John's role was cut out and clearly defined; to be a forerunner of Christ. He was more equipped than any other prophet or person to fulfill that mission. He joyfully accepted that humble position and concentrated on revealing Christ to the people, declaring consistently, "Behold the Lamb of God who takes away the sins of the world." John never attempted to contend with Jesus in anything, in anyway.

He spoke of Jesus so highly that his own disciples at a point left him to follow Jesus. When his attention was drawn to it, his response was too good to be true. Instead of criticizing Jesus and accusing him of "stealing his members", John said, Jesus must increase, but he must decrease. He publicly said he was not worthy to lace the shoes of Jesus. Incredible humility, unmatched spiritual maturity, and a lesson none of us who claim to be followers of Christ should miss. God has not called us to be everything and do do everything. Covetousness, pride, jealousy, and selfish ambition are real dangers that can drive us into asserting ourselves over and above what is our place, calling, and position in life.

Impact has more to do with calling than control and manipulation. The fact that I am a pastor doesn't necessarily mean I am supposed to do what other pastors are doing. No. Like everyone else, I have my space, time, and specific calling, and I am sticking to it. My hope and trust is in God, not gold or men. If you are trying to do what others are doing without reference to God's call on your life, I encourage you to check your motive and be sure you are not pushing where you should be pulling. There are some athletes who excel in long distance race but can never be anywhere near the first in a short distance race.

God's grace will always be sufficient for you to achieve what he has called you to do. Think big but keep an open mind regarding where God want to lead you, and how he wants to use you. Protect your uniqueness and don't be what you are not meant to be. When the chips are down, it is your fruit and impact that will bear testimony to your works. There can never be another you, so be you. Some may leave you like they left John because their time with you is over, and others may "increase" while you "decrease", but none of these has the capacity to change your story if you stay true to your calling.

God bless you.

Love is a Liberating Force

1 Cor.13:1-3, NIV

If I speak in the tongue of angels, but have not love, I am only a resounding gong or a clanging symbol. If I have the gift of prophecy and can fanthom all mysteries and all knowledge, and if I have a faith that can move mountains, but have not love, I am nothing. If I give all I possess to the poor and surrender my body to the flames, but have not love, I gain nothing

---

There is no power greater, deeper, and stronger than the power of love. Love defines God. God is LOVE. He does not have love: HE IS LOVE! Apostle Paul is admonishing us to be careful not to narrow down the love of God to merely doing good works. If the good we do is not motivated by love, it doesn't count with God. The ability to give, preach, prophesy, work miracles, or do other good works does not necessarily mean we are fulfilling Christ's demand to walk in love.

We cannot "manufacture" God's love, but we can manifest it. As long as life shall last, there may be times when we feel like "withdrawing" love from friends and family because they upset us, and that is the reason we need to keep reminding ourselves of the importance of this subject.

When we hurt, we mostly react in a negative way. It is very natural, and may be aimed at righting a wrong, but that is a clear indication of our carnal nature not having the capacity to give unconditional love. Loving others as Christ loved us means offenses should not take us to the level of wishing evil for the offender. We are bigger and better than that as Christians.

We ought to be mindful of the fact that as followers of Christ, we have no reason to hate human beings, no matter how bad they treat us. The love of Christ is the Law of God's kingdom. God hates sin but loves the sinner. He wants everyone, including that man or woman who is a thorn in your flesh, to be born again and come to a saving knowledge of Christ.

Indeed, some of the people who test our walk of love may be born-again believers like us. We assume they should know better, so we pretend to love them when they hurt us, while harboring resentment against them. Apostle Paul tells us to let all our actions be motivated by love. Let's keep reminding ourselves that this love we are being asked to manifest is beyond us; it is fruit of the Holy Spirit, and it will manifest only when we are yielded to God's Spirit.

Here's a good prayer guideline when you come to that difficult spot where it is "impossible" to love someone. Pray, "Holy Spirit, I am not able to love this person as you want me to. I yield and ask you to love him/her through me." It has always worked for me, and it will work for you too. The only alternative to love is hatred, which develops negative tentacles like unforgiveness, bitterness, division, and death.

The price you pay if you choose not to walk in the God-kind of love is too costly. Each moment you spend feasting on bad things people have done against you, is actually a waste of your life and time. Life is too short to be fixated on bad things people have done to you, and classifying them as bad etc. The only one who has the power to change a human being is the God who created him.

God has assigned us to love everyone, bringing hope and restoration to families and friends. If anyone preaches or prophesies to you a message that provokes hatred towards your fellow human being, it cannot be from the God of the Holy Bible. Yes, we have to be upset with wrong behavior, but not obsessed with the actors involved.

Love is a liberating force, because God is love. Truth is, you can't have the joy, peace, and prosperity of the Holy Spirit until and unless you are willing to let him love people (especially bad folks) through you. Try it, and you will be happy you did.

God bless you.

Passion for Praising

Ps.51:15, NKJV

O Lord, open my lips, and my mouth will show forth Your praise

---

My first consideration on reading this scripture is this; "why in the world would David who loved to worship and praise the Lord ask God to open his lips so he could praise Him?" The answer came easily to my spirit, knowing how I sometimes feel, vis-a-vis what I actually want to do. It is my desire to worship and praise God with the highest level of excitement every moment and day of my life, but the reality is that sometimes the way I feel doesn't allow my lips to "open" easily to execute that spiritual agenda. When I wake up in the morning feeling emotionally numb and dumb, praising the Lord with joy and excitement becomes a nonstarter.

Our mood fluctuates some of the times, and more often than not, we find ourselves at an emotional low tide. Anytime that happens, it shows that we need something more than good intentions and a willing heart to enter into praise and worship. It takes personal commitment and divine empowerment for our lips to "open" to offer God the praise and worship he deserves. This is exactly what King David, arguably the most celebrated praise and worship icon of all time, describes to us in this scripture. He had sinned against God by committing adultery and murder. His sense of guilt literally padlocked his mouth and deprived him of the joy of worship. His desire to worship was intact alright, but coordination between desire and delivery was missing.

Every one of us, like King David, experience times of spiritual dryness when praising God becomes like being asked to scoop all the water out of the ocean. The reason for coming to that place of spiritual and emotional paralysis may not be sin like David's; it may be sickness, tiredness, boredom, stress, or something we sometimes cannot define or put your finger on. When we open our eyes in the morning, and all we think about is going through the same mundane activities and challenges, our desire to praise and worship flies through the window. We can always get it back. All we need to do is to remember that the key to being liberated from that feeling of hopelessness and helplessness lies in defying the odds and declaring the goodness of the Lord. We say and sing it, not because we feel it, but because we believe it.

When day breaks and you feel like life is pulling you in the wrong direction emotionally, whisper a prayer to the Holy Spirit to help unlock your lips. Your freedom to live in victory lies in creating an atmosphere of praise and worship to the Lord. You cannot worship and worry at the same time; one will have to give way to the other, and because God lives in the praises of his people, it is the worry that will have to go.

If you are not FEELING like praising the Lord for some reason or no reason, you need help from above. David, despite committing adultery and murder, asked for help and got it. You can be sure the Lord will do same for you. God is no respecter of persons. All you've got to do is rise above the prison of negative emotions and face each day, including today, with hope. When you are weak, admit it, and ask God for strength to keep on keeping on. Say to the Lord, "open my lips, and my mouth will show forth your praise."

My prayer for you today is that the Lord will enlighten your path and renew your strength, so you will regain your passion for praising and worshipping him. Our God is good. Let us rejoice and celebrate Jesus Christ today and always while we have the time, breath, and space.

God bless you.

Let's Pray For Each Other

Rom.1:9-10, NKJV

First, I thank God through Jesus Christ for you all, that your faith is spoken of throughout the whole world. For God is my witness, whom I serve with my spirit in the gospel of His Son, that without ceasing I make mention of you always in my prayers

---

Apostle James once wrote to the Church these words, "the fervent prayer of a righteous man avails much" (Jam.5:16). He points us to the eternal truth that prayer is powerful and never wasted. The writer of the book of Romans was excited about reports that came to him that the believers in Rome he had been praying for, were holding on to the faith, despite the ruthless persecution they were facing. They stood tall and strong at the peril of their lives, and this became "topic of the day" in the entire Roman empire.

The writer was not surprised about that development because "without ceasing I make mention of you always in my prayers." He consistently prayed for them, and he had cause to thank God that his prayers were answered. God has not changed. If we commit to praying for each other, we will see similar and greater results in our lives and that of our loved ones. The Church thrives on prayer, and our survival depends very much on interceding for each other. Indeed, our collective prayers is key to our collective wellbeing and individual prosperity. When the going is tough, and the road is rough, there is no power greater than the power of prayer.

When your brother is sick and tired from the ravages and pressures of life, and he gets to the point of giving up, your prayer is a necessary lifeline for his survival and revival. Many of us can testify that we have come this far because of the continued prayers of family, friends, and loved ones. Some of us have experienced low points in our lives when even the prospect of opening our mouths to pray went completely caput. Somehow, somewhere, someone remembered us in his prayers, and God answered and strengthened us to stand.

Upholding each other in prayer is very important. Its impact goes beyond what the natural eye can see, impacting the spirit-realm for greater good. These are unusual times, and the prayer-door should remain open 24/7. We must be humble enough to ask for prayer support whenever necessary.

Find a prayer partner who you can trust to keep faith with you and commit to praying for each other every day. Begin with your immediate family. Each day pray for God's grace to be with each and every member of your family. Ask for God's divine presence, protection, and provision for each child and adult. Extend your borders of intercessory prayer to include the saints and those in political and ecclesiastical leadership.

Prayer does what worrying and complaining can never do. Someone needs your prayers every day for heaven to perform on his behalf. Pray, and the good Lord will give you a testimony and theme of praise. And always remember to pray for me too, as I pray for you. It's a good deal; let's keep this covenant, and we shall conquer in every challenge, and triumph in every trial.

God Bless You

Spread the Word to the World

Lev.17:11, NKJV

For the life of the flesh is in the blood, and I have given it to you upon the altar to make atonement for your souls; for it is the blood that makes atonement for the soul

---

God gave Moses specific instructions regarding the sanctity of blood, and the lesson and truth revealed in the end was that God's people should regard blood sacrifice as the highest form of sacrifice.

In the context of today's devotional scripture, the blood being referred to was the blood of animals. God made allowance for the sins of the Old Testament saints to be forgiven when animal blood is offered on the altar in Moses' tabernacle. What is interesting, however, is that the blood of animals sacrificed, could not TAKE AWAY the sins of the people; it merely COVERED them.

Scripture records in Hebrews 9:10a, "It was symbolic for the present time..." In other words, what was happening in the Old Testament was not the real stuff, but only pointing us to something higher and better that was coming in the future. The real stuff the Old Testament Law was pointing to, was Christ Jesus, the Lamb of God. He is the fulfillment of the law that demands forgiveness of sins through the shedding of blood.

Hebrews 9:11-12 states emphatically, "But Christ came as High Priest of the good things to come, with the greater and more perfect tabernacle not made with hands, that is, not of this creation. Not with the blood of goats and calves, but with His own blood He entered the Most Holy Place once and for all, having obtained eternal redemption."

Beloved, the faith we have in the salvation of our souls through the shed blood of Jesus Christ shakes the very foundations of the kingdom of hell. Satan has developed and is offering many religious alternatives to deceive men that they can be saved apart from the blood of Jesus. Beginning from the day of his birth to date, the name Jesus Christ stirred up hatred in the demonic realm.

The persecution we face for believing in Christ is not going to abate or go away. Light and darkness stand forever opposed to each other, and as long as the blood of Jesus offers life and redemption for lost souls, the forces of evil and darkness cannot go to sleep. It wets their bed and ruffles their feathers. Every believer needs to understand that this is not a time to be complacent. Souls are dying, people are confused and desperate, and God is expecting us to be the lifeline to their deadline.

This is not a time to run and hide. We have a job that must be done; reaching out to lost souls with love and compassion. God does not endorse violence; he requires your voice. Aaron did his part as high priest, while his children assisted in the tabernacle ministry. Jesus Christ our High Priest has accomplished his task. He shed his blood for us. We are now custodians of the power emanating from his blood, the message of salvation through grace.

Time is not on our side; we must put the "GO" back into the GO-SPEL. The enemy is continuously raising an army of ruthless men and women with swords and bombs, whose primary target is anyone who confess Jesus Christ as Lord and personal Savior. They are okay with anyone who choose not to believe anything; but as long as you confess Jesus Christ as your Lord and personal Savior, their verdict is that you don't deserve to live.

You cannot hate them, because you are of a different breed; you are a child of light, and messenger of life. Your weapon is LOVE.

Let us quicken our steps in spreading the message of salvation. Let us identify with Apostle Paul's confession: "For me to live is Christ, and to die is gain." Don't live all your life asking God for things; use some of your time and resources doing something for him. Learn from what our Lord said to Satan, "Man shall not live by bread alone..."

Everyone needs the blood of Jesus to make it to heaven, because no other blood can rise higher than the blood of the Son of God. Spread the WORD to the WORLD. It is a divine assignment that cannot wait. I am sold out for this call "till death do us part." What about you?

God Bless You.

Fall in Love with Jesus

Col. 3:5-6, NKJV

Therefore put to death your members which are on the earth: fornication, uncleanness, passion, evil desire, and covetousness, which is idolatry. Because of these things the wrath of God is coming upon the sons of disobedience

---

Grace does not take away responsibility. The grace of God does not endorse reckless and sinful living. It empowers us to overpower sin and Satan. We have been set free from sin.

What God gives to us, he expects us to keep and maintain with due diligence and reverence. Holiness is a gift from God, and we must appropriate and walk in it by faith. The fleshly nature which ruled us before we received Christ will always seek to re-assert itself and drive us back to live in sin.

God want us to take responsibility and "put to death" the old sinful nature. This is not a one-time shoot-to-kill exercise; it is a lifelong battle. Apostle Paul wrote, "I beat my body daily." The day you fail to put the old nature to death, it will resurrect with vengeance and cause you to say or do what you normally might not say or do. Don't make excuses for your sin, repent and come out of it.

Here are some suggestions on how you can put the cravings of the flesh to death on a daily basis. First, you have to make a conscious effort not to feed your senses with sights and sounds that are likely to influence you to sin. If you watch pornographic material, you are most likely to fornicate or commit adultery. You cannot sow mangoes and reap melons.

Secondly, you have to avoid places and persons that motivate you to sin. This is because your environment can influence your behavior. Third tip is to depend on the Holy Spirit to help you; and this calls for a disciplined and consistent prayer life, coupled with meditating on the Word of God and obeying its teachings and admonitions. The decision to stand or fall is in your hands.

The grace of God has moved you from a position of helplessness to a place of empowerment, from hopelessness to holiness. You are now a new creature in Christ and should reflect the new light and life God has deposited in you. Walk in the freedom of God's Spirit, as you seek to live to please him. You don't need to impose any set of rules on yourself. The more you fall in love with Jesus, the more you will die to self and sin.

The easiest way to live a God-honoring life is to fall in love with Jesus. Once your heart goes after him, your body will have no choice but to follow suit; you love him so much you don't want to pursue what he abhors. If you fall in love with Jesus, you will stay in tune with holiness.

God Bless You.

Pray for Long Life

Ps.61:6, NIV

Increase the days of the king's life, his years for many generations

The life we live is a gift from God and should not be taken for granted.

We ought to value each day and moment that we have the privilege to be counted among the living, thanking God for his grace and mercy. This prayer of King David (Ps.61:6) should be a part of our prayer request to God every day. He asked God to "increase the days of the king's life." David did not want to die a premature death. He had a desire to live life to its fullest, and he made it known to the only One who could make that happen.

Every one of us has the same right to appropriate the blessing of living long lives. Indeed, God has the final word when it comes to matters of life and death, but he has given us rights as his children to ask for anything we desire (including life), and he will give it to us. In the days of King Hezekiah, God sent the prophet Isaiah to tell him that he was going to die. Hezekiah prayed for mercy, and God added fifteen years to his life. That was an endorsement of the power of prayer in matters of life and death and should be inspiration for us to pray like David and Hezekiah did.

Life is precious and should be handled with care, but who can handle it better than the God who gave it to us. Making a conscious and deliberate effort to commit our lives and that of our dear ones into God's hands on a daily basis is very important. There's peace in knowing that God is in control of our lives.

Let's get our priorities right by praying for life before we ask and work for bread. We can only enjoy the people in our lives and the money we earn when we have life. Fortunately for us, we serve a God whose ultimate for us is to have and enjoy life. It is part of the divine agenda contained in the salvation package Christ offers. (Jn.10:10b).

The natural is as important as the spiritual, and we should not pursue one at the expense of the other. There should be balance between our spiritual and physical lives. As long as God want us here, we should love it here and crave his indulgence to live our full term on earth to the best of our ability, by his grace and mercy, and to his glory.

Beloved, pray for life. If it is worth having, then it is worth asking. You owe it to yourself and your loved ones to be here long enough to enjoy each other and fulfill God's purpose. No one and nothing can guarantee you good health and long life than the God who gave it to you.

Fathers and mothers pray for life for your sons and daughters. Everything else you do for your children is important, but the most important is for them to have life. Cover them with your prayers. Pray that they know Christ who is the source of life, and that they are protected from untimely death.

Husbands and wives pray for life for your spouses. Brothers and sisters, aunties and uncles, friends and loved ones; let us pray that the good Lord will "increase the days" of our lives. We all wish for life, so let's pray for it. Wishes alone cannot bring us life. Physical exercise, dieting etc., do have their place in helping us live healthy and longer, but God is the ultimate source of life, and we should connect to him through prayer.

Prayer is key. Let us pray that God will deliver us from evil, sickness, and untimely death; that we might live long, productive lives, "to declare the goodness of the Lord in the land of the living."

God bless you.

Delivered from The Grave

Ps. 86:13, NIV

For great is your love towards me; you have delivered me from the depths of the grave

---

There have been a few times in our travels around the world that we have experienced scary flights as a result of bad weather. Anytime the pilot announces a storm and ask everyone to fasten seat belt and remain seated, you know we are in for the long haul and need "deliverance." The danger that situation poses and the anxiety it brings centers around death. If we don't survive the storm, it will not be a good ending, and everyone knew that. We don't wish for it, because we were not created to die. We are spirit beings living in human bodies. Our innate desire to live and not die, comes from our spirits and transferred to our bodies. It is both divine and legitimate.

Adam's sin changed the dynamics and has subjected our fleshly nature to change and decay. Spiritual and physical death has become a bondage, and unless Christ becomes the Lord of your life, you are bound to die a double death - spiritually and physically. But no! God has a better plan for you and me.

The psalmist captures it so beautifully here: "For great is your love towards me; you have delivered me from the depths of the grave." The reason God delivers us is his love. He does it because he chose to. He does it because he loves to. He is not compelled by our performance, but his person. His motivation has nothing to do with manipulation, but all to do with mercy and love.

Jesus Christ is a good God, full of compassion and mercy. He loves us with unconditional love. He came on earth with a goal to break the power of death that has held humanity captive since the days of Adam. The chapters of our salvation are written in just one language, the LOVE of Christ, and sealed with his holy blood.

For all who accept Jesus Christ as your Lord and personal Savior, each day is an opportunity to celebrate your deliverance from "the depths of the grave." Christ has revived your spirit and restored you to himself. He conquered the grave and lives eternally, and so are you in him.

God's love is not an abstract. It is not populist. It is not subjective. It is deliberate, focused, and directed at each of us as individuals. It has no limits or favorites. It has neither color nor conditions. The arms outstretched on the cross is open to all who dare to believe.

Are you tired, bogged down with fear, anxiety, frustration, loneliness, rejection, pain, depression, and misery? I know a Man who delivered me from the mess, gave me a message of life, and made me a messenger of hope; his name is Jesus, the Christ. If you can trust him, you will be delivered today.

Receive the love and light of Christ. Experience the deliverance he offers and be set free from the power of the grave. May the love of our God and Christ protect you and your family in the name of Jesus Christ.

God bless you

It Shall Not Stand

Is.7:7, NKJV

Thus says the Lord GOD: "It shall not stand, nor shall it come to pass

---

The kings of Syria and the northern kingdom of Israel declared an unprovoked war on Judah. When news reached King Ahaz that the combined armies of Syria and Israel were marching towards his capital city, Jerusalem, he panicked and went into a frenzy. God immediately dispatched the prophet Isaiah with a message to Ahaz, declaring that indeed the two invading kings had planned to annihilate him, but "It shall not stand, nor shall it come to pass." Forget about the history, and let's do some application here. What are the things you fear are going to upset your "Apple cart?"

Maybe the doctor just announced to you that you have a terminal disease, or someone told you the project you have invested your time and effort isn't going to work. Your children may be taking on a lifestyle that is contrary to what you stand for, and the enemy seem to be winning on all fronts. There is something out there in your past, present, or future that poses a threat to your joy and peace, and you have already accepted defeat. Listen to the voice of the Holy Spirit, and don't exchange fact for reality. If you face the challenges in your own strength, the end may tally with your fears; but if you bring God into the fray, no matter where and how life twist and turn you, the victory will be yours. Even in death, you are still a winner, because in Christ you can only die the death of the righteous; transitioning into glory.

The two kings who ganged up against King Ahaz were not push-overs, and Ahaz knew that for a fact. They might have figured out how their combined forces would be too much for Ahaz to handle. The fear and panic that seized Ahaz was for very good reasons. He did not have the capacity to fight the opposing army and win. He needed something much greater and more powerful than the enemy forces and thank God he got it from heaven.

God did not send him special forces with sophisticated weapons. He sent him his Word; the infallible Word, sharper than a double-edged sword (Heb.4:12). That was the beginning of the dismantling of the enemy's stronghold. Ahaz accepted the Word, and that expression of faith in God's Word became the game-changer. Beloved, you are as free from fear as your trust and obedience to God's Word. It is not the number of scriptures you know that will give you victory over Satan and the things he throws at you; it is how far you are willing to go to BELIEVE what God is saying to you, regardless of your challenges. Can I announce to you today that every enemy army mobilized against you is not going to prevail against you. Every challenge will have to yield to your choice to trust God for victory.

Personalize the Word God gave to Ahaz and confess in faith that whatever negative pronouncements have been made against you, and challenges are rocking your world, "it shall not stand, nor shall it come to pass." You shall prevail over them. That is what God's Word says, and so shall it be in Jesus's Name.

God Bless You.

Sing Through the Storm

Amos 9:11, NKJV

On that day I will raise up the tabernacle of David, which has fallen down, and repair its damages; I will raise up its ruins, and rebuild it as in the days of old

---

Every day comes with its own challenges. Some of our challenges come with specific timelines; coming and going with the speed of lightning, while others gain "Resident" status and simply refuse to go away.

When you have a problem with your relationship, job, health, or finances and your much prayer doesn't seem to make any difference, your faith is on homestretch; like living through a COVID-19 pandemic. Your tabernacle has fallen, and all you want is to have it lifted up to its original position.

Don't throw away your confidence in the Lord. Keep the faith and stand up to the test. The God who raised David's fallen tabernacle will work out your restoration.

Once upon a time, I used to worry about the reason for the cycle of betrayal and mischief that was being visited on us by people we had trusted and loved. The best effort we put into ministry ended up with a "fallen tabernacle," and the frustration was no fun.

Today, God is reversing the order by bringing into our lives faithful and committed spiritual sons, daughters, friends and partners. Challenges still come, but God has raised our "faith tabernacle" to a higher level than it used to be in the past. All the "tabernacles" that fell in the past are being raised and restored.

There was something very unique about the tabernacle of David comparative to the tabernacle of Moses. The tabernacle Moses built had no music, no singing, no dancing, no rejoicing, and no celebration. David's tabernacle was full music, dancing and celebration, and that is what God promised to restore to us.

God's idea is to restore us to a life of joy and excitement similar to the one associated with David's tabernacle.

He does not promise us restoration of the mundane, unexciting life of Moses's tabernacle. Maybe a wall in your life has collapsed without warning. Sorrow, pain, uncertainty, fear, and frustration have all ganged up to put you on silent mode.

God has a word of hope for you; Yahweh will raise up the tabernacle of David (praise and celebration) "that has fallen down" in your life. He will walk you through the fiery furnace and it will not consume you, because he will be right there with you each step of the way. You will definitely feel the heat, but you will not fail the test. You will survive through Christ.

Beyond raising up the tabernacle of David in your life, God is promising a three-dimensional move that will restore your joy and give you hope for the future. Firstly, he promises to repair the damages caused to your life and dreams. His call to you to trust and obey is still relevant.

Secondly, the Lord says he will "raise up its ruins." Some of the challenges you are facing are in a state of ruin, so you are wondering how anything good can come out of same. The God who created light out of darkness is well able to do anything out of everything. Keep holding fast to the promise. Remember that the moment you give up, you have decided to go down.

Thirdly, God is going to "rebuild it as in the days of old." Whatever has stolen your peace and joy will have to make way for God's healing to come back to you. Even if physical healing is delayed, he still walks with you all the way to the end. The "tabernacle of David" that serves as a focal point in giving you the impetus to praise God, and which the enemy has torn down in ruins, is going to be restored.

Begin the Praise, and you will release the Presence to manifest God's Power. You may be down, but you are not out. Praise the Lord, and see his glory unfold. Sing through the storm, and see God perform.

God Bless You.

Power Belongs to God

Ps. 62:11, NKJV

God has spoken once, twice I have heard this: that power belongs to God

---

Power, to a very large extent, is a neutral force, relative to how we use it as human beings. If it is applied graciously, it becomes a blessing with immense spiritual, physical, and psychological impact; but when power is abused and used inappropriately, it kills, decimates, disintegrates, and destroys.

The wise have said that "power corrupts, and absolute power corrupts absolutely." The truism in this adage is the reason democratic governance demand checks and balances at every level of government.

History is replete with narratives of numerous dictators who under the influence of unlimited power, brought untold hardships to humanity.

Today, there are still evidence of abuse of power by parents, pastors, teachers, politicians, corporate managers, coaches et al. This can only change if we acknowledge God as the source of power, and our position as stewards accountable to him.

Whenever you find yourself in any position of power, remember you are exercising that power or authority on behalf of God. You are never an authority to yourself. The "power" you hold in the home, church, work place etc., is not a mandate to bully and abuse those under your authority.

It is an instrument and opportunity to provide leadership, guidance, protection, inspiration, correction, and direction. Anything short of these, can lead to abuse and disaster. God want you to acknowledge that all power belongs to him alone, and what is given to you is for the common good, not for controlling, manipulating, humiliating, and kicking your fellow men.

You can gain power over a person or group of people based on your having more than what they have, in terms of wealth, education, position, or social status. You may even be in that privileged position through "accident of history." Whichever way it comes, its primary source is still God.

As a child of God and citizen of the kingdom of light, you have to be conscious of what God expect you to do with his delegated authority, and tread cautiously in exercising same. If you are a parent, be mindful of the fact that you are accountable to God for your use of the position of power he has given you over your children.

If you are a pastor, prophet, or in any leadership position in the Church, you are not a god unto yourself. The people God has placed in your care are to be fed, not fleeced. Don't make demands on them that are unscriptural, unreasonable, and that they are unable to meet.

And if you are a manager in the corporate world, please the ladies and gentlemen working under you are not there to satisfy your lust. Respect their dignity, and exercise restraint in the way you relate to them. Respect them by showing enough decency and decorum towards them. Don't threaten them with demotion because you cannot control your emotions.

And to the politician, the stake is high, and you should know and understand the dynamics of the power vested in you by the people who elected you. God has given you the rare opportunity to serve a nation, not to mismanage its resources and impoverish its people. Here's a reminder: All power belongs to God.

The little and temporary power he has given each of us should be used with discretion, responsibility, and with the view to being a blessing, not a bully. Use the power vested in you via your position, to equip and empower people, not to enslave or exploit them.

God Bless You

Wisdom Is of God

Prov.3:7-8, NKJV

Do not be wise in your own eyes;
Fear the LORD and depart from evil. It will be health to your flesh,
And strength to your bones

Wisdom is a virtue, and the need to pursue it is a common theme throughout the scriptures. Jesus Christ is described by apostle Paul as "the wisdom of God", amplifying the importance to make it something worth pursuing.

In Proverbs 3:7, however, we are counseled not to be wise in our own eyes. In other words, we should be careful not to interpret "wisdom" in a subject way. The mere fact that we think we have acted wisely doesn't make it so. Sometimes, our best interpretations may be misrepresentation of facts we don't know. Experience makes us gain some knowledge, but not necessarily wisdom.

The assumption that knowledge we have accumulated makes us wiser than Solomon on a given subject is misleading. It can make us assume the posture of experts on issues that we still have to listen to minds that are better informed than us. Life is a continuous learning process, and there are varying levels of wisdom; the highest being what apostle calls "wisdom from above." It is never boasting, ever learning.

The proceeding verse (v8) gives us a head start on where our focus should be; to "fear the LORD and depart from evil." Instead of trying to run our lives according to our understanding and being wise in our own eyes, the scripture gives us two things to do. The first is to fear God. That speaks of giving God the reverence due him; living with the understanding that there are issues of life beyond our understanding and interpretation. It is acknowledgement of our limitations in terms of our human wisdom, knowledge, and understanding.

The second advice is to "depart from evil." Sin is attractive and powerful. Whether we submit to it or resist it, is a decision that each of us have to make for ourselves. The Good Book stresses the importance of walking away from evil. If there are things we say or do that undermine peace in the home, church, or community, the solution is to walk away from it. When the argument is turning ugly, you don't try to prove your smartness or wisdom. You walk away from it.

If you are in a place where you are likely to indulge in some unholy activity, apply the wisdom of God and get out of there. God never delivers a Samson who decides to hangout with Delilah at the wrong place at the wrong time. No! There is a price to pay for any evil we allow in our lives, and it is very disheartening when overconfidence and self-delusion takes the better of us, and is flaunted as wisdom.

In our dealings with our spouses, children, friends, and others, let's give them enough respect by acknowledging that we are not the wisest person in town. Let our reverence for God translate into respecting the views of others, no matter who we are, or what we know. Let's depart from any semblance of evil that is likely to make our lives and that of others miserable. True wisdom builds, it doesn't destroy. True wisdom comes from God alone.

God bless you

The Light Will Prevail

Ex.10:22-23, NKJV

So Moses stretched out his hand toward heaven, and there was thick darkness in all the land of Egypt three days. They did not see one another; nor did anyone rise from his place three days. But all the children of Israel had light in their dwellings

Pharaoh's refusal to let the children of Israel go from Egyptian captivity led to a series of judgments, one of them was the visitation of darkness on the land of Egypt. Even though the darkness covered the entire land, Bible records that "all the children of Israel had light in their dwellings." The same God is working 24/7 to keep us from the darkness that is swallowing up this generation. It doesn't matter how dark it gets, the indwelling Christ will shine in us, for us, and through us. We are fashioned to override the power and influence of the darkness of sin and Satan. From the perspective of scripture, it is helpful when we acknowledge that nothing in this world is going to get better.

The political, economic, and social structures will continue their downward spiral till Yeshua comes. Indeed, the Lord has told us what the signs of the end-time is going to be like; and for those who care to know, the chaos we are experiencing has its cure in Christ alone. If you keep dreaming of people living up to higher moral standards like we have known in the past, you are living in deliberate self-delusion.

The darkness is going to intensify, and wickedness is going to continue enlarging its tentacles, but the good news is that the Lihht (Christ and righteousness) that is in us will always prevail over darkness (Satan and sin). Sexual perversity, and spiritual adultery is already breaking all previous records of indecency and moral absurdity, but as children of the kingdom of light, we are not going to throw our hands in the air in despair and cry to God to rapture us out of here.

We will be here as long as God want us here, not as part of the problem, but of the solution. Despite the moral decadence, and the unprecedented rise in crime and other forms of demonic activities, there is nothing to be afraid of, because we are a people of the Light. Our position in Christ makes a huge difference; where the unbeliever is desperate, we ought to be determined.

Our fear, or reverence, should be directed towards God, not the darkness. As long as we obey God's Word, we are in the light, and the power of darkness cannot overcome us. Evil can dominate the "land of Egypt" (unbeliever's life), but the saints of the Lord shall outshine the gloom and doom. Wherever you are today is influenced by the light of Christ within you. If the darkness has power over you, your story would have been worse off than what you are experiencing now. God has your back and has placed you in a privileged position where you see things differently from the unbeliever who is under the control of the powers of darkness. You see from God's perspective, because you are a child of the Light and have the mind of Christ to guide you.

Henceforth, do not allow the spiritual and moral darkness of "Egypt" to undermine your joy and peace. When the darkness deepens, the light brightens; it cannot be any other way. Let us be thankful to the Lord that as the world GROWS darker and darker, we shall continue to GLOW brighter and brighter.

God Bless You.

Time to Sing Not to Sink

Is.51:11, ESV

And the ransomed of the LORD shall return and come to Zion with singing; everlasting joy shall be upon their heads; they shall obtain gladness and joy, and sorrow and sighing shall flee away

---

This is a prophetic message of hope, restoration, and comfort, given to the battered and shattered nation of Israel. This message is applicable to the Church, and to every believer, because we are the ransomed of the Lord, and God's spiritual Zion.

When things are not going the way we want, our hearts naturally grow faint, and our hands become weak. The daily challenges regarding health issues, financial crisis, family hiccups, church burdens, and attendant spiritual battles rob us of the joy of life.

Thank God for his Word of comfort; there is surely going to be a change, and we are going to "return to Zion with singing." The time for you as an individual to come into that experience is not for me tell, but the truth is mine to declare. You will surely have a good ending.

The joy that has been stolen from you is going to come back to you. The state of sorrow and sighing will change. God has committed himself to helping you deal with things you never thought you could ever have victory over. The joy God promises is everlasting; it has an unlimited lifespan, beginning from now till forever.

This joy and gladness have their source in the Holy Spirit, and have nothing to do with what you have, or do not have. Beloved, God's Presence will be enough for you. The knowledge that God is in control will break the chains that hold you in perpetual sadness, pain, and sorrow.

The time is coming when you will see going to the house of God as an opportunity to celebrate the goodness and mercy of the Lord. You will have no need to be prompted to worship, because you would have tasted the Father's mercy and love in its fullness.

Your encounter with God's grace will release in you a well of joyful songs of gratitude and thanksgiving. There is hope in Christ, because he has the answer to every crisis. Be prepared for great new beginnings in your life. Get ready to return to Zion with shouts of joy and singing.

Your days of sighing and sorrow are about to end; their expiry date is due. God will do you good. Rejoice, for your redemption is nearer than yesterday. His BLEEDING on Calvary guarantees your BLESSING in every crisis.

God Bless You.

Stand in Your Place

Gen. 3:9, GNB

But the LORD God called out to the man, "Where are you?"

God created man in his own image; that is what the Holy Scriptures tells us. Before man was created, God made provision for a comfortable life, and rightly positioned him in a GARDEN, not a FOREST. That is very informative. Fast forward, man was POSITIONED in the EAST of the garden of Eden, where God literally went to commune with him "in the cool of the evening" every day. The environment was good, the provision was great, and the weather was cool. When Adam chose to believe Satan's lie and sinned against God, the dynamics changed.

First, he began to see himself differently from the glorious being that he was. With the change in perception, came a change in position. The man God placed in the East (where the sun rises) had left that place. He was nowhere to be found within that space. That is exactly what happens when we don't see the value God places on us. Sin becomes attractive.

The interesting part of the narrative is that Adam was in the garden alright, but NOT in the East; he was not in the POSITION God placed him. Adam was missing from the divinely appointed place of meeting. When God asked, "Adam, where are you?" it was not out of lack of knowledge of what Adam had done or where he was. It was a rhetorical question that sought to highlight the fact that Adam wasn't where he was supposed to be.

The application is simple. It is possible for us to be ABSENT from our ordained or delegated places of service. You may be a teacher and be in a classroom everyday, but if you are not teaching the kids, you are absent. If you are a husband or wife and are not playing your role as lover, protector, provider, companion etc., you are absent from the position you are supposed to occupy.

For those who stand against parental authority, you are your own worst enemy. The Holy Bible commands respect and submission; that is God's place of meeting with you, so stick to it. Indeed, physical presence is part of the deal, but emotional and spiritual connection makes the package complete. If you are present, let your presence be felt in a very positive way.

Here then is the litmus test for all of us today; are we standing in the place God and destiny has appointed us to be? Can we confidently affirm that if God shows up in the East of our garden (home, church, school, office etc), he will find us STANDING or STUMBLING? Remember that the issue is not merely about being physically present; it is about making an impact.

The first question God asked in the garden of Eden is yours to answer today. Adam (put your name right there) where are you? Are you present in the East of your garden, or roaming north, south, and west? God is waiting for your answer. The message is delivered.

God bless you

Praise is a Game Changer

Dan.2:20-21, NIV

Praise be to the name of God for ever and ever; wisdom and power are his. He changes times and seasons; he sets up kings and deposes them. He gives wisdom to the wise and knowledge to the discerning. He reveals deep and hidden things; he knows what lies in darkness, and light dwells with him

---

Our God can never be controlled or confused by anything that happens in his universe. When Daniel and his three Hebrew friends were confronted with possible execution as captives in Babylon, Daniel knew exactly where to turn for help. Even though he was yet to see the answer to his prayer, he began by praising God.

The young man Daniel gives us a lesson in praising God when we are dealing with difficult challenges. He had confidence in the God who "changes times and seasons" and yet remains unchanging, unfailing, and unchangeable.

Beloved, you can rest assured in Christ that your disappointments are not going to remain with you forever. God will bring about a change. You will not die where you have fallen. Remember the revelation Daniel gives us in this passage: "he (God) sets up kings and deposes them…he knows what lies in darkness."

As long as you are committed to trusting and obeying him, you will not fail. God never promised us a life without difficulties and setbacks. Jesus said, "in this world you shall have tribulations." He did not stop there; he gave us a winning formula when the challenges come. He said, "be of good cheer, for I have overcome the world."

You can't win by whining and throwing a pity-party because things aren't going the way you expect. Praising while you wait for a better tomorrow opens the heavens to your favor. Nothing concerning you is hidden from God. No one standing against you is beyond the reach of Yahweh.

When you are tired, he knows it. When you are at your wits end, he understands it. If you trust him to change your situation and praise him in anticipation, God will respond with love, and lighten your path. Daniel did not need to be lectured on who his God was, and what he was capable of doing.

He took hold of his personal testimony of God's goodness in his life, and made that the theme of his praise. He touched heaven, and God answered.

You share the same privilege with Daniel; if he praised and had an encounter with divinity, you can also praise and experience the love of God in higher dimensions of glory.

Today I petition the God and Father of our Lord Jesus Christ to receive your praise and remove every plague in your life. Rejoice in Christ, there is hope for tomorrow, because there is help coming.

God Bless You.

Morning Praise

Eze.46:12-15, NKJV

You shall daily make a burnt offering to the Lord of a lamb of the first year without blemish: you shall prepare it every morning. And you shall prepare a grain offering with it every morning, a sixth of an ephah, and a third of a hin of oil to moisten the fine flour. This grain offering is a perpetual ordinance to be made regularly to the LORD. Thus they shall prepare the Lamb, the grain offering, and the oil, as a regular burnt offering every morning

---

The Old Testament worship rituals described here by Ezekiel have been fulfilled in Christ, the Lamb of God. The daily shedding of the blood of "a lamb without blemish" was done to give the worshippers access to the presence of God, and to indicate forgiveness of their sins.

Jesus, the spotless Lamb of God, offered Himself on the cross to reconcile us to God once and for all time. The Lord Jesus Christ offered His sinless blood, not as a temporary relief from the burden of sin, but as a permanent solution to the strained relationship between man and his creator.

The Old Testament lamb brought by men, pointed us to the New Testament Lamb offered by God, who did not have to die every day for our sins. His blood has a spiritual chemistry that is in no other blood, and therefore has no expiry date.

When each day breaks, let us put meaning to this unparalleled sacrifice of the Lamb of God by offering the New Covenant sacrifice of praise and thanksgiving. Our mornings should be marked with heavy doses of worship and gratitude to our God.

The "grain" speaks of the Word, and the "oil" represents the anointing of the Holy Spirit. As we confess our sins before the Lord, meditate on the Word, and submit to the Holy Spirit each morning, our worship, walk, and work becomes an offering to God.

Jesus said the Father is SEEKING for worshippers (Jn.4:23-24); implying it is very important for him. Do not deny God the worship due Him. Book an appointment with heaven every morning to give God the worship and praise He desires and deserves.

The morning worship will brighten your day and lighten every load you may have to carry. Ours is an extraordinary privilege, compared to what the Old Testament saints had to go through every morning to offer acceptable worship. We have no excuse to ignore this call to worship every day. This call has no rituals to bind us, and no financial costs to hinder us.

Jesus made full payment on Calvary. The way is open. Let us walk through the door and enter His throne room with hearts filled with gratitude, praise, and thanksgiving. This is the assignment for each morning, including today. Praise the Lord and give him the worship due His name.

God Bless You.

Jesus Christ Reigns Supreme

Gen.15:11, KJV

Who is like unto thee, O LORD, among the gods? who is like thee, glorious in holiness, fearful in praises, doing wonders?

Religion is a matter of faith. People believe what they believe, based on their own personal convictions, reasons, and perhaps experiences, and that is perfectly right. When it comes to the Christian faith, we move beyond religious belief to relationship. Like apostle Paul wrote, "We KNOW (emphasis mine) him whom we have believed." Knowledge of the PERSON we call "God" is the reason we follow, confess, and serve the Lord Jesus Christ. It is therefore impossible to talk us out of it.

How on earth can you ask someone to deny what he knows to be both fact and truth. And lest we misconstrue the issues, knowledge isn't limited to what we read in books or parents and teachers impart to us. The highest form of knowledge is experiential knowledge; you know it because you have experienced it. Moses was raised in Pharaoh's court and definitely saw the magical acts of Egypt. He was exposed to the spiritual gymnastics of the gods of Egypt. Indeed, when he confronted Pharaoh as a messenger of God on behalf of the Hebrews, he personally encountered the powers of the gods of Egypt. In the end, he came to the conclusion that they are not the same as the God who he represented. Yes, they are not!!

There are three attributes of God that Moses highlighted here: first, that our God is "glorious in holiness". Every spiritual manifestation called "god" can claim to be anything, but only the God of the Holy Bible is "glorious in holiness". Forget about everything else the scriptures say about God and concentrate on his manifestation in Christ, and tell me what you see; no equal, he is simply "glorious in holiness".

Moses also spoke about God being "fearful in praise". Our praise unnerves the powers of darkness and their human agents. In today's world, it's okay to talk about anything and any religion without sounding offensive and intolerant, but the moment Christ is mentioned, and the Holy Bible becomes a subject of discussion, hell breaks loose. Why? Our God is "fearful in praise." Hallelujah!!

The third declaration of Moses is, "doing wonders". We serve a God who is an extraordinary performer. He has an unmatched track record. He saves and delivers in a way nothing and no one else can. Some of the people (from scientists to politicians) who through the ages spent time and resources trying to disprove him, ended up proving, confessing, and accepting him.

The God of the Holy Bible does wonders, and that is why the persistent persecutions and unrelenting attacks throughout the ages have failed to quench the fire of our faith. Wise men sought and still seek him, in academia, business, politics et al, Jesus Christ is acknowledged as Lord and Saviour. And of course, I do too. Get this settled in your spirit: There is no God like our God. He is "glorious in holiness, fearful in praises, doing wonders." Hallelujah!!

God bless you

Rise to The Occasion

2 Chron. 29:11, NIV

My sons, do not be negligent now, for the LORD has chosen you to stand before Him, to serve Him, and that you should minister to Him and burn incense

---

Hezekiah became King at the prime age of 25 years. It was at a time the nation of Judah had fallen into apostasy. King Ahaz, his predecessor, had polluted the land with idol worship, and effectively shut the doors to the house of God. King Hezekiah's first initiative on ascending the throne was to open "the doors of the house of the LORD and repaired them." (2Chron.29:3)

The king summoned the priests and Levites and demanded immediate restoration of the worship of Jehovah. He reminded the people of their standing with the Lord, and their responsibility to worship him alone. Hezekiah hit the nail right on the head; the nation had disregarded its divine calling and become negligent in doing what the Lord expected of them. It was time to right the wrong. We see a similar pattern playing out among believers today. Many live in a closet of self-preservation; all we care, talk, and pray about, are our needs and wants. We have allowed evil to fester and flourish among and around us because we have little or no passion to stand in our place as vessels of godliness. Every public space and discourse are being taken over by a volcanic wave of anti-Christ sentiments, and we are afraid to stand up to them.

Friend, you are called to "stand before God" and on the side of truth. You are to reflect Jesus Christ to the world. Be up and doing; stand tall for the truth of Christ and his unadulterated Word. It is your primary responsibility and service to him. Scientists tell us that the moon reflects the light from the sun. The Son of God is our "Sun of righteousness", risen upon us with healing in his wings; to deliver us from fear, and spiritual negligence. Our only option is to reflect the light of Christ or be confined to spiritual apostasy.

Your prayer closet is where you draw on his light, and the world is where you reflect that light. It is not enough to be spiritual behind closed doors, and to care less in the real world. It is a rare privilege to serve in the presence of kings (rulers), and an even greater blessing to stand in the courts of the King of kings. King Ahaz shut the doors to the worship of Jehovah, but Hezekiah opened them. You are either an Ahaz, or Hezekiah; you commit to worshiping and serving the Lord, or you neglect his call on your life. There is no neutral ground for those who love the Lord and called according to his purpose.

Make God the focal point of your life. Don't use him; running to him only when you need something from him. A disciple and true worshipper of Christ does more than just asking for things; he serves the king and opens the door of salvation for others.

Come to him with your "incense" (worship). Stay with him till you are impacted. Go to the world and make a difference reflecting his light, no matter the rot of "King Ahaz."

God bless you.

Move When You Have to

Gen.12:10, NKJV

And there was a famine in the land: and Abram went down into Egypt to sojourn there; for the famine was grievous in the land

---

God gave Abram, who later became Abraham, a promise. He was going to possess the land of Canaan. As he explored the full expanse of the land, he was confronted with a challenge at Bethel; "there was a famine in the land." The challenge Abram faced was not something that could be altered overnight. There was famine. It meant lack of food, which called for a strategic response. He couldn't plant and hope for a harvest in a day or week, so he had to move. Egypt was not part of his original agenda but offered the most convenient solution for the situation at hand.

We are told in the previous verse that he had built an altar, a place of worship in the land before the famine struck. Everything was pointing to the fact that Abram was in the perfect will of God when the unexpected happened. He had no time to cast out demons when all he had to do was change his position. He had to MOVE, not to mourn.

Sometimes that's what the situation confronting us demands of us. There are times that we need to stand in one place and persevere till we break through the barriers hindering our progress, but we should also be aware that certain situations can only change when we change. That change should be defined, definite, and distinct.

We either change our mindset, goals and expectations, or the place and people we are working with. The circumstances should inform our decisions. Abram was a man of faith, but that faith did not make him stay where he knew for a fact there was no food. He operated on a dimension of faith that made him move away from possible starvation to a place of sufficiency. We are in a complex and competitive world. Every challenge is an opportunity to make a move; not necessarily physical, but also mental. We can make a move towards prosperity by using our time and talents to solve problems. That is a job-creating movement, seeing and solving problems and in the process establishing a market for success.

Those who stayed during the famine in the land might have had enough food stored away. They had the luxury of waiting until the next harvest because they had what Abram did not have. They could not move as easily as Abram did, probably because they had houses and other properties that tied them permanently to the land. Anytime you experience dryness in your life, consider the choices and their possible consequences. Be sure you know where you are going before you move. Do not assume that every move will end the "famine". In the time of Isaac, there was another famine in the land. Isaac wanted to move out, but God said no. He obeyed and prospered.

We need balance and flexibility, and the path to securing both is a closer walk with God. God loves and directs "altar builders" (worshippers). Abram was such a person and was led by the Spirit of God when it became necessary for him to move.

You may be in some hard place (famine) and not knowing what to do; whether to maintain the status quo or move on. Let God lead you. Pray about it, align your decision with the Word of God, and let your conclusions rise above emotions.

Seek counsel where necessary, and when you are sure that it is time to move on, get up and go. It may be a new territory with its own peculiar challenges, but if that is where you must be to survive the season of "famine", so be it; and may the good Lord help you to survive and succeed.

God bless you

The Voice of the Lord

Ps.29:4-5, NIV

The voice of the LORD is powerful; the voice of the LORD is majestic.
The voice of the LORD breaks the cedars;
the LORD breaks in pieces the cedars of Lebanon

The expression "voice of the LORD" is more figurative than literal. It is not how it sounds, but what it does with regard to its substance, influence, and impact. God's voice has a content. It carries a message and is performance oriented. The Bible opens in Genesis chapter one with a typical example of the power of "God's Voice." Creation would not have been possible if God never spoke.

Apart from human beings, God (according to the scriptures) spoke everything else into existence. His creative words began with the phrase, "let there be." Everything responded to that command. The seas, stars, animals etc., are all manifestations of words spoken by God. The psalmist tried so hard explain the extraordinary nature of God's Word, and in the verse 4, he highlighted two things about "the voice of God", or words spoken by God. First, he said the voice of God is powerful. Every word God speaks is backed by his power.

The prophet Isaiah knows this power of God's Word and therefore wrote that God's Word does not return to him empty without fulfilling the purpose for which it was sent. It is loaded with power to do anything and everything. No other word is above God's Word. It has power to save the lost, heal the sick, raise the dead, and deliver from bondage. You've got to apply it to appreciate it.

The second description is that the voice or Word of God is "majestic"; speaking to us of royalty or kingship. When God speaks, we are to regard his words as words of authority coming from the King of the entire universe. Even society that did not create us, makes demands on us, and we obey. How much more should we not submit to "the voice of God" which has come to us as the Word of God (Jesus Christ).

What voice are you hearing today? Is it from within or without? What is that voice saying? Is it constructive or destructive? Mark my words, the voice of our God speaks both ways. God speaks to destroy the things that stand against us and establish the resurrection life of Christ in our hearts and lives. Get excited and read the Bible for yourself every day. Victory in Jesus is in his voice (Word); for he himself has said, "the words I speak, they are spirit, and they are life." The Word of God will work for you in power and majesty, if you apply it to your life at all times.

The things that need to be destroyed will be destroyed as the Lord commands, and those that need to be saved will be saved. The voice of the Lord is powerful and majestic. It will change your situation. Your end will be glorious. God says so, and that will surely be your lot.

God bless you.

Think Beyond Today

1Ch.22:5, NIV)

David said, "My son Solomon is young and inexperienced, and the house to be built for the LORD should be of great magnificence and fame and splendor in the sight of all the nations. Therefore I will make preparations for it." So David made extensive preparations before his death

---

Generational thinking is what we find David doing here. He was well advanced in age and had done a lot for family and country. Despite his unprecedented success as the second king of Israel, David had other ideas in mind that was not part of God's purpose for his life. He wanted to build a temple to honor the Lord, but God sent the prophet Nathan to tell David to assign the building of the temple to his son and successor, Solomon. Being a good parent and father, the king thought it wise to make some resources available for his son to use for the project.

In David's own words, this is what he said: "My son Solomon is young and inexperienced...Therefore I will make preparations for it (the temple)." The king was on point, acknowledging the limitations of his son, and the solution necessary to mitigate the problem. First, he pointed at the age factor (Solomon was young), and then its implication (he was inexperienced). The lesson is not farfetched. Every Christian parent has a responsibility to walk into the future of his or her children. Responsible parenting involves more than providing enough for today. There must a clear road map leading to a better future for our children.

Like king David, we should prepare our children for the future, and prepare the future for our children. They are our greatest assets and enduring legacies. Investing in their education is important, but that is only a part of the package. As much as we can, we ought to address all issues pertaining to their spiritual, moral, and material well-being.

If God blesses you with money, don't spend it all on yourself. Put something away for your children to build on. They shouldn't go back and start where you started, that's retrogressive and a bad testimony. Give them a better head start. Make them wiser by sharing your experiences with them. They definitely do not have to make the mistakes you made in your youthful days.

Remind them of the words spoken by Jesus to his disciples, "greater works than these you shall do." Let them see a bigger vision for their lives, and greater possibilities for success. David said "the house to be built for the LORD should be of great magnificence." He gave Solomon a vision, and helped him with the resources necessary to undertake the mission and bring it to fruition.

God expect more from us regarding the next generation. He expect us to prepare them for their own future success stories; to inspire, counsel, lead, and provide at least some of the things they will need to build on solid foundations. Until this is done, the job is an unfinished business.

Yes, by all means enjoy the fruit of your labor, but do so with the intention to make life better and easier for as many children as God gives you grace to impact. You owe it to God and yourself to think and act generationally.

God bless you.

Rejoicing in Suffering

Col.1:24, NKJV

I now rejoice in my sufferings for you, and fill up in my flesh what is lacking in the afflictions of Christ, for the sake of His body

In this letter to the church in Colossae, Apostle Paul spoke of his sufferings without regret. Indeed, he rejoice in it. He had every cause to complain and vent his frustration on God, but he showed us something different about how to respond to suffering we don't deserve.

Paul's reason for maintaining his integrity in the face of suffering was because it inured to the benefit of the Church. He said, "I now rejoice in my sufferings for you." His imprisonment and subsequent abuse by Roman soldiers were richly compensated for, in the knowledge that it was benefiting God's people. Their faith was strengthened by the apostle's tenacity. Paul gave them a practical lesson in endurance.

None of us like to suffer, but the lesson here is that if our suffering is going to be a blessing to others, it is worth going through it. Parents, pastors, and leaders generally, ought to have this mindset; the burdens we carry are for the benefit of others. That which is hurting us may be the only way of bringing healing to our families, friends, and congregants.

It's true that some of the challenges we face will not be there if we are only living for ourselves, but we are bigger than that. In Christ, we are assigned the responsibility to help others in their struggles. We are "saviors" in our own right. Some may not be able to survive another day without our input, and so no matter the cost, we must answer the call.

The incentive for making sacrifices for others is in the benefit they derive from it. Jesus died that we might live. His suffering paved the way for us to be reconciled to our Heavenly Father. If Jesus has any reason to rejoice over his suffering, it is because his suffering has benefited and impacted the entire human race. The pain he suffered was the price necessary for our peace and salvation.

Whatever you are doing for family or community that is causing you to suffer one way or the other, please think about the end result and keep at it. You may be a single parent working so hard to provide for your children, and this is causing you so much in so many ways. Stay the course, because your sacrifices will pay off one day. No sacrifice is wasted, and time will prove that to you soon.

The burden becomes heavier when we are not focusing on the long-term gains and benefits. We can all do what Paul did and rejoice in our "sufferings", knowing that the outcome will be glorious. God will work it all out for our good.

Be strong and face every pain and suffering that comes as a result of the good work you are doing to benefit others. Rejoice in hope that there will be victory in the end.

God bless you.

Adapt Quickly

Lu.1:6-7, NKJV

So it was, that while they were there, the days were completed for her to be delivered. And she brought forth her first born Son, and wrapped him in swaddling cloths, and laid him in a manger, because there was no room for them in the inn

---

One of the greatest lessons we can learn from this scripture is that God usually put great things in seemingly "insignificant" places, people, or things. Beyond that, it is also important to note that those who take good care of the "little" things God give them, live to see it blossom into big things. The place where Jesus was born was so obscure and insignificant. Mary had carried what was prophetically meant to be the greatest pregnancy ever to be experienced on earth, but when time came to birth the "vision," the place of birth did not reflect the status of the product. She did not complain. She did not take her eyes off the ball. She made good use of what was available to her.

Mary recognized the limitations of her immediate environment and adapted quickly to the manger and swaddling clothes. She had no time to question God's integrity. The baby was not going to die because there was no napkins, sweaters, and diapers. What she had presently was what God had provided and must be taken for all it was worth. Her present challenges were not going to alter the future prospects of her unique Child. Yes. We all have to learn something from Mary. The place your vision is birthed has nothing to do with the position God has prepared for its future. If you cannot appreciate the resources available to you in the "manger," your baby (vision) will die. The effort you may have put into your work this year is not being reflected by the result on hand, so you are becoming jittery and discouraged.

You were expecting to birth your baby Jesus in a palace, because after all he is supposed to be King of kings and Lord of Lords. The least space you expected to get in the crowded city for delivering your baby (vision) was a five-star hospital for the elite in society. And now this; manger and swaddling clothes. What you need to understand is that God places a lot of premium on humble beginnings. Big trees usually come out of small seeds. If you have made the journey all-year round to get to where you are today, you have no cause to regret your achievements, no matter how small and insignificant it might look.

Place value on what you see and protect it until you get the opportunity to move out and grow it. Don't crave for attention from anyone. Man's applause is not God's approval. I guess nobody really took notice of Mary and her baby in swaddling clothes, apart from the wisemen from the East, and the shepherds who were cued by the heavenly hosts. Keep your heart and mind on what God has put in your spirit. This is not the time to give up.

Christmas is the season of rising up and appreciating God's grace on your life. Christmas is not a time to look down on your little baby in swaddling clothes and mourn. God has shown us through Mary, that every vision he places in our lives, has the potential to grow into a "messiah," if we can keep faith with him and trust him. Keep the faith and kick the fear. There is a great future awaiting you. It begins with taking good care of your baby in swaddling clothes.

God bless you.

His Faithfulness Is Forevermore

Lam.3:22-23, NIV

Through the Lord's mercies we are not consumed, because his mercies fail not. They are new every morning, Great is your faithfulness

---

We are at the threshold of another Christmas season; implying the end of another year is close at hand. Every one of us has gone through different experiences. We have had our ups and downs - days of excitement, as well as seasons of disappointment. Life keeps some of us on edge, as we witness the year race past us without seeing our dreams fulfilled. Nonetheless, we owe God tons of gratitude because his grace has sustained us. We are here; therefore, we have hope. God's mercy has seen us through unpredictable, and sometimes uncomfortable days, weeks, and months.

Thanking God for all the mercies bestowed on us should be an obvious choice. Instead of looking for your wounds and licking them, turn towards God and praise Him. God may not have given us everything we believed for, but even his denials deserve our appreciation. Remember, He is THE LORD, not our errand boy. He is faithful and just. This new day is another testimony of his mercies towards you. The opportunity to see the break of another day is given to you by Him. You neither earned it, nor deserve it. You did nothing to qualify for it. His grace and mercy raised you out of bed, and even though you may not be in the best of moods today, God's faithful and steadfast love is there for you to access.

The prophet Jeremiah is a perfect example of how we can be thankful to God despite our challenges. In this book, appropriately called "Lamentations", he tells of the frustrations he had to endure, but was quick to recognize and acknowledge that God's mercy and faithfulness helped him through it all. You can also do same. Count your blessings and say with boldness, "through the Lord's mercies I am not consumed. They are new every morning (including this morning). Great is his faithfulness." Feel his presence and be released from the pressure as you make this good confession.

God bless you.

A heart of gratitude

Ps.126:3, NKJV

The Lord has done great things for us, and we are glad.

It helps to take a break sometimes and just reflect on what life without Christ would have been like. Considering the fact that despite the price paid for our redemption, we still have a lot of negativities to contend with, we can begin to appreciate how unbearable life would have been, if Jesus Christ had not come. That is why Christmas should mean a season of celebration and thanksgiving for you and me. Indeed, "the Lord has done great things for us"; sending his Only Begotten Son into this world of sin and darkness to die for us. This is the season that marks the entrance of Divinity's greatest gift to humanity.

Saints, let us come into agreement with the Psalmist that the Lord has indeed done great things for us, and be thankful to him. Some of us may have begun the year on a brighter note than we are ending it. You may have lost loved ones you wish are still here with you. You may have lost your job, investments, relationships, or struggling with very serious health challenges etc. All of these are serious issues that cannot be glossed over, but the truth still stands that God has done great things for us. You are alive because he took the decision to keep you here for this long. He has provided an anchor for your soul. The little spark of hope that keeps you going, is a gift from heaven.

The air you breath, and the occasional smile and laughter that bubbles out of your soul, are all part and parcel of God's great work of grace, meant to hold you above the ferocious waters of untimely death! God has indeed done great things for us, and we must dare to be glad to overcome the gloom. Count your blessings and you will realize that even though you lost some things, you did not lose everything. You have God, and you cannot lose him. That's how blessed you are.

Take a stand to be joyful this Christmas, despite the challenges. When the enemy tries to depress you by drawing your attention to what God has not done, confuse him with a song of praise to God for the great things he has done for you, in you, and through you. That way you stay on your feet and refuse to faint or die before your time. Lighten your world with joy in what God can do and will do. Do it, and you will be glad you did.

God bless you.

Allow yourself to be mentored

Lu.1:39-40,56, NIV

Now Mary arose in those days and went into the hill country with haste, to a city of Judah, and entered the house of Zacharias and greeted Elizabeth...and Mary remained with her for three months."

Victorious Christian living involves SACRIFICE and SUBMISSION. If you are not prepared to sacrifice, you are not prepared to succeed in anything. Mary found herself in a very awkward situation at this point in her life. She was pregnant and it was not easy explaining the scientific basis for the pregnancy. She needed inspiration, instruction, and impartation. These she could not get from anyone at her level or age group. Mary reckoned that she needed a mature person whose experience of an "embarrassing pregnancy" was similar to hers. She located Elizabeth, a Godly woman who was also carrying a pregnancy "at a wrong time" - in her old age, way beyond her season of menopause.

To reach Elizabeth and tap into her strength, wisdom, and guidance, Mary had to do FOUR important things, which we all must do if we are to be able to carry through our own "pregnancies" (dreams, goals, visions etc.) to its logical conclusion. The first thing Mary did was to ARISE. The scripture says, "Now Mary AROSE..." If you sit in the same place all your life, the only change you will see is disillusionment and deterioration. If you want your situation to change, then YOU must change. The change you desire must begin with YOU and in YOU!! Nobody is responsible for you but you. Arise and make a move towards your goal.

Secondly, she "went into the HILL country". It was not a low-lying place. She had to climb a "hill" with the pregnancy. Do you catch the drift? There are seasons of lifting your "eyes to the hills" and waiting for help like David, but I bet there are other times when God expects you to climb your hill to receive what you need. Only the three disciples who climbed the hill with Jesus saw His Glory on the Mount of transfiguration. Leave your comfort zone. Pay the PRICE to win the PRIZE! Thirdly, Mary did not only climb the hill, but the Bible says, she went with "HASTE". There was no hesitation. Her mind was made up, and the hill was not going to slow her down. She turned her stumbling stone into a stepping-stone.

If she was going to be sluggish about this trip, the flesh could set in and give her a thousand and three reasons why it was not worth making such sacrifices to sit at the feet of an old pregnant lady. Mary went in haste. If there are some "mountains" confronting you that you need to climb, get up and climb them in haste. Procrastination will paralyze your passion and steal your blessing. The fourth lesson is that Mary "REMAINED" with Elizabeth for THREE MONTHS!! She had left Joseph behind. She was the one carrying the pregnancy. She needed his consent, but not his control. It is interesting how some of our young people today literally refuse to submit to mentorship by mature Godly ministry.

This "Computer Generation" (don't be upset with me) submits to technology and ignores the human-touch that goes beyond head-knowledge to heart-wisdom. Many of us have come this far because we dared to leave everything we seemed to have achieved behind, climbed our own peculiar mountains, and sat at the feet of Godly men and women for years. At my age, I still have spiritual parents I look up to, and who form a wall of protection for my family and ministry. They are a source of strength and inspiration when dark clouds assail our way (thank you Lyle and Lu).

Beloved, step up your game like Mary and you will find grace to carry your "pregnancy" through. May God continue to bless and give you strength to arise, climb your mountains, and submit to spiritual mentoring, counseling, and leadership for your own good.

God bless you

Rise up and Work!

Is.28:24-26, GNB

No farmer goes on constantly plowing his fields and getting them ready for planting. Once he has prepared the soil, he plants the seeds of herbs such as dill and cumin. He plants rows of wheat and barley, and at the edges of his fields he plants other grain. He knows how to do his work, because God instructs him.

Here is an inspiration to progress in whatever you are doing. Another year is phasing out. You have to get ready to add value to your life. For some things, you must maintain the routine; like eating, taking a shower, praying etc. These are things you cannot or should not stop doing. There are other things that demand stepping up to the next level, and that is what the prophet is alluding to in this passage of scripture.

The farmer cannot keep preparing the field all year round, but that is where some of us are. We claim to have faith, but never act on our faith. God has supplied us seed, but we prefer to sit; we don't want to take the next step. Even though we have entered the promised land, we keep going out looking for manna from the skies. It is good to prepare for the exam, but if you never get to a point of deciding to take the exam, then you can never move forward and be recognized as qualified person in that field/career.

Some are in relationships as old as Methuselah. You have told everyone over the past many years that you intend to marry. Your intention attracted everyone's attention, and yet you are still standing at the same junction singing a lullaby. Break the vicious cycle of procrastination. God has instructed you enough. Once upon a time, Peter went fishing and caught no fish. Jesus asked him to go back. He obeyed, but he did more than just rowing his boat. He cast his net, and that was what brought the ultimate result; he had a bumper harvest of fish.

God is happy about your preparation. It is now time to step up your game. Do it, and the good Lord will make the coming year more fruitful and exciting for you in Jesus Name.

God bless you.

Wait, Your Herod isn't Dead Yet

Matt. 2:19-21

Now when Herod was dead, behold, an angel of the Lord appeared in a dream to Joseph in Egypt, saying, "Arise, take the young Child and His mother, and go to the land of Israel, for those who sought the young Child's life are dead." Then he arose, took the young Child and His mother, and came into the land of Israel.

What an amazing display of the fruit of patience and long suffering revealed to us here! Herod was a threat to the life of the baby Jesus. God had the power to snuff the life out of Herod in order to put a stop to his intransigence, but he did not. God neither cursed nor killed Herod. The Lord of the whole earth waited for a created being, who was posing a threat to His divine plan of salvation, to play the boss until his appointed time on earth came to a conclusive end.

Meanwhile Joseph and Mary had to suffer all the inconveniences associated with being non-citizens in a strange land. Remember they had to feed, pay rent for accommodation, provide for basic needs of the baby etc. They were in the perfect will of God alright, but certainly not in a comfortable environment. Before you give the devil too much credit for the challenges the couple went through, let's agree on this one thing; they were in the perfect will of God. We are seeing therefore, that being in the will of God does not insulate us from pain, difficulties, and disappointments.

When you point to the challenges in your present situation and use them as evidence of God's disapproval or judgment, it may lead you to take decisions that will not be in conformity with the will of God for your life. Sometimes the place of comfort may not be the place of safety for you and the "baby" (vision) God has given you. God can turn your Egypt (negative circumstances) into a preparatory ground for a better future. You may have waited for so long. Indeed, you may even have waited for "too long", by your reckoning; but God may be saying, "you've got to wait a little bit more, because your Herod isn't dead yet."

That is usually a hard one, especially when you are in "Egypt", but as long as God has the red light on, there is nothing better to do than to wait. Your Herod has an expiry date, and one day he will die, and then you will be free to leave Egypt. Until that time comes, keep doing your best for family, church, friends, enemies, and country. There is an angel assigned to appear in your dream when the time is ripe, and Herod is dead. In the silence, God is still working for you. Trust God for the best.

God bless you

But you have come to Mt. Zion

Heb.12:22-24, NIV

But you have come to Mount Zion, to the heavenly Jerusalem, the city of the living God. You have come to thousands upon thousands of angels in joyful assembly, to the church of the first born, whose names are written in heaven. You have come to God, the judge of all men...to Jesus the mediator of a new covenant

---

Three times in Heb.12:22-24 we read: "You have come." This means we were in some other location, spiritually speaking. It also means we have transitioned from the first place of abode, to a better place of existence. So where have we come to, and how unique is this new place? The writer of the book of Hebrews says firstly, that "you have come to Mount Zion;" a place of worship, an environment of peace, and a life where God's presence is ever-present.

When you receive Jesus Christ as your Lord and personal Savior, there is a paradigm shift in the spirit; fear of Satan, demons, men, the future et al. should no longer hold you captive. You cannot confess Jesus Christ as Lord and continue to remain under the yoke of fear. God pronounces you "not guilty," and no one can reverse that verdict. Your Father in heaven says he is too good to put his own children in jail. If you look to the earthly Jerusalem, you may wallow in disappointment. God promises something new, something unique, something better, and something that will last throughout eternity. This is the peace of Christmas, not for a season, but forever for all times and for all mankind.

Secondly, it says, "you have come to thousands upon thousands of angels in joyful assembly..." As you go through the hustle and bustle of each day, remember that you are not alone. Even when you don't see anyone around you, be assured that you are in the midst of "thousands upon thousands of angels." God is keeping his promise to give his angels charge over you, to keep you in all your ways (Ps.91:11). Ultimately, the scripture adds, "you have come to God the judge of all men...to Jesus the mediator of a new covenant." That should seal the deal for all of us who dare to believe in the faithfulness of God.

We have come to where it matters most; we have come to God the JUDGE of all men, and to Jesus the MEDIATOR of a NEW COVENANT. There is no place beyond where you are in Christ. Everything begins and ends with him. Satan's accusations and the lies of men cannot change anything "God the judge of all men," has decreed regarding your life. No tag of condemnation placed on you can hold, because the ultimate judge says you are not guilty.

You have a mediator in Christ, and for heaven's sake, he is your advocate. Do not settle for anything less. Celebrate the new life and freedom Christ has given you. Don't plead guilty when God says you are forgiven. Come to where you are supposed to come; to Mount Zion, to the joyful assembly of angels, to God the judge of all, and to Jesus Christ the mediator of a new covenant. God bless you and your entire family with greater peace, joy, and gladness this Christmas season and beyond.

God bless you.

Greatness in You

Lu.2:6-7, NKJV

So it was, that while they were there, the days were completed for her to be delivered. And she brought forth her first born Son, and wrapped him in swaddling clothes, and laid him in a manger, because there was no room for them in the inn

---

One of the greatest lessons we can learn from this scripture is that God usually puts great things in seemingly "insignificant" places or people. Beyond that, it is also important to note that those who take good care of the "little" things God gives them, will eventually live to see it blossom into big things.

The place where Jesus was born was so obscure and insignificant. Mary had carried what was prophetically meant to be the greatest pregnancy ever to be experienced on earth, but when time came to birth the "vision," the place of birth did not reflect the status of the product. She did not complain. She did not take her eyes off the ball. She made good use of what was available to her. Mary recognized the limitations of her immediate environment and adapted quickly to the manger and swaddling clothes. She had no time to question God's integrity. The baby was not going to die because there was no sophisticated medical equipment, qualified doctors, or diapers. What she had presently was what God had provided and must be taken for all it was worth.

Her present challenges were not going to alter the future prospects of her unique Child. Yes. We all have to learn something from Mary. The place your vision is birthed has nothing to do with the position God has prepared for its future. If you cannot appreciate the resources available to you in the "manger," your baby (vision) will die. The effort you may have put into your work this year is not being reflected by the result on hand, so you are becoming jittery and discouraged. You were expecting to birth your baby Jesus in a palace, because after all he is supposed to be King of kings and Lord of Lords. The least space you expected to get in the crowded city for delivering your baby (vision) was a five-star hospital for the elite in society. And now this; manger and swaddling clothes.

What you need to understand is that God places a lot of premium on humble beginnings. Big trees usually come out of small seeds. If you have made the journey all-year round to get to where you are today, you have no cause to regret your achievements, no matter how small and insignificant they might look. Place value on what you see and protect it until you get the opportunity to move out and grow it. Don't crave for attention from anyone. Man's applause is not God's approval. I guess nobody really took notice of Mary and her baby in swaddling clothes, apart from the wisemen from the East, and the shepherds who were cued by the heavenly hosts.

Keep your heart and mind on what God has put in your spirit. This is not the time to give up. Christmas is the season of rising up and appreciating God's grace on your life. Christmas is not a time to look down on your little baby in swaddling clothes and mourn. God has shown us through Mary, that every vision he places in our lives, has the potential to grow into a "messiah," if we can keep faith with him and trust him. Keep the faith and kick the fear. There is a great future awaiting you. It begins with taking good care of your baby in swaddling clothes.

God bless you, and Merry Christmas to you and yours in Jesus Name!

Serve As you wait

Lu.1:5-8, NKJV

There was in the days of Herod, the king of Judea, a certain priest named Zacharias, of the division of Abijah. His wife was of the daughters of Aaron, and her name was Elizabeth. And they were both righteous before God, walking in all the commandments and ordinances of the LORD blameless. But they had no child, because Elizabeth was barren, and they were both advanced in years. So it was that while he was serving as priest before God....

It is not too difficult loving Jesus and serving in the Church when all your needs are being met. The real test of your love and commitment comes when your feathers are ruffled; when you are offended, your needs are not being met, and God doesn't seem to answer your most urgent prayer. Zacharias passed that test, leaving us an example of how to serve God selflessly and without any preconditions.

Both priest and his wife, according to the scriptures, were righteous. The record of their character and level of their commitment speaks volumes about where they stood with God: "And they were both righteous before God, walking in all the commandments and ordinances of the LORD blameless." What else can a person do to gladden the heart of God? Our natural inclination and interpretation of Zacharias and his wife's predicament would be that God is either unjust, unfair, or the couple are not righteous after all. Meanwhile in the divine plan of God, they would get a child only during the "extra time" of their lives.

Zacharias showed that he was not serving God because of a need, but out of love. Some of us would take an early retirement from incense burning (serving) in the House of God if He dares delay in answering our prayers in such "slow" fashion. As another year closes in on us, strengthen your hands in whatever you are doing for God. There is no prayer that God does not answer; his answer is sometimes a loud "wait!". This "wait" answer usually comes without explanation. Don't let it discourage and stop you from doing what you're called to do to advance God's kingdom. It is in the place and hour of ministry that the angel came to Zacharias.

What would have happened if Zacharias had quit on God because he was not getting a child at the time he was most likely to get a child? It would have done nothing to God; He would still be God. The ultimate loser would have been Zacharias and all the generations past, present, and future, who have been blessed and would be blessed by the ministry of their son (John the Baptist).

Friend, life is not about you and your immediate needs and family alone; God will give and withhold in accordance with what he wants to do with you, in you, and through you. Ask for grace to wait, if that's all you got to do, for as long as God wants. In your waiting, work and worship till your angel Gabriel shows up.

God bless you

Yea in Christ

Lu.1:45, NKJV

Blessed is she who believed, for there shall be a fulfillment of those things which were told her from the Lord.

Mary received a promise from the Lord, and based on that promise, stepped out to visit her senior auntie. When Elizabeth saw Mary, the fire of the Holy Spirit within her was ignited, and a prophetic word burst forth. Among the things the Holy Spirit revealed through Elizabeth was that God was going to fulfill the promise made to Mary because the young lady believed. Her faith was going to serve as God's vehicle for bringing the promise to fruition.

Let's make a connection here. With the year racing to a close, you might be pre-occupied with the downside of events over the past 12 months. The point is this; what has happened has happened, and what did not happen did not happen. You cannot change anything about the past, and that is why you should confine the past to the past. Your prospects and opportunities for a better life are in today and tomorrow, not in yesterday. There was no scan to confirm what kind of baby was in Mary's womb, but she believed what the angel told her; that she was carrying the Savior of the world.

Nine months of anxiety, possible ridicule, and pressure to explain the strange circumstances surrounding her pregnancy; something that never happened before since the eons of time. The message she received was from a total stranger. It was more likely to be her first time seeing an angel. The tendency to doubt the message and question its credibility is greater, given the circumstances surrounding her life at the time. She was a young lady blessed to have a young man proposing to marry her and going ahead to engage her. Why would she risk her "society wedding" to carry a hard-to-explain pregnancy for nine months? It was simple faith in a faithful God that did the trick.

Mary believed God and cared less what society thought about her situation. It is your turn. Begin a serious mind-transformation exercise from today. Look forward to the coming year with anticipation for the great things Lord will do, because of what he has promised in his Word. Keep in mind that God is not a man that he should lie. He always watches over his Word and performs it. If you can believe it, the coming year is your time to glow. It is going to be your year of extraordinary testimonies. God is the guarantor; the devil is the loser. Keep the faith and kick the fear, and the good Lord continue to bless you and yours in Christ's wonderful name!

You are God's Star

Matt.2:1-2, NKJV

Now after Jesus was born in Bethlehem of Judea in the days of Herod the king, wise men from the East came to Jerusalem, saying, "Where is He who has been born King of the Jews? For we have seen His star in the East and have come to worship Him."

Accumulation of facts about Christ, and the ability to see visions and operate in the gifts of the Spirit does not necessarily amount to knowledge of Christ. The wise men who came looking for Jesus, had all their facts right. They knew by divine revelation that Christ had been born. They were "wise men" so they could not have been fooled into making such a long trip, leaving the comfort of their homes, looking for a baby without any significance. Their journey was deliberate, because the revelation and information they had, was very credible.

Indeed, the Bible never said they were "three wisemen"; it only said "wisemen" so they could be anything from two, three, or a hundred. And given the fact that the entire city of Jerusalem noticed their presence, the number of wisemen must have been bigger than tradition suggests to us. This is just food for thought. Now to the substance of the message. These wisemen had a correct vision which propelled their mission but locating the exact place to find and worship the King of glory became a problem. Even so in our world today, there are huge numbers of "wise men" (both male and female) who have heard the gospel, been convicted of their need of Christ, but find it difficult locating a true place of worship.

The reason is that the Church in many places has lost credibility. The ministry is now a career, no longer a calling. Shepherds are being replaced by butchers. We have too many "wolves in sheep clothing." The principle of iron sharpening iron no longer applies because nobody wants to be accused of being judgmental. The Church is saying by its loud silence when it comes to issues of sin that getting the CROWD is more important than following the CHRIST. The problem, however, is that if Jesus Christ says he came to "convict" (not condemn) the world of sin, and the Church he is building has no sense of conviction, then how do the lost "wise men" of our generation locate him?

We cannot de-populate hell by pampering ourselves when we should be pinching ourselves. We are the "star" that must lead the lost "wisemen" of this world to the Savior. If we shine bright enough, they will not be attracted to "Herod" (secret societies, false religions, occultism etc.). Enjoy your Christmas party; but do so with a mind to let the Christ in you attract, not distract. Jesus is counting on you to call the wanderers' home. You are God's star, and you must shine wherever you are located.

God bless you.

His Ways are not Our Ways

Rom.11:33, GNB

How great are God's riches! How deep are his wisdom and knowledge! Who can explain his decisions? Who can understand his ways?

If you are someone who has walked with God long enough, you will agree with this writer that it is impossible to always correctly interpret or understand why God does things the way he does. You can't understand why God wouldn't routinely take quick action in resolving issues that need immediate attention, as per your opinion. Sometimes you have to go the extra mile to believe that God cares at all. Looking at the pain, suffering, untimely deaths, setbacks et al., you wonder why he wouldn't do things the way you would have done them.

The answer you get from God regarding an issue may not be satisfying or gratifying, but it is the only one there is to contend with; God's wisdom, knowledge, and ultimate actions are not subject to full human understanding. Things may happen that we can easily put meaning to, while others may be beyond our understanding. Sometimes the righteous suffer, while the ungodly look happier and healthier. "Who can understand his decisions?"

The answer to this question, is the solution to our confusion. The difference between our understanding and God's wisdom is too wide to measure. Indeed, it is exactly what makes him God. We cannot understand all he does or doesn't do. To try and explain the reason for every act of omission and commission of God, is to pretend to be God when you are not.

As a pastor, I have had too many occasions when my spiritual children have asked for explanation for challenges in their lives. I have always taken the position that what God has not explained, I cannot explain. Apostle Paul told the church in Corinth, "our understanding is in part." Anyone who attempts to explain everything happening in everyone's life cannot be truthful. The Bible and prayer are my best resource materials, and bottom line is that if I don't know why God is allowing something to happen that I think should not be happening, I accept his will and submit to his unsearchable wisdom.

I decide to keep trusting him, because that is the only option I have. If you cannot trust God in the bad times, you will find it difficult believing him for what he has for you in the future. The fact that you may be ending another year with so many unresolved issues, doesn't mean God has turned his back on you. It is a part of our walk of faith. When the pressure mounts on us and we don't know what to do, we can do what we know; we keep trusting, praying, and praising till the darkness gives way to light.

God bless you and give you peace in Jesus' Name.

Your future is Hidden in Him

Eccl.11:5, NKJV

As you do not know what is in the wind, or how the bones grow in the womb of her who is with child, so you do not know the works of God who makes everything.

When we had opportunity to visit the beautiful island of Puerto Rico a few years ago, I did not miss the chance to take pictures of the beautiful night scenery of buildings, ships, and lights. Little did I know that a wave of hurricane was going to reduce most of it to rubbles in October 2017. Even those who through scientific means forecasted the upcoming wind surge, could not tell the exact details of the damage it was going to cause. The secret "in the wind" is known to God alone.

With the help of an ultrasound machine, medical doctors can know a lot about a baby in a mother's womb, but they cannot tell everything about that baby, in terms of what his life's pursuits, purpose, triumphs and failures would be. The full details of the real issues of a baby's life can never be picked by any scientific equipment or logical means. Issues relating to who and what he will become, and his eternal destiny, are beyond the remit of science and sense. The secret "in the womb" belongs to our God.

If we have all knowledge of all things, it may take out the adventure that comes with a life of living by faith. Not knowing all that the new year holds for you, should not stop you from joyfully embracing it. Your preparation for healthy living, peace, joy, and prosperity in the new year, begins with your mind. A mind that trusts that God is working on your behalf is what you need to win in the coming year.

If you don't know anything at all about the future, you do know a few things; first, that God holds the future. Second, that he has already assured you of a safe landing in your flight towards the future (Jer.29:11). Third, that he will be with you always, even to the end of the ages. Gird yourself spiritually, mentally, emotionally, and physically (even if you are on a sick bed), to ride upon high places. I am lacing my boots to run into glorious blessings I never experienced before, because the Holy One of Israel, who knows what is "in the wind," and knows what is "in the womb" is running ahead of me.

I am simply unstoppable, stubbornly focused, and aggressively pursuing heaven's agenda for my life. Welcome to the Jesus team, where the fabric for our jersey is always faith, and nothing else. We are winning now and forever, whether in pleasure or in pain. All things will continue to work together for our good because we serve a good God.

God bless you.

New Possibilities

Mk. 2:21, GNB

No one uses a piece of new cloth to patch up an old coat, because the new patch will shrink and tear off some of the old cloth, making an even bigger hole.

A lot has changed since I was a young boy. Old things were repaired instead of thrown away. Growing up, it was quite common to see people wear shirts and trousers which had patches on them. Discarding a dress because of a little tear in it wasn't the norm. On the contrary, you find an old fabric similar to the torn dress and use it to patch the dress. That practice is what Jesus is referring to here when he makes the point that "No one uses a piece of new cloth to patch up an old coat." It would be a mismatch and wouldn't take long to come apart.

Another year is phasing out, and there are some things you should not take into the new year; they will be a mismatch for the next level of your life. There are old garments of disappointment, anger, unforgiveness, bitterness, sinful living etc. that must be discarded. The onus is on you to choose the life you want to live in the new year. Whatever dress (attitudes) need to be changed, make the decision and determination to change it. Avoid making excuses because God will only operate within the space that you give him. He neither dictates nor imposes his will on us.

The Word is clear; God and the world have nothing in common (James 4:4). If there is a time to do a sober reflection on your life, it is today, the last day of the year. Look at what has not helped your growth and maturity in Christ and get rid of it. They may be things, people, or places you go to that contradict the principles of God's Word. They are old "dresses" that won't fit into the new year fashion-line. If you must do patching in some areas in the year, the fabric must be of same quality. Patching old dress with new fabric isn't going to work.

The fear you have entertained all year long, must now give way to the faith that is able to unlock new possibilities and changes in your life. The unforgiving spirit that only produced toxic poisons and kept you frustrated should be confined to the garbage can of deliberate forgiveness and possible forgetfulness. It may be difficult to forget all the negatives and nuances of the passing year, but I bet God is ready to give you the grace to rise above the rot, and reach out to a greater, better, and happier life than you ever did.

Erect a mental wall of separation between your past disappointments and your future possibilities, beginning in your present position. Some things will not change until you change, so change if you must.

God bless you!